HACKING THE AFTERLIFE:
PRACTICAL ADVICE FROM THE FLIPSIDE

By

Richard Martini

Table of Contents

Introduction

To Be or Not To Be; That's *THE* Question

"Ascent of the Blessed" by Hieronymus Bosch
This detail has been cited as an example of a near death experience, complete with a tunnel of light and souls venturing through it.

A "Life Hack" refers to *"any trick, shortcut, skill, or novelty method that increases productivity and efficiency, in all walks of life."[1]*

Or in this case; "and beyond."

I've been examining near death experiences, between life hypnosis sessions, out of body experiences and speaking to mediums and others who report relatively the same things about the afterlife. These reports point to the conclusion; that we don't die, that those who've gone before us are accessible on the other side of the veil.

---

[1] Detail from "Ascent of the Blessed" by Hieronymus Bosch. Wikimedia.

I've been filming people under deep hypnosis for a decade and I've expanded my research to include people who've had near death experiences, as well as interviewing people who appear to be able to communicate with people no longer on the planet. At some point, by asking questions about a person's "memory" of a past life, I realized people appear to be able to access and explore a "between lives realm" without being under hypnosis at all.

The unusual premise of this book is that what or *who we are* as individuals does not disappear upon our demise and this bundle of "what we are or were" is still accessible to our loved ones back here. Reportedly, our core essence doesn't turn into bits of fairy dust and vanish after death, nor does our life's energy drift into a Jungian pool of unconsciousness. These reports claim our "life energy" moves from this reality into another "reality," reportedly like walking from "one room to the next." Like using the transporter room from a Star Trek episode.

Of course, our physical bodies eventually dissolve, turn to ash. But the energy does not; as the "law of conservation of energy" argues in physics.[2] Reportedly, our energy exists *here* during our lifetime, like a smaller piece of a holographic image. When the plate of a hologram is broken into pieces, each part contains all of the information from that holographic image, but "in a diminished fashion." Once we are finished here with this lifetime, our energy apparently leaves the body and "returns home" intact to reconnect with the rest of the energy left behind.

According to the hundreds of sessions or cases I've examined, dozens of near death experiences, hundreds of hypnosis sessions, along with the 30 or so that I've filmed – when we return "home" we reconnect with that portion of our energy we left behind coming here. What was startling to learn, and a bit disconcerting, is that most people claim we only bring a relatively small portion of our overall life force to our lives; the average is "about one third."[3] Further that each lifetime is a choice.

---

[2] In physics, the law of conservation of energy states that the total energy of an isolated system remains constant—it is said to be conserved over time. Energy can neither be created nor destroyed; rather, it transforms from one form to another.

[3] I examined these reports in "Flipside: A Tourist's Guide on How to Navigate the Afterlife" and "It's a Wonderful Afterlife volumes one and two." There are many other sources, a partial bibliography is at the end of this book.

To decide to incarnate or not to incarnate. Good question.

This book will explore "life planning" sessions, where under deep hypnosis, people access that decision to come to the planet, why they chose their particular persona, and what they hoped to accomplish in doing so. That our life choice is not based on previous lifetimes or karma, or difficulties we've had in the past – although we certainly can choose to explore those arenas - but the choice to do so is based on free will. We can always say "No. I'm not returning. I have better things to do back here than to go down there with the rest of you."

But for some godforsaken reason, because our soul group convinces us to do so, or our guides convince us that it's a journey we should take on behalf of others, we agree to participate. Indeed, those of us here have *all* agreed to come here, to get back on stage, to play our parts as requested of us. We may not like it once we get back here, but how we perform is entirely up to us. When we leave this mortal coil – it's not that we drift like a "wisp of smoke" into a *bardo* as Buddhism argues, but a full third of our energy heads "back home" to reunite with the other two thirds of our energy that is "always back there."

It's bit like the liquid robot from in the film "Terminator 2." When a piece broke off, the liquid sought out the rest of the robot so it could reformulate the whole machine; our energy seeks out and finds the rest of our energy and melds with it to make us "whole" again. People have described this event of "resynthesizing" with their higher energy as "mind blowing" and "intensely healing." When we reconnect with our *literal* selves, we remember the motivation behind our adventures here, and all of our previous adventures with other members of our soul group. We can see why we chose this lifetime, we understand why we chose our previous lifetimes, and understand the overall theme of all of those choices.

They report that each lifetime reflects the overall discipline that our soul group is working on. Like being part of a university class in a chosen discipline; one soul group's overall theme might be medicine, healing, compassion, forgiveness, loyalty, any of the various themes that are explored in literature and the theater.

In one between life session a woman reported that her "soul group examines what addiction does to people" and recalled various lifetimes that include addictions in all their forms. She was able to see that the overdose of her brother, the sexual addictions of her father, and her own life's addictions all had a theme to them, of understanding the fundamental energy behind addiction and how to transform it into healing energy.

In some cases a soul may not want to return "home" right away, may forestall the trip to stick around and see how things play out. It's up to us whether we stay or go, after all, just as it's up to us whether we come here or not. We might see these souls who haven't left in some energetic, etheric way. They're usually referred to as "ghosts" and in popular media appear with eerie music. But in many cases, after a person checks out, says goodbye to their loved ones, they can't wait to get back home. They report they usually can't wait to return to their friends, "back home."

To be clear, this isn't my belief, philosophy or religious bent. I have a background as a journalist (written for Variety, Premiere, USA Today and Inc.com) I'm a documentary filmmaker ("White City/Windy City" "Journey into Tibet") I'm a film director ("Limit Up," "Point of Betrayal," "You Can't Hurry Love" among others) and I'm just reporting what the research consistently says. I'm not an expert on the afterlife, nor an expert on *anything* really. I've been filming and interviewing people about their Flipside experiences for a decade. The reports are essentially the same.

These eyewitness reports are a bit like the explorers who took ships across the sea, then came back with fantastic tales of what they'd seen. Some went with an attitude of reinforcing their religious beliefs, some made up stories to get money for future trips, while others kept diaries and reported verbatim what they'd witnessed. But when the reports were consistent and could be repeated, their destination became "the new world." What these people report about the Flipside is both consistent and replicable, which is pretty much what science requires for something to be considered data.

The main difference here is that when these explorers return from their trip abroad, *they refer to that other place across the sea as "home."*

Further, the research shows that while we are on the planet, that two thirds of our energy back there, on the Flipside, isn't just floating on clouds. It's reported that our higher selves "attend classes," "learn how to manipulate energy," even report playing "games with our soul mates." In one case, a person reported finding her soul group playing an elaborate "game of tag."

She said the game required a person to track down and "capture" six other soul mates. They could hide "anywhere in the universe;" the added complication was that "everyone is invisible" and they can hide "in any realm" they wanted to. Like an incredible multi-engine version of a Google search, but using their mind's engine to *search for the energy pattern of invisible entities in multiple dimensions.*

They also report that on the Flipside, our higher selves can tune in, watch, enjoy or be horrified by our performance back here. A bit like watching a play in the theater where we are both *in the audience and on stage* at the same time.

The people on stage have a filter that prevents them from knowing there's an audience watching them, or from knowing why they chose a particular part or costume or prop, or why they agreed to the part in the first place. Of course, it would ruin the play if they spent most of their time shading their eyes to wave at the audience and say *"Hi Mom. Look at me! I'm in a play!"*

From our seats "back home" we can cheer, applaud, cry, laugh with those onstage acting out these roles. When our friends exit, it's reported we often congratulate them for a job well done. When the actor who plays Romeo meets the actress who played Juliet backstage, he doesn't chastise her for screwing up his life and causing both of their deaths. He embraces her, congratulates her for a job well done. "Great acting tonight, Julie." "You too Romy; see you at the after party."

"It's not your time to exit the stage yet."

Some people have a near death experience, find themselves "back home" with their soul group, but these folks are usually told *"Hey, get back on stage! You're not supposed to be here yet."*

I've spoken to a number of International Association of Near Death Studies groups[4] and I've met a number of people disconcerted they felt so wonderful "back home" and are upset to be forced "back here." They saw loved ones back there, experienced the unconditional love many report backstage and have no desire to put on the makeup, and step into the limelight.

---

[4] lands.org is a great place to share and listen to a variety of experiences like this.

We live in a world where we try to own time, manipulate and change time. We may not be happy we have more work to do onstage, work that we aren't prepared for, or want to do. *But hang on.* What if I told you it's possible to "go home" while you're still here, still on the planet?

What if I told you it's possible to visit your friends who are no longer on the planet, and you can ask and get information that you didn't know was possible to learn? What if I told you that anyone who has ever walked the Earth is available and accessible, because their energy never dies? It transforms, as per the first law of thermodynamics, from one form to the next, but the essence of that form, since it's outside of time, will always exist.[5] So if you want to ask Will, *"What did you mean by to be or not to be? Is that a rhetorical question? Or are you talking about incarnation?"* you can.

We've all heard fantastical accounts about the afterlife. From visions of satanic fires to angels riding on clouds, we've been inundated with these reports since humans populated the planet. But in reports of the afterlife, isn't it unusual that no two of these reports are ever the same?

As scientist Dr. Neil deGrasse Tyson points out, a rainbow is different for everyone who sees it. No two rainbows are alike. *"The exact Rainbow any of us sees in the sky is entirely our own -- a personal, yet communal gift from the laws of optics."[6]*

The same is true for visions of the afterlife. Two people may visit a "Library of records" but no two descriptions are alike. People may visit a "soul group,"[7] but exactly where it's located or how it's constructed varies from person to person.

We may even see the same person in the afterlife others have seen. They may appear to us differently than they appear to another person, it appears to depend on how they want to present themselves.

---

[5] The law states that "energy can be transformed from one form to another, but cannot be created or destroyed."

[6] Neil deGrasse Tyson tweet @neiltyson 12:41 PM - 14 Jun 2016

[7] "Soul groups" are spoken of by Michael Newton in "Journey of Souls." His reports suggest 3-25 people in the immediate circle, with the average being about 15.

Sometimes we see them as older, sometimes younger, depending on the person we're visiting. Yet we have a feeling of *knowing* that we're actually seeing the person we once knew. I've filmed first hand reports of these encounters with people from all walks of life; different genders, beliefs or lack of belief - who are consistent in their reporting. With different hypnotherapists, different accounts of near death experiences, different experiences as we'll see; all describe the same "place" in a different way.

Caveat Emptor!

As I've mentioned in "Flipside: A Tourist's Guide on How to Navigate the Afterlife" and "It's a Wonderful Afterlife" a skeptic is someone who "doesn't believe in the prevailing school of thought." I'm a skeptic in the truest sense of the word. Science considers accounts of past lives to be *"cryptomnesia"*; something a person imagined, heard, or read about someone else's life, that they forgot -- but their subconscious did not. Or, science argues people may tap into what Carl Jung referred to as the "universal unconscious" - a place in the universe where the energy from our lives supposedly comes to rest, floating like an island of non-biodegradable detritus in outer space. Past life memories are people merely "tapping into" that island.

Further science *believes* near death experiences are due to *Hypoxia*, lack of oxygen in the brain which causes hallucinations. (As happens in high altitude.) I know about *Hypoxia* – I've been at high altitude in the mountains of Tibet and had some pretty fantastic "visions" up there. But science "believes" this because, well, there's no data on the topic.

Finally, materialist science *believes* consciousness begins and ends in the brain, as if the engrams contain all the information we need to know, and if someone has enough of them – or a computer does – it can become "sentient." To quote my former Oxford/Harvard alum Boston University professor Julian Baird; *"I'd agree with you, but then we'd both be wrong."* The simplest way to prove past lives, out of body experiences, near death experiences are actual events, not imaginary, is through the evidence of "new information." If a person sees, hears, learns something during one of these events that they couldn't possibly have known - that there's no "known example" anywhere in books or the internet or in "some other person's mind that perhaps they were accessing" - then it must come from somewhere *else* other than the brain.

If that *new information* turns out to be accurate -- then the person could **not** have gotten the information from the Jungian unconscious, from the energetic memory of some previous person, from the hidden recesses of their subconscious, or from not being able to breathe atop Mt. Everest.

It's not up to me to convince anyone either way. I'm just a reporter here. *If that's your final answer* on the matter, as they say, I recommend putting this book back on the shelf, returning it to the kindle app or whatever dime store bin you found it. You should be able to get your money back. After all, buying books is not like being alive – they come with a *money back guarantee*. There may be solid reasons for you not to venture down this avenue, and I appreciate that. I'm not writing these books for everyone. No really, if you're feeling the slightest bit uncomfortable, it's going to get a lot more freaky up in here. Maybe this amusement park ride isn't for you.

Apologies in advance for syntax mistakes, typos, and any other errors I make here; someone complained of my reading of my books on Audible, I sometimes laugh, am overcome with emotion, correct myself or as one wag put it, could "hear my cat meow" in the background. If meowing bothers you, then I'm not your guide. Get a refund, please!

That being said, there are people who may *need to hear these reports*, and need to hear it in the tone and syntax I express. For whatever reason. *Now, for those of you who have stuck around:* I invite you into this world of the afterlife, where we can query people no longer on the planet with specific questions and get some pretty amazing answers. *Care to follow me? But* **you have been warned.**

Giordano Bruno, philosopher burned at the stake for revealing his out of body experience where he saw that the earth goes around the sun.
"L'asciate ogni speranza voi ch'entrate"
"Abandon All Hope Ye Who Turns the Page."

CHAPTER ONE

Hacking the Flipside

"A sunset here is a sunrise somewhere else."

#1. Afterlife Hack: *We don't die.*

That's pretty much the most important detail I can impart from these eyewitness reports. I have set out to prove it false on many occasions. Which is pretty funny when you think about it; "We don't die? Oh, that's crazy. He's out of his mind. We do die, doesn't he realize he's claiming something that can't possibly be true? We're born, we live; we die. It doesn't get any simpler than that."

But do we? Yes, our physical body crumbles, but the spirit, the thing which animates us, our soul, our energetic construct – call it what you will – does not die. In fact, in continues on quite nicely, *thank you very much.*

I base that factoid on the thousands of cases I've examined of near death experiences, between life experiences, experiences with communicating with the afterlife, experiences out of body. These experiences are all connected to the fact that when our body stops functioning, who we are as individuals does not.

In some cases, people might be upset about that. Think of all the bad people who *needed* to be killed, executed; "taken out." We may think we've killed them, executed them, dispatched "the bad guys" – but they are not dead either. *Not killed.* And you're likely to run into them in the afterlife, because their problem is some deeper, more interesting connection between the person doing the killing and the one who got "killed."

That can be disconcerting to others who've spent their lives in mourning, suffering, in angst over how their relatives died, were tortured, butchered -- and they may have spent a lifetime vowing revenge, seeking revenge, living and breathing and ready to die to avenge their loved one's death. I don't mean to offend anyone who is offended by the idea that we don't die.

It's just in the data.

Our consciousness continues on, unabated, with or without our bodies. We may wish that wasn't the case – we may wish that we could "end it all" – but I'm sorry to report; we cannot. It's not physically possible to "end it all." There is no ending when it comes to something that already exists.

It's not that I'm claiming this – I'm reporting this.

I'm also not reporting what people have said previously about the religious aspects of existence; "in the beginning there was the word" or "there is no beginning and no end." Neither of those sentences bear fruit within the context of these reports.

Reports are that souls are created. They weren't "always here," and they don't "always remain the same." What's reported is that they are created in a complex process that's a bit difficult to use words to describe, and that they progress through their many lifetimes and experiences, grow from young souls to old souls, and continue a progression that may or may not include "returning to the source" and disseminating all of their energy so that souls can be created again.

A bit like water. It evaporates, goes up into the clouds, comes back down again. A lot happens along the way. Ice happens, condensation, fog, snow... but ultimately every drop of water that is on the planet has always been here. Was it here prior to Earth's existence? Apparently not. The same water cats drink dinosaurs once drank. Every drop of water on the planet has always been here. So that cup of joe I have next to my computer may have been consumed by Genghis Kahn. Or Shaka Khan. It's been here before and will come back again.

In the beginning there was consciousness, or the energy construct of consciousness. That conscious entity, or entities, put things into motion to create what we know as our universe. They didn't do it once; they've been doing it for a long time. I can't say it's been an eternal process, because that's not what's reported either. There is a beginning with regard to souls, and there is an end – but after a long, long time of learning and eventually going back to the source.

The research I'll be referring to, citing in this book is from people who claim that consciousness continues on after we die. But more important than that, consciousness didn't come into our existence with birth, in fact it's been a part of our experience prior to that. And I'm not talking about our birth as a human, I'm talking about our birth as a soul – or energetic construct.

There's a process for how that occurs, I've reported it in the books, and will refer to it here. But in essence we didn't all begin with the big bang – we can come into existence at any point in time as a soul – and there's reports from the Flipside that there's more than one big bang as well. That the mechanism that is the universe has done this before, and will continue to do it again in the future.

Don't shoot the messenger. I'm just the piano player in this honkytonk.

#2 Afterlife Hack: The afterlife is *home*.

I've examined thousands of cases, and filmed over 30 between life sessions now, observed a number of other ones from folks who've sent them to me, and the second most important concept I've come across is that this world we live in, this planet Earth is not our home. When people are asked where they want to go after remembering a previous lifetime, and the scene of their death, they nearly always respond "I want to go home."

I know that sounds a bit off and odd. And no, I'm not talking blues or grays or off world experience, other planets, or UFOs. What I'm talking about it the idea that "over there" or the place where we go when we die – we don't all go to the same location, but we do go to the same arena, eventually – that place over there, the one we think of as "in the afterlife" or "after death" is actually what we all consider to be "home."

When I first heard a person say it while under deep hypnosis, I was startled. The therapist conducting the session got to a point where the person was able to recall a "previous lifetime that had some significance on this one" and then, after hearing a description of the death scene from that lifetime, asked a simple question.

"Where would you like to go now?" The person said *"I want to go home."*

At first I thought.. "Wait, what? Where's that? You mean Poughkeepsie?" This person had just recalled a lifetime growing up near a farm in upstate New York, so naturally, I assumed she meant she wanted to go back there… but hang on, she had just remembered a previous lifetime where she had died in the Holocaust, and had been from Warsaw. Did she mean "Warsaw?"

Then she described that journey that so many folks describe during a between life hypnotherapy session, during an out of body experience, or during a near death experience. "Traveling towards a bright light" – appearing at the light, going through it, then experiencing "Profound joy" and seeing "loved ones" and others who greeted her as if she had just returned after an extended trip… somewhere else.

Here, this is the somewhere else. Earth. Life. Being human. Being alive. Going through a lifetime. When we're done with it, we have the desire to go "home."

A skeptical friend of mine said *"Oh that's what everyone would say! Everyone wants to go home."* I pointed out that you'd think people would be imagining some form of heaven or paradise. But they say "home." There is no common agreed upon version of home – everyone sees home differently, including twins.

We don't experience the world exactly the same, how could we experience home the same? He insisted that it would be the most natural thing in the world while under deep hypnosis, after "imagining" that you've just witnessed, experienced, felt, a lifetime that you aren't currently aware of, that at the moment of death – whether its dramatic or mundane – the natural thing to say when asked "So where do you want to go now?" is to say "I want to go home."

But which home? The home from this lifetime? Or the home from that previous lifetime? Turns out *it's neither.*

#3 Afterlife Hack: What you expect generally dictates what you'll experience in the afterlife, at least initially.

I'm a fan of Dr. Eben Alexander's books "Proof of Heaven" and "Map of Heaven." It's interesting to read Dr. Alexander's journey into this realm via a near death experience. He's a scientist, a surgeon, he's been a believer in all things material for a long, long time. And now to watch him as he faces these events that are... well, let's call them "post materialist science" is a joy to behold. "Material science" argues that everything comes from something. "Post material science" includes quantum theory, arguing "just because we can't observe it doesn't mean it's not there."

It's worth pointing out that when you compare near death experiences to between life hypnotherapy sessions, out of body experiences and other events – they're all talking about the same medium. Like painters talking about paint and a canvas.

But everyone's experience with the Flipside is different. Not everyone *hears music* during a near death experience; Dr. Alexander's is the first account I've seen where someone described dancing. That doesn't mean that everyone else "just wasn't looking carefully enough" nor does it mean that everyone is going to see dancers during their afterlife experience. Just as there are no two definitions of "home" that are identical, every journey into the Flipside is different. The only thing that connects them is our ability to describe feelings like "unconditional love" "healing light" "people who are no longer on the planet" etc.

We experience reality differently, why not the Flipside?

There are numerous accounts of hearing music during a near death experience and some between life sessions – from symphonies to profound musical interludes, to musicians actually being able to perform. These musical experiences are akin to putting paint on a canvas. It depends on who is holding the brush, where the paint came from, what hue and colors are involved, what the brush strokes are like. Because everyone doesn't have the *identical* experience, doesn't mean they're not having an experience. In fact, the preponderance of accounts about the afterlife say basically the same things.

We just have to read them.

But in general, if you've lived a happy, generous life, people claim you're going to experience that upon your departure. If you've lived a fearful scared life, or been suffering from guilt, or depression or some other negative experience, you may very well experience that upon your departure. If you're riddled with guilt as to how you lived your life, it will take a while to shed that emotion as well. That said, some who've had a tough life – claim they find themselves greeted in the most wonderful way.

In "It's a Wonderful Afterlife" one woman remembered being a Sioux warrior chief who died while racing into battle. She stood around (after her death) and watched as her friends and loved ones killed by the tribe they were fighting – but once she departed, she went back into a realm of happiness and remembrance of things past. Her tone and demeanor changed from that of a warrior, to one of awe and acceptance. She saw her loved ones from all of her lifetimes, and her core group of souls that she normally incarnates with. People she recognized then as part of her life, people she recognizes now as again part of this existence.

There are no hard fast rules about what kind of afterlife you'll experience. Many people are convinced that they're going to suffer and feel the pangs of guilt – and they may experience that upon their life review with the help of their elders. But it's completely dependent upon the individual, and what they want to experience. Could be unpleasant. But in the vast majority of cases I've examined, people by and large are amazed, in awe, and happy to be home.

#4. Afterlife Hack: Good and Evil are relative terms that generally have meaning on Earth, but don't over there.

Again, that's just in the data.

There are near death experiences where people felt or witnessed something "scary" or "dark" or difficult just after their beginning the journey. Dr. Alexander experienced being stuck in some kind of "mud like" environment. David Bennett ("Voyage of Purpose") experienced a pitch blackness at first, film director Jeremy Kagan experienced something similar at the beginning of his spiritual journey – fear, darkness, being "trapped."

People do report experiencing some kind of hell experience in some of their near death experiences. In all the between life sessions I've examined, I've only run across a few where someone experienced something in a realm that might be considered "hell" – at least to them.

It's never the same; the descriptions, the experiences are not the same. Just like the depictions of "home" or the "between lives realm" or "heaven" are not the same. It's not like going to Walmart, where no matter where you are in the country, you'll see the same unhappy workers, wearing the same drab colors, and see the same low cost items in every store – exactly the same. Or McDonalds where the menu in Mumbai looks just like the menu in Sacramento – even though you can only dine on lamb or goat and not cow. If you're looking at the menu, you can't tell the difference. But in these experiences, no two accounts are the same.

During his near death experience, Dr. Rajiv Parti experienced a journey to a "hell" place – where he saw people with horns. (As I asked him, *"Why would seeing someone with horns be negative? What is it about the horn –* which is made of matted hair – *that has negative connotations? Why couldn't seeing someone with a horn be pleasant?"*) During a few of the sessions I've filmed, during the first few moments of leaving a "previous lifetime" they experienced something that can only be referenced as "hellacious."

But was it a physical place? Was it the same place for each individual? No. What happened in these sessions I filmed, people would experience the negativity; one said "It smells like Sulphur, I can feel the fear here, or I'm in a dark frightening place now." But when the therapist asked "So why did you choose to come to this place, what are we here to examine or experience?" the place itself dissolved.

As if was the place they expected to go to after their life, they'd been told so many times they were going to end up there, that upon their passing, wound up in a place of that kind of creation.

One could argue that these places do exist, "lower realms" as they call them in Buddhism, and they're filled with unhappy souls. That there are terrifying frightening beings flying around and scaring the hell out of the individuals.

Put it this way; if upon stepping over to the other side you run smack dab into a fellow with horns and a pitchfork, do what I would do. Examine the horns (Made of matted hair? Same on earth. Go figure). Check out the fork. Steel? Or plastic? There's no pain, no experience that you can have that isn't created in your mind – here or over there. Then tell your Uncle Pete to take off the costume, it's a funny idea, but you have places to go and people to see.

In a number of sessions, I've seen people experience sudden discomfort upon re-experiencing the death from a previous lifetime. Especially if it was in an era of fear and delusion. And when the therapist asks "So why did you choose to come to this place after your death? What are we doing here?" They realize that they've chosen to be in this fearful place – they aren't forced to be there. And every time they've been asked the question, the illusion disappears. Like a CGI film that's been suddenly stopped and redrawn.

If a question – "Why did you choose to come here?" – can make our experience disappear or dissipate, then *how real can it be*? Certainly some people might want to experience that kind of fear, or want to stick around and be part of that fear – but because they're in a hypnotherapy session using hypnosis to examine their journey – they realize it's temporary. That the reason they've brought themselves to a therapist's office is because they want to be able to move beyond that experience.

Which is a version of hacking the afterlife.

You don't want to wind up in some kind of place that is negative? Then consider for a moment that the more you stress over something, or worry about something, the more you've created that world for yourself. If you're going to meditate on something, meditate on the place you'd like to be if tomorrow, or even today, was your last day on the planet. Where would you like to be? Who would you like to see there? And what would you like to experience there? And what would you like to experience here?

#5 Afterlife Hack: We're fully conscious between lives.

"Fully" is a relative term. I'm not talking about omniscience. I am talking about how at some point you can be fully conscious of all your lifetimes that have led up to this one. That you can see and learn and experience all the lessons that you've learned over all your lifetimes.

That's a pretty profound and humbling experience. Certainly it's one that shakes up your world view if you were a person who believed this was the only lifetime you'd had. Especially if you're a person who wishes that they'd done more with their life than what they thought they'd accomplished.

Which leads us to the concept that if we're fully conscious between lives – how conscious can we be during this life?

But once you return "home" to your loved ones – the people who've been reincarnating with you for millennia, you get to see what role they played in your life, and what role they've played in all your lives. And once you're back there, you're not limited to only seeing your core soul group – there's basically everyone who ever existed hanging out back there – sometimes they've reincarnated as different people, but if you want to visit them – you can.

Got someone you'd like to meet on the Flipside? Take your pick. They're accessible. They may be busy, they may be working on their current lifetime, at the moment, they may be teaching or doing something completely different than what you imagined – but they're usually accessible. If you can get the proper link, you can ask questions. They don't have to worry about revealing anything that would upset your path or journey because you've already done so by asking the question.

Everything that's happened in your mind still exists. It doesn't get "deleted." *Everyone who ever has lived on this planet still exists. They don't get deleted either.*

#6 Afterlife Hack: The veil is thinning.

I've heard it often enough in these various sessions that I no longer ask "What does that mean?" *It is what it is.* The veil, or the filters that prevent certain brains from accessing information, appears to be thinning. There are many factors that could be responsible:

Rewiring of the brain due to external factors. I've read that severely autistic children benefit from watching themselves on video acting out. That their actions allow them to alter the chemistry of the brain merely by watching the actions. If this is the case, then perhaps discussing concepts about there being another reality than this one, allows for the brain to access those concepts in a different way.

Could be that brains are being rewired because of the preponderance of microwave towers wherever we go. Our brains function as a receiver of these waves, a study was done in Finland about blue tooth units, and it was reported that 70% of reported brain tumors in Finland could be linked with blue tooth use. These are the obvious negatives of being bombarded by radio waves – but are there possible benefits?

People who fly in airplanes regularly (pilots and stewards) have had a rise in incidences where they flipped out, or had some kind of mental break. Is that because the ozone layer is thinning, is it because they're closer to sun spots, or does being at that high altitude somehow affect the brain in a deleterious way? I'm not suggesting it is the case, but it's worth examining why there seem to be increased meltdowns for those in flights. Could simply be that it's the time of some kind of quickening. I've heard the term more than once, and always said in reference to a shift in consciousness. "Over *here* we call that *the quickening.*"

What does quickening mean? Well it means things are moving at a faster rate. Every report I've heard or seen about the Flipside notes that things over there "move at an incredibly faster rate" than over here. That the energetic vibrations over there make movement over here seem like it's in super slow motion. So perhaps there's some physiological reason things are speeding up in our brains, or our perception of reality, and therefore making it easier to access this information.

It could be none of these. But I've heard it often enough – the veil is thinning, best thing we can do is try to examine it why.

#7 Afterlife Hack: Everything happens for a reason.

This has always been a conundrum. How could it be that everything has meaning? I used to believe that chaos and coincidence ruled behavior and actions. But it's free will that rules our actions.

You can't predict what an outcome is going to be no matter how much information you might have. It's a bit like asking a question to a billion ants – "What are you doing today?" Every ant is going to have a different job or task to accomplish – and there appears to be some overriding consciousness with regard to the size of the ant colony – research shows that once a colony reaches its full size, around five years, it somehow generates a message to the ants to leave and start a new colony.

How does it accomplish this message? Ant mail? (Is that faster than snail mail?) It could very well be that the accumulation of ants, like the accumulation of brain cells, combined with some form of consciousness, dictates what's going to occur next.

When people under deep hypnosis are asked "How much of your energy did you bring to earth?" they generally respond with a figure that's between 20 and 40%. About a third of our life energy. I'm told the reason for that is the human brain couldn't function with more energy or the brain would be overloaded. I imagine if that's the case, then those who have come here who had the natural ability to move people's hearts may have shown up with a higher percentage of energy, which allowed them to do things that were considered miracles at one point in time.

I'm not saying they did perform miracles, I do believe that miracle is a relative term. It's a miracle that my cell phone rings for example – and also a miracle that some doctors are able to heal just by touch.[8] I've seen it happen, and I don't question it – but try to realize that there's an energetic world I can't see and there are people who are more in touch with that world than I am.

I've heard stories of Tibetan monks who through deep focus and meditation could "move through walls," I've heard and read accounts of Tibetan monks "sky walking" – or running with such long strides that they could cover a great distance in a few leaps. I don't know how that physiologically works – but I don't discount that it has happened in the past.

I've also seen fakirs pretend to pull solid items out of thin air, or out of their mouths for their faithful, and using a camera, am able to slow that footage down to see the trick they're pulling off. I'm not interested in proving people are false or true based on their relation with material objects. I can report that people in the afterlife take classes in energy construction, and these classes teach a number of things including how to move objects telepathically, how to create objects through intention, and how to help doctors on earth with their healing arts.

I'm open to the reports that people claim that "everything happens for a reason." Of course they're talking about good and bad things. That those bad things were agreed to in advance, and the good things as well. No one can pinpoint everything that's going to occur in a lifetime – because of the concept of free will – people are free to screw things up. But by and large, every event that happens in a lifetime is part of the classroom experience.

Perhaps its syntax. "Everything happens for a reason" implies someone greater than ourselves forcing events to happen. That's not in the research. What I've found is that **we have the power to make things happen for ourselves** – based upon many factors that could occur suddenly based on free will, but from a spiritual perspective. Someone else changes their mind, breaks their agreement, and we decide to adjust to that change – and our path is altered.

---

[8] Tibetan medicine has a number of case studies where people are cured of illnesses using ancient methods. See 2004 "Knowledge of Healing" on Netflix.

From a spiritual perspective – *which is something we're not aware of or tapped into unless we spend our lives in meditative equipoise* – we adjust accordingly. "Everything happens for a reason," but the particular reason may be beyond the capacity of our brain to comprehend, especially when the events seem tragic. We may be able to comprehend it, however, if we "open our heart" to the solution, as from the Flipside perspective, we may be able to understand events as part of a larger theme in our soul's journey.

#8 Afterlife Hack: You chose your parents.

I hear quite a bit of flack about this one. *"Choose my parents? Are you out of your freakin' mind? They're the last people I would have chosen!"* At which point I say "I presume that's why you chose them. So you could be here at this space and time making that statement." Otherwise, you would have stayed by their side, never left them, and wound up doing exactly what they did, and be living next door to them. As they did in the old days. Instead you got away as fast as you could. Consider for a moment they gave you that gift – agreed to play their roles *so well* - so you could do what you've wound up doing. *Away from them.*

It's something Michael Newton found in his research, and something Dr. Helen Wambach also found in her prior research with thousands of patients. She asked them while they were under hypnosis about why and how they chose their lifetimes; she got a variety of answers, but all of them were conscious decisions.

It brings to mind the story of Dave Schultz's father Phillip. Dave was the wrestler featured in the film "Foxcatcher," who was killed by the crazed billionaire Jon DuPont. An interesting detail the filmmakers missed is that at his son's funeral Phillip gave a eulogy that pointed to another reality altogether. He said that when Dave was around 5, he asked his father if he could "keep a secret?"

His father said he could, and Dave walked him out into the woods, away from their home to say "I spoke to my *council* before I came here, and they told me I would come to teach a lesson in love, but that I won't be here very long."

Phillip Schultz forgot that particular conversation until his son's death.

I've interviewed dozens of people who had similar conversations with their "council of elders" (he actually said "council" – as it jumped out at me when I read it in the Philadelphia newspaper's account) where people ask their council about the life they've just led, and later at some point, about the life they're about to lead. Imagine if you will that we all have this conversation at some point, and they ask "so why are you choosing your parents?"

Good question to contemplate, even if you can't believe it.

#9 Afterlife Hack: You're doing pretty much what you signed up for.

When I did my first of four between life hypnotherapy sessions, I got to a place where I never thought I'd get to – standing in front of my council. I saw eight people standing in a semi-circle, it felt like I'd known them forever, and it felt like they were generally happy to see and hear from me. And I asked the same question that all of the people I've filmed asked – *"So how am I doing?"*

I've heard variations on this answer; "You're doing exactly what you signed up for, you've gotten this far, try to congratulate yourself for getting this far, as not everyone does." "It takes courage to come to the planet, and it takes courage to choose as difficult a life as you've chosen, but you have to give yourself credit for doing such a great job of it."

But beyond that, I wanted to know: "Why did I choose Rich Martini?" The answer I heard was "Every thought, action, word or deed contains energy. If you write a poem, write a book, sing a song, paint a painting, help someone with tax returns – some part of your energy on a quantum level is associated with those actions. So literally a *part of you* is going into the work you're creating. That can be a healing energy. You've chosen many lifetimes where healing was involved, and in an "outside the box" kind of way (I actually used that cliché') you chose a lifetime as a filmmaker."

I said that "Film can have a healing effect on people. If you can make someone laugh, you can change their disposition instantly. Tears work, but require catharsis to have the same effect." It was funny, as when I got around to transcribing this session, I realized I'd never used the word catharsis in a sentence before. But I then said *"I'm just sorry I didn't choose someone who would be more successful at it."*

And when I said this, my council laughed, and the hypnotherapist laughed, I had the odd experience of hearing laughter in two different realms at the same time. I was reflecting on the fact the despite having spent 30 odd years in the film business, I've written and/or directed a handful of theatrical films that pretty much no one has seen. "But" I added "I think that's eventually going to change."

So there is hope. But this sentiment applies to everyone reading this sentence. You chose this life for a reason, and part of the journey is to understand why you chose it. Sometimes, people ask the question before their council and hear "You need a course correction. The reason we brought you here is to make you realize you're not doing what you promised you would do." A course correction is possible. Perhaps that's why you picked up this book.

#10. Afterlife Hack: Just let go.

At the end of my first session, the therapist, Jimmy Quast of Easton Hypnosis in Maryland, asked if there was "anything else" I wanted to see or experience while I was there. Mind you, I was convinced I would not get anywhere, not respond to this form of therapy, and had been determined to "not say anything to appease the therapist" if I didn't see anything. I thought as a journalist, it would be a perfect way to disprove this was an effective tool at examining the subconscious. And for about 20 minutes, I kept saying "I don't see anything. Just black" when Jimmy asked. Then he said, "Just look down."

And as I've recounted elsewhere I saw myself as a Native American, a Lakota Sioux medicine man, and later I was able to verify a number of details about this man's life. But that aside, I was humbled by the experience, awed by traveling into the between lives realm, and amazed to be able to get anywhere, including having direct discussions with my spirit guide, my council of elders, and my friend Luana Anders who had inspired this trip in the first place.

So as he asked if there was "anything else I'd like to see" I said "Let me ask them a question." And in my mind's eye I asked "Is there anything that I can say or bring back to people who will hear my story so that I may help them in the healing process?" The lead guide sort of smiled at me and said "Tell them to just let go."

And in that moment, I saw what he meant – to let go of the fear of death, to let go of the fear of life, to let go of the fear of illness, or abandonment, of every fear that exists on the planet that keeps us in a delusional state. Because once we let go of fear, let go of anger, let go of emotions that are attached to an event, let go of revenge towards people and events that are beyond your control or even comprehension as to why they occurred – once you can truly let go, you can be free.

That freedom resonates with me to this very day. To this very sentence. *Just let go.*

"Every man has his own destiny: the only imperative is to follow it, to accept it, no matter where it leads him." Henry Miller

"If you just think of me, I'll be there. But please - get on with it." – Luana Anders as quoted via medium Pattie Canova.

CHAPTER TWO:

The Architecture of the Afterlife

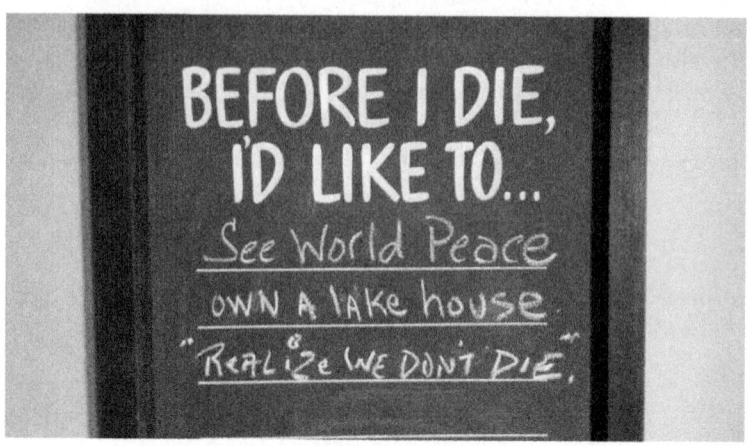

"Hello. From the other side…"
Lyrics by Greg Kurstin and Adele

My father was an architect and my mother was a concert pianist. One taught me how to read a blueprint, the other how to read a musical score. Both of them had the ability to look at lines and marks on a piece of paper and see things in three dimensions. A blueprint after all, is just an outline for an imaginary building; how it comes together is based on a myriad of factors, including construction materials, the weather, quality of workers, etc.

The same holds true for a musical score – my mother could read a score the way I read a book. I bought her a copy of the difficult Rachmaninoff piano concerto #3, she read it in the car on the way home, then sat down and played it, haltingly, but all the way through when she arrived at our family piano. She was that good at "sight reading" and he was that good at visualizing what was right or wrong about a blueprint.[9]

---

[9] If you want to hear my mom play the piano, visit AnthyMartini.com

Later in life, my father worked as a Construction Manager – a bit like a film director – overseeing giant construction projects worldwide. When he took over the King Fahd University project in Riyadh, Saudi Arabia, he found that all the toilets in the University were facing Mecca; a detail the original architects had missed (or not, depending on your sense of humor.) My father's solution saved his client both money and face; by having all the porcelain in the university turned slightly so they were no longer facing a sacred direction. *It pays to understand blueprints.*

What's a blueprint for the afterlife? Well, it's a bit like a musical score *and* a building design. It's an idealized version of what we might expect to find on the Flipside, without the snafus and bad notes that can occur during a performance or construction. These observations are based on the many sessions I've filmed, and hundreds of accounts I've examined. It appears that everyone will experience the Flipside based on their own set of filters and perspective, however, there are a number of familiar hallmarks, signposts, literal places we create that we can visit, when we're no longer on the planet.

But first, let's agree on some nomenclature, shall we?

How can offer *proof of the afterlife*? Before we can answer this we first need to ask, "How do we define *proof of life*?" We have a number of obvious answers; "We're conscious and we can observe things that are alive or dead." But there is no real definition for something that's "not dead." Here's the dictionary definition of what it means to "be alive":

Merriam-Webster's:
    adjective
    : having life: living: not dead
    : continuing to exist
    : not yet defeated: still having a chance to win or succeed

The Oxford Dictionary:
    Adjective
    1. (Of a person, animal, or plant) living, not dead:

The definition of being alive is… *"Not dead."* Seriously?

Then the definition of dead is… what? "Not alive?" It's a conundrum to be sure, since no scientist or division of science has been able to define what consciousness is. It follows that no one has been able to define what "being alive" is as well. (Other than "not dead.") If we can't define consciousness we're stuck with material science's definition that claims if you have enough engrams, robots can be sentient. Or it argues that consciousness may be related to quantum theory, which argues that it takes consciousness to determine what is or isn't real.

Which is it fellas? Is life real or imaginary? Can't be both. Can it?

It all seems like complicated word play. The use of language severely limits our ability to impart a complex concept, since it's easy to say "He's alive" or "He's dead." Is a rock alive or dead? Well, what's the difference between the atoms agreeing to hang together in the inhabited space of a stone, or the atoms agreeing to inhabit the space of a human? What does "I think therefore I am" really mean? Does it mean "I am alive?" Certainly, when we come upon something dead or "no longer alive" – decaying perhaps, being gobbled up by ants perhaps – we can argue it was once alive, but that it is now no longer alive.

But that's a pretty poor definition, isn't it? Because it doesn't help us at all if we're discussing the concept of what it means to be alive. The answer to the question "What is life?" appears to depend upon the person who is asking the questions as much as the person who supplies the definition.

I came upon a dead gecko the other day. I leaned down, thinking it must be a toy; large gecko, on its back, legs akimbo. I got closer and realized this poor fellow had somehow darted across a staircase at the very moment someone was stepping onto the stonework. Not very easy to do, but it nailed him. He was as dead as a doornail. (Has anyone seen a "live" doornail?) Physically still intact, so much so that I thought it was a rubber version of Signor Gecko. But was he *really* dead? Or maybe not breathing?

I've seen animals who appeared to be dead, after getting hit by a car for example, suddenly leap up and run away. Were they having a near death experience (NDE) while lying there prone? Perhaps "playing dead" instead of "playing alive."

Certainly a person who is in a coma is "still alive" although people who are related to that person can argue about what being alive means to them. We get down to the level of "brain function." If the brain is functioning – if blood is carrying oxygen to the brain and we're getting electrical signals from the brain, even a person in a coma is considered alive.

Years ago I was on a plane talking to a woman from Australia who told me the story of her brother who was in a coma. His physical therapist also happened to be a psychic medium. She told the sister that her brother was asking for "yellow shades." The sister realized he was trying to say the sun was too bright in his room, and he needed his old sunglasses. She put them on him. No doctor believed her brother was capable of consciousness; there was nothing that pointed to a functioning brain. Yet, apparently, he could still ask for his shades.

There are many medical cases of people who've been dead for a number of minutes – even hours – and they "come back to life." People who've been frozen, remain barely alive, and yet are able to recover fully. There are examples of yogis who bury themselves in snow and have trained their bodies to take on the barest of oxygen – the amount that might kill the rest of us, and yet they remain "alive." Then we have the thousands of cases of people who've had near death experiences – as catalogued by scientists like Dr. Sam Parnia, Dr. Bruce Greyson, or Mario Beauregard PhD. All cite cases where people had no oxygen going to their brains for a specific amount of time – the amount of time that is normally associated with being dead – yet recover from those events.

Not all of them are conscious while they're "dead." Some remember nothing, or have the feeling that they were in "blackness" or some form of "darkness." A few of those people are happy to declare that "there is no afterlife" because *they certainly didn't experience one* – and of course the logic goes since we are all exactly alike, then all of us won't be able to experience it either. Just because I like spaghetti carbonara in Rome more than the same dish in the U.S., doesn't mean anyone else will agree. They're my taste buds after all.

As noted, some doctors claim near death experiences are *hypoxia* – a hallucinatory condition that occurs when there's a lack of oxygen to the brain (typically among climbers in the Himalayas) and therefore people who claim to have experienced "seeing a light" or "meeting a loved one" are merely hallucinating these events.

As we'll see in these reports, there are many cases where people have had near death experiences, have learned information that they did not know while conscious, could not have known in their lifetime, were not privy to, or had no idea about – and yet during their near death experience learned this *new information* from someone or somewhere else.

That is what this book is about. Learning from the Flipside. What we might be able to learn from those no longer on the planet. Not in terms of where they are, or how they are – the answers to those questions are fairly obvious. "If I'm answering you, then I must be here with you, right?" Or "I'm fine, that's why I'm able to respond to your question." But questions such as, "How can we manipulate energy in such a way that it benefits mankind?" requires a different level of understanding, and openness to the question and answer. *But we'll get there.*

I base my conclusions on a number of sources; people who've had near death experiences who remember their experiences, people with NDE's who have done deep hypnosis or whom I can ask to consciously remember their experiences, people who've been under deep hypnosis who recall not only past lives but the between lives realm, transcripts of those sessions or interviews with participants, and people who claim to be able to communicate with the Flipside.

As mentioned in "It's a Wonderful Afterlife" I spoke to the Department of Perceptual Studies group at the University of Virginia, led by Dr. Bruce Greyson. During my meeting, Bruce pointed out that "hypnosis is not considered valid science" to which I replied, "but that doesn't account for the fact that thousands of people across the globe say the same things about the between lives arena while under hypnosis; no matter who asks the questions, no matter their background the results are the same, relatively. How could so many people be saying the same things about the afterlife?"

I found this article from Ian Stevenson, the famed past life researcher at the University of Virginia, who spent his peer-reviewed career hunting down some amazing cases, and his work is continued by Dr. Jim Tucker at the University. Ian was not a fan of hypnosis gained information.

Concerns about Hypnotic Regression

Hypnotic Regression to Previous Lives
A Short Statement by Ian Stevenson, M.D.[10]

"The following remarks have been written in an effort to reply
most effectively to the large number of letters and inquiries that I

---

[10] https://med.virginia.edu/perceptual-studies/concerns-about-hypnotic-regression/

receive from persons who wish to apply to me for hypnotic regression to previous lives, wish me to recommend a hypnotist to them, or wish me to investigate some material that has emerged from such an experience.

*Many persons who attach no importance whatever to their dreams--realizing that most of them are merely images of the dreamer's subconscious mind without correspondence to any other reality--nevertheless believe that **whatever emerges during hypnosis can invariably be taken at face value**. In fact, the state of a person during hypnosis resembles in many ways--although not in all--that of a person dreaming.*"

"I'd agree with you, but then we'd both be wrong." He's talking about the kind of hour long hypnosis sessions done since Freud. Surface hypnosis, done with a doctor and client trying to "affect a cure." These sessions I've filmed are often four to six hours, the questions asked are neutral ("Where would you like to go?" "Is it day or night?") and when people get new information – something they could not have known prior to the session - they can prove its accuracy.

*"**The subconscious parts of the mind are released from ordinary inhibitions and they may then present in dramatic form a new "personality."** If the subject has been instructed by the hypnotist--explicitly or implicitly--to "**go back to another place and time**" or given some similar guidance, the new "personality" may appear to be one of another period of history. Such evoked "previous personalities" **may be extremely plausible** both to the person having the experience and to other persons watching him or her.*"

The exception is when two people attend the same event in their past life memory. I cite a case from Brian Weiss later on, where during a past life memory, his patient said *"and I saw that you were there,"* although Dr. Weiss had told no one of his own past life regression where he saw himself in the exact same location, wearing the same clothing cited by his patient. If two people independently remember seeing each other at the exact same event, it's *implausible* that it's coming from their imagination.

In "Flipside" I cite a case where a man did a past life regression, saw himself living in Boston with a woman he'd met earlier in this lifetime. At my request, we arranged for that woman to have her own past life session, with a different therapist on a different continent, who knew nothing of the man's past life memory, and the woman knew nothing of the man's session. In her past life memory, **she saw the identical details; being married to this man in Boston in the 1840's.** Not statistically possible, other than that they were "remembering their previous life together."

> *"Experiments by Baker and by Nicholas Spanos and his colleagues have shown **how easily different suggestions given by a hypnotist can influence the features of the "previous personality"** in conformity with suggestions."*

This would be true of past life regressionists who ask leading questions. "Is this boat the Titanic?" "I bet you're Cleopatra." I've found in the six hour sessions I've filmed; the hypnotherapist asks neutral questions about a person's surroundings. Further, it's the person doing the remembering who clarifies the memory, as if they're driving this bus. "Oh, I see, I'm not the man being tarred and feathered, but I'm a person who is watching this man, and feeling empathy for him."

> *"In fact, however, nearly all such hypnotically evoked "previous personalities" are entirely imaginary just as are the contents of most dreams. They may include some accurate historical details, but these are usually derived from information the subject has acquired normally through reading, radio and television programs, or other sources.* The subject may not remember where he obtained the information included, but sometimes this can be brought out in other sessions with hypnosis designed to search for the sources of the information used in making up the "previous personality."

Well, that's a mighty leap, Professor. *"Entirely imaginary"* or from "reading, radio and TV programs" – he's describing *cryptomnesia.* As I point out in numerous cases, when a person *remembers* a specific detail about a previous lifetime that they could not have known – that is not common knowledge, is not in the public eye, but later can be proven to be true, it shows the fallacy of this argument.

When a person during a near death experience blind from birth identifies to his doctor that the doctor's tennis shoes are orange – it's *new information.*[11] When a person on the Flipside talks about the death of a

---

[11] From "Brain Wars" by Mario Beauregard PhD

person, and it's only later the person finds out their friend has died, that's *new information.* And as we'll see in this book, when someone who is dead tells us something specific about the manner of her death, not common knowledge, and it's later proven to be true – that's *new information.*

> *"Experiments by E. Zolik and by R. Kampman and R. Hirvenoja have demonstrated this phenomenon. **A marked emotional experience during the hypnotic regression provides no assurance that memories of a real previous life were recovered. The subjective experience of reliving a previous life may be impressive to the person having the experience, and yet the "previous life" may be a fantasy, like most of our dreams.** Also, benefit (even dramatic improvement) in some physical or psychological symptom does not provide evidence that a real previous life has been remembered."*

"Benefit... does not provide evidence..." Well, that is, *unless it does.* Michael Newton, in his interview in Flipside, pointed out he didn't believe in past life regression, like Ian Stevenson, so when a client came in and complained of a phantom shoulder pain and spontaneously went to the lifetime where it occurred, the skeptical Newton didn't believe him. Newton peppered him with the questions of a skeptic, and after the session, wrote the British War office and discovered that indeed, the man lived and died *exactly* as he described, in 1916. Just because the therapist doesn't understand or know the genesis of past life memory, doesn't mean it isn't accurate.

> *"Persons with psychosomatic symptoms and psychoneuroses recover following a wide variety of psychotherapeutic measures. There are many general effects of any psychotherapeutic measure. **Improvement may be due exclusively to these and have nothing to do with the special technique, whether hypnotic regression, psychoanalysis, or whatever, of the psychotherapist.**

> *It is worth emphasizing that very young children who remember verified previous lives often have phobias, such as of water, even though they remember the event that seems to have generated the phobia, such as a death from drowning. **Thus remembering the cause of a phobia or some other symptom does not necessarily remove it.**"*

"Remembering the cause of a phobia... does not necessarily remove it." *Unless, of course, it does.* In "Flipside" I filmed a woman with a severe aqua-phobia; she had never been able to swim, and she remembered a recent lifetime drowning. She remembered being a German sailor aboard a ship who was thrown overboard by the crew. (Many of the details were researched and found to be accurate.)

But in her between life memory, she saw the ship had run aground, she'd been stealing food and was "voted off the ship." Further she saw the Captain come to her and say "You have no idea how hard it was to *do that to you* in this lifetime." She realized it was a "contract" they had made so she could experience that event for her spiritual progression. After the session, she was "cured" of her phobia; I filmed her swimming with her family in Connecticut a month later. (Perhaps not all phobias are curable but wouldn't it be worth it to see if it was possible? To the patient?)

> *"Persons considering hypnotic regression experiments should ask themselves:* **What benefit would there be for me in coping with my present difficulties if I did remember something that seemed somehow connected with them from a previous life? Would such a memory, even if it were real, remove the difficulties?"**

In "Many Lives, Many Masters," Dr. Brian Weiss talks about curing a number of people from psychosomatic illnesses. Paul Araund, former President of the Newton Institute spoke of a client in "Flipside" who cured himself of a lifetime of sinus problems by remembering the life he drowned in Greece. He also had a professional athlete who lost her ability to use her arm but through past life memory of being stomped to death, was able to regain full motion of her arm. It's not enough to say "Even if it were real, (how would it) remove the difficulties?" if it actually does.

> *"This being a brief statement, it cannot do justice to all the complex aspects of the subject,* **but I will mention that very rarely something of value may emerge during experiments with hypnotic regression to "previous lives." Examples occur in instances where the subject proves able to speak a foreign language not normally learned.**
>
> *The procedure of hypnotic regression to "previous lives" is not without some hazards.* **Instances have occurred in which the "previous personality" has not "gone away" when instructed to do so** *and the subject in such cases has been left in an altered state*

of personality for several days or more before restoration of his normal personality. "

It would be great if Dr. Stevenson cited these instances. But it's simply not in any case I've ever seen or read about (or have cited in my books) where people have "accessed a personality" that has not "gone away." When you see that you've had "many previous personalities" the question is "why did you choose that lifetime, why did you choose this lifetime and what do the two have in common?"

Because once a person sees that they chose this lifetime, that they chose that previous lifetime, they can understand *why* they made those choices. Once a person gets to experience that we have had multiple lifetimes, and understands why they made those choices, and what those choices have to do with their soul's progression, then there's no point in not enjoying the current choice.

"Not gone away" implies voodoo here, or some other idea of "demon" visitation - which is not in the research. If ever a "stranger" shows up during a session, the simple solution is to ask *"Who are you? What are you doing here?"* and then *"Why did this person agree to have you show up today?"*

> *"I am not now engaging in experiments with hypnotic regression to "previous lives." I do not recommend hypnotists to persons who wish to have this experience. **I do not approve of any hypnotist who makes promises to clients that suggest they will certainly return to a real previous life under his direction. I do not approve of anyone who charges fees for acting as a hypnotist in such experiments.***
>
> *I do not undertake verifications of details that may emerge from such experiments except in the extremely rare instances that seem to me to show strong evidence of some paranormal process. **Instances of responsive xenoglossy (speaking a foreign language not normally learned) may be included in this small group that I am interested in investigating.***
>
> ***Although opposed to commercial exploitation of unwarranted claims for hypnotic regression, I am in favor of serious research with hypnotic regression. "***

If Dr. Stevenson had started with this statement, it would make more sense. But because it's buried in this diatribe; he may claim *"I am in favor of serious research with hypnotic regression"* but everyone who follows his research is stuck in the rut of trying to figure out how to finance it, and not by using hypnosis. The only case I have knowledge of xenoglossia was a film editor I met on one of my films. He had a recurring dream of living and dying as a German soldier during World War II and his wife said he "often spoke in German" during the night.

This was years prior to my doing these reports, but it's not something you easily forget. In my own case, someone spoke to me in Latin, a language I don't speak or know, and it turned out to be a phrase in Latin that was not in current use. ("Vanum populatum" - "annihilate vanity") Six months later, while under hypnosis, I was able to quiz the person who spoke to me. I asked why I was spoken to in Latin, in essence the answer was *"Because if I said it to you in English, you never would have looked it up and contemplated why someone was saying it to you."*

> *"The above remarks apply with some modifications to amateur experiments with Ouija boards, planchettes, and automatic writing. In most such experiments the persons concerned tap into nothing more than the subconscious layers of the minds of one or more of the participants. The dangers of deception and self-deception are perhaps greater than in experiments with hypnosis, especially when the persons experimenting become convinced that they are being guided by discarnate personalities.*
>
> *Here again, in rare instances some paranormal process may be involved in the results of such experiments and very rarely they have produced evidence suggestive of actual contact with a discarnate personality. But in the majority of instances such evidence is totally lacking."[12]*

On this note I heartily agree with Dr. Stevenson. Ouija boards are a form of "asking for trouble with the spirit world." (If your kid owns one, throw it away.) I've heard some parents have had a miserable experience after someone played around with one. For that reason alone, they're not worth toying with.

---

[12] For further info: Stevenson's "Children Who Remember Previous Lives (McFarland & Company, 2001). "A Case of the Psychotherapist's Fallacy: Hypnotic Regression to 'Previous Lives'" (American Journal of Clinical Hypnosis. Vol36, pages 188-193, 1994).

However, the point should be made – there are "no bad spirits" out there. Michael Newton claims these "paranormal events" are based in the subconscious of the person closest to where it happens. (Meaning if they had a previous lifetime as someone who created mayhem they may be allowing that person to continue the pattern.)

Just what the heck are ghosts anyway?

I've been haunted my whole life. Well, that's not really true, but it's been a long time since I saw my first ghost, and it wasn't until I began this research 45 years later that I realized what they are. Folks who can't leave the party.

I've seen them in a lot of places. Old hotels, old apartment buildings. Usually sitting on the edge of my bed, watching me sleep. I wake up and look around. "That was weird." I was sleeping on the couch of a friend's place in Santa Monica, and awoke to a pretty blond hippie chick crying on the couch. As I blinked, she disappeared. So I casually asked my friend; "Who's the ghost?" I described her and he turned white. "That was the wife of my friend who gave me this place. She committed suicide here."

Later, I had a fellow waking me up in my apartment in Santa Monica. Then one day a new neighbor came running into my apt at 8 a.m. screaming. She'd just seen this same guy in her mirror while she was brushing her teeth. I said "Oh, he's the dead guy who lives here. Just ask him not to scare you, he'll leave you alone."

I've mentioned these in my other books. The painter in Sydney who woke me up while hanging from a rafter. Said "Terribly sorry, it's just something I feel the need to do" then stepped onto the ladder below him, pulled the rope down and disappeared. My friend Jan Sharp told me that the guy who painted their house in Darlinghurst had indeed, hanged himself. But not in their house – in his own. So I guess he just liked to hang around his old workplace, so to speak.

Or the Mohawk Indian in full battle gear who woke me at The Workshops in Maine where I was teaching film. Screaming at me in some language I don't know, blood, or red paint dripping down his arms, a tomahawk in one hand and an axe in the other. Scared the *BeeJeesus* out of me. Slept with all the lights on, TV, clock radio on. Said aloud "Dude. I'm only here a week, so go bother someone else, would you?"

This was all prior to my Flipside research. Now, if I run into a ghost, I'm more proactive: "Hey, thanks for stopping by, but what are you still doing on this side of the veil when all your friends and loved ones are waiting for you on the other side?"

I was staying with some friends in New England and whenever a rainstorm came in, would hear "knocks", lights going on and off, stairs creaking. I "opened myself up" to whoever was visiting us, and saw an image of a nasty British soldier from the Revolutionary War era who had been in charge of the jail that was near the site of the house I was staying in. He supervised the prison and gallows, and showed me some horrible sights. (I later found that there was a British garrison on the site during the Revolutionary War.)

Since I'd done some of these reports by this point, I was able to say to him, "Look, I appreciate you experienced a lot of pain in your lifetime, brother. *But you're missing out on something quite wonderful.* Look around you. Can you see a light? If you go towards that light, every friend of yours, everyone who ever loved you is waiting beyond that light. Just go there, and you won't have to suffer here anymore, you can get back home where you belong."

I didn't know how effective that imaginary speech was, but a year later, I was back in the same house, had a dream where this fellow came to visit – looking quite different. Happy, radiant, and thanking me for "showing him the way home." I don't know if *really happened* – I'm not claiming it did – but I am agreeing with Stevenson here that "toying with the afterlife" isn't a thing to encourage people to do. You're here for a reason. Try to enjoy it. But if it does have value for it, there's no harm in exploring it.

I have had *new information* imparted from the Flipside that I was not aware of nor could have been. Like when our two-year-old son said *"Dad! I was a monk in Nepal!"* (As reported in the chapter "My Son the Monk" in "Flipside.") It was his first full sentence to me, we were on the phone – and I said "Put your mom on the phone." I asked her, "Why did he say that?" She had no idea – they weren't watching a "reincarnation" show on TV, nor reading a book about Nepal. He'd just said it to me as if he'd been *waiting two years* to report it to me.

A year later, I asked my 3-year-old son if he had "known me from before."

He nodded and I asked *"so where did you meet me?"* He said "Tibet." Startled, I asked where in Tibet. He said "On the path." Then I remembered three years earlier I had been on a path around Mt. Kailash with Robert Thurman, the former Tibetan monk who was in charge of Tibetan studies at Columbia University. Robert told me we were at the spot where "if you make a wish it will come true." I chuckled and thought of wishing for a "million dollars" or a "three picture movie deal."

But out of my mouth came "I want a son." I was startled when I said it, as startled as when I asked my son in the car, "Was it Mt. Kailash?" He shook his head "No." I asked him "was it Kangra?" Kangra is the name of the path (in Tibetan) where I made the wish. He nodded and said "It was on Kangra."[13]

Then a year later, while working on the film "Salt" I'd sublet an apartment in Greenwich Village. Our son had found some books in the library of the home we were subletting, pulled two out and put one in the trash. She had said to him, "What are you doing?" and he said, "That book is worthless, this is the important one." He held up Robert Thurman's book "Circling the Sacred Mountain" with a photo of Mt. Kailash on the cover. Our son pointed to the place where I made the wish and said, "That's where I found daddy."

I had never said the word Kailash to him other than that day in the car a year earlier. And besides, he didn't know how to read!

One night, his mom had gone upstairs to bed, and called him to follow. I saw him hesitate, looking upstairs as if something up there was frightening him. I instinctively said, "Is there something up there that scares you?" He nodded, took me by the hand and led me to the refrigerator and pointed to a photograph of my friend Luana who had passed away 8 years earlier.

I said "Did you see her upstairs?" He nodded "Yes." "Does she frighten you?" This was years before I'd begun my research into this field, I was worried he'd never go up the stairs again. He said, "Yes dad, you can see right through her!"

---

[13] I filmed our trip across Tibet for the documentary "Journey Into Tibet with Robert Thurman" available at Amazon.

I fished for something to assuage him. "Does she say anything to you?" He nodded. "She says, "I love you R.J." I said "Well... that doesn't sound very scary, does it?" And he looked at me and sighed, as if I had won this argument, said "Ohhhkay" then walked upstairs.

My father came to see me the night he crossed over. I had flown into Chicago and was asleep when I felt him come into the room and put his hand on my shoulder. I heard his voice say, "I'm experiencing indescribable joy." He said, "I need you to write something down." I turned on a light, got a paper and pencil, and then turned the light off in case that had some effect on my hearing his voice. Wide awake.

He said "I'm here with Mama and Papa," his brother, two sisters. "It's beautiful here" he said. He said he was with "Harry" and named some other people. I wrote down names of people I'd never heard of. I asked "Why are you telling *me* this?" *"Because you can hear me"* he said. The next morning, I told my mom about the vision of hearing him, and asked her who the names were. She said "Oh those were friends of his who died in World War II."

I didn't know these people, had never heard them. They were new to me. But they weren't *new* to Mom. It's *new information*. I had never heard their names, had no idea who they were. My mother knew but they all died decades before I was on the planet.

Our daughter also saw my father in our home, about a year after his passing. We were in the living room with the new baby son, when our daughter came running in. She announced, "Grandpa's in the kitchen!" I wanted to jump up and look, but tried to stay calm. "Oh really? That's nice. Why is he here?" She said "To see the baby!"

I looked at my wife who had tears in her eyes, as did I. I said "Oh, that's great. Anything he wants to tell us?" She said, "He loves you very much." After a pause, I said "Is there anything else?" She looked around the apartment at all the toys and furniture, as if listening to a voice from someone I couldn't see. "He says "You guys need a bigger house."

Just like my architect father to notice the chaos in our place. Yes, dad, we do need a bigger house. But we're happy to have you in it. I've reported, since my father's passing, he visited me a number of times. Once to dictate a letter to my mom, (with names of his friends who died in WWII that I didn't know), while I was under anesthesia in a doctor's office, and when I was skinny dipping in an ice cold lake in Tibet, which was something people did to "wash away the sins of a lifetime." I heard his voice clear as a bell in the cold Tibetan night say "Basta!" (Italian for "Enough already" which he often said when on the planet.) I've done five hypnosis sessions, and seen him (and Luana) in nearly every one. I don't mean an image of him; but a breathing, speaking, hold-your-hand, give-you-a-hug version that only someone who knew a person would *feel beyond a shadow of doubt* that it was their loved one.

"No man ever steps in the same river twice, for it's not the same river and he's not the same man."
— **Heraclitus**

Mom and Dad, circa 1960, Dad looks pretty much as I saw him after he passed in 2004. Reportedly, we appear to people here in whatever guise we prefer to be seen.

CHAPTER THREE

Interview with a Flipside Tour Guide: Scott De Tamble

Scott De Tamble, clinical hypnotherapist.[14]

Some years ago, I was talking to the former President of the Michael Newton Institute, Paul Aurand, about someone he recommended I could speak to in Los Angeles about life between lives hypnotherapy, and Paul recommended I give Scott a call. Our first phone conversation lasted over two hours, and I've spent many more hours by his side filming sessions that he's conducted. We've had some amazing adventures together. In addition to guiding individual sessions, he also trains people in Hypnosis and General Hypnotherapy, Past Life Regression, and Spiritual Hypnotherapy. Scott was trained by Dr. Michael Newton in the technique of between life therapy.

For those familiar with my books, Scott is a frequent contributor. He's a clinical hypnotherapist, has had many years of training in a number of techniques, and I can honestly say that in the decade that I've known him, From the over 30 clients that he's worked on that I've either filmed, or watched – he's had a 100% success rate.

That's not normal.

Most hypnotherapists will admit that sometimes someone comes along who "just can't be hypnotized." It's a bit of a misnomer actually, for those who have tried this process realize that you're never "under" hypnosis.

---

14 Lightbetweenlives.com

You're just relaxed enough to say whatever pops into your mind, pretty much like what people do during a guided meditation.

I think Scott is a virtuoso at what he does. I've watched him spend five hours helping a person relax, and then when the person has given up "getting anywhere" in the session, he doubles back and begins to ask questions that force the person to expand their point of view. He has the patience of Job (not Steven Jobs, but the biblical fellow), and the instincts of Columbo. Scott does play the role of a detective – asking questions about where you've been, what you have been planning – and it's hard to see how he carefully, cleverly pulls on the thread, paying notice of everything said, until he springs the questions only your spirit guide can answer.

He has his own chapter in "It's a Wonderful Afterlife" talking about his path and journey to the work. Recently, I caught him speaking at the International Association of Near Death Studies group in Tustin, CA, and he always presents this information in a fresh and different way.

Scott is like the excellent tour guide into the afterlife who has been there enough times to know the blueprint. He seems to never be thrown by what happens during the journey, no matter how outlandish the story might appear at first. He's always able to guide the client back to the pathway, to help him to see why it is that person came to see him in the first place and what they might need to know.

I've filmed and interviewed a number of hypnotherapists, and each have their own talents and techniques. Just like on a tour, no two guides are identical – and you go with one or the other because they've been recommended to you, or you trust their abilities to take you somewhere you've never been before and to get you safely home.

Scott De Tamble

"I'm a clinical hypnotherapist, and one thing that got me started in this field of work is that I was always fascinated by past lives. I was also drawn to earlier time periods in our world's history, and I was excited to learn how to guide people into their past lives through hypnotherapy.

I had read Michael Newton's book "Journey of Souls," and years later I found out he was training people in these deep hypnotic techniques. I took that training and it changed my life. It opened up the concept that the research and study of past lives is just the tip of the iceberg.

Let's talk about between-life therapy, what it's about, the realms we visit between our lifetimes, and explore "How do we get there?" Most of my clients have personal issues in their life that they want to examine and heal if they can. It could be relationship issues, career issues, maybe health problems, or something else. We'll ask the client to bring in a list of their personal questions, and we'll talk about what they're looking for in the session. Then we'll talk about hypnosis and hypnotherapy and how that works, and we'll give them some tips on how to get the most out of their experience.

When it's time to get started, I'll dim the lights, light some candles, and we'll do a hypnotic induction, which is just a fancy way of saying we're getting a person relaxed and into the zone, to help them open the gates to deeper parts of themselves.

What we're looking to do is access the soul's memories. Not just the memories of the human being, which are probably in the brain, but we're going to delve into the soul's own memory. As we all know, we are more than just a body, more than just a physical organism. There is some kind of essence, energy, soul, or spirit which animates this body, and that's what we're really looking to access in these sessions.

We want to retrieve the memories of other lifetimes, and memories of our existence between our lifetimes. We want to open the doors to the soul.

Age Regression and Back to the Womb

We'll do some memory warm-ups to help the person get in the groove of talking and remembering. Michael Newton PhD developed this process, which he stumbled upon from working with some of his psychology clients. Through trial and error over the years, he developed a fine framework to take just about anyone into this arena. It's not quite a one-size-fits-all method; we do have to adjust and customize to some degree, depending on the person, but that's the fun of it for me. Together we get to be creative and see where we can go together, and what we can find.

We start with an age regression, where we walk a person back in time down a stairway of their life. If they're 50 years old, we'll start at 50 and move backwards, asking them to imagine growing younger and younger;

and then we'll stop around the age of 11 or 12 and move off the stairway to something they're familiar with. Perhaps we'll go to their home and get some details about their life as a child We want to begin to open them up to recalling and speaking about their earlier memories.

After eliciting some details about that time, we'll return to the stairway, and guide them deeper, to 5 or 6 years old, and I like to ask them about finding themselves doing something fun. Again, these are memory warm-ups to get the client in the mode of traveling back in time. After that, we again return to the stairway, and we'll regress all the way back to the womb, to the time before they were born.

We'll go back to when they were just a fetus growing in their mother. There is a lot of amazing information to be found there. At some point there's a child growing, and there's a soul which has been assigned to that baby. When I say "assigned," I'm not suggesting that souls are ordered or told to go in this baby. We actually choose our lifetimes in concert with advisors and counselors, and with the advice of our personal spiritual guides.

Prior to making that choice, we have a life planning session where we look at the state of our soul. We look at the qualities we want to develop and maybe look at more than one possible lifetime to see which life would offer the opportunities to stretch and to grow, and challenge us to move in the directions we want to go. For example, say we're having trouble with forgiveness… we may choose a life in which we might get stabbed in the back a couple of times, to see if we can forgive and move forward. There are various lessons and qualities we choose to work on in order to further the development of our souls.

In our hypnosis session, we'll explore the pre-life planning meeting where we're advised on what we should or could be doing, and we'll explore the choices that we made. We'll ask when the soul first visits that fetus, that baby, and when that event occurred. Sometimes it's within moments of conception. They come in and say "Wow it's dividing… okay, this is going to me! It's 8 cells, 16 cells, it's dividing." Souls can come in very early to see that, "Bang! It's on! This is going *to be me*." **Sometimes souls are busy doing other things in spiritual dimensions, and so they may pop in at three months of gestation to see how things are doing: "Ok it looks good." Then they'll go out and have various spiritual experiences before returning later to merge with the child.** We have a lot going on as souls; we're multidimensional beings, and we can have many things occurring simultaneously in different realms.

We have some clients who move in and out during the gestation… they'll stop in to get the feel for how the muscles work, the neurons work, the various systems of the body… then they go out and have spiritual adventures or work… and then come back in a few months later. At some point we do need to park ourselves in that baby. Although, I've had some clients who claim they show up after the baby is born. They say "I didn't really want to go through that bloody painful thing, just let the mother and the baby sort of do that and I'll come in a couple of days later." Some people don't like to get their hands dirty!

It's fascinating in that it's so different for every one of us, and perhaps different each time we incarnate. **Each time it's a unique path, depending on so many factors and variables.** It's fun and educational to explore that during a session.

We can get lots of fascinating information from the womb about why a person chose this life, this family, this neighborhood, and these conditions. We may learn that the body has certain qualities. For example, the body may be very athletic; or perhaps there are infirmities. There are reasons for all of this and we can explore these reasons during a session.

Another fascinating aspect of the soul coming into the fetus is that sometimes they'll say that the soul can employ modifications on that fetus, particularly on the brain or nervous system. We encounter this from time to time in sessions. The soul will say "This is a pretty good specimen, but I need to tinker with its mind a little bit." I recently had a fellow who said **"I'm going to insert packets of information into this baby's brain, which are going to lie dormant for about 45 years. Then later I'm going to open these up and I'll have this information in my possession."** It's pretty amazing what souls can do.

Past Life Regression

Moving through that womb process, next we'll take a person into a past lifetime… a previous lifetime or a previous incarnation that they have lived, one that is connected to their current life today. We want to learn from that experience, that past life, and bring that information into the present.

It's fascinating to look at past lives and say, "Wow, I was a farmer, I had 20 kids, that was really neat." But how is that connected to now? That's what we really want to explore. We'll look at a lifetime, usually a lifetime on earth… though there are other places in the universe to incarnate. It's a very big universe, and existence is very long, if not forever. As Carl Sagan would say "There are billions and billions of stars…," and scientists are discovering new planets every week: "Found another earth-like planet in such and such sector," etc. The numbers are incredible. How many stars are in the Milky Way? Something like 200 billion. How many galaxies are there? At least as many. There are a lot of stars and a lot of worlds out there.

There are other dimensions, perhaps other universes in which to incarnate. So the opportunities are perhaps infinite for us to come and have experiences of lifetimes. Some incarnations might be in a purely mental world, or an emotional world, or an energy world… we have lots of opportunities to have amazing experiences. This is what we love to do as souls, and it is a way to accelerate our soul's understanding and growth.

In our session, in the past life regression portion, we'll explore the lifetime, we'll explore the personal relationships they had… we'll explore the conditions: "Was I poor or wealthy? How did I deal with that?" We'll look at some of the milestones, and explore how they spent their time, what were some of the major turning points. **We'll look at the major theme of that lifetime. Sometimes it's service to the community; or, working on personal issues; or perhaps it had to do with looking after a family member.**

We'll move to and fro through the lifetime. We can go back to their childhood, then work through adulthood, and ultimately move forward to the last day of that life. We'll look back and understand the meaning of the life, and then, in that final day, we will observe the death of that past life personality. That's a very interesting thing… going through the death experience. It's very unique for each of us, each time we live a lifetime, and each time we explore this through doing a regression session.

Life Between Lives

This is where the life between lives adventure begins. As Near-Death Experiences (NDEs) show, there are lots of ways that people cross over. One common theme, similar to NDEs, is where a person may experience moving through a tunnel, seeing a light, and often someone in spirit comes to greet them. But we find a wide spectrum of experiences.

As a soul rises up from the body, I'll ask them "How are you feeling now?" The response is typically "I'm so relieved that it's over!" Because living a life is a struggle. **We have these physical needs and experiences, such as hunger, thirst, survival, pain; and we have emotional experiences such as loss, longing, need for acceptance... all of these intense feelings, so leaving that life behind is often a bit of a relief for a soul.**

It's like taking a rather difficult class in college that bends your mind, like calculus. "I don't care if I got an 'A' or a 'D minus... I made it through!' It can be such a great relief to be finished with some of our incarnations.

Crossing Over

In terms of crossing over, sometimes a person will need to take a little rest period. As we're going to shift from the physical to the spiritual dimension, there's a shifting of vibration, a shift of frequency that our soul needs to accomplish. In our sessions, and in reality, sometimes people need a little time to make this shift, to acclimate and make this adjustment. Sometimes people will say "I was moving, but now I've stopped. And I'm just resting." That's perfectly fine. Folks often need 'way stations' to take this all in baby steps, in making this vibrational shift from the physical life to the spiritual dimensions.

We'll take our time. While they're resting, I'll talk to them about the lifetime they just lived. Maybe they need to process some of that information. I'll help them to shed some of the earthly experience... kind of like taking off your clothes at the end of the day and dropping them on the ground and saying "It's good to be home." **Eventually they will complete the shift into the spiritual world, the spirt realm, where there are many fascinating experiences waiting for them.**

Spirit Guides

Often a Being of Light will come to meet us. This is usually the client's personal spiritual guide, a soul energy who is something like a guardian angel. Other times, a spirit meeting us could be a loved one who has preceded us in death, like Grandpa, or Mom, or Uncle John. A family member or loved one will come to meet us and say "Welcome! You made it! You're going to be okay. Come with me, I'll take you where you need to go." That spirit will escort us to whatever experience they feel is needed, or wherever they are directed to take the person. Sometimes a person meeting our client in spirit is a sort of impersonal attendant, like a valet, or a nurse in a hospital, someone who escorts you into the waiting room.

But **usually people are met by their own personal spirit guides.** We all have spirit guides of various types. but we usually have one primary spirit guide who has been teaching us for a long, long time. This guide knows us better than we know ourselves really, knows what we've been working on, what we need to learn, and has the ability to easily see into our soul to ascertain what is needed for the next step in our development. So this primary spirit guide will often meet us as we enter the spiritual realm once again.

In our sessions, we'll often sit down with that guide, and he or she will orient us to the spirit world once more. **When a person incarnates, they partake of a certain amnesia, because they need to focus on the task at hand in the lifetime. When they return home, to their home in spirit, they may need some time to re-orient.** They may visit with friends, visit with teachers, all the while beginning to recall who they really are as a soul-spirit; and begin to understand why they were having an experience in the physical plane.

So as a therapist, I'll sit you down and talk to your spirit guide about the life you just lived. What did you accomplish? What did you not accomplish? We'll discuss the purpose of the incarnation, and discuss what was learned. **Overwhelmingly, our spirit guides are very supportive and very positive, even if we didn't exactly achieve what we set out to do.** They seem to say, "It's all right, you'll get 'em next time kid! At least you got in there and gave it a go." So this spirit guide chat is a very accepting and loving experience. Sometimes they'll enfold us in their energy to help us acclimate to the spirit world.

It's an honor to witness in these sessions the moment when the client is re-meeting their guide and rekindling that relationship which has existed for eons. The guide may be cradling that person with pure love and understanding, and the client may sometimes shed tears of emotion. **To feel such a pure emotion, a heavenly, unconditional love -- we don't get that very frequently in life. As you know, love often has conditions in this world; and so, to feel this unconditional love and acceptance in a session is a beautiful thing.**

Healing and Restoration

We'll do our orientation with the spirit guide. They may have particular things they want to show us; and often they'll direct us to go to a place of healing or restoration, as they want to restore our energy to our full spiritual power. Places of healing take many different forms. Though it is all energy and light, people tend to perceive and interpret these experiences in earthly ways. A common scenario would be to go to a temple of healing, where you lie down on a flat surface. There is light coming from all directions, and it's filling you with energy, restoring your soul's energy. In the sessions, it's amazing to watch these people lying on the couch receiving this healing. The look on their face is priceless; they're glowing, it's just incredible.

While they're reliving this spiritual healing before they were even born in this life, because of the 'now' nature of time in the spirit world, and the mysterious link between the spirit world and the current life... it's like they're experiencing it all over again! They're getting healed right there in the office. It's an honor and blessing to be present during these healings.

I've had people describe other forms. For example; "I'm standing under a shower of light, it's rejuvenating. It's washing the mud of earth away from me, it's cleansing me and restoring my energy." My first experience with this was in my own first session. After the death of that past life persona, I went to a place like a Roman bath, in a beautiful classical setting. There were few people around, and I just kicked back in this bath for a while. Comfortable temperature and all, very relaxing.

I've had other clients report things like, "I'm in a field of daisies and the sun is shining, and I'm playing with bunnies." Maybe that's what's really healing for them. It's different for everyone. Once this healing restoration takes place in a session, the client becomes even more fully immersed in the soul's memories, It's a good experience for them to have in our session. It paves the way for deeper spiritual experiences.

The Council of Elders

After the healing is accomplished, I'll usually talk to the client's personal spirit guide and ask them, "What do you feel this person needs to do next?" There are many interesting station stops in between our lives in these sessions. One important station stop or experience we can have, is to go before a panel of very wise and exalted beings. Dr. Newton calls this panel the "Council of Elders" **These are highly evolved beings who may be a couple of steps beyond a spirit guide, very wise beings who no longer incarnate, but continue to serve in spirit.** They are in service, helping younger souls to grow. So often we'll go before this panel of wise and compassionate souls for an evaluation of the past lifetime.

Again, because of the mysterious nature of spirit time, we can ask questions about the current lifetime, and the current situation. The Council will give us all sorts of information and guidance. We have the client bring in a list of personal questions, and during this meeting with the Council, we'll go over the questions, seeking the wisdom of the Council.

We have an interesting technique for interacting with spirit in these sessions. While the client is relaxed and in deep hypnosis, we can facilitate a way to help them to channel this information from their guides or Council, or whatever wise Beings we may encounter. **So the information is not coming from the therapist; it's coming through the mouth of the client.** This is my favorite part of the work. I get to talk to these wise and loving exalted spiritual beings through my clients. It's what I live for in doing these sessions. I get to rub elbows with some very high souls, and I know that it's a great honor.

While I have utmost reverence and respect for these wise Beings, I will question them tenaciously. I will put them through their paces, and, honestly, probably annoy them! But they understand that I'm trying to get as much information for my client as I can. And my client is their client, so to speak, the guides and Council often sent the client to me in the first place! I find that these spirits are very generous to us in these sessions.

A Council meeting can take various forms. A typical setting is walking into a building that has a feeling of grandeur and sacredness about it – a temple, say, or a cathedral. And as the client walks in, they have a feeling of awe. It's something like going before the throne of God, though of course the Council are not nearly that high. **We stand before these beings, and they look at us, read our souls, and can tell us what we need in terms of our development.**

It's quite meaningful to access this wisdom for my clients. Towards the end of a session, a really great question is "Why was Annie brought to this session today, what does she need to know?" The Council will say "We'll we dropped that book on her foot in the Barnes and Noble bookstore; now, we're trying to get through to her, and give her a course correction about her life."

The Hall of Records

After we finish up with the Council of Elders, there are various other activities which may await. One thing we can do, is go to a Library, like a hall of records, which some may call the "Akashic Records." We can go to this place and consult the records regarding the person's soul history.

I recently had a client who was visiting the library, and they were given a book that showed all of their previous lives. These books can take different shapes, and may even contain moving pictures, something like a spiritual iPad. It's a magical situation when you're not turning pages, you're watching scenes from other lives. It's an amazing thing. Most souls want to research their own lives, but there are other uses. If someone is science-minded, for example, they can seek information about technology. All knowledge is available to us in these records; and we can touch base with spirit and bring this information back to our current lives.

Soul Groups

Another important stop in these sessions has to do with soul groups. We have soul groups just like families on earth. These are groups of souls who are brought together at some point and bond like brothers and sisters, become close, and tend to incarnate together in various roles over and over. **Soul groups may be from five or six souls, to 15 or 20 or more, and there are larger affiliated groups. But there is usually an inner circle, with a few souls that we're really close to.**

Meeting up with your soul group in a session is a fun and sometimes emotional experience. It's like meeting up with your lost sisters and brothers. Maybe a particular soul was your mom in another life, and in this current life she's your daughter, and in the next life she's going to be a best friend. The roles can change, but the bonds of love and friendship are always there.

We have these really close soul relationships, and it's a beautiful thing to commune with our soul group. **It's a feeling of unconditional love and complete acceptance, though there is humor and teasing as well.** We can talk to soul group members. We can have them come up one by one, asking them "Who wants to come forward and talk to Mary today?" And someone may come forward and say "You did well in that life."

We can ask them questions about how Mary is doing in her life today. Perhaps Nancy comes forward to give information; "You know, Mary, she takes things too seriously, we wish she'd get out and smell the roses more." We can obtain meaningful information from all of these different soul friends.

There are different types of soul groups. Remember being in grade school, when you had one class? Mrs. Miller was the teacher and we had 30 kids in there. Similarly, when we're younger souls, we generally have a single soul group. Later on, as souls grow and develop, they make affiliations with various other groups. We'll still have our 'homeroom,' which Michael Newton calls a 'cluster group.' Then maybe we have an interest in healing, and we can join a healing group. **We'll have a teacher or guide who overlooks the group, and we'll work on each other, and learn about healing and energy work. Or say you have an interest in art, or in music, there may be an affiliated group that you'll work with.** So there can be several soul groups or working groups that we participate in, as we progress.

As you can see, these sessions, and indeed our actual life as spirits, are full of activities. While Dr. Newton has written about many things that appear in sessions, there are always new experiences to explore. These are as varied as we are as individuals. For example, during one of the sessions that Rich Martini (from "It's a Wonderful Afterlife") filmed in my office, a woman went to a celestial music center, somewhere in another galaxy. And she visited this celestial music hall and gave a concert!

Everyone can access different experiences. Another thing we might do is to take a field trip into other dimensions, other worlds; and perhaps take a class to learn how to manipulate energy, or how to use energy to form matter, or how to use energy to heal. There is so much learning available upstairs, it's really beyond our imaginations while we're down here on Earth.

Pre-Life Planning

As the session starts to wind down, we may go to visit the time of pre-life planning. We may choose to understand why a person chose the current lifetime. **'Why am I here now? What am I supposed to be doing? Am I**

totally off track or what?' We can go to revisit the life planning session and meet with counselors and advisors and guides. A person can remember, "Oh yeah, I wanted to have this relationship with this and such soul, but in the second part of the life, I wanted to work as a space engineer; then the third part of my life I wanted to volunteer at a homeless shelter." We can go back and examine why people made these choices. And we can look at, for example, certain contracts or plans we made before incarnating.

Wrapping Up

By the time we have explored many of these things, it may have been three or four hours in the office. Sessions are lengthy, and they have a life of their own. I never know how long they're going to last. I've had sessions last three hours, and I've had sessions last six hours. Again, each has a life of its own and it's not over 'til it's over.

Toward the end, I'll talk to the spirit guide and ask "What else do we need to find today?" They'll say "This or that…" or eventually, they may say, "She's had enough for one day." We'll wrap up the session. Sessions tend to wind down naturally, and I'll bring the client back to the here and now. They've been visiting in spirit for hours, so by the time they open their eyes, they may feel a little woozy. I'll give them a chance to come back to themselves. If they want to talk about what they explored, we will do so; or if they just want to sit quietly for a bit, that's fine too.

As clients walk out of the office, they know they've had an unusual experience. Indeed, so much ground has been covered – these sessions are so deep and far reaching – that it could be weeks, months, or even years before it all sinks in and they fully understand the import of what they learned on that afternoon. They need to take some time to let it sink in, and to integrate it into their current life.

I want to mention NewtonInstitute.org. This is the website for Dr. Newton's training group and therapist base. We have over 200 therapists worldwide who are doing this work. The entry requirements for therapists are stringent, and the training is intense. So this group is highly recommended. Even if you just want to do a past life regression, I'd recommend going to a Newton Institute-trained therapist, because their spiritual background knowledge will help deepen your experience.

Thank you. I'd like to open this up to questions from the audience.

Audience question: Do we remember what happens during the sessions?

Scott: People generally remember most of what occurs, although as I mentioned, we do cover a lot of ground. We audio record each session, so people will have a record of it.

By the way, I just had a client who became inspired to create a between-life session transcription service, so people can obtain a written report of their session. This makes it easier to study, compared to listening to audio, stopping and starting, etc. She is at LBLTranscription.com.

How long do people spend between lives?

It varies. I think it also varies throughout history. Say 10,000 years ago, where there wasn't much change going on… kind of living a cave man existence, a person might go a thousand years between lives, because there might not be all that much to explore.

How do you know that?

We've asked people and they've told us. There's not much advancement going on between let's say 30,000 years ago and 20,000 years ago, although that depends on where you are in the world. We find a faster turnover rate now. People are coming back within two or three years. But it varies - the times they are a changin' – and we appear to come back more often at this juncture of history, because it's just more exciting and there's more to do.

Recently in a session, I asked a client's spirit guide about time. I asked them if time existed in spirit. **They explained that time does exist in the spirit world; but the physics are so different, that I wouldn't understand it!**

In the grand scheme of things, where are souls going? Are we gaining experience for the sake of experience?

I would say we're looking to grow and expand our awareness. And our compassion expands our wisdom.

But is there an endgame to all this?

Rich Martini: During one of my sessions, there was a discussion about a soul's trajectory being like a painter with a blank canvas. All the experiences we have in life, each lifetime, becomes color on the canvas – and your overall journey is like a painting of who we are as souls. The paint represents all of our experiences. Perhaps we have spoken with our spiritual guide, in advance, to discuss what shades and colors we might want to experience in painting this portrait... You might experience a difficult life with an illness so that you can gain that experience, or access that particular color for your portrait. The endgame is to achieve that multi-colored, multi-faceted portrait of who you are as a soul. If that makes any sense!

Scott: Healing is related to the word "whole." In life, we sometimes get knocked off balance, and these spiritual experiences are placing us back into the cosmic blueprint.

RichMartini: I had a spirit guide say that when he had graduated from all of his lifetimes and his journey, his "graduation gift" was …me. Perhaps after I go through all of my lifetimes, I'll graduate as well, and perhaps get a soul to look over as my graduation gift. Then I'll move from my soul group to another group – the endgame seems to be to move up, to graduate from your class – until we get back to the source.

Scott: But is there really an endgame? I don't believe there is one. It's like when you travel over hills, you get to the top and you see, "Oh there's another hill over there. I couldn't see it before. I wonder what lies beyond that?" What is the endgame of existence? I don't think there is one. We simply keep expanding our consciousness.

What about negative souls?

What's a negative soul?

People who've committed crimes. How does that work in the spirit world?

If someone does some negative acts, how do they what?

How do they reconcile that with their path?

Good question. Basically if someone does "negative" acts – well, what's negative? I feel like I don't know. To kill someone is probably not a good thing. However, it could be the very best thing under a certain circumstance. Would you kill one person to save ten million people? Perhaps that's a question for ethicists to debate. But okay, if someone commits an act that they feel was wrong, they'll review it between lives.

The counselors might say **"Right here you had a choice: you could have put the gun down and walked out of the liquor store. What do you think about that?"** So by looking at their actions and talking it out with advisors, they can see that maybe they could have made different choices. The guides and counselors may offer alternatives.

"What would have happened if you put the gun down and apologized? What would happen then?" **Souls can be shown various scenarios. This is a way that souls can learn.** Then they may be given another chance to face that test again during a lifetime. They get to see if they really did incorporate that spiritual lesson… or perhaps not, and will have to face it again until they do.

If you're on mental or physical medications, how does that play into your path?

In terms of medication, if someone tends to function better on a medication, they should take it. I'm not going to judge it. They don't judge it in spirit either. **God is not going to get mad at you if you take a medication, or even if you're addicted to heroin. No one's going to judge or be upset with you. There's just acceptance… though they're probably going to talk to you about it.**

Do we have to come here to incarnate?

No, we don't have to come here. No one is forced to do anything. You are not forced by anyone or by karma to incarnate. On the contrary, souls 'up there' are clamoring to incarnate! Souls in spirit are like, "I'm so excited, I can't wait to get back down there and mix it up!"

Coming into a life is like going to Disneyland; there are thrills, chills, and spills, it's just a great time. In the spiritual realms, we take in lectures and classes, and we can learn all we can about these wonderful concepts, ethical, metaphysical concepts. But it's somewhat intellectual, mental, or cerebral, in a sense. **We come down into a life and a body, which is full of instincts and hormones and needs, to test our learnings, to feel them, to live them, to see if we really learned them.**

But we don't remember those lessons, do we?

That may also be part of the plan. Some of us do have memories of lessons, and other lives, and even our existence in spirit. Before birth, we determine how much we are going to remember. It may be 3% or 50%, or nothing. It depends. Every person in this room, at different points of their lives, may have feelings or *remembrances* about who we really are.

But for the most part, we partake of spiritual amnesia, because we need to focus on the task at hand, and live the current life the best that we can. If we're thinking about all these other things, you know, "Hey, remember those good old Roman days? That was so much fun, but then you got drunk and fell over and cut me with your sword!" That may interfere with our current mission of taking care of whatever business we are focusing upon.

So, no, we don't have to come here, but we choose to, because we want to test what we've learned. And we also want to viscerally experience life. Souls can learn many things upstairs, but they don't really progress in the way that we do when we come into these earthly incarnations. Living a life accelerates our advancement. **Because how can you really know anything until you've experienced it?** Like if someone was losing a child, you can have compassion for them; but until you've lost a child. you don't really know what that feels like. We also come down here to feel; to feel what it feels like to live and to have these experiences.

Do people incarnate on other planets?

Oh yes. Earth is a beautiful, amazing place, very precious and unique; but it's just a speck of dust in the universe. **Many, many people say in sessions that they have incarnations in places other than Earth.** There are other physical worlds, where the bodies may be humanoid, you know, with two arms and two legs, that kind of thing. There are reports of water worlds where people are like dolphin beings, and other worlds where people fly in these crazy pterodactyl bodies... there are lots of places to go and have wonderful experiences.

Is there a future on Earth?

During sessions, I've had people flip into future lives here on Earth. I don't know what to think about that. We think Homo Sapiens developed around... what? 200,000 years ago? Our species, Homo Sapiens, or the

Cro-Magnon, developed about 40,000 years ago? With the current state of our technology, and the incredible leaps with that, who knows what we might come up with in 50, 100, a thousand years? I'm a science fiction fan, I think we'll eventually branch out to other places. I think we'll find ways to overcome the vast distances between the stars. Is there a future on Earth? It's up to us. Every decision we make in our lives affects and alters that. I'm hoping for the best.

I had a client tell me this is the 39th iteration of this species. It was planned, and it was seeded; there are creator beings, other beings that are working on us and helping us. Will we evolve, will we develop into a new species? Who knows what we'll evolve into? As souls we're already doing it.

Are there spiritual reasons behind suicide?

There's not one answer, there are always different reasons in different cases. Some souls make a plan to live, say, 68 years, but then the life turns out poorly and they just bail out. Others actually plan to commit suicide, in order to give a lesson in loss to others around them. Not a fun lesson. But we have free will, and even though we've made certain plans, we can always turn left instead of right.

How are suicides handled by the spiritual guides and Elders? They'll talk to the soul. They'll say "Hey, we created this great life for you, and you bailed out. We're a little disappointed in that. We're not going to spank you or anything, but we want to talk about this… next time you take a life, you're going to have to show us that you're really going to stick with it!"

Thanks Scott.

You're most welcome. Thank you all!"
……

Recently a scientist contacted me about my research; I put this PhD in touch with Scott. During her past life regression, she remembered a lifetime where she thought she was playing for the Boston Red Sox, including the player's first name.

The cool thing about professional baseball is they keep records of everyone who played the game. During her session she said "What felt familiar was a moment in my reading when I said how amazing the ball park feels to me, how baseball is in my blood, my DNA. In the recording during hypnosis, you can hear me talk about what the ball park felt like on (the) opening night of a very big game, a big, big game, like the World Series. I told Scott about the other team, I said (their) name; "Bluejays.""

The actual *bird name* of the other team was the "Robins." She's found footage of that World Series game; the Red Sox versus the *"Brooklyn Robins"* – who eventually became the Brooklyn Dodgers. Not a detail this professor knew (or many know) prior to her session with Scott; a small but important detail in the newly accessed memory from a previous lifetime.

Scott De Tamble is a clinical hypnotherapist specializing in Past Life Regression and Between Life Therapy, and can be found at lightbetweenlives.com

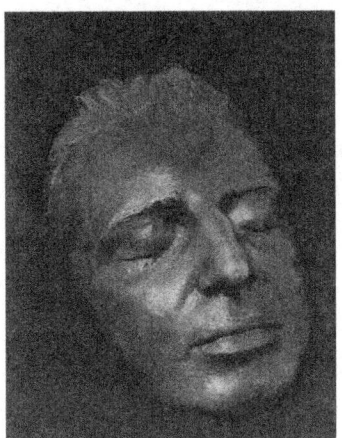

Mozart's death mask
"Just curious. Did your musical gift come from relentlessly practicing piano or from a previous incarnation?"

CHAPTER FOUR

Speaking of Edgar Cayce

Kevin Moore and his Skype guest; me with hand signals.

"The life of the dead is set in the memory of the living."
— Cicero

Recently, I appeared on Kevin Moore's alternative late night talk show via Skype in the UK. It's easy to find the original show online; I've edited my remarks, and clarified a few.

I'm reproducing it here because I touch on a number of points of how I came to these reports and what I'm learning from the research. At the end, there's a point where it appears we access someone on the Flipside who claims to be Edgar Cayce, "The Sleeping Prophet."

Edgar Cayce was famous for healing or helping people with illnesses that they couldn't identify. He went into a trance and "channeled" a cure for a number of people who claimed to be healed by his advice. According to Wikipedia, the people who came to see him, included Woodrow Wilson, Thomas Edison, Irving Berlin, and George Gershwin.

In the case of Cayce, there are many cases researchable at the A.R.E. center in Virginia Beach, so people can see for themselves how accurate he was in his diagnoses. From what I've been able to gather from reading about him, and checking a number of his reports – is that when it came to helping people who were ill here on the planet, he had a pretty good record of helping or healing people. He wasn't 100% accurate – and later in life, people sent him stories about people who were no longer on the planet, and when he went into a trance and prescribed some medical answer, it was pointed out that he was writing about a dead person.

So, in the skeptic's world; Cayce *was not accurate*. Further, when Cayce was asked about predicting the future, he gave a number of fantastical answers which for the most part did not come true. So there's that as well. If you're a person who is looking for 100% accuracy, I would say Edgar doesn't fit in that category.

But that would be ignoring other aspects of his journey in life that were accurate. He had an amazing ability to fall asleep and recount the content of books for example. He had an amazing ability to go into a trance and talk about the health of someone he'd never met, recommend a cure, and that person would later verify everything that Cayce had said. So there's that aspect – which is that in terms of spiritual events, Cayce was correct, accurate, absolutely right a number of times that aren't explained by how the materialist world appears to work. *Which is where I come in.*

Interview with Kevin Moore

Kevin Moore: On today's show I'm joined by Richard Martini, author and award winning filmmaker. Richard's written and or directed 9 theatrical films, has been a freelance writer for Variety, Inc.com, Premiere and other magazines, is also a graduate of the masters of professional writing program at USC. His first book was "Flipside: A Tourist's Guide on How to Navigate the Afterlife."

Martini went on a quest to find out what the prevailing science of the afterlife might be; he journeyed into Tibetan philosophy, made documentaries in India and Tibet and was eventually introduced to the work of The Newton Institute, founded by renowned author and hypnotherapist Dr. Michael Newton, author of "Journey of Souls." Welcome to the show.

I came across your work on Coast to Coast radio. I think what you've done with this documentary "Flipside" is wonderful; I really recommend it to anyone into this subject. How did you get involved in the paranormal and the near death and life between life experiences?

RichMartini: It was some years ago, a close friend was passing away and I started to experience visitations from her. She would appear as a younger woman, before I'd met her. Ultimately, my friend did pass away, and at some point, about a year later, I started to wonder - if she could physically appear to me while I was asleep, (I heard her voice at least once) then is it possible she could she still exist? If so, where is she?

If there is a continuity of consciousness, where does it go? At some point, I had an out of body experience while living in New York City. I had the unusual experience of leaving my body, traveling through deep space, going somewhere which seemed to be another universe.

I can only say it felt like another universe, because I had the actual feeling of traveling through space at a great rate of speed, then suddenly turning and going in another direction. That new "universe" seemed different than the one I'd just been traveling through; wherever that was. That's as best as I can describe it – and then… there she was. She opened her eyes as if to say "You wanted to know where I was, here I am."

At that moment a truck outside my window honked his horn and I had the experience traveling back to Manhattan and seeing it come up at me with great velocity. When I woke up, I thought "wow." I could have dismissed it, like we do, as an odd dream… but I felt like she'd taken me to where she was currently residing.

I began to ask, "How do I go visit her - if she still exists? Where is she?" That become the genesis of my search; because she had been a Buddhist, I began studying Tibetan philosophy. I thought perhaps they had a road map on how to get there, with their "Tibetan Book of the Dead." I had some wonderful experiences, but ultimately I stumbled upon another path.

I was in London, visiting my friend Chuck Tebbetts who introduced me to his friend, Robert Beer, an Oxford professor; he turned me on to the work of Michael Newton. Newton was a psychologist who lived in LA in the 1960's and didn't believe in past life regression. He was skeptical of it until one day when working with a client, the person spontaneously remembered a previous lifetime.

The man had come in with shoulder pain; his doctors told him, "We have no idea where the shoulder problem is coming from, it must be in your mind, so why don't you see a psychologist who can put you under hypnosis?"

During the session, Michael Newton asked him to take him to the source of his pain and he remembered being a British soldier in the 4th corps in the Battle of the Somme in France in 1916. The man saw himself being stabbed in the shoulder by a German soldier. But Newton, the skeptic, didn't believe him, so he was asking him questions "What's your mother's maiden name?" "What's your regiment?" As Newton told me in his interview, while this poor guy was writhing on his couch, he was grilling him for details. But ultimately the client was cured of his problem and he called to say to Michael "My wife wanted to thank you as my pain is gone."

But that didn't satisfy Newton, so he contacted the British War Office and asked "Did you have a guy in the 4th corps?" etc, and it turned out this guy did exist. So Newton opened his practice to past life regression, as many hypnotherapists will tell you they don't really care if the past life existed or not, it's all about helping their clients to heal.

That's also reported in Dr. Brian Weiss' work ("Many Lives, Many Masters") He had a person who spontaneously cured herself by remembering a previous lifetime, and as he put it, it wasn't important whether or not the past life existed as he was just trying to help his clients. But somewhere along the line in the 1960's Newton's work took a turn.

A woman came in who was very depressed, and Michael asked her about taking him to the source of her depression. He added the words "Especially if there's a group around." She said "Oh I see, in my life planning process, we all agreed not to be together. The people that I normally incarnate with, we all agreed to not be at the same time and the same place." Newton was confused, and asked "Who are these people what are you talking about?" She said "They're here. I see them all in your office."

As Michael put it in the interview, when the session was done, it blew his mind – what was she talking about? Where are these people? In the past? In the future?" She said it was not a past life memory, not a future memory, but was occurring "right now."

Basically Newton closed his public practice and for the next 30 years saw 7000 clients who took him to this place; "between lives." Through deep hypnosis – 4 - 6 hour sessions – Newton ultimately cataloged that work and published a book in 1994, "The Journey of Souls."

After reading his book, hearing about people finding their loved ones through hypnosis, I thought "Well, if you're looking to find Luana, my friend, then this is the place to start." I thought that making a documentary on the topic would be interesting – it couldn't possibly be true that 7000 people would say the same things about the journey of souls, and a camera would reveal whether or not that was the case.

I contacted the Newton institute, and to my surprise they said "Bring your camera; we're doing a conference in Chicago." Since it's my home town, I went to this conference even though they told me that Michael is retired and doesn't do interviews anymore.

But we met at the conference, he said "Ok, I'll give you my last interview." He's retired, just doesn't want to do interviews any more. I interviewed him for a couple of hours, I'd read his books, I asked him everything I could think of. I interviewed his wife Peggy, which was interesting for me as I was able to corroborate some of the more unusual things he was saying about his work.

I asked his wife, "So what did you think when your husband came home and said; "this is what people are saying about the afterlife." She said "I thought he was crazy." She thought they were going to take him away – that's the way she put it - but then she said "Then I heard the tapes. All these people coming in and saying the same things about the journey of souls - people who'd never met - how could that be?" I realized I needed to make my own tapes.

Nowadays you can film for 8 hours on one digital tape, I asked "can I film some of these sessions?" Because I thought the camera was not going to lie, you'll see on camera if someone is manipulating people. Which of course, is the common complaint about questioning people while under hypnosis. "Are you sure you weren't someone famous?" "Doesn't this boat look like the Titanic to you?"

I got to film and document the process. I started filming people in 2004, I've filmed about 30 sessions since then. I've created my own construct – which is that I choose the person generally, choose who is going to do the session. Because I know them, from my life, I know their background – I've chosen people who are skeptics, some are religious, chosen people from all walks of life. I've chosen different hypnotherapists, because then you can eliminate the possibility that one person is asking these questions might influence the outcome.

Over the course of those 30 sessions, everyone has said, basically the same thing the 7000 people said. Then Michael Newton and Paul Aurand, then President of the Newton Institute offered me my own session, saying "You know, maybe you should try it." I thought well, okay, like George Plimpton did in his books like "Paper Lion" or "Paper Tiger" – why not?

I did. All I can tell you, it was like taking the red pill. Suddenly the world shifted for me because I had the exact same experience, (others did) I was there... my skeptical mind, my conscious mind was constantly saying "This can't be real, you're a screenwriter, you're making this up" and my subconscious mind was saying these things; "I'm seeing this, I'm seeing that."

Then afterwards I did the forensic work to see if it was possible that my memory of that lifetime and those events existed. I found it to be the case. Since then I've done four different sessions with different hypnotherapists. I did it to eliminate the possibility one therapist might be influencing questions in myself. At first I thought, maybe I'll have a different past life memory – but no, it was like I had left a garden gate open, and when the session began I was suddenly back in that garden. As if I'd left for a few seconds even though the time between sessions was two years.

By the way I went and found my friend Luana Anders the actress, the one who passed away. Where I thought she would be. I've had the experience four times now of holding her hand, looking her in the eye, her saying things to me that doesn't feel like I'm making them up, it feels like her sense of humor. She's younger over there than when I met her over here, **but I know it's her. It's like knowing someone is part of your family in the dark. When you hear their voice, you know who it is.**

Kevin: She's passed on, of course.

Yes, Luana passed on in 1996. But the first time I ran into her she was in this big classroom. As mentioned, before she passed away she told me she had a recurring dream she was in a classroom where everyone was dressed in white, speaking in a language she'd never heard before and somehow she understood. At the time I thought – that's the morphine drip – but her close friend called me the day she died and said "I had this great dream about Luana. She was in the 4th dimension, she's in a classroom and everyone's dressed in white." I mentioned the phone call to Luana's hospice nurse and she said "That was Luana's recurring dream."

Then later, when Robert Beer turned me on to Michael Newton. I opened his book and this guy was talking about classrooms in the afterlife. When I was filming myself I had the experience of going not to just one classroom – but a number of classrooms. *Classrooms! In the afterlife!* My conscious mind is thinking "enough already" I've been to school for two thirds of my life – do we have to keep going to school over there? But I found that while you're in these classrooms, you can actually ask questions while you're over there. It's a very unusual method of inquiry.

While I'm under deep hypnosis – which is a misnomer, as you're never "under" in this therapy – you're always fully conscious – you're just very relaxed. It's a lot like a guided meditation during a yoga – you know "picture yourself on a boat on a river." It's identical, but it's up to six hours. Basically you're leading the therapist. They're asking "Where would you like to go?" Nearly all of the sessions I've filmed people said "I'd like to go home." Where's "home?" Well.. it ain't here. They're not talking about Chicago – they're talking about "home." What they would agree, or we could all agree is "home."

Of course, Kevin, your idea of home is going to be different than my idea of home – because you know all different routes from your background and experience. **But it's a bit like when people in Newton's work claim they're visiting a library. What do they mean, a "library?" A physical place? There are no two libraries alike, but they'll call it a library anyway.** People say they see stacks of books, others see scrolls, people say they see video screens or film – holographic screens – each one is different.

But people say "I'm in the library" and someone is "showing me this book" and "inside this book" is this information. By the way, you interviewed Erik Medhus, I've read his book "My Life After Death" – I highly recommend it, where he talks about one of these libraries.

Another book I recommend is by a young boy named Galen Stoller. Galen died some years ago and his father with the help of a medium, wrote this book with his son. Galen writes the introduction to "It's a Wonderful Afterlife" volume two. He's an unusual case, because it's been verified by people on the Flipside that Galen wrote a book.

There is a woman in St. Louis who wrote Galen's father, Dr. Ken Stoller, a renowned pediatrician in Arizona. She wrote Ken and told him this story. That her husband had passed away and then some time later she was doing a session with a friend who is a medium. Her dead husband came through loud and clear and said to his widow **"You've got to pick up this book called "My Life After Life" written by a kid over here named Galen Stoller. The book has a picture of him on the cover (it does) and he's wearing a red shirt (he is) – and the husband said "everyone over here is talking about it. It's probably the best description of what it's like over here."**

When I heard this from Galen's father, I couldn't help myself and said "Oh, the medium must have seen your book or read a review of it online." So Ken wrote to the woman in St. Louis and asked her if it was possible she or the medium had heard of his son's book previously. I've seen her reply – she wrote that she and the medium have been friends a long time, and no, the medium had never heard of this book and yes this is precisely how it happened, and this is what my husband said, very specifically; "Seek this book out because it kind of describes what my experience is over here." That's *New information* from the Flipside. They can read what we write.

Actually I'd run across the book through a friend, sought out Dr. Stoller, we've become friends. I wanted to know had he or his son read any books about or was aware of Newton's work – because in Galen's book he describes going to classes in the afterlife, and I wanted to know was he aware of Dr. Newton's work? He was not, and neither was his son. The descriptions of the classrooms he's attended are fascinating, and mirror my own experience visiting them, albeit mine being an visitor and his from being a student.

While writing "It's a Wonderful Afterlife" I asked Ken if his son might write the foreword to my new book.

Through a medium? (Is that how he wrote it?)

Yes, through a medium or through his father, I'm not exactly sure of their process, but Galen wrote the foreword to "It's a Wonderful Afterlife Volume Two." I'm fond of saying it's the first foreword I'm aware of written by someone not on the planet. That being said, I recommend Erik Medhus' book, "My Life After Death" and Annie Kagan's book "The

Afterlife of Billy Finger's." If someone wants to contemplate the architecture of the afterlife, those books sort of corroborate what I'm hearing while people are under deep hypnosis.

How did "It's a Wonderful Afterlife" about?

I wrote Flipside based on the footage from my documentary of the same name. I had been filming people under deep hypnosis, Then I did transcripts of the sessions and made chapters out of them. But when I presented this evidence, this data to the Department of Perceptual Studies at the University of Virginia, which includes Dr. Bruce Greyson, Dr. Jim Tucker, Ed Kelly PhD, these are the guys who wrote "Irreducible Mind" and other books – they're scientists on the cutting edge of consciousness research. They said, "this is fascinating stuff, but science doesn't consider hypnosis a valid scientific tool." The reason is that it's hard to put these sessions in a clinical setting.

I said "Well, that doesn't account for thousands of people across the planet saying basically the same things about the journey of souls no matter who asks the questions, or who answers them." The two key points to science are that something is consistent, and it's replicable. In the case of these questions, they are consistent and replicable. Then you have to ask why would it be that people never exposed to this form of hypnotherapy or have had any contact or awareness of it say the same things?

Yes.

But I took that admonition into my next book "It's a Wonderful Afterlife" – I interview people who'd had near death experiences, out of body experiences, and people who'd had both NDE's and then done hypnosis to see if they could clarify the things or experiences that they saw. That research has led me to this premise for my new book: "Hacking the afterlife." The idea is I'm trying to access new information from the Flipside.

I love the title. Great title.

Well, you know "life hacks." These are "afterlife hacks." Let's say you're going through a stressful period in your life, and let's say wouldn't it be great if you could talk to grandpa and ask "Why is this happening to me?" or "Why can't I find my soul mate?" These are questions that we all carry. What if we ask people who are no longer on the planet to help us find the answers? When you talk to someone who is on the Flipside, of course the initial reaction is they're giving me information – it's "Woahh! What is this?"

It's important to note that this isn't channeling. Or mediumship. In both instances, a person "shuts off" their conscious mind and allows whatever they're seeing or hearing to come through. In this case, I'm asking questions to people who are no longer on the planet. If they don't know the answer, which is often the case, I ask them if they can bring forward someone who does.

What I've learned is that people who were here on the planet who are over there are not suddenly omniscient. They can access a lot of information, including most if not all of their previous lifetimes. However, they often answer a question with "That's beyond my capacity" or "That's above my pay grade." They don't suddenly see or know everything when they get back there.

However, they can also access the lifetimes of people that are in their soul group. Remember the woman I mentioned Michael Newton spoke of, talking about her soul group? It's possible to can access their lives, and get all that information, that's a lot – and there are also spirit guides who can share with you their journeys, here, or according to some of these people – on other planets. Other places, other realms.

You may be able to access all that information, but that still doesn't make us omniscient. The mind appears to be this unusual place that remembers everything from your lifetime, even though you think you can't access it - if you ask questions about it you can get into a newer deeper insight into it. Which is all hypnotherapists are doing – asking specific questions about the journey and path that the person has been on.

What about the issue of time on the Flipside? Heard anything about that?

There's a lot of people in new age circles who say "time doesn't exist over there. Once you're outside of this realm it doesn't exist." That's mentioned in the Seth books.

Of course.

But in my research I'm not hearing that. I'm hearing something slightly different. Which is that "time" is *different* over there. Extremely different.

Relatively different. There's a linearity that happens because people start in one place and they may wind up over in another place in terms of their souls' progression. Let's say they begin as a younger soul and they go through experiences in lifetimes and they end up over in the older soul group. That's a linear progression, albeit under a completely different time frame. There are young souls and old souls on the Flipside, they had a progression from young to old. Not everyone is on that same progression – but in general, they all eventually get old.

I was talking to somebody yesterday, oddly enough, and I brought up this question to his spirit guide. I was talking to a person I've never met before, who has not read any of my books, who has seen my film, and who contacted me through a friend and said I've had these lifelong issues. "Is there any way we can access them?"

I said "let's try." We're both fully conscious speaking on Skype – as we are doing now. He's at a university back east, he's never done hypnosis, and I just start asking a series of questions about his life and his journey and eventually we get to a place where it appears – that's all I can call it – that I'm talking to a higher self of his. I'm asking questions like "Does time exist over there?"

His response was "**Think of time as a string, and when you're looking at a string from outside, you see it in a linear fashion, but when you turn it and it's now you're looking at the string, it's a circle – you're looking at the whole thing. A whole piece – he said "it's a matter of perspective"** depending how you look at the string. His point being; reality is the same. It is both linear, and it is also not. Depends on your perspective.

That goes into quantum theory on some level, or quantum consciousness, whatever you want to call it – but looking at things from a different perspective. That's why I'm calling the book "Hacking the Afterlife," because I'm asking specific questions to someone "not on the planet." A question might be, "tell us about fossil fuel, how do we change salt water to fresh water in an economical way?"

I don't know how that would work, but if I could get a chance to talk to scientists who understand chemistry – then ask questions, and say "I want you to ask your higher self, ask your guides, how do we do this and show you the process so you can bring it back to us?" You see?

That's an amazing idea. I love what you're trying to do and we'll fully support it here as well.

I was sitting around thinking, "what am I doing? I'm a filmmaker, a journalist and this stuff kind of fell into my lap over and over again, I started to think "Well, is there a reason for this that I can help people with, or help the planet with?" We all hope the work we do here has some positive influence.

Yes, to be of service and give back.

Once I started to film people under hypnosis and interview people about consciousness, and broadening the research, I thought, "Maybe the next step in this process is to ask them to help us. Help us help each other."

I set aside the religious aspects of it. You know the old joke. You go into a church and talk to God, you're spiritual. But if God replies to you, you're crazy. I know it's a controversial concept. *Talk to the dead.* I had a film friend say to me sarcastically "Oh you're the director who thinks he talks to the dead." I said "No, I'm the guy who talks to the people who talk to the dead."

Hypnotherapists, mediums, other folks who have access to these reports. I'm not doing the asking myself because I have a hard enough time discerning who just told me to have vanilla or chocolate ice cream. I mean I feel bad for mediums who are accurate; why wouldn't they consult with their guides above every little detail?

But I am aware of the religious aspects of these reports, and understand the possible "heresy" of what these reports might show or point to. Not that God is dead, but God isn't who we thought he or she was. Not that any particular religious figure was right or wrong – but perhaps just inaccurate. At first I thought these reports shows that all religions are inaccurate.

But that was the first reaction, then I realized "Wait a second, that's not correct; all religions appear to be aiming at the same thing – that the Flipside is much closer than we imagine, that we are all connected, that we do experience unconditional love, and that we should love your neighbor as ourselves. The golden rule applies here because on the Flipside we're all equal. We all come from the same source.

We just choose different costumes to wear while we're on stage here. We grab different props, there's different props that one needs to fulfill whatever it is they're trying to do – but backstage... no props. All equal. No hierarchy. Young souls, older souls, but total respect for everyone unequivocally.

If that's true – if that is accurate, then why do we suddenly pretend like it's different when we get here? Why do we pretend that somebody's famous for something? For the way they look, act, talk, sing, dance, move around the room – why do we pretend that's better than anyone else? What's the construct involved We can – not destroy – but look at so-called reality from a different perspective.

Have you ever heard anything out loud from the Flipside?

We've all had this experience where you're waking up from a dream and you hear something. Well I have, and I'm sure many people have. You hear like a voice or something. One morning I heard the words "Vanum. Populatum." I opened my eyes. "What the heck? What was that?"[15]

I wrote the words down – then a few weeks later I found the note, "oh right, let's look this up." I was googling away... "Vanum... oh. It's an actual word in Latin. It means vanity. That's interesting. Populatum. What does that mean?" Then I saw the definition. "It means to annihilate, to destroy, to utterly wipe off the face of the earth." Wipe out vanity? I live in LA. *Where do I begin?*

I couldn't get my mind around who was talking to me in Latin. I don't speak Latin. Then six months later, I start this documentary and they offer me a between life session. I remembered that I was supposed to come up with some questions, but I was convinced I couldn't be hypnotized. So, on a lark, I came up with ten possible questions "if I got anywhere." One of them "What's the meaning of Vanum Populatum?" I figured if the hypnotherapist was trying to lead me in any fashion, he couldn't answer the question, as I'm pretty sure I'm the only person on the planet who knows the meaning to the phrase.

Then lo and behold, I actually did get somewhere, I was in this mental construct of being in a large room with these wise elders and I ask –

---

[15] Vanum: vanity. Populatum: to annihilate, to utterly destroy; to wipe off the face of the earth.

"What's the meaning of vanum populatum?" The lead elder, sitting in the middle said *"Why don't you ask Richard? He knows the answer."* As he said my name, an image appeared above and to the right, like a thought bubble, of myself sitting on the couch in front of the camera.

I was looking at myself in this vision from the point of view of the camera. In that moment I realized two things; 1. He didn't say "You know the answer to this question." He said "ask Richard." So he wasn't talking to "me" per se – he was talking to the higher version of me. The older, wiser soul that they've known forever, 2, I realized that my "higher self" had cleverly disguised the phrase in Latin, knowing that I would puzzle over its meaning and look it up. Once I looked it up, I would realize how important the concept was – the wipe out vanity.

If I'd heard "annihilate vanity" it wouldn't mean anything – but because I looked it up, then I understood it. After all, what is vanity? It's not just money and fame – it's that for sure – it's "things." **It's all those levels of what we aren't while we're here. All the things that we frame in our mind about ourselves and others based on surface things. That process of judging people for things that don't exist really – those things only exist here, not over there.** So by wiping away vanity we get a closer idea of who it is we really are.

Yes, which is scaling back to that understanding of - well we can't understand it, we have to feel it. But it's unconditional love in a sense.

Well that's an interesting concept. "Unconditional love." What is it?

I don't know.

I mean versus what? Conditional love? Which is how we navigate the planet. We conditionally love our car, until it fails, we conditionally love quite a few things until they fail us. This is a stretch – but Robin Williams, one of the greatest, most beloved people on the planet decides to check himself out for whatever reason. Might have been the influence of the drugs he was taking for Parkinson's, might have been that it was time for him to go, whatever… but because we have conditional love of how people behave, when you mention his name, people say "he checked himself out."

As if – chastising for how he got off the stage. He gives this incredible performance, and then he tripped as he went off the stage and we go "eh, I can't accept that." I'm just saying when we judge other people for what they wear, who they are, what they do – we can't be in their shoes. Give them a break. Once you see them on the Flipside, you can ask them point blank; *"So why did you do that?"* They'll be happy to tell you.

I was filming a session with a woman who's a film producer, a skeptic, and she decided she would do this session because she was having an operation done and heard that hypnosis would be helpful to her recovery. So that's why she agreed to do it.

On the way to Scott De Tamble's office (lightbetweenlives.com) she announced that she didn't believe anything I had said about there being an afterlife, and didn't believe she could get anywhere during her session, but was willing to try. Of course, she not only saw a previous lifetime but went into a really profoundly, amazing between lives session. Here she was experiencing her journey between lives, being with her soul group and she got to a point where she was in a vast library and was talking to this wise person and she'd only brought three questions to ask. Since she didn't believe she'd get anywhere, they were all skeptical questions. Questions of a skeptic.

She asked "Is the universe a machine?" She asked, "What's the meaning of the shift in consciousness that everyone seems to be so excited about? What's a shift in consciousness?" and "What or who is God?"

Great questions.

Here are the answers; "Is the universe a machine?" "Yes," the spirit guide answered, "it's a mechanism. However," he said "it is sentient." So the mechanism of the universe is sentient? I took that to mean that if I learn something, the universe learns it – I'm not really exactly sure what he meant, but that's what she/he said. The second thing was the shift in consciousness, he said "Oh you humans" – (I love when someone starts a sentence with "You humans")

He said, "You humans always feel the need to name these things. You think you can get a better handle on it." He said "In terms of the cosmos – it's no big deal." He said "If you want to understand a shift in conscious, imagine yourself a little crab walking along the ocean floor and you suddenly realize you're in an ocean. That's a shift in consciousness."

I was startled by the answer. I had been thinking we don't really see oxygen as what it is – it functions like water, like we're in an ocean of oxygen. It has all the same characteristics and properties – clear, fresh, dirty, etc – we don't really see it that way, we cut down trees, which are like our lungs – our source of oxygen – we cut them down like they don't matter. So a shift in consciousness is like seeing "Oh my God! We can't do that."

All right – so "What or who is god?" I was on the edge of my seat. He said "God is beyond the capacity of the human brain to comprehend, it's just not physical possible." I thought "Okay, he's either ducking the question or he's saying the brain is like a computer that can only take so much information – if you give it too much input it just stops – it will freeze or crash. Like Skype.

Then he said "However, you can experience god."

This made me think of the South African Bushman that I'd met. A native of the Kalahari Desert, who spends most of their lives looking for water. They have something like 27 different words for it. We were talking about the experience of a swimming pool, and he had no concept of what I was saying as he'd never done that. Jumping in a pool was beyond his conscious mind, so my explaining it, or talking about it – it's fun, you float, there's gravity, *it's like flying but wet* – just not in his consciousness. Too much information.

However, he could experience jumping in a pool and then "know it." This is what my brain went to when her spirit guide said "**You can't know God, but you can experience God.**"

He said. **"To experience god you need to open your heart to everyone and to all things."**

I realized that concept "god is love" is a wonderful bumper sticker, but it's the Flipside of that. "Love" which has no definition, it's the thing that we can't define, that we can't agree upon what it is, but we once we experience it, we know it – well, that's what God is.

Call it the prime mover source of the universe – or that interconnectedness between all of us – **unconditional love.** When you open your heart to everyone, even to the guy pointing a gun at you, the guy who cuts you off in traffic – the guy who stole the donut out of your hand while you're trying to take a bite – opening your heart to everyone and… to all things. What are "all things?"

A desk. Trees. If your heart was open to all things with unconditional love, then you would have an experience of what god is. In some near death experiences, people describe being back home and having that feeling of unconditional love. It's a feeling of opening their hearts to everyone... and to all things.

That's incredible, Rich. You've touched on so much here as well; there's so much we can talk about. You spoke of laughter being important; I think that's so true, yes, we may be talking about deep subjects, but having fun and enjoying ourselves is a major part of this experience as well.

I think of it as a stage. My wife doesn't like this analogy; she prefers to call it a classroom. But when I say it's a lot like being on a stage, we choose our roles, etc, but what makes a stage interesting? **The essence of drama is conflict.** That goes back to Aristotle... the essence of drama is conflict. The idea that the people on stage who are the conflict people are the ones who draw our attention, right?

However, while you're on stage certainly the ones we remember the most are the ones that make us laugh, or the ones who get us out of our mind. When you're laughing you're no longer thinking about whatever the troubles are that you have. If you can make other people laugh, then you get that wave of benefit... right? In front of you.

When we talk about death or talk about the afterlife, unless we use Twilight Zone music to accompany it, people can't get a handle on it. My experience is that there's a lot of fun over there, there are a lot of laughs over there – because you're no longer carrying all that nonsense around.

Did it feel quirky? Or realistic?

At first it seemed foggy, and then things become clear – clarity, certain things were very clear. Some faces. The guy I was talking to yesterday couldn't see a face, only energy and light, but we sense everything differently.

Everybody has a different experience, like we were saying, libraries whatever – but in my case, I was looking at eight people that I could see in my mind's eye because they're now part of my brain. Men and women, some androgynous, some had colors, they all seemed very amused by me. I thought that was interesting. Because even while I was doing this sessions, I assumed like anyone would – "Oh, I'm going into the afterlife and I'm going to experience something profound and mysterious... I won't find any comedy here."

How important is it to be here rather than being back home?

I think if you go back to that construct of a play – we're all backstage, let's say. We're all sitting around and I say "so, Kevin, what are you doing? What's your next gig?" and you say "I've had enough, that was really difficult. I had a stressful life" and your friends are saying "You were really good at that thing you did, and that fun stuff you did was great too!"

"You went skydiving and we were all with you. We experienced that with you." Then they might say "So listen here's the deal, we want you to come with us and we're all going to have this really cool adventure – these things will happen, you may not be there for a long time, but it's going to be a great adventure for all of us."

But you have free will at all times. You can say "Sorry, no, I'm out. I have to rest." Your friends might say, "Yeah, yeah, you always say that after a difficult lifetime, but c'mon man, we need your help."

You're saying that people might opt out of a lifetime?

There's only a third of our energy here, so two thirds are always back there – so just think about that for a second. It's a little bit like sitting on a couch, eating popcorn and watching yourself on a screen. If two thirds are back there at all times and a third of us are over here – how emotionally involved can you be watching yourself?

Well, some stuff you might say "Oh, that's so painful!" Or other events might feel like "Oh, you had this same problem with this person before, I thought you were going to fix that..." But for whatever reason we don't fix it. We have the same outcome. But when we return home, they'll tell us "It's okay, it's all right. We'll fix it next time."

There's also a time element involved. When people say "There is no time on the Flipside" or "Once we're off the planet, time doesn't exist" that's giving us a pass. People may feel "well if everything is happening simultaneously, then whatever I do doesn't matter, if there's no time and everything is happening at the same time. But there's an inherent problem with that construct. I'm saying it's not in the data – it's not accurate, and that it's related to a quantum perspective of what time really is.

In one of the sessions I was filming, a friend had this incredibly vivid memory of a lifetime where she was captain of an English ship for the East India Company in 1610. Later, I was able to find a reference to this person, as the Old Bailey in London has the records online of every lawsuit filed since it opened. I found this person's name and address in a lawsuit in 1610. She remembered being this captain who died at 25 years old, she described living and dying on a ship which was boarded by pirates.

Then at some point she went back into the between lives realm. Of course, consciously she's never been there to the between life realm, so this experience was all new to her, even though she's "returning home." She describes climbing a hillside and finding a class of students who had been waiting for. She told me it felt like her consciousness just melded back into the teacher of the class. She said that lifetime felt like 15 minutes, "like the amount of time it takes to go out for a cigarette."

I spoke to her about it later, and just for the sake of reference, if 15 minutes equals a 25-year lifetime, then how long does 100 years feel like? Let's say "about an hour." From that perspective when we talk about people living 2000 years, from our perspective over there it might feel like 20 movies ago. An event that happened 500 or 2000 years ago might not seem so foreign of different to our conscious mind when you look at that way – because time is certainly very different over there.

You are full of so much knowledge in this field, it's great to have you one, you're oozing info here, I don't really want to stop you, it's such quality stuff... just going back to what you said earlier on, about every experience everyone has in their regression is different, in the sense that it's descriptions are different. People bring things forth in channeling – a lot of things you were saying I wanted to say "Yeah, that's what they've told me."

What are the things that seemed similar to you?

In these sense that every truth is different – there is not just one truth there are... -- we all have an individual truth and that when we get to the spirit side, or home, whatever we want to call it, we are still trying to work it out on that level. Still trying to work out the truth of what this is all about – yes we may be more in tune with who we were before we came down here, and there are infinite levels to go to, even on the level we initially go to, we have challenges on that level as well, that's what I've been told.

It's like we're working towards something a bigger infinite picture let's say – that reality there or here – maybe there is no difference, we don't understand it, there's not words to give it justification of what it is or give it meaning, but it's just as real as it is here, or maybe we're more aware. Other things – they've talked to me about how important it is to have a laugh, being spiritual is not without laughter as well.

In my experience, when I get to a point where I talk about what's the architecture – how many levels are there – we do have a tendency to do what that one spirit guide said – we try to put things into words, whereas they don't communicate over there from just syntax, because it's so open to interpretation. **The idea of multi-verses, multi-lives, we get caught up in trying to define it, and over there, as I've heard from many different people and my own experience, they're describing something to you, like an event by touching you on the shoulder and you'll see the whole image of the event, experience it firsthand.**

It's a way of avoiding using these archaic sounds that we take to be meaning and words – so even there, you want to bring it back to the microcosm which is "what's my experience?" When you examine "what's my journey?" It's individual journeys – I'm just focused on what I've learned.

When you get back to the other side, you see your loved ones and soul mates, and you might experience all of your previous lifetimes, maybe not right away, it might take a while, you might still be here working stuff out. In Michael Newton's book, there was a client who remembered a lifetime where she stuck around on the planet for a couple of hundred years after passing. She remembered haunting a building for a number of years, and Michael Newton asked her why.

She said "It was just something I felt comfortable doing. Going outside standing on the porch waiting for my husband to return." Michael asked, "So what was the process of actually returning when you finally went home?" She said, "My spirit guide showed up and he pointed to his wrist as if to say "have you had enough time?"

As if to say "Your friends are waiting for you back home." I thought that was funny; there's no watches over there, per se, and why that gesture would mean something... But you know when you're outside of time, it means the same thing to everybody.

But that experience was her own private journey, and knowing we don't die doesn't make it any less painful for our loved ones, the loss of a child, loss of a parent, loss of a loved one.... These are powerful real things, that are hard to get our minds around, and I'm not mitigating it in any way.

But I am saying that when you sort of shift your perspective a little bit to know that we don't die – nobody dies – and if we can't die than therefore, we will not only see our loved ones again, but we can still communicate with them now. That's really a profoundly powerful tonic and shift of perspective.

So what about those people who are having it really hard on themselves, very depressed, not happy with their life? Perhaps they feel like everything's wrong; they may not see it from a spirit perspective, it's still just as difficult sometimes, and yet they want to check out early, they want to leave, they've had enough. Why is it important for us to stay here?

I think it is because we've chosen to be here. It's like we have to remember that we've signed a contract to be here, and we need to read the fine print. Which is to say that it is difficult to be here. Sometimes we sign up for difficult lifetimes and think we can handle them, but we get here and we realize they're more than we can handle. During one between life session there was a description of what it's like to shift from being an energy form over there, to merging with the fetus over here – for lack of terminology.

To move your energy from back there into a body here. **The description I heard was "Imagine being in a fast fighter jet and you're dropping down into a sports car, say a Ferrari, that's moving at 200 mph. It's a tricky maneuver and when you climb into the cockpit, you start checking the toggles and you realize not all of them hook up correctly. You may have thought they would, but when you get here, they just don't all work – perhaps for genetic reasons, or for other environmental reasons.**

Or perhaps you know that choosing this lifetime you were going to have some form of depression while you're here and you figured "Well I can overcome that this time around." But when you get here, as we know, once you're in the experience of something intense you may really feel "I can't overcome that. I feel different. I feel awkward."

It's part of the reason I talk about this stuff. Because it requires a certain amount of faith. It is an issue of faith – knowing or believing that your spirit guides, and everyone is with you at all times, they're aware of what you're going through at all times – and there's a reason you're going through what you're going through, even if you can't fathom it at the moment.

When people are in the midst of these sessions they'll often ask their spirit guides, "So how am I doing?" The guides nearly always say the same thing, "You're doing exactly what you signed up for."

But some people do get to a point where they say "I can't take this anymore" and check out early. When they get back home, their friends may say "What did you do that for? If you had only waited until Wednesday, when the tickets to Rome were coming, we were all going to live together for the third act of our lives. I waited my whole life to connect to you, and you left in the middle of the play!"

Generally, people who do remember lifetimes where they checked out early are hard on themselves. They realize the mistake they made, and are sorry for it. They'll say "Oh my God, I screwed up, we were going to do this thing together, and if I had just waited until Wednesday!" But you're loved ones know you pretty well, and may say "Look, we love you, you're okay, you're back home, we'll work it out – we'll do another lifetime again where we'll do all this stuff again. It's a lot of work, but we can do it because we love you."

I was talking about this topic in Virginia Beach and a woman came up and said **"I'm a Wednesday person."** I asked "What do you mean?" She said she was really depressed, went on line to found out how to do herself in, and went down to the hardware store to buy the chemicals. She said she was in line with the stuff when she overheard these two boys behind her.

They were two boys from Uganda whose parents had been killed in the strife over there, and they were at a loss of where to go what to do. She turned and realized in that moment "This is why I'm here" and now she runs an orphanage in Uganda where she takes care of these kids. She waited until Wednesday.

The reason you signed up to be here on the planet – it may be very difficult to fathom, very difficult to understand - but you signed up for a reason. You're here for a reason. It might not just be to help you, it may be to help somebody else and you have to allow that to a be a possibility in your life no matter how depressed you are. Like I say, there is a way out of depression by learning about Richard Davidson's work at the University of Wisconsin and understanding that meditation can cure or alleviate symptoms of depression.

It's not an SSRI drug, like Prozac or Zoloft, even though a lot of people say those drugs help them, there's a percentage that they don't work for. In my books I note that every single mass killing since Columbine, the shooter either was on this type of medication or had a history of it – I'll just leave it at that.[16]

But this idea that meditation can help people who are depressed because it affects the serotonin release in the amygdala. It's not wishful thinking. It's science. It's not just a matter of me saying "It's all going to be ok;" you can be proactive and you can learn a way out of something that's very difficult to get out of. Perhaps not a very funny topic... but.

I just love the way you put that. Thank you. As Edgar Cayce would say; "We're all here to be of service." It's one of the most important ideas – we don't have to be, but it is the way we should try to be, because it makes you more fulfilled than anything else would.

I've spoken at the Cayce Center in Virginia Beach and I've met the guy who runs that wonderful group, but I use Edgar as an example of that premise that we're not omniscient on the Flipside. While Cayce was alive, he helped many people while channeling or connecting to someone on the Flipside – either a doctor who used to be on the planet, or perhaps a medical professional who is over there, or perhaps his own higher self.

I think that's why he was so successful at healing so many people around the planet. People would write him letters and talk about their illness; he'd go into trance and find the cure; find how to alleviate the problem.

But he wasn't omniscient – when it came to predicting the future, he was pretty inaccurate. "California falling into the ocean" etc. Those kinds of predictions. For whatever reason, he might have been seeing events on this

---

[16] Serotonin release inhibitors help many people, but according on Dr. I interviewed, 10-15% patients can't tolerate the drug which side effects include violence to self or others and suicide. Richard Davidson's study at University of Wisconsin shows meditation can change the amygdala, and effectively "cure or alleviate depression." Every doctor who prescribes SSRI drugs, especially for teens, should let patients know there is a proven holistic alternative, that does same thing the meds do, but HAS NO SIDE EFFECTS.

planet – he might have been seeing it through someone else's eyes, someone in another realm – I don't know.

But Edgar Cayce was literally hacking the afterlife. Healing people by getting information from someone on the Flipside, and passing it along. But when it came to predicting the future, "not so much." I think that's because the future is not set. We have free will. Two thirds of me is back there and can change his mind no matter what the contract was.

I will say this, the one thing that the Edgar Cayce Institute does do well, as I've gotten to know it more, it is a healing center. That's primarily what any good medium is, is a healer.

Exactly and I'm not mitigating it in any way.

A lot of people seek out mediums to know the future...

And they can't; because the future is not set. They can give you "likely outcomes." My point is, people go to a medium to ask "What's my love life going to be like?" "Is my loved one okay in the afterlife?" It's great to get affirmation of that, but what about the deeper questions a medium could ask as well – "What's my purpose for being here?"

What is the meaning of all this? How do we fix the planet?

Yes. I've spoken to mediums and they are inundated with mundane questions; there's so much more information that can be tapped into. When you find a medium you can work with, try to ask questions not just for yourself, but for the planet. "Can my loved ones tell me how can we help other people back here on the planet?"

I've got so many more questions. We were going to do an experiment, weren't we?

Sure, we can try, if you'd like.

As people out there (in my audience) know I've been channeling a bit, not even a year as of yet, I don't mind doing this, giving it a go and see what comes through.

Let me ask you in terms of your meditations - I'm sorry you said you were channeling? What's the process? What do you do?

(Note: I had no idea he was channeling someone while on the air, I just assumed his was a radio talk show about the paranormal.)

When I channel I take a few deep breaths, and then I have the analogy that it's almost like there's a circular tunnel and a door opens and I'm greeted by people.. and then there's a connection made.

Okay. So can you do me a favor?

Yes.

Let's go to wherever those people are.

Okay, I'll take a couple of deep breaths to do that.

You can close your eyes if you want – whatever makes it easier for you to go there. I'm not a hypnotherapist, by the way; I'm a filmmaker and a journalist, I'm not somebody who's trained in hypnotherapy, and I highly recommend the Michael Newton method because people there have been trained… My premise here is recurring dreams, or the people that you see – not only to do they exist, (you could argue they exist relatively) but they exist somewhere in your consciousness or perhaps in some other place.

I want you to focus on getting to the end of that tunnel. As you walk outside the tunnel, get to a place where you're now seeing these people. Who do you see? How many of them are there?

(Closes his eyes) I believe there's three.

Whatever I ask you, try to not judge it, just allow whatever comes to be your mind to be the first thing to come to your mind. We can examine it later. So allow that there's three people there – are they male or female or something else?

No, they're all golden beings.

Is there one that's sort of more leading than the others? Or are they all kind of equal in stature or import?

They're all equal but there's one that's sort of making a connection.

Can we ask him or her, this golden person to come forward?

Yes.

Just for the sake of our experience between Richard and Kevin here… thank you for coming forward. Can you give us some kind of a name we can refer to you as? Just put any name in Kevin's mind.

"I'm part of the group called "The One." (Kevin's voice changes at this point, speaking slowly and clearly)

Okay, I understand that – that could be the colors that you're wearing and your jacket – the one – just in terms of you, give me a name for you, if I can. A first name. Whatever comes to mind.

"Edgar."

Very good, I appreciate that, just for the sake of our discussion, your name may be a subconscious name in Kevin's mind, it's okay either way. For the purposes of our conversation let me ask you – can I ask you some direct questions that you can have Kevin answer for you?

"Of course."

How do you think Kevin's doing? What's your opinion about his path and journey?

"His path was one of free will as we all have free will on our path."

Have you ever incarnated on our planet?

"Yes."

When was the time period of your last incarnation?

"I passed away in the early 40's."

Can you give Kevin a visual image of where that was in the 40's. What continent it might have been on?

"America. Virginia."

So let me ask you Edgar, in your lifetime on the planet, what kind of work did you do?

"I was a healer."

(Note: It's at this moment that I realize that Kevin is "channeling" Edgar Cayce. Edgar Cayce died in 1945.[17] When someone claims to be talking to someone on the Flipside, I assume A. They are making it up using their subconscious, B. They're talking to someone who in their conscious mind appears to be that person, but is actually someone else, like a spirit guide/advisor, or C. It actually is that person. If I assume the third premise, it doesn't change the first two; I can address my questions directly to whomever it is that is appearing. If I try not to judge their answers, I allow for the construct that *it might be* that person, and later research what they've said. It may not be the most scientific method, but the results are consistent.)

RM: All right, I'm familiar with a few healers who lived in Virginia in the 1940's named Edgar, I'm going to assume for the sake of this conversation, and clarification, that you are this person (I'm thinking of – Edgar Cayce but not actually calling him that). So let me ask you Edgar; "Why was it that when you predicted things in the future, they didn't occur?"

(Note: Edgar Cayce was successful at going into a trance, accessing information, then offering it to people suffering from an illness. There are many recorded cases of his giving advice in this manner, and curing or healing people who've written him. Eventually, people started asking question about the future during the trance. When it came to predicting the future, he was pretty much completely wrong. Also, by leading with this question, I'd see if Kevin was going to try to protect Cayce's ego or reputation.)

(Speaking slowly, deliberately) There are strands of possibilities. What I mean by that is that there are an infinite number of possibilities, infinite number of multi-universes, and with each gift (prediction) that was his, it was only as good as they (he and his guides) were able to tune into the correct frequency, the correct light, in a sense."

---

[17]"Cayce was an American mystic who answered questions on subjects as varied as healing, reincarnation, wars, Atlantis, and future events while claiming to be in a trance. A biographer gave him the nickname, "The Sleeping Prophet." ... Cayce became a celebrity toward the end of his life, and he believed the publicity given to his prophecies overshadowed the more important parts of his work, such as healing the sick and studying religion." (Wikipedia)

Thank you. I assumed that you were accessing possible future outcomes and I appreciate allowing us to hear that was the case.

"Not all predictions have come true – and not all predictions have come to pass."

Yes, that's right, "strands of possibilities that can allow us to change them or alter them if we need to."

(Note: I'm referring to the idea we have free will, and are allowed to change our mind about a future outcome. I don't know if Kevin is familiar with this concept, but I'm assuming Edgar is.)

Let me you ask a specific question; in your lifetime, when you were channeling or trans-channeling information for people or helping people, were you accessing a doctor (who had passed over)? Who was this person you were accessing? Were they someone you were in a previous life or was it someone else entirely?

"A group. There is a group."

(Note: At this moment I'm assuming these individuals are part of Edgar's "council.")

I see. Can I ask you to do me a huge favor; can you bring that group into Kevin's consciousness so he can see how many people are in that group?

"Of course."

How many are in that group you were accessing?

"Eight or more."

Primarily was there one person? Or would all eight weigh in and help with your prognosis?

"Absolutely."

(Note: I assume he means the group.)

Were these people, were they people who had incarnated on the planet or not?

"No."

Had they incarnated on other planets or other realms?

"Yes."

Were they bringing their expertise to help you while you were on the planet to heal people with their expertise?

"You could say that."

This is a wonderful opportunity for us to be able to access information from you. I'm going to ask specific question about the healing light of the universe. How healing occurs. Is there any way people on the planet can access that healing light? Or what is the best method for people to try to access that healing light?

"All the light is contained within each of us. All of everything, all of consciousness is contained within all of us. All one has to do is go towards the light within us."

I see.

"Move towards the light within one's self. The light of the divination of creation, of all-ness, of all-knowingness. Use and bring that light around us. Light is all we are. It's all there is. It's everything."

In terms of being able to focus that lens, because of course in the human condition we have a lot of distractions that keep us from being able to access that light – what would you describe as a good method for us to be able to access that healing light?

*"It is very simple. It is the use of meditation. The use of quiet space. The use of calling your divinity towards you. **Calling the oneness of who you truly are towards you; your true soul self, your father in heaven you may call it – some (call it that), or the oneness of the universe.** Using quiet space… to bring that towards you."*

If you could just walk just walk us through, how if someone who is not feeling well or has an illness, can focus this light. If you could just give us a step by step simple process.

*"Absolutely. **Just focus the light on part of yourself that needs the healing the most. It may be an emotional healing, it may be a body healing; use the light and focus it on the area of the body that needs the healing the most. Do this even once a day for a minimum of 15 minutes on the area, even using your own hands to focus the light, and you will**"*

see a transformation over a period over a number of weeks towards that area, or less. ”[18]

That's really sound and practical advice, Edgar. Have you incarnated since your demise on the planet? Are you here?

"Aspects of me is here."

I see. What aspects of you?

"This aspect of me."

(Note: I'm not sure if he means "at this very moment being channeled" or the diagnosis part where he gives advice.)

In terms of the people who work in your name, and there are quite a few, there's your organization, A.R.E, based in Virginia Beach - it's worldwide; is there anything you'd like to say to the people who are focused on your work and the stuff that you've done?

"I never once dreamed that my work or the aspects of my work or the aspect that was me doing that work would ever have accomplished what was or is still here now in this time frame. **I would never have believed in my wildest dream that such things would be done in my name.** *I am most grateful and humble for what has been done and the healing aspects of what has been done in my name. The only message I can give at this moment as has been said through this entity, is that there are many truths, there are many mansions; there is not just one truth. There are many ultimate truths to this."*

(Note: By entity, I assume he means Kevin, who has been channeling Edgar for some time (unbeknownst to me). There are a number of individuals who claim to channel the "Sleeping Prophet" and one would have to do a study of all of them and compare what they had to say, to see any common threads. I assume "mansions" is a reference to the Bible quote from John 14:2: "In my Father's house are many mansions: if it were

---

[18] (Note: Thirty years ago in Sweden, I met an Icelandic healer told me a story of his motorcycle accident, and then, recuperating at home, he prayed for help. He awoke to see an "etheric doctor" working inside his leg. He said after that incident, his leg was fine, but his bedroom was not. From that point forward "energetic beings dressed in white" would enter his room and take him out of his body and transport him to a place where they taught him healing powers. I asked him to describe the process of healing a person, and he described, pretty much word for word what Edgar just said.)

not so, I would have told you. I go to prepare a place for you." Interesting to note, in the interview with "Jesus" in "It's a Wonderful Afterlife" volume two, he uses the same metaphor of many mansions in the afterlife, but adds how each room may be a different realm in the afterlife.)

Thank you and I appreciate this information. It's so unusual and it's really great to meet you. Even the construct of where we are; I'm in Santa Monica, Kevin is in England and... where are you? Just in terms of physical space – are you in another realm? Or are just outside of our realm?

"I'm outside of time and space as you understand it, as your science is of "this moment." I'm in a dimension you could call "home." A dimension that some would call "the spirit world." Channeled through this entity has been this message we've always said, as the one has always carried, that there are multiple, multiple infinity dimensions to go to. I would classify (here) it as a lower level dimensions compared to those I have channeled in that dimension."

On behalf of those individuals in this lower dimension; if somebody wanted to access your information, or talk to your group of eight healers; what would be the best method for them to connect to that healing group to get that information that you have?

"We try to communicate through many people. There are many channels to work through, that we can try to work through, this particular channel now that you're speaking through (Kevin) has agreed before coming to this level to hold this work up, hold the light of this work up; it was his choice to do it or not. There are many other channels that we can speak through but we are currently speaking through this channel at this time.

That doesn't mean that when the usefulness of this body is gone, that we will not seek to go through other channels. That is one method, another method is if you believe, if you trust, if you know, if you're true to yourself, then you can speak to us and we will come through (to) you. You have to really have the truth in you. That it is your truth that we are speaking with you. If it is not of truth to yourself, we cannot communicate with you. Your vibration of truth lies near our vibration; when the two meet, communication can take place."

(Note: By "truth" I assume he means a variation of the word "true" as in "authentic, sincere" in motivation. If you ask the question to them with authentic sincerity, they'll find a way to communicate. Interesting he uses the idea of being "true to oneself" in order to communicate with him or his healing troupe. In this instance, he identifies "truth" as a vibrational one. Vibrating on a frequency of "truth" allows for "communication to take place.")

Let me ask you - in terms of your work and methodology, (your work) seems to be in the healing arts in terms of healing individuals and people. In terms of our planet, we have a lot of issues with carbon, we have issues with climate change, issues with salt water turning to fresh water – is there anything you can help guide us just in terms of something we might focus on to help others on the planet?

*"Yes, of course. **The help that you seek is the help of love.** And peace. Knowing that the planet you live on, can stem from a more peaceful existence than it is now. We have always said through this entity how hard and how difficult you humans, we shall call you, do things. We have always said, through this entity, that we do not care of the outcome to a point. **But we do care that you harm yourself and the planet by doing things the most difficult way possible. If you came from a former understanding of oneness and love towards your fellow man, half the problems you have now would be eliminated overnight.**

(Note: I think "A former understanding" means being able to recall the between lives realm, where we do have an understanding of oneness).

There… is not enough. (Meaning not enough "there on your planet Earth.") There is not enough. There is always enough. (Meaning on the Flipside there is always "enough unconditional love?") Enough for everything. For everyone.

Enough peace. Enough love, enough justice, enough knowingness. But you have cut yourselves off from your true nature, which is partly the essence of incarnation, you could say. It doesn't have to be so painful though. There is an easier way for mankind to treat itself and others. Just look at the animal kingdom for a refreshment (Seeing with new eyes) treatment.

(Note: This passage is worth examining with regard to the concept of getting help from "love." He says "You seek the help of love." Love as either a verb or noun is more commonly thought of as an action that we can do or direct. "Send love," or "give love."

He appears to be saying to "tap into love" –**considering love to be a substance, like an energy or a solid. If we think of "love" as a liquid for example, we can see how "tapping into love" might be something that could alter or change a disposition or change how we view the planet.** In this case neither an action nor an object, but a resource.

Like saying "If you access more oxygen you'll feel better and more energized." If you access more love – or the energy of unconditional loving, we can address problems of the planet more directly. If we didn't have the filter of forgetfulness, forgetting how much unconditional love we normally experience on the Flipside, we would have an easier time of accepting that as fact. As noted earlier, one spirit guide in response to the question "who or what is god?" replied "you can experience god by opening your heart to everyone and all things." If you include that in a definition of "love" – opening your heart to everyone and all things – then love becomes a resource. A fountain that gives us the power to change our own paradigm.)

Okay Edgar, I have an odd question for you, this goes along the lines of prediction, but it also goes along the lines of helping someone on the planet. So there's someone listening to this show right now, listening to this interview with you, who if they suddenly won a lot of money or had access to a lot of money, they could help the planet. Is it possible to ask, could you give us some lottery numbers? Is this too much to ask?

(Note: It's one of my standard ways of breaking up the seriousness of the communication. "Hey, if you're actually over on the Flipside talking to us, how about if you throw me a bone from there?")

"There is nothing that we can do to affect the outcomes of such predictions, as you understand this level of incarnation is done with free will, from the level of incarnation where this is being channeled from. We are not able to interfere with contracts that were laid at a space and time beyond where this communication is taking place now."

Aw c'mon Edgar. Give it up. I want some numbers! (Kevin laughs) Ok, I'm teasing you. I just wanted to see what kind of sense of humor back there. Are you having any laughs back there with your friends?

"You have to understand, that coming through this nature of reality in a sense, is very difficult to maintain. I may be laughing myself, at myself at the state that I'm in, where this is being channeled from. But coming

through a platform like this, through this entity, is almost impossible to maintain, but it is…"

Sorry, it's just in my nature to see if I can get you to laugh.

"It's also difficult to… even right now, there are blockages in this communication as you can see, sometimes it is free flowing as it is now, other times it is very difficult for the message to come through. We find your comedy quite pleasing."

I just wanted to add some levity to this unusual conversation where you are outside of time, where I am inside of time. Is there any kind of feeling or sensation that you can place into Kevin's mind or body at this moment so that he understands that when he feels this experience that you're communicating with him? Could you place a feeling or some kind of sensation in him in his conscious mind right now?

"Yes."

In Kevin's world, I would say that when this occurs, this is something for him to pay attention, almost like an alarm or signal, or a loving gesture that whatever he's experiencing or seeing or sensing or being or hearing is something for him to pay extra attention to.

"Yes."

Very good, let me ask you Edgar, do you have any questions for us?

*"The only question we would have for you is today (is to ask) **"How much have you loved yourself and others around you?"***

Good question Edgar. (Anyone?) All right, here's the most important question I can ask today. Who is going to win the world series?

Kevin laughs.

Ha. I made you laugh! It wasn't easy. It's okay, you don't have to answer, I know who's going to win, just wanted to see if I could get you to laugh. I got a chuckle – from "Edgar who's outside of time." How about you Kevin? Any questions for Edgar? Maybe something personal?

(sighs. Voice changes.). Uh.. what I would ask probably – woah, God this is so difficult – "How many more of them are there that Edgar is in contact with?" I suppose that's been answered really.

I think when you're outside of time you can be anywhere simultaneously – it's a time construct, you could be in a thousand or a million minds at the same time because you're not longer constrained by a linear path.

All right Edgar, one more thing. Is there anything you can ask us to do on the planet's behalf? From your perspective you understand out journey and path better than we do, Is there any one thing you'd like to mention – an admonition, a sentence of some direction, of something that could help us back here?

(Long sigh) *"To know that you are loved unconditionally from the spirit side as some would call it. And .. to give as much light and love to the world as you can do, by just sending love and light to all those out there, even those that you may accuse of causing atrocities; send the love and light out to them the ones who need it the most and the ones suffering in silence, whatever that silence may be.*

Send the love and light to them by just projecting it in your mind, thoughts are creative, thoughts are reality, thoughts create reality, thoughts are more powerful than you can imagine; think and choose wise and careful thoughts. Much love."

Excellent. Thank you Edgar. Kevin, thank you for taking us on this quite unusual journey.

(Kevin laughs, breathes.) Wow.

Did you have any idea that Edgar Cayce was going to be at the end of the tunnel?

Yes, I've dealt with him before... he's been coming through the channeling quite often. I can't explain it.. there's a big part of me that feels like I've made it all up; I don't feel silly for it... I've gone beyond that stage. I tried to get lottery numbers out of (Edgar), I tried. There was a point where you said that and he was saying "I'm pissing my pants laughing" but I didn't want to say it, but that's what he wanted to say.

You've got to say whatever comes into your mind, because that is funny.

I'll be honest with you. I found that really interesting what we've just done – I'm in the UK, you're in California, and this... other thing..

I'm not a hypnotist, there was no hypnosis or suggestions - I'm just asking you questions. You're free to say no to any one of them. The key thing from my perspective, is that I don't judge the answers.

I specifically asked Edgar "So why were all your predictions wrong?" He didn't seem to take it personally or have a reaction to that. He said that there are many different strands and possibilities… In essence saying that the future is not set.

I just wanted to say thank you for that Rich, that was the weirdest ending I've ever done to a show I've ever done. I just want to say thanks so much I really appreciate you coming on the show.

………

When asked recently about how this interview had affected his world view, Kevin wrote: "I'm kind of taken back; I will say much has changed in the way I do the channeling (now). I know now it comes through my higher self and I guess Cayce is an aspect of that."

So was I talking to Edgar Cayce? I have no way of knowing if that's true or not. I've never met Kevin before, I have no way of confirming his accuracy about channeling Edgar, or that I was talking to someone no longer on the planet. (As we'll see later, I do get the chance to do that).

But what Edgar spoke of in terms of healing, in terms of getting advice from "higher souls" who have more knowledge on topics, being able to help people on the planet who need help – these are all things that I've found repeated in the research of people who've been under hypnosis and speaking with someone on the Flipside.

But Kevin was live on the air, talking from London to someone in Santa Monica who merely asked him questions, and advised him to "stay open to whatever is said, try not to judge it." At one point he says **"I'm outside of time and space as you understand it, as your science is of this moment. I'm in a dimension you could call "home."** I'm pretty much the only person who refers to the Flipside as "home." I said it during my first session, and then started noticing it in many others. People referring to the Flipside as "home." *Glad to see that Edgar feels the same way.*

CHAPTER FIVE:

The Martini Sessions

Clockwise; Me, Craig Ottinger, Bill Meyer, Dave Siebert, Paul Tracey and Mark Caplis. Three of these pals have unfortunately exited the stage early.

"There will be today, there will be tomorrow, there will be always, and there was yesterday, and there was the day before..." — Leo Tolstoy

At some point, friends of mine would hear about what I was doing with regard to filming people under hypnosis, and they would inevitably say "I want to do that, can you do that with me?" I'd explain that I'm not a hypnotherapist, I haven't been trained in hypnosis, and I have no business pretending to put anyone under hypnosis.

But a couple of friends insisted. "Just try it." I fumbled my way through what I thought was an appropriate session, trying to get them to relax, but generally spending too much time talking about whatever it is they might have seen or heard. The results were predictable; "I don't see anything. I can't tell you what my name was in a past life because I'm not there, I'm here."

When I was interviewing people for "It's a Wonderful Afterlife" I would talk to people who had an LBL (a between life session) done with someone trained in Michael Newton's method, and while I was asking them questions about the event, I would ask them to revisit what they'd seen or heard.

The first time I did it was while interviewing a shaman back east over Skype. As she said she had been in a large room where she had visited her council, I asked if she could remember what that looked like. She closed her eyes and started spontaneously looking around the room. "The floor is like an ancient mosaic..." she said, and went on to describe the architecture in great detail.

I hadn't asked her to close her eyes, but she did so, and as she began to describe this place I realized she wasn't describing a "memory" of an event, she was actually describing what she was seeing "in present tense." I asked if there was anyone around who could answers some questions about her journey and path.

She said there was, I directed some questions at these individuals. I was startled that "they" were answering. Sometimes the answers were sentences or ideas that the person later said were not in their consciousness, but appeared there simultaneously as I asked the question.

I asked if we could go to her "life planning session." She said she was in a room that looked like a laboratory with her spirit guide. He was showing her various possible future lifetimes that she might choose. I asked how he was doing that. She said it was a "hologram, about two feet tall – of the person he was talking about."

I asked what this person looked like, and in this case, he was showing her a holographic version of herself. I asked her to freeze the action of what she was witnessing and to ask her guide some direct questions. I asked what the hologram was composed of, and she replied "fractals of energy" – and she saw inside the hologram to see multiple images of geometric shapes, each containing information about the lifetime and journey of this soul.

I had not filmed this woman under hypnosis, actually I had met her at a wedding in Connecticut. I had spoken to her about a Tibetan tattoo she had on her shoulder, and that led to a conversation about Tibetan philosophy and my research into the Flipside. She said she knew someone who had training in the Michael Newton method, and that she would contact him to see if he was available to do a session with her.

Some weeks later, she allowed me to transcribe that session, which I put into "It's a Wonderful Afterlife." But the interview we were doing was over Skype, and like I say, she was accessing etheric images and memories, and examining bits and pieces of her session without any hypnosis, or my suggestion there might be some hypnosis.

This event has led to me doing the same during other conversations with people who've had a near death experience or some other consciousness altering event. At some point I say "Can we try and access this memory?" They say "Sure, but I don't remember it." I reply "Well, let's just see where we get." The only thing I ask them to do, which comes from the hypnotherapy sessions, is to say "whatever comes to mind, try not to judge it. Just say the first thing that comes to mind, and you can judge it later."

Off we go. *Into the wild blue yonder.*

"Stage hypnosis" the kind we see in County Fairs, is done with a minimal level of depth and a lot of suggestion (sometime with confederates). The kind of deep hypnosis that Scott and Michael Newton work with, is clinical, and if you want to examine your reason for being on the planet, I highly recommend doing that. Seek out a hypnotherapist trained in the Newton method, there's a searchable database at NewtonInstitute.org

But as an experiment, I found to my chagrin, that I could ask questions and get actual answers. By its very nature, we're not getting anywhere *deep*. However, the fact that we can get *anywhere* is pretty deep. They aren't under hypnosis, I'm not giving them a command or a suggestion. We're usually drinking coffee and they're free to say "Sorry, I can't see a thing" or "It's just not there."

But that's not what happens.

I've found that past life memories are so close to the surface, so present in everyday lives, that just by asking some simple questions, and asking the person to answer "without judgment" they access more information than I ever thought possible.

One can argue that I'm "leading" them with questions because I know where I'd like to go. I do my best not to do that by asking questions that are "either/or" answers; "Is it day or night?" If you ask the conscious mind questions about the subconscious, it tends to block that kind of information. Besides; we're just two friends having coffee. If I've accidentally led you into a memory that makes you realize how choosing this lifetime was related to a previous choice, how cool is that?

Here is a series of conversations I've had with friends. I was not recording them on tape or video because, after all, it was an experiment over coffee, but I took notes and then reported back to them what I heard, and asked them to fill in any other details.

"Roger"[19]

Roger is a friend from "across the pond." He's been all over the world, has worked with NGO's in countries across the planet, is also an accomplished website entrepreneur.

He'd never done hypnosis before, and asked me about the process, and then one afternoon while having coffee, I said "Do you want to try and see where we go?" He said he would.

In this instance, I did spend a little bit of time getting him to close his eyes and relax and "clear his mind." I also asked him to think of himself traveling through a tunnel – in this case, I think I suggested a section of a dark forest where it was hard to see. I told him that once he got down to the end of the dark wood, he'd see light, and he would be "in another lifetime that has some significance to this one."

I had no idea if this was possible to do sitting outside near his office. But when we got to the clearing, he said he could see himself as a young male, living in the 19th century. He said the family name was Smythe and was from a small town in Scotland. He said his father was a vicar in the small town, Presbyterian, and he felt he had a relatively happy upbringing in this small town.

---

[19] I almost always use pseudonyms in these reports. I'll leave it up to my friends if they want to reveal they've appeared in my books or not. If they've checked off the planet, then I have no qualms about using their real names, especially when they have something they'd like to impart.

I asked if he could go to a significant moment in the memory of this fellow, and he said that he saw himself standing at the edge of a mine in South Africa. That he had taken it upon himself to seek his fortune in South Africa, and had become a leading citizen.

He said it was diamond or gold mine – that he never married, but that he felt he had accomplished something by taking that risk to leave home and seek his fortune elsewhere. (I've found a Smythe family of Methven in Scotland, whose tree includes a vicar and someone who went to South Africa. His son became President of Natal.)

We were both surprised that we got as far as we did during the half hour we sat and chatted about it. On one hand, he went from someone skeptical that there was such a thing as past lives, to wondering how it could be that he could experience that previous lifetime in such a visceral way. Not that he was seeing it from a distant perspective, but feeling those feelings that someone felt in a previous lifetime. *For him, that amounted to proof of concept.*

The experience also made me realize that I didn't need to try to put some "under" while asking my simple questions. In fact, it seemed to be more helpful if I just bounced around with specific questions, not worrying whether or not the person speaking was maintaining focus. The focus seemed to come just from asking them specific questions about where they were and why.

Bill

Bill is the son of a doctor who has worked in comedy as a writer/performer/director for most of his life. Currently, he's writing and directing comedy films. I've known him for over 30 years and we've worked on many hilarious projects together.

We were sitting at a Starbucks up in Beverly Glen, and he asked about this research. I asked him if he had ever tried "hypnosis"; he said "Once in college." He said the experience seemed shallow, and nothing came of it – other than seeing a "man's face" during the few minutes while his college buddy was trying to perform a version of "stage hypnosis."

I asked him "Do you want to explore that a bit?" He said "Sure." I asked "So who was that man whose face you saw back in college during this fake hypnosis session?"

He said "I haven't a clue." I responded with "You do have a clue. Everything that happens to us is filed away inside our brain – it may go from short term to long term memory, but science tells us *that every experience we've ever had in this lifetime is embedded somewhere in our brain.* There is no delete key." If this is true, then the face he saw during a "stage hypnosis" event back in college, is stored somewhere – it's not deleted or swept away by sleep.

I asked him to picture the face in his mind's eye. He kind of stared into the distance and blinked. I asked "Is it a man or woman's face?" He said "a man." I asked "What color hair does he have?" He described the man's black hair, with a beard and brown eyes. I asked "What's the name of this fellow?"

He said "I want to say "Prince." Or "Duke." I offered that may have been his title; we could refer to him as "The Prince" for reference. I asked why this Prince's face appeared to him. Did he know him?

He said "I feel like I'm supposed to assassinate him." We examined that for a bit. He gave me a time period – the 1830's. I asked him what his occupation was, and he said "I'm in the Spanish government." I asked him if he could name the town where he was living. He said Taormina.

For those who are fans of history, I know two things about Taormina. One that it is on the boot of Italy, the north side, and two, that it was part of the Spanish empire, as Spain ruled the "Kingdom of Naples" for over 200 years. If he was working in the Spanish government, living in Taormina in 1830's, he would have been working for the Spanish royalty.

I asked him to describe his home, what he wore during the day. He did. Then I asked if he was successful in his killing the Duke or Prince. He said "no." I asked "What happened?" He said "They tortured me for information." He was staring off into the distance as he said it, and I was worried about his having to experience that again.

I said "So without feeling any of the pain from that experience, tell me, what did they do to you?" He said "They threatened to take out my eyes if I didn't give up the conspirators." I asked if he did. He said "Yes, I did, and they were all executed." I could see that he was distraught over this detail, I asked him to let that memory go and to advance forward to the last day of this man's life.

He said he saw himself in the castle "overlooking the water" and his daughter was keeping watch over him. He said as he died, she threw her body over his. When I asked where he saw himself after that event, he said "I'm floating above."

At some point, he went towards "a bright light." After that happened, I asked if there was "anyone around who could answer some questions for us." He said there was, and I asked if it was a male or female presence, or a bit of both? He said the presence was a light, but it felt more female. I asked him to give her a name, and he spelled out *Mari*.

I asked Mari directly; "So Mari, why did you show this lifetime to our friend here today? What is he supposed to know or learn from being able to observe it?" She replied, (through Bill) "To show him that there is no action or deed in life that you can't recover from."

Again, this fellow has never done hypnosis, has no clue as to what I'm going to ask him – has never spoken to anyone about a memory of some bearded fellow's face, never seen or experienced anything related to the plot against someone, nor was he ever aware of any spirit guide in his life. But when he said those words, tears welled in his eyes and I could see that he was distraught over saying the sentence.

"There is no action or deed in this life that you can't recover from."

For me, that's an afterlife hack. If you know that there's no action or deed that you can't recover from – then no matter what anyone does to you, or whatever mistakes you've made in your life, there is no mistake that you can't recover from.

Of course in this case, he's still recovering from it, obviously, if it's so close to his consciousness. I've known this fellow a long time, and he's one of the funniest people I've ever met. He's sharp and bright and has incredible comic chops. I know he wasn't planning to come up with some fantastical story about being in Spanish Royalty 200 years ago – but it just came up. Over coffee. At Starbucks of all places.

Eddie

Edward is a successful post production supervisor from Austria. We met about 20 years ago working on a low budget film and have remained friends. He's made his career in a number of places including cutting edge work in 3D environments for films. He even shares the same hometown as another famous Arnold; the former Governor of California.

I hadn't seen Edward in a year or so, and we literally ran into each other in Santa Monica, and decided to have a quick coffee. He asked what I'd been up to, and gave him an update on all things Flipside. He said he'd never done hypnosis, hadn't read any of my books, but said he'd like to "try it sometime." I told him how I'd been having some success with people remembering things not under hypnosis, and he said he'd like to see if he could as well. "Why not?" I said.

I asked him if he'd had "any recurring dreams" or visions during his life. He said he had recently – in fact the night before he had this image of a young boy who had been tarred and feathered and wondered what that could possibly be.

I offered that we could ask and find out.

I asked him to describe this boy in his dream. At first he said "I have no idea" but when I asked "say the first name that comes to mind." He said his name was "Ed" and that he was in Budapest about 1849, and was covered with black tar and feathers in the vision or memory. (None of these answers came directly, they come from asking "What century is it? Do you have a specific year? Where on the planet is this? Do you have a country? How about a city?"

If the name doesn't come easily, I'll ask "What's the first letter. Second letter?" Until something comes forth. In this technique, you ask the person either/or questions. "Is it day or night?" "Are you a man or woman?" "How old are you?" etc.

He said that this boy's "crime" had been stealing bread. That the tar was now "cold and sticky" and really uncomfortable. That he was on the road away from Budapest. He felt like the boy was aged around 17 years old.

I asked him to go backwards, prior to the event where he was tarred and feathered. When I asked that, Eddie said he realized that it hadn't been him who was tarred and feathered but someone else; another boy. That he had been observing that scene and that it affected him emotionally.

Eddie had watched the boy who had been tarred and feathered, and felt what this boy had gone through. That the memory was a form of empathy to really examine how this boy felt. That the person doing the observation was a younger boy, about 14, and his named was David. He couldn't access the last name, but said it was something like Eddie's own last name.

He said he was aware there had been 100's of people in the streets of Budapest observing this event, as if it was some form of entertainment - everyone would show up to look at the tarred and feathered person who'd been convicted of a crime and sent out of the city.

I asked "If you could be with David outdoors, where is he?" Eddie said that he him by a lake. He was able to look at the shore, saw that David was barefoot and wearing "rags."

I asked him to go to the place where David lived and he described a large structure, not a castle, but a large building, which appeared to be a type of boarding school. The school was in or near Kiev, and he saw lots of silk everywhere - colors of red silk, velvet, purple and blue... when I asked about his father, he said he saw an "onion tower-like-hat" on a person - no face.

Eddie said that David had a gift for observing the suffering in others, and feeling that. The school may have a been a monastery of sorts, but it wasn't a military school, more like a monastery, but not a monastery. That people may have gone on to become priests or philosophers.

I was able to find a reference to the "1st noble boarding school of Kiev" - A reference to the "noble boarding school" of Kiev - pretty famous for philosophers - the lyceum.[20]

I asked if he had a teacher in the school and he named Sergey - or Sergei - with black hair and brown eyes. I asked if we could access Sergei directly, and then asked Sergei to take a look at David. He described a "very calm young man." David said that Sergei had a big moustache and a large nose.

---

[20] http://www.prlib.ru/en-us/History/Pages/Item.aspx?itemid=1173 Here's a link to an interesting history of "Kyiv University" which was a popular place for intellectuals in 1850. http://www.encyclopediaofukraine.com/

We spoke of how David never married and died at age 21. I asked him to picture the death scene and Eddie said it was a "very small room" that he died from "fever" and the death process he described as "dissolving" - almost like going from something to a "cloud of dust."

Asked for a visual, he said the particles of dust looked metallic - sparkling. At some point we moved from that scene to where Eddie said that he felt that he was bathed or covered in a pool of light... which made him feel "happy," "healing" - with love. I asked him to describe that love feeling, what that actually meant and he said "it's (a feeling) beyond love.. it's all encompassing and complete." At this point, since his eyes were open, and we were having coffee, I spoke of how others had called that emotion "unconditional love."

I suggested that Eddie "Take a holographic photograph in his mind of that experience so that you could access or call upon it in the future at any time."

I asked if we could go further and see if there was anyone around who could help us answer some questions. Eddie said that he sensed a presence, when I asked "male or female" he said "both." When I asked for a name we could use for this person, the name "Tiresias" came to mind.

(Note: Tiresias is the name of a famous character in Greek history, a "blind seer" who helped people see the path in front of them.)

I asked if it was possible to ask him questions directly and Eddie said "Go ahead." When I asked if Tiresias was Eddie's guide, Eddie replied "I am not." I asked him a number of follow up questions to which he replied continually; "I am not." I laughed and told him that I understand the concept behind saying that he was not, (as in he's not Edward's guide but is someone who is a friend of his) but he was also "*not* not, I was going to do my best to ask him some questions, despite his insistence that he was not."

He eventually corrected me about the term "Guide" and called himself an "usher" - I realize that may have been his response to the "spirit guide" question - "I am not his spirit guide - I am his usher."

In other words: "Are you his spirit guide?" "I am not. I am his usher." Those were two sentences he said, just (cleverly) out of order. I said that I understood "usher" to be something like a "guide" since they serve the same purpose - guiding people to where they're supposed to go.

I asked Tiresias "Have you ever incarnated with Eddie in other lifetimes on earth?" to which he replied "I am not." I said "I understand you are not, but I'm asking if you and Edward shared lifetimes either here on earth or elsewhere." He said "You would not understand."

(Note: It's interesting. Because I've heard so many of these memories, there's pretty much nothing that I haven't heard in this arena. But for his guide to say "You wouldn't understand" implies that the guide doesn't know all, doesn't know me. He's assuming I wouldn't understand, but I pressed on anyway.)

I said "I appreciate that, but could you show us that lifetime - was it on Earth or somewhere else in this universe, or in another realm?" He said "In this universe." I asked "Was it on an Earth like foundation or in a gaseous state or under water?" He said "Underwater" then described what it was like living under water. I asked if the bodies were animal-like or humanoid and he said they were "humanoid." I made the observation to him that breathing oxygen on our planet is the same as breathing underwater somewhere else - that oxygen functions the same as water does.

I asked if there was anyone else who could come forth to be with Edward and Eddie said "My mother." Tears instantly came into his eyes. Eddie said that he "sensed more than saw her," but was able to see her as a younger girl "before Edward knew her."

I pointed out that was a common experience - meeting people no longer on the planet who present themselves in their most comfortable version of their energy - younger, thinner, etc. Eddie said he "sensed her in his aura" - not separate but part of the same energy. I asked if Edward and his mother had incarnated together before, and Eddie said no. Then I asked if his mother was part of Edward's "soul group" and he said "yes." I asked if I could speak directly to hid mom, and he said "yes."

I asked her how she was feeling or what she was up to. I asked her to describe why Edward chose her as his mother and she said one word; *"Trust."* I asked if that was something her soul group was working on? (Note: Often members of a soul group work on the same topic, like scientists working in a lab on the same problem.)

Eddie said he was getting a sensation of guilt or of sadness associated with her. I asked what that might be, and Eddie said it was in regard to a baby she aborted or lost and how that was stressful to her throughout her life. That the even caused her deep sadness.

I asked if that baby, the one who died, could make its presence known to his mother. Eddie said "Michael" was the name... but that it was a female presence. "I said Michaela perhaps?" Eddie replied "No, just Michael." I said it wasn't important to get the name correctly, as most names over there seemed to be composed of sound or energy rather than a word - and Michael appeared but would not speak. I asked Michael if she was someone who had incarnated with his mother before, or if they were otherwise connected. Michael would not, or could not reply. (At least through Eddie's consciousness).

I tried to point out to his mom, that despite her sadness for losing Michael, it was clear from her presence that she isn't dead – "In fact, she is here with us at this very moment, presenting herself to you. That makes it clear that she did not die, and that she still exists and is still here; therefore, she should not be a source of pain or sadness for losing her, as she isn't lost - she's here." Eddie seemed to smile, through tears, to acknowledge this to be the case.

Then Eddie heard Tiresias speaking to him in Latin, but couldn't make out what the words were. I thought that was interesting and told Eddie the story of how I had heard someone speaking to me in Latin prior to my first between life session, and during the session was able to get clarity on how that came about.

At that point Tiresias spoke up with some advice for me directly. He said *"Serious-ity is not your vehicle"* – (seriousness "is not your thing.") That because of my playfulness with language and life, that's made it difficult for others to connect with me... that the use of comedy served to keep them at a distance, because people feel they can't get a handle on whether I'm being serious or not. Tiresias added "It's important to speak from the heart - and one way to do that is to not speak, just to look into another person's eyes..."

Eddic said that he was seeing an image of two sets of eyes looking in a mirror – he noted "**By looking into another person's eyes you can transcend language and reach them in a direct fashion that's beyond words.**"

He said "You're asking good questions. By being smart and using comedy, you avoid sadness - when sadness is also part of the equation, and is as important as laughter. **On one hand you think that by using laughter you can help others avoid sadness, but there is an important quality in sadness that is healing."**

I told Eddie that I understood what his guide was saying - specifically with regard to how sadness is also healing energy and is important for people to experience. **Eddie shrugged, and said he didn't have a clue as to what I was talking about, or what Tiresias was referring to, as he'd not read my book.**

Finally, I asked Tiresias to tell us why Edward was being shown these lifetimes. He answered "Time." As in "*it's about time*" - meaning it's the right time for him to tap into these voices/influences that are in his life and to open himself into them. Eddie then held his chest, and described an intense feeling that had just gone through him - a powerful feeling that came from both Tiresias and his mother. Eddie said that Tiresias was giving Eddie that intense feeling to let him know "It was important."

I've known Edward a long time, and he's a sober, serious guy, not prone to flights of fancy, or "belief in the unknown." He's more of a scientist than a philosopher, and having this experience profoundly moved him, but also confused him. He had no idea where it came from, or how it came about.

I paraphrased this event, and emailed it to Eddie, to which he replied: "Interesting discovery to look at – how the dots connect – **I was so surprised what came out of my mouth. I have had no previous knowledge of how you do what you were doing, or what you were doing."** He wrote **"the weird part is that when I read your notes, I just copied that into a google search engine and up came the "Gymnasium in Kiev."**

"For whatever reason, as I read these words it gave me that same emotional reflex, it tickled me, a physical reaction which I associate as a fond memory of something. Like when you smell something you cannot resist or a tune of music takes you into a place which you can't ignore."

He observed "It's only music and senses, or smell that can do this to you – bread or mother's milk takes you back to that space – not geographically but emotionally – I was reading the Wikipedia version of that gymnasium (school) in Kiev and **I had the same reflex from the experience – but it's not just the thinking, but if it reflects like a reaction with no conscious attitude. I never was in Kiev; (I have) never studied any of this – (these are) complete virgin territories."**

"When you questioned me – "If this is always available, why don't we do it all the time"?" (The answer) came clearly to me, the way we lived those lives, we do actually do that (during our lifetimes, but) we don't do it consciously. Dreams and other things we process (during our conscious hours) those (are based on) previous experiences and that is the quality of the current lifetime. This is what makes Richard, Richard and Eddie Edward." Either way, a fascinating journey that happened over a cup of coffee.

John

John is from the Midwest, and has a successful career in Washington, D.C. Having been an assistant to a Congressman, he's had a long and successful career in the nation's capital in a number of different fields. He's read "Flipside," has never done hypnosis, but one morning he had a couple of hours for coffee and we started talking about this idea of "brief past life memories over coffee." He dubbed them *"The Martini Sessions."*

I asked "Have you had any recurring dreams or people show up in your dreams?" He said "Ghosts." I said "When was the last time?" He said "Last night."

I said "Great. Let's see who that is. Do you mind?" He shrugged, I said "Was it a male or female?" He said male. We went through those basic descriptions, "Where are we? Is it night or day? How are you dressed?" until I asked "Can we talk to this fellow directly?" He said "Sure." I said "What's your name?" He said without thinking, "Joseph Ferguson."

We got that Joseph had died in the Civil War, that he was in his 20's - we went back to happier times on Joseph's farm in Tennessee, when he dined with his family, etc, then went forward to his last day on the planet when he was shot and bleeding in a house in Virginia.

Again, John hadn't come to me for a "past life regression." I'm merely asking what apparently is just under the surface of his consciousness. He had a recurring dream, and it's my contention that every memory is stored, everything we dream of, we have a context for, if not consciously, then subconsciously. Whatever we think we can't understand, it just requires patience and asking the right questions to get to the answer.

I asked him to go to the "next event" after his passing. He said "A cloud of light – I see streaks of blue - streaming down." Asked what the light was composed of, how it made him feel, he said "I feel a tingling sensation and it makes me feel loved." I asked about that feeling, to put it into words, and he said **"unconditional love."** I said "Explain that. What's a feeling of unconditional love?" He said "It's all encompassing."

It's at this point I know we've gotten somewhere. He doesn't know that this is a recurring theme in my work, in the sessions, in anyone I've ever spoken to about what it feels like to "go into the Flipside." **At some point – either while traveling through a "bright light" or afterwards, people talk about this feeling of "unconditional love."** Which I think is odd because they aren't two words we use often. It's not a feeling many of us have ever felt, or ever made others feel. But we know it when we feel it.

I asked him to memorize that feeling so he could return to it later in his meditations. Then I asked him to skip down to another event if someone was nearby. Two guides came forward - one female - Victoria, and she started to speak about John. I asked "So how did John do in this life as Joseph?" It startled John, as he said "You mean "How did Joseph do?" I said "Well, how could you remember Joseph's death scene if you weren't Joseph?" He saw the point and shifted his perspective at this moment.

Victoria, at my request showed him a few lifetimes - a knight in England and then one in France - he talked about the battles that they fought. I asked her "Why is he being shown these lifetimes?" and she said "Humility." I asked "What does that mean?"

"So he can see that before you send someone into battle, you have to understand what it's like to be in battle yourself, what it's like to kill or be killed." (Working in or around many who work in various defense department industries, you could argue that he's still involved with sending people into battle).

That was pretty cool. I asked if there was anyone else around we should meet and she introduced us to this other guide – Michael. He said that he had lifetimes with John "on other planets."

I said "In this universe?" to which Michael replied "There's only one." I said "Well, I've heard about lifetimes in other realms - but specifically where was *this lifetime*, was it on land, on water, in the air - a gaseous existence?" and he said "(It was) in the water."

I asked "Is there a place of healing that you could take John to or show to him?" and John said "I can see it. It's a monastery on a rock in Bhutan." I said "Have you ever been there?" He said "no." I said "Why are you showing this to John?"

He said "He needs to go there, to find peace, to connect with what he's supposed to do on the planet." I said "What is that?" He said "Write books. Write about his experience." I said "You mean in life - his journey like an autobiography? Or do you mean spiritual books that show the path?" He said "That show the path. He has it in him, he just has to get them onto paper."

Then I asked Victoria to give him a sign - an incontrovertible sign that wasn't coming from me, but that was coming from her, some place in his body so that he would know when he feels that, they are in communication with him. John said "I can feel it in my heart."

Again, another unusual journey that occurred over a cup of coffee. Maybe it's something in the coffee.

Sophie

I met a woman from Australia recently, whom I'll call Sophie, who has spent a number of years of her life helping the Tibetan people and their cause. She befriended a Tibetan Rinpoche (Tibetan for "Precious Jewel" – an honorific often given to the reincarnation of highly realized Tibetan monk) who despite having to escape from his home some years earlier, was able to slip back into Tibet and see his old home and monastery with her help.

It was during this trip, she had visions while walking around Tibet; statues seemed to come to life, dragons would appear and stones seemed like they had spirits moving in and out of them. She only mentioned this to the Rinpoche, and he let her know it was a common occurrence. The history of Tibet is filled with people seeing dragons and other mystical creatures;

while I was on the roof of the Jokhang, Robert Thurman told me we were on the spot where Tsong Khapa, the founder of the Dalai Lama's Gelupka sect said that he saw the "sky filled with flying dragons."

One might ascribe those kinds of visual events to *hypoxia*, that medical condition from lack of oxygen that causes hallucinations. Of course that may be possible, but I'm more interested in "new information" during one of these events – things that they couldn't have known prior to seeing or hearing from someone or something that appears to be "an hallucination." If we can find the new information, then we know for certain it wasn't brain created.

We were sitting in my local café when she spoke of a recurring dream where she felt she was visiting Mt. Kailash in Western Tibet, a place that she's never been to physically, but has read about. Kailash is considered the "most sacred spot on Earth" by four major religions; Buddhists, Hindus, Jain and the Tibetan ancient religion of Bon. As noted, I've been to Kailash, filming a documentary for Tibet House in New York, and it was the sight of some pretty unusual magical events in my life.

One was speaking to a friend of mine who is no longer on the planet – my lifelong pal Paul Tracey who commented in my ear about how difficult the journey was for me. I was carrying a backpack at altitude, moaning to myself how it was "the most difficult trek" I'd ever been on – and I heard Paul's voice say clearly "Imagine how hard it was for me to get around." Paul had his hip replaced twice as a young man, and went from the best athlete in our grade school to walking with a cane in high school.

I hadn't been thinking of Paul, but he directed my thoughts to an afternoon where we had spent at a swimming hole, and called it *"the happiest day of my life."* I hadn't remembered that day, or that swimming hole in all the years since we'd gone there; I found it startling for him to be reminding me of it while I was walking at high altitude in Tibet.

Later, while camped under the north face of Kailash, I was visited in my tent by someone who wasn't dead, but whose voice I could clearly hear. It was the actor Michael Gough (the first Batman's butler in the Michael Keaton version) who said in a clear voice "Richard, I think what you're doing is just fantastic!" He said it in his English accent, and I was startled. I knew he was elderly at the time, but I wasn't sure if he was on or off the planet.

I opened my eyes in the tent. "Mick? Is that you?" He said "Yes, darling. Sometimes I travel around with our friend Luana around the universe, and I just wanted to stop and say this trip you're taking around Tibet is fantastic." In my mind's eye, I could "see" our mutual friend Luana – the person who inspired "Flipside" after passing away and coming to visit me. She was hovering behind Mick, didn't come forward, as if waiting for him to end his conversation with me.

As soon as I got around the mountain to Darchen, where there was an internet café I wrote his wife Henrietta and asked "how is Mick doing?" She wrote back the next day, "He's fine, sends his love." I had no idea (at the time) how it could be that my very much alive friend could "travel around the universe" with our mutual friend who was not very much alive (on this planet anyway) and how the two of them could be enjoying "trips" together. I do now, but this was in 2004, and I didn't have a clue.

Finally, I had an unusual visual experience while Robert Thurman was doing a fire puja at the base of Kailash (it's a traditional ceremony that is supposed to protect the pilgrims – and all I can report is that the group just behind us, lost two tourists in a freak snowstorm). The fire ceremony that required 6 hours of reciting prayers while seated next to a bonfire (we tied Bob to his chair in case he accidentally fell into the fire). I was standing a few feet away from Bob, listening to him pray, and closed my eyes.

In my mind's eye, I saw a funnel – like an electrified tornado funnel, it was swirling, with its bottom twisting where Bob was doing the fire prayer. The top of this funnel reached up into outer space. It was like a funnel of light with sparks and energy, went from Bob's bonfire straight up into the sky, with a roaring sound that I could hear when my eyes were closed.

I've never had such a visual experience before or since. My eyes open, I'm standing behind Robert Thurman as he's throwing seeds and other objects into this fire, I close my eyes, and I'm standing at the base of a tornado of energy that is roaring with energy that reaches into the heavens.

Certainly anyone experiencing or seeing that kind of visual would assume its related to hypoxia – high altitude hallucinations – or because Kailash is considered the "center of the universe." It's the "original Mt. Meru" – the "birthplace of Krishna" etc. but it's also the place where I found my son.

As recounted earlier, this was also the location where I was told I could make a wish and it would come true – and so off the top of my head I was about to say "a million dollars" but out of my mouth came "I want a son." But that's another story; I'm only trying to give some context for this next story; it involves Mt. Kailash.

Sophie was having this recurring dream where she's walking down a flight of steps to the bottom of a darkened staircase at the bottom of Mt. Kailash; she could hear people chanting somewhere else in the cave. She told me when she arrives at the bottom, there's someone who bars her entrance from going inside. She had no idea why she was being barred entrance. I casually asked if she'd like to explore that dream.

Without changing my voice, or trying to put her in any kind of altered state, I merely asked her to describe the person who was blocking her entrance. She could have said "I don't know" "I don't remember" or even "It was a dream, how can I remember that?"

I first asked about the staircase, what that looked like, and whether she could see her way down or not. She said she could, and I asked her to describe where the light was coming from. She couldn't pinpoint it, but said that it was bright enough so that she could see a man sitting in front of a door at the bottom of the stairs, barring her entrance into that room.

She described a man in his 20's, dark hair, who was "dirty" but wearing "purple robes." (The deep vermillion robes of the Tibetan monks may appear purple to some, when searching "Purple robes" I find numerous references to Tibetan monks wearing their crimson colored robes.) I asked if this fellow had a name, and she said a word that sounded like "Ningee."

(Note: Ningee is a common Tibetan name; Thubten Ningee, for example, runs the Tibetan Children's program in exile).

I asked her to view the scene from the point of view of this fellow Ningee, to look and see who it was that he was denying entrance to. She said that it was an older man coming down the stairs - a man in his 50's, named "Phurbu" (Tibetan for "pin" or "nail.") and that he too "looked dirty."

I asked about the color of his robes, and she said they were brown. (Common color for a layman's outfit in Tibet: "The Khamba tribesman from eastern Tibet is generally to be seen wearing a brown knee-length robe (called a chuba) with long sleeves."[21] I asked Ningee, the monk at the door why he was denying entrance to Phurbu, and she/he said "Because I hate him. He killed my mother."

Part of the idea of asking these questions is to not judge the answers. If I got caught up in why or how Phurbu may have killed Ningee's mother, we might spend the entire time figuring that part of it out. Because it appeared the Ningee was never going to let Phurbu past him, and because I'm familiar with this aspect of the journey, I skipped ahead and asked if his mother was available to come forward to speak with us.

His mother did step forward and she/he described her as a medium height woman with black hair. I tried pointing out to Ningee that indeed, his *mother still existed*, even if he saw Phurbu as a person "who killed her." (If everyone who's ever been on the planet is available on the Flipside, then it's only a matter of asking for them to step forward. They may or they may not, as we'll see...)

I asked if I could speak "directly" to his mother and said "Please show yourself to your son, so he can see that you're not dead, that you still exist." I asked her if she was happy or sad; she said "Neither." I said, "I'm wondering if you can escort us inside this room, bypass your son and take us inside the room that Sophie is trying to gain access to?"

She said that was fine. Sophie then described entering a giant room. She said the room felt like a "large auditorium" and that had about "a thousand people." I asked if there was anyone around who could help us understand what was happening in this room, and someone did step forward, that she identified as "the Rinpoche."

I thanked him for coming, and asked if he could explain who these people were and what they were doing. He said "**they're trying to elevate the energy of the planet.**" I asked if there was anyone doing that kind of work who could speak to us.

A boy stepped forward, about 26 years old, dark hair who called himself "Sam." I asked Sam who these people were in this room. He/she said "Boddhisattvas." I said "Have they incarnated on Earth?" He said "No, they've always been here."

---

[21] (From "Presence of Tibet" 1963, Lois Sims, pg 22)

I pointed out that there is no "permanence" on this side of the veil, nor as reported on the Flipside. That we all are in the process of change, of becoming, and that even the bodhisattva's in this room at one point were younger souls. **He said that was correct.**

I asked what he was working on. He said "the grid." I asked him what the grid looked like. He said "Like a spider's web." (Note, in Flipside, the first person I interviewed spoke of seeing people on the Flipside as if they were in some kind of luminescent "spider web." Then later, in this book, we'll hear about my friend Luana "working on the grid." I don't know what that means, but I'm pointing out its repetition.) I asked him about the web, and asked **if this was the web or "grid" that connected all people and all things.** He said **"Yes."**

I got the feeling that Sam wasn't happy answering these questions. I said **"You seem annoyed, Sam. Are you annoyed?"** She nodded. I said "Why?" He said **"Because I have work to do."** I said "I apologize for taking you from your work, but I felt it important to share this with our friend Sophie here, as well as others, the kind of work you're doing elevating the energy of the grid."

I suggested he go back to work while we examined the room. Sophie said the walls of the auditorium were "made of stone, with paintings on them." I asked what the paintings were of; she said "Tara." Tara, for those familiar with Tibetan mythology is the "Mother/Healing" deity that is most like "Mary" in the Christian religion. She's called upon to help heal people when they're ill or a time of need.[22]

Having had the experience to speaking to "avatars" whom are considered deities, I asked if Tara could come forth and speak directly to our friend. Sophie nodded yes.

I said **"Tara, could you come closer to our friend her, so she can see you clearly?"** Sophie's face turned red, her eyes began to fill with tears, and she looked like she was having difficulty breathing. (Later, she said she felt like she was "going to explode.") Sophie suddenly said "I can't. I

---

[22] (Tara is a person in Tibetan Buddhism known as the "mother of liberation." (Somewhat akin to the Christian cult of Mary.) Tara is a tantric meditation deity used "to develop certain inner qualities and understand outer, inner and secret teachings about compassion and emptiness." (Wikipedia: Tara) She's called upon by people to cure what ails them, or help in general.)

can't do this." I asked Tara to "Step back to a distance that was more comfortable."

(Note: As mentioned elsewhere in this book, when people come upon some kind of deity or avatar in these sessions, they all have the same physical reaction – shortness of breath, red face and tears.)

I apologized; "I'm sorry for asking you to come closer, Tara, I see that had a strong reaction on our friend." I said "In my research, I've heard that when a person appears on Earth and is considered an avatar, it's because of their energy construction, as if they're closer to the source, that causes such a reaction. The energy of their presence can be overwhelming." She said matter-of-factly; **"That is correct."**

I asked if the Rinpoche could come forward and answer some questions, as Sophie seemed distraught. As soon as I asked the Rinpoche to step forward, Sophie seemed to regain her composure and spoke normally. I asked the Rinpoche if there was any formula for healing – something that we could pass along to others; **"A "one, two, three" if you will" for how to help heal people on Earth who might need it."**

He said **"Awareness."** Then he said **"Kindness"** and finally **"Focus."**

I asked the Rinpoche to place a feeling inside Sophie's body so that whenever she felt that sensation, she would know he was near. She nodded and said **"I feel it."** I asked if there was any message that he could pass along to our friend Sophie that would help her in her progress. He said **"Just let go."**

(Note: As noted before, this is the same thing that was said to me in my first LBL session. I was asked if there was "Anything I might be able to report back to the planet?" The answer was "Just let go." Either it's the same writers up there, or someone is trying to get us *to let go*.)

I said **"By letting go, do you mean letting of negativity, or letting go of the human emotions that cause distress with regard to what she's doing?"** I was trying to clarify that concept, since Buddhism uses "detachment" as part of its practice; "Some people feel confused by "detaching" from positive emotions as well as negative ones." I tried to further clarify the question: **"You don't mean to severe the ties with the grid, so to speak, do you?"** He said **"That is correct."**

I thanked him for coming to our small café in Santa Monica, to give us such wonderful insight. A few moments later, we came back to our normal conversation over tea in a coffee shop in Santa Monica. Oddly enough, I've had so many of these spiritual conversations at Caffe Luxxe on Montana Ave, my friends started calling it "The Vortex."

Billy Meyer

One of my oldest friends checked off the planet a couple of years ago. He had a long struggle with the bottle, and the bottle finally won. But when I heard about it, I was in the middle of an interview for a German filmmaker Jessica Hahner. She'd asked me to talk about the Flipside, I brought along Jennifer Shaffer, my pal who happens to be a medium and is interviewed later in this book. While they were setting up for a shot on the beach, I got a text from my pal Dave that Billy had died. I yelled "Oh shit!"

Director Jessica: What's wrong?

RM: Oh, one of my best friends died.

Jennifer: I'm sorry.[23]

My childhood buddy. Listen, you're talking to "Joe Death" here – I'm someone who doesn't see it as death, I see it as he "got off the bus before I did." Billy had a long bout with the bottle... and I'm also thinking about my friend Howard Schultz who died from a sudden heart attack last week.

Howard was the one who gave us some names earlier...

(Note: As we arrived at the location, I talked to Jennifer about Howard's sudden passing. Jennifer spoke to Howard, gave me an accurate description of him, talked about his love of cigars. I asked Howard what he thought about the memorial service, as it was a massive ceremony with a full orchestra and many of his beloved pals sharing memories. I was standing in the back of the room listening to his associates memorialize him but didn't tell that to Jennifer. I was startled when she said "You were standing

---

[23] JenniferShaffer.com She works pro bono with law enforcement around the country, helping parents and police with missing person cases.

in the back of the room. He was standing behind you watching the ceremony. He loved it.")

(To Jennifer) Do you hear anything from Billy?

(Matter of factly) **Billy Meyer.** Did he have blond hair?

That's his name. It was sandy blond in his youth.

He smoked cigarettes? He wore a leather jacket and would say "fuck it" a lot?[24]

Pretty much in his youth. He's here?

Did he like bourbon? I can smell it. Like he's having a Jack and coke in his hand.

(to Bill) Hi Billy. Anything you want me to tell your family?

He has a daughter? **He said he has two sons and a daughter … He's telling me that his daughter is going to have the harder time of it.**

(That's accurate. She said Bill's full name and pointed out the makeup of Bill's family. A detail Jennifer could not have known.)

Okay, I'll talk to them. (Let them know about this conversation)

He said "Don't cry at his funeral."

Who said I would cry at his funeral? (Trying to keep it light).

Is he in Wisconsin?

Close. Back in Illinois. (Bill's boat was on a lake up in or near Wisconsin. I got an incoming text, as I'd sent a text to Dave telling him what I was doing, speaking about the afterlife on camera). Dave says "Hello Billy…"

Tell Dave to stop drinking.

---

[24] That's more of a description of Billy in high school years; had a leather jacket, did say "fuck it" a lot and we all smoked cigarettes. He was always a bit of a rebel.

125

He doesn't drink anymore. At least I don't think he does. (Dave was one of our first friends who stopped drinking altogether after our party days in high school.)

He showed me Diet Pepsi. Maybe it's a health issue. (Or a joke.)

Say, Bill, what do you want to do with your boat? Does Mark get the boat?

Is Mark his son?

No, Mark's a mutual friend. He owned a boat with Bill.

He says "They can have it." He says "It's a piece of junk." He's showing me something is wrong with the front. (Gestures as if to show the front of the bow).

Well, I guess the next time I see you Bill, we can go fishing together again like we did in high school.

He just showed me a jar of worms…

So what happened, did his heart give out? Or was it the alcohol? (By way of explanation) Billy we're on camera.. filming this thing about the afterlife at the moment.

He said "Hi." (She looks around at the beach) He never liked the sand, I don't think, but he loved the water though.

Well my kids love you, my wife always loved seeing you!

She feels him…

So what was it? Heart attack? Or were you drinking?

Something wrong with (a valve).. one… of the heart, a condition since he was little. Something closed, like a heart valve.

Say hello to (our mutual friend) Paul Tracey.

Is he dark haired, unruly?

Yeah.

He's here.

How about Patrick?

He's right there as well. (points)

His little brother Patrick died some years ago. A drug overdose.

I'm getting the number 18. Either 18 years ago... or he died at 18. (I don't remember what age Patrick was when he died, but 18 sounds about right).

Billy found him. That was hard on him.

Oh, Billy was mad – so mad. He's showing me how mad. (aside) I've never seen someone do that before.

Billy raged over Patrick's death. He was pretty furious..

Jessica (film director): Can I ask one question – how is the feeling right now, right after dying?

Jennifer: He feels a little more evolved – uh, hold on, I'm speaking for him. Let me ask him. (A pause. Jessica is a few inches from Jennifer now, also on camera, and Jennifer smiles at her.) He thinks you're cute. He said to me: "Tell her she's cute."

RM: So Billy.

Jennifer: He says **"It's fun. I (can) travel fast." He says "I don't have to worry. About myself (anymore)."**

Bill, isn't your birthday around now?

Yes. Could be the 19th. (It was a week earlier, on the 20th).

Am I going to your funeral?

Is it on the 5th? (It was on the 4th)

I don't know, it just happened. You want me there Bill?

"You're my best friend."

Yeah... okay. I think I can go... (I couldn't but visited his grave later when I could). Okay Bill, we'll speak again soon buddy. Another time. Bye. (End of Interview)

This exchange happened on camera. Early Jennifer had been talking to me off camera about my friend Howard Schultz (lived on my street, grew up to be a successful reality TV producer. Appears in "Flipside.")

Here she was telling me accurate details about Howard's life and his passing, including a private message for his wife, which I passed along. Then some minutes later, she sees Bill Meyer appear, and begins to speak on his behalf. Knew his name, and his children. Pretty amazing.

With Billy Meyer in Santa Monica

"Homeward bound,
I wish I was,
Homeward bound,
Home where my thought's escaping,
Home where my music's playing,
Home where my love lies waiting
Silently for me."

Paul Simon

CHAPTER SIX:

TEXTING THE FLIPSIDE

Giralomo Induno. "Triste Presentimento" 1862
"Sad incoming texts."

"I don't believe in an afterlife, I don't have to spend my whole life fearing hell, or fearing heaven even more. For whatever the tortures of hell, I think the boredom of heaven would be even worse."

- Isaac Asimov

A few years back a person contacted me on Facebook about my book and work. She lives in another country, married, a professional who wanted to chat about her enthusiasm for the research. She reminded me a bit of my grandmother Mimi, so for the sake of this chapter, that's what I'll call her.

Mimi said that she had started to listen to my "book talks online" before going to bed, and she had the experience or impression that somehow the instruction continued during her sleep. She said "I literally can't go to sleep unless I'm listening to one of your talks."[25]

My wife and kids usually nod off while I'm talking as well, I'll just leave that comic thought there. But for whatever reason, her subconscious felt it

---

[25] (https://www.youtube.com/user/MartiniProds/playlists)

was important to hear what I was saying in these book talks – which I would imagine are pretty repetitive. For whatever reason, her subconscious felt a need to access this information.

That led to an unusual conversation. I've not spoken to "Mimi" in person, and our communications have only been through Facebook instant messaging. Since I was using my thumbs to write and respond, normally I can't text for more than a few messages before I give up. In this case, I had about an hour before an appointment when I heard that "Facebook bell" signaling a message had come in. (Apologies for the syntax, we are speaking in *text* after all).

Mimi: Hi Rich! Any new projects? I had a very strange dream last night. Thought I could share it with u. I saw some shiny girls with wings (like cartoon characters) landing slowly in front of me from the sky and said hi to me while smiling. They were transparent and I could go through them.

RM: Angels? Cool! What was the vibe? Had a discussion with a fellow from India who had a dream, an out of body experience of being at a wedding on another planet, but only the animals saw him. They were odd animals, (that's how he knew he was on another planet or another realm) and wondered if animals who see "ghosts" might be seeing beings who are dreaming they're here.

Mimi: Could be Angels! Good call! They were so calm and relaxing. I felt comfortable seeing them. But they didn't surprise me. It felt like it was something normal. Now that I recall it and think of it, I get goose bumps. I dream strange things often. **Sometimes I dream of other dimensions.** Like the ocean is going upward to the sky instead of going towards the horizon. Or I've dreamt of holding someone's hand and run over a wall full of greens. Towards sky again lol

Interesting. Well, who are they? Just answer with the first thought that comes into your head. Try not to judge it.... Whose hand are you holding? Male or female, young old, who is it? Someone you know?

I thought of angels this morning. But I didn't find myself holy enough to dream of angels. It was a Caucasian young guy. Didn't know the name. He was Very tall. I remember his face. Brunette.

Are u running thru flowers on earth or somewhere else?

It's definitely somewhere else.

What's the first letter of his name? What color are his eyes?

His eyes were kind. Don't remember the colour. Maybe brown. R or M. Tough to find out. His name sounds like ... He sounded either a lover or brother. The name sounds more than 2 syllables. I don't think he's here.

(Note: When someone says "I don't think he's here" then it's possible they're experiencing someone on the Flipside, perhaps from their soul group. By asking "is it here or somewhere else?" allows for the possibility that she knows him from "somewhere else" – back home where she would know him quite well.)

Ask him a question.

He belonged to somewhere that looked very different from earth. Like different dimensions. It felt like I was there for a visit. What should I ask?

Ask him who the fairies are or where he is now. You're stepping back into the memory. You can ask and get answers from that perspective.

I don't get an answer. Maybe cuz it's crowded here (at work) and I can't concentrate. I asked where he was with my eyes closed. I saw his head and his smile.

You can ask "where do i know you from?" "Where did we meet?" Whatever pops in your mind.

He has messy brown hair. Like this: (sends a picture of a messy haired Marco Polo) His smile is deep. I feel like I've known him for a long time

Where did u meet, here on earth or there in the spirit world?

I don't think it was on earth.

Squeeze his hand, *let him know you're here to speak with him. Have u ever incarnated together?*

He sounds too good for earth. He's full of something. Knowledge maybe.

(Note: "Too good for earth" isn't a positive or negative comment. Just that the feeling she's getting from him at this particular moment is on a more pure level, hence why she senses that he's "full of knowledge.")

Ask him why he showed up? What's he here to tell u?

I don't think we incarnated lately. It sounds so long ago.

Seems long ago to u, but not to him. When? First date that comes to mind.

He was in my dream to help me find peace.

(Note: That's interesting. As reported in "Flipside" and "It's a Wonderful Afterlife," people accessed on the Flipside claim that they can enter our dreams energetically to give us a message. In this case, he "entered her dream" to help her "find peace.")

Ok. That's good.

1800's.

Not long at all. Country?

Could these answers be my brain making up words?

Try not to judge. First country that comes to mind.

(Note: As mentioned when "new information" comes into the brain from the subconscious, it enters the same way that imagination creates things. At first they seem to be self-created, but later, with the passage of time, they feel more like memories than imaginary events. It's possible that she's making these details up, but they appear in her mind the way a memory does.)

He's dressed like Europeans in 1800s. Somewhere Latin.

Ask him for a name… Italy, Spain, Albania…?

Italy.

Ok. What city? First letter. Second letter.

Somewhere rainy. He's in a yard of a castle. With other ppl. He's not a king. He's someone normal.

Ok. Somewhere in Italy? Ask.

N… A… These are the two letters.

Na... ok.. Napoli? Naples?

Ever since I squeezed his hand my hand is full of energy. It's static…

Keep squeezing. Na... poli?

I don't know :(

Ask him for the third letter, no stress.

Omg

I don't know that city (jk).

I just googled Napoli and in the image I saw the castle I was telling u about. (She sent a picture of a Castle in Naples).

Castel dell'Ovo, Naples (Wikimedia)

Very good. Ask him his name. One letter at a time. First and last.

His name sounds romantic. Romeo, Roamo. Something with that rhythm.

Last name?

Medalio. Sounds like this.

Medaglio. Means medal. Romeo Medalio or Medalia di Napoli. Now, who were u back then? Male or female?

Female. Young wearing a long skirt.

Your first name? What color hair, eyes? Tall, short? How old?

I seem tired. I'm pulling a rope. Average. Brown hair. Early 20s.

What is Romeo to u? Boss, friend, lover?

People are not dressed well here. We are all poor.

What's the rope attached to? Donkey? Horse? Goat?

To a gate… He's my husband. We both work very hard. We have a little kid. I think boy. 2-3 years old.

Ok. Is Romeo anyone in this life to u? Or the boy? Look at the boy's face.

Sleeping. He's sleeping in my arms. Chubby little boy. The three of us have white skin. (Romeo) works so hard I feel so bad

What is the year in the 1800s?

1817.

Describe your face, body, hair.

It's rained lately. My hair is wet and messy. I'm not skinny.

Parents? What does Romeo do for a living?

He's a laborer. I am too. He works more than me though.

What kind of labor?

He's a porter I think. We have a very difficult life. He loves me and the kid so much.

Signora Medalio in Napoli, 1817. What's your first name?

N. It has an N in it.

(Thinking of names in Italian) Natalia?

Ya I think.

Natalia Medalio.. or Medalia?

I've always thought I was French before. I've dreamt of speaking French a couple of times. Sorry to interrupt.

It's ok. Naples was Spanish, and French. In fact, could have been around this time. King Louis of France took it from King Ferrante. That could be one reason why your skin is white and not olive colored.

Interesting.

Ok, let's go to Natalie's last day on the planet. Where is she?

Bed.

With?

By myself. Coughing.

Ok. Does she pass alone?

Romeo comes home late. Takes his hat off. I'm still young.

Ok. Describe what happens.

He comes home and I'm on bed. I'm sick… I don't see what happens next.

Ok, try to examine the moment after her death. Where are u? Above, to the side?

I don't think I will die. But I will die on a bed. Sometime later.

Ok... so let's go to her last day on the planet, when she does pass away.

Romeo is not giving me these answers (by the way). I'm seeing it in my mind.

Good. Be there now. Where are you?

Cemetery.

Ok, are you standing, floating?

Yes. There are 20ish people, standing together. I'm watching them from afar. Neighbours. Romeo and the son.

Ok. How do you feel?

Neutral.

Very good. What happens next? Anyone to say goodbye to?

I'm looking at them. Something inside me is laughing loud out of happiness. It's like I've heard a very funny joke. I go to Romeo and the son. He's 5 now.

That's funny. You're feeling a bit giddy. What do u do? Speak to them?

No, nothing. I look at them. And expect them to understand. But they don't.

What's your feeling about this lifetime as Natalie?

I worked a lot. I was tired every day.

Did you accomplish your goals?

I accomplished my family. To be strong. Romeo helped me so much. He talked to me every night. I was upset that we were poor.

Ok, i want u to allow yourself to experience what comes next. Where do u go?

Back. (I'm soaked to the back). And up.

Back... describe the journey.

I was kissing my son goodbye and then I was pulled back. I turn my head to see that the sky is rainy but…

What do you see? Where are you headed?

Something pink or light purple shows up. I'd like to follow it. Now I'm running towards it. Running on air.

Is there someone around?

No one. It's me. Just me. Trying to reach the pink light.

Examine the light more closely. Can u step thru it?

Yes. **I'm inside it.**

What's that like?

My hands are wide open. I'm smiling and spinning. The Rays hit me and I love it. I don't want to leave it or here. But still think of my son… But the fun is way too much than worrying for him…

(Note: This is what many people say about the feeling they have when they reach a "tunnel" or light. They experience **"unconditional love."** If I was sitting with Mimi, I would have suggested she talk more about that feeling. However, I'm getting texts on a blackberry while I'm sitting in my car in Santa Monica. I used a blackberry back then, it was the last cellphone keyboard that allowed me to type fast.)

It's ok. He's ok. This is your path and journey. Is there anyone around we can speak to? Check your surroundings. Look around. Anyone nearby?

Yes. But far away. I see their shadows. (There are) four.

Male or female? Ask if we can speak with them.

One looks like my mom. (Mimi's mom) She smiles and hugs me. I would cry. But I don't.

Come a little closer, describe them… anyone that seems like a group leader?

A guy. **All are wearing white. It's like I'm back from a trip and people are waiting for me at the airport. I'm telling them I have a lot to tell them.** They smile as if they know it already. The guy is in front of me. Keeps smiling. I jump into his arms. He hugs me gently.

Is he the spokesperson for this group?

Yes, he is. The rest are aside and looking.

What's his name?

D..

Can we speak to Dee directly?

Yes.

Hi Dee. Thanks for showing up.

He nods. He has a cane.

This is an odd way for us to talk. But why was Mimi shown this life today?

She's sad. And stressed. **She's done this stage before.**

Ok. About?

About work and school. (I can't stop crying.)

Just breathe. That's normal. This is odd to do this in this way, but no worries. Dee knows the answer. How can we show her to let that go?

"We just showed her the tough life she had. It can't get worse."

Dee can you put a feeling in Mimi's body so she knows when you are near?

"It's up to her."

Please show her what happened with her 5-year-old son.

He grows fine. He joins the army.

Is he in her life time now?

He says "It's Mimi's husband."

Very good, thank you for that.

But it could be Mimi's illusion.

Mimi, try not to judge what you see or hear you can always examine it later.

Ok.

So what should we tell her today that will help her in this lifetime?

"Keep helping. This is why you are here."

Could you please be more specific for her? Who does she need to help?

"Make others feel comfortable. Take their sorrow away. Make them laugh."

I understand. Thank you for that.

He nods. (I'm shaking. Is it normal?)

Yes. Can you please show Mimi new or a feeling or sensation on her body somewhere so that she knows when you're nearby?

I always have. I'm always with her. She feels me when she's relaxed.

Very good. Can you describe that sensation for me?

The 10-second goosebumps that she feels occasionally.

Ok. Very good. Mimi, do you have any questions or is there someplace you would like to visit? Or some person you would like to visit?

No. I'm exhausted. I saw my mom that was joyful. She's one of my guardians? I think she is. She hugs me.

Ok. Very good. Let's ask her. Or ask D.

I think the answer is yes.

Nice. Thank you all for helping today.

They smile.

Any messages you want to give to her?

"She's fine. Just worrying too much. She keeps telling people "you are fine." But she doesn't say it to herself."

Very good. I think you've helped her very much. Do you have any messages for me?

You are a good man.

Just asking. Ok, thanks.

"Mimi needed this today. We kept talking to her but she didn't listen. You helped her hear us."

Glad to help. All righty.. Thanks everyone. Mimi, are you ready to come back?

Yes.

Give everyone, all four a big hug. Take as long as you like.

I did. They are fading.

Very good. Count to ten aloud and when you're done thank them. (After a pause) That was fun.

What was that? Wow.

We did a shortened version of a past life regression.

I day dream a lot. But this was strange.

Believe me, you had the same hallmarks. Same bullet-points - seeing a past life, then between lives, meeting your soul guides...

I knew it from somewhere that you (would have) an amazing role in my life when I messaged you the first time.

Nice verification. It's all part of you, just under your surface. Pay attention to what your guide said. "Relax, lighten up" and "we're always with you."

True ... I had always thought I was experiencing God when I got the random goosebumps.

Goosebumps are not things your conscious mind can do. Not physically possible. If only we could consciously create them! That's proof that the story is real.

Interesting. You make a film based on Reincarnation. ("Flipside: A Journey into the Afterlife") You have the skill and facilities… Ok, will work on that!

……………..

Just rereading this, I'm amazed at how far we got via texting.

It's always a bit thrilling to get anywhere when people get a chance to learn something from it. But I offer it here to demonstrate that I wasn't using hypnosis, I wasn't even in the same country as her. **I just asked questions based on my experience with the architecture of the Flipside.**

I had no idea we'd get anywhere. I was as surprised as she was that this "random face in a dream" turned into a past life memory and then a message from her spirit guides on how to relax. Amazing!

One can argue none of it is real, all of it is imaginary – but there are bits in here that were **"new information for her."** Information that can help her with her current life.

I contacted Mimi about reviewing this chapter, asked how she was doing. Said she was having a lot of stress at work, feeling distraught and overworked, at her wit's end as to what to do. I suggested "Ask your guides." One method I suggest, before she went to sleep, **"Reach out and ask someone, a loved one who has passed over, for help and guidance."**

The next day she wrote to say her mother (who passed 15 years ago) had come to her in a vivid dream and tried to counsel her. She didn't remember what her mom said, but that it was powerful. The next day, a co-worker came over to her desk and said, in effect: **"Let go of what you can't control."**

"The odd thing," Mimi wrote, "is that the co-worker is about the same age of her mother, and as she spoke her face morphed into my mother's face." As if her mother were directly giving her the advice. She said she wept at how much she missed her mother after the incident.

Did the co-worker's face actually morph? Well for all intents and purposes, yes, in Mimi's mind's eye. We honor those who come to us in dreams or in visions by listening to what they have to say, instead of wondering how the heck it happened. Suffice to say it isn't easy for them to "morph" or put their energy into our heads – otherwise they'd do it all the time.

As I'm fond of saying – "You're loved one isn't missing you the way you are missing them. They're right here, trying to tell you something. Are you going to listen to your loved one? Or spend a lot of effort questioning how it happened?"

Saul Vazquez snapped this photograph of a fatal motorcycle accident in July, 2016. Note the spectral image between the trucks. His spirit leaving? Perhaps. (Image via Saul Vazquez / Facebook)

CHAPTER SEVEN:

Someone On The Flipside Who Calls Himself Prince

From the 2016 New Orleans Jazz fest. (Photo E. Gundersen)

"You can't connect the dots looking forward; you can only connect them looking backwards. You have to trust that the dots will somehow connect in your future. You have to trust in something - your gut, destiny, life, karma, whatever. This approach has never let me down, and it has made all the difference in my life." Steve Jobs

Some years ago I came across ChannelingErik.com. It's a website created by a doctor in Houston, Dr. Elisa Medhus, who lost her son. When her phone rang one day and her son's voice spoke to her, she lost her skepticism about the afterlife, and reached out to some very talented mediums to speak with him. Her blog has some fascinating interviews with her son and other folks, and her books are wonderful as well.

Recently she put out a book "written from the Flipside" by her son Erik, called "My Life After Death." I highly recommend it.[26]

Dr. Medhus doesn't make any money from her work with her son. She has written a couple of books, but being friends with her, I know that she's barely making ends meet in this work that she does.

It's an unusual construct, that exists in some realm not quite of the Earth, and not quite on the Flipside. Elisa crafts the questions, asks them on mic, the medium hears the question and gets the answer. The answers are pretty unusual; for the most part, they're in align with what people say under deep hypnosis about the afterlife.

I was listening to one of the interviews that Elisa and Erik were doing and could hear some voices speaking during the recording. I contacted Elisa about them, she said she didn't hear them, and asked if I could send her a copy of what I heard. Using my film equipment, I slowed down and sped up the voices and sent them off to her. There are clearly some voices that appear on the tape – I noted that when I sped them up, I could hear them more clearly. I have no idea if they are "voices from the Flipside" but will address them later in this book.

Recently, Prince Rogers Nelson died. I reviewed one of his earlier shows when I was a music critic for Variety.[27] I'd seen him backstage, but didn't speak with him. But I had a dream just after his passing that I was in a giant auditorium, sitting with some friends in the audience. Up onstage in front of us was this tiny figure, sitting in a spotlight, talking to someone or some folks who seemed to be spiritual guides.

As this person spoke, everyone in the audience could experience exactly what they were saying – as if we were all tuned into the same event. If he told a sad story, we all felt it, or they were showing him an event where he changed someone's life, we all experienced that as well.

---

[26] "My Life After Death: A Memoir from Heaven." By Erik Medhus, Elisa Medhus M.D. (Atria books; 2015)

[27] My review: "The King of erotic funk slammed into the Universal Amphitheatre Thursday for the start of a three-day stint. There was plenty of glitz and glam, and when the sparks settled, Prince again proved that, beyond the hype, he's a master showman..." http://variety.com/1993/legit/reviews/prince-and-the-new-power-generation-1200431966/

The event in this dream was the "life review" of the individual known as Prince Rogers Nelson. At some point I felt myself waking up, coming back to consciousness, and turning to my friends as if to say "Oh, this is fun, I'm sorry I have to go" and my friends said "Don't worry, this will be going on for days."

When I saw that Dr. Medhus had asked her son to interview Prince Rogers Nelson after his passing, I couldn't wait to view it. With her permission, here is an excerpt of that interview. [28]

As a caveat, no one is claiming that the person identified here is "Prince" nor is anyone trying to profit from the artist's likeness, or music. For the sake of this article, I could just as easily call this person "Nelson" and it would have the same import. While you're reading this interview, try to remember that this is a person speaking from the Flipside who "identified" as Prince Rogers Nelson in this life, but has had other lifetimes before, and will again one day. So to make that easier, let's call this person "Prince."

INTERVIEW WITH SOMEONE WHO APPEARS TO BE PRINCE

Interviewers: Erik Medhus, Dr. Elisa Medhus, a Medium that works with Dr. Medhus and the Artist formerly (and currently) known as Prince. Dr. Medhus asks the questions from Texas, and The Medium answers them from her place in Ohio.

Dr. Medhus: Hi Erik.

The Medium: (speaking on behalf of Erik) "What's up, mom?"

(She gives him a couple of options of people to talk to) Where would you like to start?

He's showing me images, "We'll talk about Prince, we'll go there."

Can you go get him?

---

[28] Full video is at ChannelingErik.com. All copyright belongs to Dr. Medhus. For further information, please visit channelingerik.com Permission to use, copy or disseminate must be in writing from Dr. Medhus.

He's making fun of you; Erik says "I can get him but I don't have to "go anywhere." "Let's just connect to him. Think about it like that."

Ok, let's think about it like that.

I'm going to shift and tune into him – he's definitely stepping forward next to Erik, coming in next to him. I'm seeing images that look like Prince. It's funny - I did a session one time for a client where Michael Jackson came through, and the energy coming from Prince feels the same – very calm, very gentle, extremely gentle in his approach.

Initially – he's expressing gratitude. He says "I already know what this is going to be about." There must be a lot swirling about how he passed. Why he passed.

First, thank you for coming forward. You are missed.

He was leaning into that (as you spoke), he was thanking you. He says "Thank you for giving me an opportunity like this to have a voice. Maybe to clear up a few things…" and he kind of takes a bow and goes like this (hands in front, bowing) He says "You have the floor." He's being very um… chivalrous.

I don't know that much about you Prince, but that seems right.

(Medium, aside) Me neither.

What was your state of mind when you passed over?

He's going like this with his hands (indicates passing over calm waters). "Very calm." He's giving me a sense of feeling very calm. He says – again not telling me how he passed, but he says he didn't fight it. It didn't feel like there was a fight or struggle, it felt very natural. "As far as my mindset -- where my heart was, it felt natural with the timing and all."

Was it one of your "exit points" that you designed for yourself?

He quickly said "Yes." [29]

---

[29] "Exit points" refer to the idea that we agree to sign up for a lifetime for a certain amount of time, or to accomplish so many tasks. We may have fulfilled all of our duties and when the time appears to check out – some have claimed we choose an "exit point" the way someone might choose an off ramp at the last second.

What did you die from?

He looks down at his body and he says "frail" - making me feel his health was frail, not superior, somehow his health was compromised. But I also feel like this is.. he's speaking with images, with energy, I see his body as unwell. I feel like because his body was in a compromised state, it must have been medication that he was taking...

He said "Yep." Or medication that he was on and its' effect on that compromised body – like someone who takes heart medication and they die from it.

It was medication to a frail body that caused your demise?

He says "Yes." He's very soft in his *yes*.

Any particular medication? Or several?

He wants me to see there were several, but I don't feel like it was abuse. I asked him if it was any kind of abuse... he says **"Perhaps they shouldn't have been used together."** Perhaps it was some prescription for him? (Note: Apparently this is accurate based on his autopsy. This interview was soon after his death.)

One of the members of our blog asks "Why are so many musicians dying?"

He's so sweet. He tipped his chin, smiled real big and says "No matter who you are when you come to Earth -- and then when you come back home -- once you make your mark... It's not like it's planned," he says, "that we (musicians) all leave in waves... (But) **once you make your mark and accomplish what we need to, you transition back... you come home. That's why some people design different or later exit points."**

He makes me feel like (he's demonstrating) "Here's an exit point in my 50's -- but I still have some work to get done, so my exit point (over) there if I accomplish what I want to - with freewill thrown in - or (over) there's another one that I have in mind."

He says "I felt like I was a voice for many - based on my actions - or for many who couldn't speak (up, but) who were introverted or afraid to express themselves. **I knew I made an impact, I know I left an impact, (and) that has something to do with the timing of my exit**."

Were you a devout Jehovah's Witness?

Hmmm. He said "Yes" then gave two words to describe why… - and he's giving energy that says something different. I'll try to break it down for you… He said "Safety and comfort. It felt safe and it's where I felt comfortable with beliefs." But now he's making me feel like he understands the framework that kept him within – "It doesn't mean it is wrong, certain types of beliefs…" He's laughing (now), says "…**It doesn't matter who you worship or what avenue you worship through, we're all truly worshiping the same thing; it's all just different light.**"

(Note: Here again the concept of "light" being the source, or web of the universe, how all are connected. We'll see many references to God as "light" to other souls as "light" to the "healing light of the universe." What is light? It's both particle and wave, and apparently some form of consciousness.)

Was it just a comfortable belief for you??

He says "Yeah, it was conditioning." He says "Comfort and conditioning." (Aside) He gives really short fragmented answers. I'd describe him as a man of little words; just very direct and to the point. Not someone who speaks a lot.. just someone who speaks directly to the point.

Have your beliefs changed since the transition? And did you refuse (medical) treatment because of your religious beliefs?

He says "Many times, yes." He says "In his lifestyle there were many ways that he chose to live. Maybe not so much tied to my religious beliefs, but who I was and what made me happy or what made me comfortable." He says **"Often you can get you picked on for choosing to not be like all the rest – sometimes you get picked on for that."**

Did your beliefs change after you passed? Did you see Jehovah's Witness differently?

He says "Widely; his beliefs have widely changed." He says "Think about it like this: **You go through life with a set of beliefs that you're really attached to, or tied to them - and when you come here, you see all the rest, all the other perspectives that you didn't accept or align with in your physical life. So here it's more of accepting (of) all ways. You see it that it's all the same thing."**

He uses a painting as an example; "You can have two different artists paint the very same picture with different color paint; over here you have this artist show through paint how people express themselves, **but over here it is just the same; still the same thing. This is no exception with (regards to) religion. Then when you come (back) here, you break free from what you're tied to and realize you're all one."**

That it's still the same thing.

 "Yes, this is the same. Over here you (can) break through and see that it's all one."

When you look back on your old beliefs as a Jehovah's Witness, do you see it as negative?

 "Not as negative," but how it (those beliefs) kept him with "tunnel vision and how that affects so many (people)." This (experience) was really eye awakening, really moving for him to see. He smiled and said matter-of-factly **"Just to realize that it's really all the same thing."**

Describe your transition. What happened? Did you go through a white room or tunnel?

I heard him say **"I was greeted by my grandparents."** He says that it was very quiet. He says "I'm a quiet person." He kind of laughs, "Imagine that!" -- based on his lifestyle that he lived. "I'm a quiet person;" so his transition was very quiet, it was extremely subtle.

He shows me like **traveling through a tunnel.** He says **"Like constant movement through what looks like a tunnel, feels like different shades of white, if that's possible."** He says "Go ahead and repeat that for everybody because it sounds ignorant – because it's not "shades" - it's vibration."

He said he felt pulled, like a pulling sensation, and it **looked like a tunnel.** (When he got to the other side) **"There were not many there, I get overwhelmed easily, I like my space. Then it happens… there's a sense of "all-knowing" there's a sense of comfort that envelops you and welcomes you into…"** -- he calls it **"The homeland."**

(Note: In most of the 30 between life hypnosis session I've filmed, after a person remembers the last day of a previous lifetime, they're asked "Where would you like to go now?" They all say what I said when I did my first session. "I want to go home." Interesting that Prince felt "pulled" to this location (some folks say the same thing, while others feel the sensation of flying to. One person described it as "magnets pulling steel filings across a table.")

He's giving me a big picture, almost like stepping into it (the picture) – **"Traveling is not the right phrase, but then (when I arrive) I see all kinds of people and plants. But it's not a world like ours."**

(Note: Again, a common refrain from many near death experiences. Dr. Eben Alexander saw rolling hills and grass, others have seen trees, flowers, gardens, in many of the between life hypnosis session they see intricate architecture, trees and flowers. In Erik Medhus' book "My Life After Death" he describes seeing grass, and in Galen Stoller's "My Life After Life" he describes being out in a place that looks like the desert near his home. The point being – no description is identical, but they are all similar.)

The Medium: He says "I never questioned what was happening." It was like he knew, he was never scared, and he was never like "What the heck just happened?" (That fear) It never carried with him.

What was your life review like?

He says that he is still learning from a multitude of perspectives. He says -- he kind of looks back like he's looking at his life review – (It was) **"More profound, more deep, the depth of which I connected to people. I couldn't have imagined." He says "I didn't realize the impact (I had on people), you truly don't realize the impact you make (on others) until you feel it from an outside perspective."**

He's giving me the word "**Grateful.**" He's almost kind of speechless. He says **"Don't get me wrong; there's a lot I don't want to look at that, I don't want to reflect on, but you grow and you understand that you're (over) there in your physical life, and you don't always understand (why things happen to you) -- you just have to suck it up."**

What was your spiritual mission in this lifetime? What were you here to learn and teach?

He says "To move people. I guess I would call myself an example; to move people, to be a voice for people to express themselves however they felt comfortable (doing so.) **To be true to who you are, no matter what that means."**

Like Erik (has said) "Be your true authentic self."

"If you try to hide something, (or) try to be something you're not, you'll live a life of misery and that defeats the whole purpose of being in life." His spiritual mission was to teach…

"To help pull you out of your comfort zone. Because if you stay there you don't learn -- you don't know who you are." (Aside) Woah. That was a strong statement with the energy that he's giving. **"If you stay in your comfort zone, you truly don't know who you are."** He's so sincere (when he says this.)

Where you here to learn anything?

He said "Just that. How to trust myself in moving outside of your comfort zone. **If so many eyes are upon you at once, imagine the ridicule you could face -- that you can face; that's uncomfortable. You'll never learn about yourself if you don't pull yourself out of your comfort zone."**

Do you think you accomplished that?

He's so kind – he keeps saying (to me) "Make sure there's no ego" (in these replies) He says he **"Wants his messages to be conveyed with authenticity and sincerity."** (In response to your question) He says "I think so." He says **"I hope people learn from me to truly express who you are, don't hold back, it doesn't matter… Meaning others' judgment of you doesn't matter."**

Were you killed by someone? You know when someone like you dies, all sorts of conspiracy theories bubble up.

He says that's true, conspiracy theories bubble up when you have the spotlight on you, (but) he says "This was divine order." He's pointing (his finger) up.

What about what Erik has been teaching? Are you in alignment with what he's saying?

He says "A lot of what Erik teaches now coincides with who I was, how I tried to live my life. Being in the public eye and being famous can easily pull you away from your own beliefs and knowing who you are. The thing I like about Erik is that he speaks truth, no bullshit. **I wanted to live my life with no bullshit. I don't bullshit people; this is who I am, you can take it or leave it.**" He says there are lot coincidences between the two of them.

Talk about the angel who cured you of epilepsy (when you were a child). Can you talk about that?

He says **"Yes."** He's referring to this angelic being as **being very much like a guardian angel but very motherly towards him**. This is how he's explaining it, he says "This goes back to the foundation of truth being *in* truth, believing it and accepting it. If you can find the core of what truth is…"

(Note: He clarifies this point – not a "guardian angel" per se, but "very much like a guardian angel.")

So for him in that moment (it was) believing that you can be healed, and releasing (disbelief) at that same time, anything can happen. Anything's possible; it's a miracle that miracles can happen, people are too cynical, too sour to believe in miracles, but it was the belief in truth…" He says this very matter-of-factly.

You believed this angel could heal you. You were able to let go of epilepsy?

He said "You put it perfectly. **If you believe and just let go, miracles can happen every day.**"

What's your favorite instrument?

He says probably guitar, there's also … it looks like a saxophone, but (he prefers) the expression through the chords. **I hear** a guitar playing; it sounds like an electric guitar.

You should jam with Erik!

(Laughs) That's what's happening right now.

What about your will? Did you leave one?

He makes me feel like he did – or, he shows me the start of a will, but it's not complete, not finished, like he intended to. He didn't have his estate or belongings covered, it wasn't complete.

But it's only money. What inspired "Purple Rain?"

He says -- he's using images to talk, he's pretty good at it, I'm quite surprised -- he says "Purple rain" (was about) connecting to an understanding something outside of yourself. He says, "It's feeling like, Elisa…" he's using your name, **there's something bigger and more powerful than you. (And) it represents my sense of wonder; this was to try to shine light on things that are bigger than us."** And he sends his energy outward, (to demonstrate) "Trying to find or connect to things that are bigger than us, a sense of wonder, to move people the way that I felt moved at times."

(Note: In Michael Newton's research, he discovered that people can "look at themselves" if asked to. They noted that people saw themselves as a light or color, depending upon the "experience" of their soul. The lighter colors represented younger souls, but the darker colors, specifically purple, represented souls who had deep wisdom.)[30]

….Why did you say "Don't waste your prayers" at your last party with regard to your health?

He says (about prayer) "It's a belief. Sometimes people take that very literally, but it's not like 'don't waste prayers cause they aren't answered.' There's energy there (in prayer), there's creation there, keep praying." But he means "Live it, be it." He's showing me someone praying for something they want, he's (showing how they are) pulling their energy into themselves. **"So don't just pray it, just be it."**

….Tell us about another lifetime that you had that most influenced your one as Prince.

He gives me the word "orphan." He looks like an abandoned child, homeless, no family, no anybody and wanting to have a voice. He says "Having a voice not just in who you are, because there's a validation in just knowing someone (has) heard you." He felt very un-validated in his

---

[30] Newton categorizes these colors (same as a rainbow, from light to dark) in his second book "Destiny of Souls."

being "**In who I was (then), because I didn't have anybody to listen to me. Not that I needed that in ego, but I needed that to sort of just validate my existence.**"

He said he was born to a poor family who couldn't afford to keep him so he was abandoned. (That lifetime) looks very primitive, his clothing is primitive. The way it affected this life, as Prince, is kind of taking that to the complete opposite; "Being able to have a voice and being heard and the way that people responded to me, by records selling or whatever…" (This life) validated him - but also what he was trying to say to people. It's like this extra validation in essence of who he was.

Any final message or advice to us or humanity as whole?

He's very subtle with his energy here. **He kissed a peace sign (two fingers to his lips) and said "Live your truth."**

Three words that are important, thank you for that. Erik, you want to ask him something?

Erik looked at him and said **"If you could directly change humanity like that (snaps fingers) – How would you do it and what would you do?"**

Prince says "**I would give them vision to see what the hurt (is like) when they… what it looks like when they hurt someone, what it looks like when they cause hurt. Energetically. I would give them that vision, because then we would all be kind, we wouldn't cause that hurt. So with the snap of my fingers, if I could change something, it would be that.**"

Then he kind of pulls back and just says **"Be kind to one another."**

Awesome, so many have wanted to hear from you - they'll be very excited about this.

He says "Thank you for the love, the continual outpouring of love for who I am and accepting who I am." He just keeps saying "Thank you Elisa." And he keeps bowing.

You're Welcome and thank you Erik

…….

"Live your truth." "Be kind to one another." "Don't pray it; be it." "If you believe it and let go, miracles can happen." Wise words indeed. I include this interview for the simple reason that it includes *new information* from the Flipside. **"Then it happens... there's a sense of "all-knowing" there's a sense of comfort that envelops you and welcomes you into..." -- he calls it "The homeland."**

I can only point to the fact that Prince is saying the same things that everyone else says. Once you "get through" to the other side – you see plants and flowers, you see that all religions come from the same light, you get a sense of all knowing, a sense of comfort (or unconditional love) that envelops you, welcomes you to the homeland."

He uses a painting as an example; **"You can have two different artists paint the very same picture with different color paint; over here you have this artist show through paint how people express themselves, but over here it is just the same; still the same thing. This is no exception with (regards to) religion. Then when you come (back) here, you break free from what you're tied to and realize you're all one."**

A pretty eloquent way of putting it.

We are all one. How we choose to express our memory of the Flipside, the memory of having unconditional love – is up to us. But eventually we get back to "the homeland" and see that we are all one, and all religions are the same thing. Referring to the light that connects us all, that is who we are, and who god is.

That it's still the same thing.

> "Yes, this is the same. Over here you (can) break through and see that *it's all one*."

There is it again; "Just let go." I offer this works as well; "Just suck it up." Then there's this important passage:

> Erik looked at him and said "If you could directly change humanity like that (snaps fingers) – How would you do it and what would you do?"

> Prince says "I would give them vision to see what the hurt (is like) when they... **what it looks like when they hurt someone, what it looks like when they cause hurt. Energetically**. I would give

them that vision, because then we would all be kind, we wouldn't cause that hurt. So with the snap of my fingers, if I could change something, it would be that."

In "Flipside" I spoke of a man who saw during his NDE a review of when he beat up a man who had cut him off in traffic. He experienced the beating from the man's POV. He could taste the blood, feel the broken teeth, and experienced the humiliation this poor man felt while the man who was having the NDE beat the shit out of him.

In David Bennett's NDE ("Voyage of Purpose")[31] he recalled being in a cowboy bar in Texas where a man made a pass at him – and he reported it to the bartender, who along with everyone else in the macho bar proceeded to beat the living daylights out of this gay man. Bennett said he could "feel the wave of rage, anger and hostility" that came from everyone in the room. He said it felt "horrible."

Paul Aurand, hypnotherapist, talked about his first LBL where he was shown a lifetime where he had been a slave owner, and experienced whipping his slaves. Treating them "as if they were less than animals." Paul was sick to see that behavior, something he knew nothing about in this lifetime, but learned from his council of elders, was "something he'd been working on for many lifetimes." That he had finally only directed that kind of rage at himself "but you're getting better."

If Prince could give us one gift – it would be to see the effects of our actions. Now I ask you. Is this new or old information? You want to understand what it means to be alive? *Check out how your actions affect others on the planet.* Prince with Tavis Smiley in 2009:

> Prince said to Tavis: *"I've never spoken about this before, but I was born epileptic… I used to have seizures when I was young. And my mother and father didn't know what to do or how to handle it but they did the best they could with what little they had."*[32]

[31] "Voyage of Purpose: Spiritual Wisdom from Near-Death back to Life." David Bennet and Cindy-Griffith Bennet. (Findhorn Press, 2011)

[32] http://www.pri.org/stories/2016-04-22/tavis-smiley-ill-never-know-why-prince-chose-me-one-his-young-prot-g-s

On the show with Tavis (and also referenced in the afterlife) he said *"I've been having to deal with a lot of things, getting **teased a lot in school**... **You know, early in my career I tried to compensate for that by being as flashy as I could and as noisy as I could."***

He said *"My mother told me one day when I walked in to her and said 'Mom, I'm not going to be sick anymore.' And she said 'Why?' And I said 'Because an angel told me so.' Now, I don't remember saying it, that's just what she told me,"* he said. Teased a lot in school. Pretty much the same thing that Prince said during this inter-life interview.

Here he is saying the same things to two different people – one is Tavis Smiley on television, the other is a medium – same topic, nearly the same words. More importantly, he was "visited by an angel" who told him everything would be okay. (If I had a nickel for every time I've heard someone in my Flipside research say they were "visited by an angel" that told them everything would be okay... including myself!)

Some months after I wrote this chapter, I had lunch with "my friend the medium" Jennifer Shaffer who will appear in a big way in the second half of this book. Jennifer works often with law enforcement agencies (pro bono) to help with missing person cases. Later in the book, I go into detail how we met, and what happened in our first meeting; but here it is a couple of years after that first meeting, and I'm editing this book when we catch a quick bite at a restaurant in Manhattan Beach near her office.

When we first met, the actor Robin Williams showed up as I was interviewing her; just after he passed on. After he showed up, I told Jennifer I had dinner with Robin once; he was the shyest most polite guy at the table. Steve Martin and Charles Grodin were at the table as well, and we all took a back seat to their lightning wit.

I'd wished I'd spoken to Robin about the Harvey Lembeck comedy workshop, we both had that in common as well as memorable lunches with his mentor and pal Jonathan Winters. Pretty much every time I interviewed Jennifer, Robin would show up for a minute or two, say something funny and depart.

But at this point in our lunch, Jennifer and I were catching up, talking about how the "veil is thinning" when she looked up said "Robin Williams just showed up." I said "Your pal! He shows up for you all the time." And she said "Well you're the one who met him, I've never met him." I asked him *why* he showed up, for me or her? She said "I just saw the word "Love." I said, "You mean "love, as in "love your neighbor?" Or love as in "the essence of what we call God is what love is?" "As if the word refers to the connections between all of us on the planet?" She said "He just showed me the word *love;* it appeared, coming out of "the Matrix." (I guess she means a mass of numbers and digits that turns into letters).

I turned on my cellphone camera and asked her to recount what we had just been talking about that brought him forward:

RM: So what did you just tell me about Robin appearing? What did you see?

Jennifer: Robin showed up when you were talking about the planet. All of a sudden, he came in when you described how everyone has this gift, (i.e., of accessing the afterlife, not only mediums) and when you said how in my work, I had taken this information to a different level. How I've learned how to use it and how others can learn to use it as well.

RM: Also that you are able to open yourself up to the idea that no one can be hurt here because we are always fine back on the Flipside...

Right. Which took me a long time understand. And then he showed up.

You mentioned how the word "love" appeared out of the Matrix form. Then I asked if we could ask Robin a question about whether the Akashic records kept a list of everything people had done before, good or bad, and his reply was to appear as Santa Claus. You said he was holding a giant scroll which rolled out endlessly. On the scroll, there was this long list, like the ones where people's names appear in the "naughty or nice" columns, but then you saw the lines where the names would be.

They were all blank.

I guess the idea is that the Akashic records people keep a list of everything that happens in our lifetimes, but God does not...

Right. It would be like God keeping a record of himself. That's in my view, where I go to. God doesn't keep a list of *himself,* he just retains everyone's experiences.

So Robin, let me ask you, is it accurate that the universe is sentient, that the universe learns things from our experiences?

(Note: This came from a discussion with a spirit guide in "It's a Wonderful Afterlife." He was asked if the universe was a machine, and he replied, "It's a mechanism, but it's sentient.")

He just showed me a map... hold on. He just showed me something on the board... a bunch of.. (listens. To Robin) What does that mean?

What did he show you?

He just showed me like a Matrix. (Laughs.) He's like "Come on!" He showed me the Matrix, like three different holographic TV screens, they're light blue... they're sentient? (He says) "Everything is celestial." (to me) What does that mean?

Everything in the sky, the heavens or perhaps the idea of heaven?

Oh yeah, I've heard that. Mormons use the term "celestial kingdom."

(Note: His answer, for me, seems to imply that everything on the Flipside is "heavenly," that it is all sentient or conscious. Looking into the afterlife would be like looking through multiple holographic images. Each piece of the hologram contains all of the information from that hologram, no matter where you look. I've also heard a description of reality as a "multi-tiered 3D chess game, where one move affects all the rest.")[33]

So when we act down here, do those celestial things learn, or are those lessons learned by the rest of the universe? Like planets learn?

He's showing us on a stage. He puts the planet on a stage, then he put some big chairs on the stage, then a bunch of people on those chairs... They're all learning from us, (on the Flipside) just like when we're "The Learning Planet," like in my session when I got crushed? This is us, now, for another planet.

(Note: Jennifer is referring to her past life memory (in a future chapter) where she lived a long time ago, and was tasked to help people cross from one realm into the next. She was in the process of helping people when her world was destroyed. The idea that people on the Flipside observe what

---

[33] See Michael Talbot's "The Holographic Universe: The Revolutionary Theory of Reality" by Michael Talbot. (Harper's Perennial 2011) He explains how holograms mirror reality.

lessons we learn here, and that knowledge helps people on the Flipside as well. We teach and learn from each other in a symbiotic way.)

So they're learning from us and we learn from them?

How we can co-exist.

So it's like a mutual existence – we learn from each other. They're pulling information up from us, but allowing information to come back down to here?

Yes.

(Note: This is something that's recurring in these reports. In one of the sessions, a guide spoke of how the souls who are no longer on the planet are also experiencing and learning from those who are still on the planet. But that the process is both ways – we learn from them as well. "As above, so below.")

*So **why is the veil thinning?** Why is that thing between us becoming easier to access?*

He just showed me Prince.

Prince the musician? What about him?

I don't know.

*He's in the new book. (**This book**. I was still working on it.)*

Is he? Give me a second**... When you said "why is the veil thinning," he showed me Prince**. (Pause, listening.) He said "Prince just wanted to go home."

What?

"Prince just wanted to go home."

Okay I understand. I include an interview with him in the book. In the interview, he talks about what it was like when he got home.

Yeah.

Are you guys friends? (Robin and Prince) You guys hang out?

(Laughs.) They're both laughing. **"We go way back."** They're laughing about the whole concept of "way back." Like *what does that mean*? In their world, where they're at, way back is like… (laughs).

Let me ask Prince a question. Are you aware of your interview that you did with Dr. Medhus and her son Erik that I'm using in my book?

He's showing me something with the number 149.

A page number?

Could be.

(I thought Jennifer said either "a page 49" or "page 149." It was a noisy restaurant. Page 49 is the interview with Scott De Tamble, but page 149 is the section of his interview where Prince talks about being bullied growing up.)

I used the interview where you talk about going back "home," what it was like arriving there, and the journey. It's funny, I asked Dr. Medhus' permission but I didn't ask yours. Is it okay to use you in the book?

He says "Yes, of course." He's showing me reading a book. Page 149. (or 49).

What's he reading?

I don't know. (pause) **He says you're very good at not taking things out.** He's laughing; he says "It's a good thing." I asked (him) "Is it a good or a bad thing?" And he gave me a look, said "It's a good thing."

You mean not taking things out… you mean like I'm allowing everything to be in?

Yes, everybody else takes bits and pieces out.

Well I think I understand the architecture of what is going on up there. I leave everything in so people can experience this research as I've experienced it.

He says **"Love is what it is."** Now he's playing his guitar.

"Love is what it is." What kind of guitar is he playing?

Right now, he's showing me a classical guitar, before it was one of those…

Electrics?

Yeah.

He's quite good guitar player.

I don't know, I haven't seen him play before.

He's amazing. Like Hendrix or Clapton. So, Prince what are you and Robin up to?

"Surfing the ethers."

Surfing the ethers? Cool. Do you go around and check out your fans, reach out to them? Or do you guys hang around and do your own thing?

(Listens) No, what? (Laughs. Nods. Smiles.) They're both teaching (the class) **"How Not to Leave the Earth Early."**

Excellent, well that's a great class. I'd like to take that class. I know a few people who need to take that class.

(Note: When people ask what I teach in film school, I tell them my class is called "How Not to Have a Career in Hollywood" because "*I'm really good at that.*" The idea they'd use the same context for the same kind of joke is doubly amusing -- to me anyway.)

Again, he showed me time doesn't exist. (Note: Meaning that it's not a big deal for them both to exit the stage early.)

Right, but if you're down here to learn something, if you've chosen to learn something, it's important for the people who look up to you, to not see how easy it is to check out.

Right. **My bad.**

No, look, we've all done it before… (Note: I think it's pretty funny if I try to reassure someone on the Flipside and they reply "My bad.")

Everything is perfect timing.

Any plans on what your next incarnation will be?

(Laughs.) That's funny. (To Robin) Why'd you show me that?

What did you see?

He shows me a little African American kid. Then I saw Eddie Murphy. That's funny, hold on.

Maybe he's saying in the future he'd be a comedian, an African American kid who is a comedian?

That's right.

Prince or Robin?

Prince wants to be a female. Robin wants to be a comedian, an African American; he'll bring back more information, (I think she means *"material")* because he'll be able to access more. Prince is more attuned with Versace' – the designer? Is she alive?

Gianni's gone but his sister is alive.

Prince wants to be a female.

(Note: I assume this means "in his next life." Prince was quoted as saying "I'm not a woman. I'm not a man. I am something that you'll never understand." It's up to us who we want to come back as or why.)

A female Versace'? Oh I see, like a clothing designer?

Yeah.

(Note: Needless to say, Prince was an amazing fashion trendsetter. As Stephen Colbert noted: not many people *own an entire color.")*

Dude, you were already a designer, already a stylist.

He says "Music hurts too much;" it hurt his joints. He said **"It hurts."**

I understand, you had those amazing dance moves; all that rehearsal must have taken its toll. That's pretty cool he wants to be a designer next time around. So guys, anything else you want to impart to us sitting here in this restaurant in Manhattan Beach?

They've got their arms around each other. (She rocks back and forth to show me, like two happy sailors.) They said **"Thank you for not questioning our existence... from your guides."**

(Earlier I had been teasing Jennifer over the fact that during her between life hypnosis session, (later in this book) she quoted her spirit guide as saying "We get exhausted when you keep questioning whether you're really tapping into spirit or not. And we *don't get exhausted*!" I thought that was pretty funny.)

You mean, thanking you for not questioning whether or not you're hearing them?

Robin wants to know where his part is in the book... (laughs) He's kidding.

I did mention him in "It's a Wonderful Afterlife." He's the last chapter of volume one. I met a postal clerk in NYC who was crying the day after his death, I told her I'd been doing this research that showed people don't die, that Robin's spirit would always exist, just not here on the planet. She loved hearing that. How about Prince, any last words?

"Live and let live."

Thanks. You're both welcome to come and visit either of us in a dream or whenever.

Prince is so sexy. Wow. He's something else. (Blushes. Laughs)

Especially Jennifer, since she needs your sense of humor during those difficult sessions when she's doing these helpful things for people.

I do apparently.

Thanks guys I appreciate it. "Live... and let live!" .

(A pause, laughs.) Oh my god, that was so funny, Robin, dressed as Mork just got into that space outfit from "Mork and Mindy" stepped into his flying saucer and Prince just flew off on his guitar!

Wow.

.....

As per Robin's request (or my imaginary friend's request):

"Let's nominate July 21st, Robin Williams' birthday as "Mirth Day." I don't have a candy company, or a card company, it just popped into my head on his birthday. *"HAPPY MIRTH DAY."* It's a day where you try to make people laugh, and you get credit for doing so. You don't have to make merry, make out, but you do have to make mirth.

Mariel Hemingway, Robert Towne on the set of "Personal Best." I was Robert's dog's personal assistant. Making movies is a tough gig. Photo: Steven Vaughan.

David Letterman ran a tribute to Robin after his passing, where Robin was shown throwing his head back, roaring like a lion with laughter. David had said something that allowed him to release that laugh which included a kick back of the head, chin pointed skyward, his legs stretched out - literally *roaring*. I urge everyone to take Robin's death not as an example of someone who is depressed who did themselves in, but as someone who gave us something to learn from. *Because he's not dead. He's just not here.*

Suicide is a tricky subject. I can only weigh in on the Flipside research. We all choose to come to the planet to learn and teach lessons; we are not here by mistake or happenstance. Each has their own path and journey, each has a myriad of reasons how they choose to experience the journey here or for exiting the stage. Once we wrap our minds around the fact that we don't die, or in this case can't die, then the matter of our leaving the stage is one of logistics. Do we judge an entire life or performance on how an actor leaves the stage? "Yes, I loved the play, the first and second act were great, but you tripped as you came off stage and that I cannot forgive. Two thumbs way down."

We tend to write reviews on how an actor exits: "*A belt, a plastic bag, a box of pills*" and ignore those who are checking themselves out with each cigarette, each shot of whisky, each time they drink and drive and/or text. Are they any less "guilty" of choosing the manner of their death than others just because it happens to be a slow lingering exit? We applaud those who managed to stay on stage until the last breath, surrounded by loved ones and wag our fingers at deaths we don't applaud, whether Robin or a child in a wedding party taken out by a drone.

We've all got a myriad of exits and entrances behind us, and ahead of us - suffice to say it's up to us how we manage them. Again, the research shows that we don't die. That each life is a sacred, precious choice, that we come here to learn and teach and love for many reasons, and the manner of our passing has roots in our own path and journey. Robin is ok, he's fine, he hasn't gone anywhere - he's just not here or visible to us. And that's a damned shame because he lit up the stage, made the entire planet stand laugh, and *there's nothing more healing than laughter.*

The mask used in "Mrs. Doubtfire."

CHAPTER EIGHT:

"Where do I renew my Library of Souls card?"

Fra. Lippi. *"Sorry, your name is not on the list; come back next life."*

"I have always imagined that paradise will be a kind of library."
- J.K. Rowling

In the afterlife research, people often talk about "visiting a library" while experiencing being on the Flipside.

"Akashic Records" is often used, the word appears in the Hindu holy books "The Vedas." There are reported rules and regulations of who can or can't access these libraries, that it's a holy place of reckoning, and where karma can be seen doled out across the centuries.

Actually, this information is accessible to anyone. The library of records has an all access pass. That doesn't mean that everyone who visits there is going to understand where they are. It appears to whomever sees it, as they need to see it. Of course they aren't seeing a structure in "outer space" but an energetic design, made by older wiser architects. It could be that they're creating the structure themselves. There is no literal location for a library. Everyone who visits a library tells a different story about what the interior looks like.

I won't see it the way you do. You won't see it the way I do. But like the rainbow that is different to everyone who sees it, it still exists. Every single thing you've ever done in any lifetime you've ever led is there. There are future possibilities there – but since the future hasn't been written they're "likely events." Like in the "The Adjustment Bureau" with Matt Damon.[34]

The premise of that film was that there were these books where the events of everyone's life was written down, and you weren't supposed to screw it up. "If I signed up for a particular life, what happens if I want to change it?"

Seems kind of hard to fix it now, doesn't it? I mean if we sat down and said "I'm going to play this role, and you're going to play that role, and we're all going to work hard at this same thing" – at some point you may say "Hey, I'm not happy with how this play is going. I think I'm going to improvise a bit here."

That's okay. There is no hall monitor that will come and pull you off stage. You want to change your mind about your contract? You can. You may screw things up for *everyone else on stage,* but if you really think you can do some good by changing what you signed up for, then all means, show us how it's done.

But in order to see what it is you signed up for, you might want to organize a trip to the library of souls, the library where you figured out what your next life was going to be, based on what your previous lifetimes were.

Here's an excerpt from my own life planning session. I had done a little digging during my first between life session, but was so busy wondering if I was "making it up" I didn't examine it too closely. In my case, I saw that I was going to be wherever my father the architect was going, or at least

---

[34] "The Adjustment Bureau" is a 2011 American romantic science fiction thriller film loosely based on the Philip K. Dick short story, "Adjustment Team." (Wikipedia) Matt Damon discovers his life was pre-planned, but a chance encounter with Emily Blunt has screwed up his "time line" for this lifetime.

that's what I said. But some four years eight years later, I revisited the event with the help of Scott De Tamble.

MY LIFE PLANNING SESSION or *"What the hell was I thinking?"*

After walking me back through some scenes of my youth, we get to this exchange...

Scott: All right then. We're going to go down the stairway. Here we go. Two, one, 9 months, etc... back in time. Before birth and in the womb now.. Be there now. I'm curious. Do you sense that it's tight and cramped, or snug or roomy – what's your first impression?

RM: Comfort. Like I'm comfortable in that kind of papoose environment, I'm aware of sounds – because my mother laughs a lot, a laugher and she's a concert pianist I heard the piano – muffled – imagine what that sounds like. Very lovely.

Pleasant?

Very pleasant. I can feel that she's a joyful kind of person - no stress with her... she's happy. Doesn't seem to be any stress involved.

Curious about her happiness, does that affect you in some way?

I'm just observing it. Like "What's that?" Oh, there's the sound of the piano – that's interesting – "What's that?" "Oh, that's the sound of the piano." I'm in a happy place, no stress involved here.

First impression. At one month did your soul enter the womb, the first month of gestation.

The fourth.[35]

In the 4th month, what do you sense about this baby or body? How do you feel about it?

---

[35] This is the 5th sessions I've done. This is the 4th time with Scott. So I'm familiar with my previous answers to some of the key questions. But some I am not.

A feeling of shifting. Shifting gears from… a feeling of shifting - into this environment that is completely different from the environment I was in; a complete adjustment.

How?

It's like being outside of a tank and then climbing down into the tank – outside, there's wind and everything else, and when you climb in, you're in this submarine environment. It's familiar and comfortable, you feel like "Oh here we are again; that's right -- this is what happens." It's a little unusual - you have to alter your energy…

What do you do to alter your energy?

Slow it down. Almost like putting on a brake – putting on the brakes full speed, imagine a train going superfast and then everything has to shift so the brakes screech, you're not going to stop just slowing down to the right rhythm to the physicality of this dimension or experience…

It's a slowing down of vibration or energy?

I think (it's like) a James Bond movie, dropping out of a plane and landing into a car – the plane was going super-fast and you have to get the stunt right. Then you drop down into this other realm - the physicality of that, and then you adjust… not to throw so many metaphors, but like jumping into cold water, your senses are alive, you have to adjust to that.. like being pushed into ice cold water.

It's not a negative image, it's just a different, it's a take-your-breath, give-you-breath kind of experience, and you have to adapt quickly and suddenly, to all of the variations. **Because you can plan what it's like jumping into cold water, but once you do it, you're there!** And it's moving; the creature, *the Richard animal,* is alive and you're shifting into that reality. Everything's gonna be awake, sort of – I can't think of the word – sort of "present."

When you make those connections, you're focused enough, you do it properly. It's okay if you show up and the toe isn't working the way it's supposed to work… – or (you realize) "What are they shouting about? I had no idea this was an Italian home!" You make an adjustment to whatever it is when you get here.

Let's talk about the Richard body. How do you feel about that body and the brain?

Feel very comfortable, like a nice fit, like getting into a good shoe that fits about right. You're sort of feeling around to see if the emotions are strong, or inaccurate, or whatever the gears are... – if all the gears are working properly. Everything seems to be okay, I don't sense an "Oops, what was I thinking?" **I guess if I'm trying to examine this particular body, I feel like it's a comfortable glove that fits really well, it's warm, comfortable – no judgment involved.** Just "We're going into this glove, here we are!" If that makes sense.

When you try out the levers of the mechanism make sure everything properly, what do you do?

It's kind of like a liquid pouring into some other liquid. When you pour one liquid into the other, one gets colored and then that color sort of blends – it starts off with a particular intensity and then kind of dissipates out. That was my experience; I'm blending out – because I'm familiar with toes and fingers, I'm just getting into this blending mode.

(Note: These metaphors I'm using are *new to me*, I've never heard anyone suggest that moving from the Flipside to this realm is like blending paint or liquid. These concepts are new to my mind – but apparently not new to my consciousness. In other words, what I'm saying doesn't feel generated from my brain or any memory I can access; these metaphors and images aren't familiar to me on any level. It's as if I'm "receiving" the information from my higher self, and using words and syntax to explain what I'm trying to impart. The images, words and syntax aren't the kinds of words I'd normally use, or have ever used. It's as if my "higher consciousness" that I'm accessing is aware of these concepts and elucidates them. At least that's the feeling I'm having while speaking extemporaneously.)

Your physical energy is blending?

Right. I'm not feeling anything is here that shouldn't have been here – Well, that's happened before, one might say "Oh, this person is very emotional, intense, what was I thinking?" But in this case; it feels very comfortable.

In that 4th month you come in to check out this body, do you stay put from then on in or move in and out?

I feel that I stay put – it's like the old adage "In for a penny, in for a pound." I'm comfortable, sort of just realizing… I feel I'm learning more information than I was aware of, while I'm here. It's like you can plan everything, but it all goes out the window once you arrive.[36]

I am tapping into my mom, her emotions and stuff going on and feeling out from her, the energy of my dad and my brothers and getting a sense of all that. And kind of like "I'm into this journey and I'm here." **A bit like hopping into a train traveling across Europe, even though the train stops and you could get out -- you're comfortable just staying in and looking out the window.**

Are you comfortable being a male this time around?

I feel comfortable with this choice, as if this choice of being a male and being with my dad, whom I've been around before (in other lifetimes.) I think it was more about the decision to be with (my dad) Charlie - to hang out with my dad – and had things gone differently, I would have been fine with being the girl. It would have been a great adventure, but it didn't pan out that way. **I wasn't involved with their creating the male, and had I shown up as Betty, it would have been just fine.**

More about being with this family?

Things would have turned out differently; it's a good question, because it takes my mind into the planning part of it. Maybe I always knew I was going to be a boy.

(Note: When discussing these pre-life sessions, or anything that might happen in between lives, I've noticed that often a person is saying in effect "This is the way this happened, and this is why this happened…" and then suddenly they see more information and realize they don't have that answer correct. With more insight or information, people often change their story as to why certain things happened "as it becomes clearer.")

If that takes your mind in the planning, we need to go look at that. I'll count from three back to one – and I want you to be somewhere some when before you were born – working things out, perhaps there's counselors or

---

[36] I used "In for a penny, in for a pound" in my first session. I heard my old boss Robert Towne use it once, but even then it sounded odd to my ear.

advisors around.. three two one.. be there now. A meeting or gathering or a study...

I'm in a classroom, but a classroom of that's been kind of designed to be more comfortable. Like with oriental rugs and settees and comfortable places to sit. It seems like a room full of about 20 people. A lot of (the) people here are talking about where I'm going; it feels like there's more people involved. I'm getting the sense of a larger amphitheater just off stage, this setting *where we are* is on stage – but out there is an amphitheater filled with people who can raise a hand or make a suggestion to something they hear; like saying "Oh that's a bad idea, and here's why."

So there's an inner circle?

Yeah, I can see my dad, my mom is onstage, but off to the periphery of this inner circle, I can see Sherry...my wife.. um.. what appears to be my kids, off the periphery, not center stage, they're here because they've agreed to participate.

So there are those souls who are going to be participants, and also souls who are overseers or teachers. Is that right?

That's what it feels like.

How many of the 20 are teachers?

It feels like maybe four or 5 that are part of my life, but it feels more like we're having a general discussion – and we're presenting it to the others, and..

The ones who are participating are presenting?

Yes, like presenting a finished product to people who aren't teachers per se, they have no relation to giving a yes or no, they're just observing this elaborate plan that we're laying out for them. As if the planning was already happened or... we're so in synch with how we work together, as we present this plan, it all seems to coalesce.

Or maybe it's just my ego saying this. I present this idea and the teachers are saying "Yeah we've heard that plan before..." – but (at the present moment) I'm saying that my occupation... explaining how (filmmaking) it's going to somehow heal people; this path is going to use the healing energy to help people on the planet.

I have no idea how I would have felt if someone said "Ooh. This is a bad idea, remember when you screwed it up before?"[37]

Let me ask – there's a moment where you're making this presentation, almost like you do in the current life, stories to people...

Yeah; pitching.

Yeah, but before you do that, there's a moment where this story is just a seed – so this Richard life is just a seed. Let's go back to that moment, the idea for this life first comes to you – where are you who are you with?

Let me rephrase this in a way; I'm feeling from what these choices were, that it was much more improvised than planned the way you (normally) plan things. Normally you sit down and say "I need to go here and here" or to here – it's like this group of people have been doing it for so long and they're so adept, myself not included; it's like being in a room with a bunch of Mozarts and Beethovens.

They're creating or making out their journeys as well, not just mine... they're all going to intersect. Charlie's (my dad) talking about his life as an architect, my mom is talking about her life as a concert pianist; it doesn't spawn from a deeply thought journey of "Do we need to do this?" It's more like "Hey I got an idea, why don't we do this?" and they're attitude is **"That's a good idea, he'll figure it out as he goes along. We'll all participate in that creation at the same time."**

Like a room full of comedy writers? "I got an idea for a skit?"

Right, there's no one there in the room that we're pitching the idea to, because they know (each other) all so well. I guess there's no one here to say *"What, are you crazy?"* as opposed to a room full of comedy writers. They're more like musicians really, people good with their instruments. You've known them forever and you've seen them forever and they say they're going play a little *leitmotif* in your life here, and I'm going to bring

---

[37] I had a glimpse of this event in my very first session in 2006. I saw myself in this environment, but it was dim, not clear. I saw myself standing and explaining why I was going to choose an "outside the box" form of healing through film. My counselors seemed amused by the idea, but supportive. Now it's coming through much more clearly.

it into a crescendo, into something more passionate and you're going to help me with that.[38]

Allow me to add**… this kind of unusual improvisational method is** *always* **being overseen.** Not by a higher entity, **but by our higher selves, because we're always back there together in the between lives realm; we're always discussing how the lifetime choices will pan out.** We have that freewill where people back on the Flipside are looking on and commenting on our lives on Earth.

(Note: This observation isn't in any of the cases I've read or seen. Nothing is set in stone, and even when we're on stage performing, we have the ability to make adjustments to our scenarios and performances while we're mid-play.)

So let's say our good friend Larry has decided to check out early – commit suicide. To leave the stage right in the middle of the play. We don't all just stop at that point, because we all have the capacity to continue on this improvised play. **You could say this is also like the life planning journey or session; that it's always ongoing. It never stops. You're always adjusting, improvising, changing, trying to do things out of compassion for everyone in the group while they're living their lives.** Like a group of theater critics in the balcony looking at their friends while the play is going on and observing "Wow, look what kind of pickle you've gotten yourself into! How can I help?"

(Note: The point I seem to be making here is that we have fully conscious selves back in the afterlife that are always aware of what we're doing and creating in our lifetime, and that we can ask for help. Ask our higher selves to change circumstances if they agree with our assessment, or haven't already signed a contract to perform. It appears to be an ongoing discussion while the play is on the boards and being performed. I'm saying here that we have the ability to improvise during the play and change the paradigm, no matter what we signed up for.)

In some way, that pre life planning conference is even now in the current 60-year-old life?

---

[38] A leitmotif is a "short, constantly recurring musical phrase" (Wikipedia)

Still in process.

Very interesting. You mentioned that this improvisational process is always supervised...

I'm aware that other groups have supervision during their life's journey; more direct, more finger wagging. **That's a result of older souls perhaps, or the temperament of those that guide those groups.** But somebody in the group, perhaps a teacher, may observe that "My experience has been different, perhaps take my advice before you make that choice you're about to make."

"Because if you go down this path, these (are some) life options I'm going to show to you, you may need to see these options or choices while you're making them." And (even) they might even be hesitant playing that role as overseer, or "theater critic" in the middle of the play.

I myself like to be more immersive... on one level. **I'm aware of other groups that are supervised, that's their process. In this particular group, for whatever reason, it's less supervised;** it's more along the lines of "Dude, we get what you're doing, bring it back, show us what you have in mind."

You've created this scenario with your friends, and you're presenting it before these people. Do these people have some say or power?

I would say that they don't exert it.

Then why are you presenting it for them?

Because they're wiser, older.

Let's zero in on the oldest wisest being. I'm going to speak directly to that being. Asking that being to speak with me, or to respond in the mind of my friend here. Or through his voice   I'm going to speak directly to that being and asking that person to respond through my friend here.

(Voice changes) Certainly.

Okay with them?

Yes.

Excellent. I greet you and I thank you and I would ask you for a name or title. Some way to address you? This overseer, teacher.

(My voice changes) Rayma.

(Note: This is the name of my spirit guide. He appeared in my first session in Chicago with Jimmy Quast, another Newton trained hypnotherapist, and has appeared in almost all of the sessions I've done with Scott. He's an older man, kind eyes, polite, but humorous. He's the one who said that "after he graduated all of his lifetimes, I was his "graduation gift.")

Ah. It's good to speak with you again Rayma.

Good to speak with you again, Scott.

Rich is telling us that his life planning sessions are different.

He's describing the process correctly. But it is filtered through Richard. (Meaning, it has "my spin" on it.)

So give me the unfiltered version. How would you add or correct him?

(Scott asks Rayma direct questions, and I find myself answering them without a thought in my head. I'm aware that when answering Scott's question, I get a feeling of intelligence when I'm speaking, as if I know the answer to his question, but it's as if I am trying to find a way to make the *answer easier for humans to understand.*

I've had some startling conversations courtesy of Rayma, including the one just mentioned where Rayma described my birth as a soul and when I was "gifted" to him for guidance over all my lifetimes. Once, Scott asked him a question, and I felt my conscious mind literally shift into his. I saw *myself* through his eyes as those on the Flipside see me. (I looked like I did at 20; long hair, suede vest, a larger sized head and an unruly beard.)

Rayma tends to tease or mock me in a loving way. Scott once asked him to show me an event that had happened two years earlier during a session, where I had made my council laugh uproariously. Rayma replayed that event in my mind, and from his point of view, the council chuckled; no uproarious laughter. From my perspective I thought they had "roared with laughter" but from Rayma's perspective it was mild chuckling. Rayma then said "Richard tends to forget we've been here before the council many times. They're used to his humor. But we like his enthusiasm; he's always pretty excited to be here." Nothing more humbling than to see yourself from another person's perspective.)

He's correct in that in this particular group, Richard's group; it's a democratic process. No one steps forth to impose their will on other people here who are the ones who've been planning this lifetime for a long time. They are aware of all the permutations of a particular lifetime. **So even when they're presenting what they're going to be doing (during this life), we're judging it from terms of many, many, many lifetimes.**

But we've come to conclusion that this particular group should have unfettered ability to plan their journey as they see fit. They'll gain the most benefit from doing it that way and for us to impose our idea of what would be best for them, won't allow them to learn from having an unfettered experience.

So planning this journey is part of the process is part of the learning and their education?

Yes.

How is that helping them by planning it themselves? What is this soul who is Rich gaining from planning his own life?

You gain the most from experience, you gain the most from mistakes when you've had those experiences with falling or failing; in the many lifetimes that he's had, he's had many failures. But he only learns from the failure if we impose or ask him to consider other lifetimes based on our idea of what he should learn. **It doesn't allow him to experience it, you see, because sometimes when they come back here, they can claim "Well that happened because we didn't plan that episode. How can I learn from random mistakes I had nothing to do with?"**

However, some groups benefit from that.

Yes, there are many, many, many groups. Think of it as a university – we like it this way. **Some other groups *like* having the feeling of a paternal or maternal presence saying "We are here for you and you to need to learn these lessons." Others learn from hearing "We're not here to help you, you're here to rise or fall from your own will."**

So why did this soul take this life at this time?

Part of it, is that everyone was making their choices of their participation and he wanted to participate in that trip and fly by the seat of his pants -- however that would work.

But every soul has a task or primarily mission or task, so what is his?

Primary reason for Richard to choose this lifetime is to learn how to use other methods of healing. **There are many methods on the planet that you can use for healing; medicine, shaman. There's teaching in his path and in his case he wanted to do something with words music and image – his primary mission was to find another way to use the healing light of the universe through his work. Not everyone believed it was going to work, we found it amusingly different, fraught with many pot holes as a choice...**

(Note: He's talking about my life choice of being a filmmaker, and how I argued that I could use laughter through film to heal people, as reported during my first LBL with Jimmy Quast in "Flipside.")

What sort of potholes or problems?

In terms of self-identification when you choose a particular work place or journey, there are so many things that happen that cause a person to be caught up in the egotism of their endeavors. **Quite a bit of vanity is involved with people working in the arts;** those potholes, we wanted to keep forefront in his mind. All of it is vanity and should be annihilated whenever you can.

(Note: Another reference to "Vanum Populatum.")

It's very difficult on this planet for people to have a successful career and not be caught up in the vanity of possessions. He's experienced that before – he's been a doctor (in a previous life) and the vanity of money altered his path of what he tried to accomplish. **Which is why I say it's amusing for someone to be a film person and try to be a healer; he's made an unusual choice of a path for himself.**

So how has this soul fared with those potholes?

Safe to say that he's done what he's set out to do on some level – it's always an improvisation, there are always things that come into the path that change the journey. **That's no denigration of what he's been doing,** it's the path he's gone down, it's just part of his lessons… he's navigated them fairly well.

Any advice for him now?

Just wanted to add something, **he's here with us at all times** – (back here on the Flipside) **He's also observing himself at all times; so we try not to interfere on any level. He's aware of what's going on, he himself (is) here – (and) he can influence or see where things have failed.** We're always a little amused by the journey, because certainly the journey is amusing – **what can we impart to him (now)? It's the message we impart to you as well – "You're on the right path because it is healing people."**

(Note: wow.)

As you know, Rayma, we were having a gathering today. Having a class. Taking people to wombs and past lives. What would you share with our group today?

The idea that you're all absolutely on the right path. **It's a little bit like learning how to sew a complex garment – it can be incredibly frustrating when pieces fall away and a stitch isn't right, but you have to have that focus and faith (that) you're creating things for people that they can wear, (and that knowledge is) the armor against injustices of what they feel. (Your work) will change their life as well as theirs; no matter how many times you stick yourself with the needle, (while sewing) you will always be rewarded with healing other people.**

Anything else you wish to share with Rich today before we let you go?

(Laughs.) Just to take himself **more seriously. As opposed to taking himself less seriously, which he's really good at.** Be courageous in these endeavors, focus on the work, there's a tendency – this has been a debate (back here on the Flipside) for a long time, that allowing this information (to be known) and saying "to allow" is difficult because it also a natural progression of events.

Allowing this information to be available to a planet that thrives on not knowing what happens after they die; it's part of how the planet has been functioning. But this group idea that we came to (here on the

Flipside) -- that people *should* begin to (be able to) understand the nature of reality for a variety of reasons – **that's why it's important, and you people are on the forefront of passing along this information.**

Thank you Rayma. And thank you for being here today. I would give you a space to speak to this group a final word or message for today.

(Sighs.) There was a question that Richard had the very first time he had this experience, speaking with his guides, and he asked if there was one sentence or concept he could pass along – to everyone – not knowing that he could pass it along to anyone.

The concept he was given that he got from his higher self was to "just let go." **We tried to show him that was a concept in so many dimensions; letting go of anger, of suffering, or of attachments that don't progress your soul, letting go on so many levels is a metaphor for helping people. But it's people like you (Scott) doing this kind of work (to teach) that letting go doesn't mean giving up.**

It isn't a negative thing – you're helping people to let go of their fear. **That's a noble cause, because fear is the thing that's ruled the planet for so long – to helping people let go of fear.** For your patients, friends and loved ones, (that teaching) is something they will always appreciate.

We thank you. We wish you well. And we support you in any way that we could.

Thank you Scott.

All right then.. time to come back to the here and now. Before we come back all the way.. why is Richard's right ankle moving in a circle?

(Apparently my foot was drawing circles during the entire time that Rayma was speaking.) Focus. It helps him focus.

You focused very well today.

Afterwards:

RM: It's weird because I gave up my parent's house 5 years ago and every moment that I just spent there (in this session) was so emotional to me. So when I travel there in my mind, I feel so present when I'm there, even in my mind. Perhaps that home might be related to that group of individuals.

As you began to speak to me, I heard a voice say **"We're waiting for you, we're all here."** As you were regressing me in age, **I saw myself growing younger, but of course I was getting bigger, taller, and my friend Luana came and took my hand, walking me down these stairs during my 40s; she walked me down to (the time) before I met her, and then passed my hand over to my mom and dad, who took my hand and walked me all the way down the stairs.**

They were all waiting for this conversation. As you can hear – my conscious mind is saying "I remember these stories" and my subconscious mind is saying **"It's okay you can see it from another angle."**

I have been in my mother's womb during previous sessions, but this time I heard that experience more clearly, the muffled sounds of the piano. (Mom was a concert pianist who played every day) Then to see the time before, the experience of being in a life planning session. When I first visited this event, it was amorphous, cloudy, or foggy – this time it was much clearer.

I could see the cushions where people were sitting, the carpets, the layout of the room and seeing my dad – but this time, seeing that the event was more like an improvisation. I have no idea what that even means.

My spirit guide Rayma was ready to stand toe to toe with you about the nature of this planning session. **To let you know that "It's okay, Scott, this class, this planning session was less structured than ones you've heard before, it was more like an improv."**

People's lifetimes over here go by at a different rate over there, what feels like 50 years here, **feels like 25 minutes there** – if you can allow that for a second, and shift yourself to that altered state of time. While we're over there watching a lifetime here, it may feel like 90 minutes over there.

If someone screws up during their lifetime, from the perspective over there, maybe it's not that big of a deal. "Let's try it this way instead" seems like a way of saying "It's not that big of a deal if we screw up."

(Note: Even as I edit this chapter, I'm amazed by what I said during it. It's not part of my memory or conscious mind, I think because part of it wasn't generated from my mind. It's like I was speaking on someone else's behalf. *Who knows?* It sure makes for compelling reading, even if I do say so myself.)

My life planning session included me picking a lifetime of writing and directing films most have never heard of. This Xmas card was during "Point of Betrayal" in 1996, with Rod Taylor, Ann Cusack and Rebecca Broussard, the last film I made with Luana. As I said to my council during my first between life hypnosis session; **"I just wish I had chosen a lifetime of someone who was more of a success!"**

CHAPTER NINE:
Other Life Planning Sessions

"Look, Abe-ola. Good news; you go down in history as the greatest President. Bad news; you don't get to see the end of the play. Are you in?"

"Death - the last sleep? No, it is the final awakening." - Walter Scott

Recently I attended a seminar where Scott De Tamble spent three days teaching how to do past life regressions as well as visiting each life planning session.

During Scott's class, two licensed therapists explored this unusual aspect of a past life regression; the life planning session. I've edited their questions and answers with their permission but for the sake of anonymity, I'm going to call these two individuals "Paul" and "April." Neither had ever had any recollection of a life planning session, and this information was as new to them as it was to me behind the camera.

Paul and April

April: Let's go back to a pleasant moment at a very young age...

Paul: My dad is stationed at an Airforce base in Boston... I'm 2 or 3 years old – still in diapers, I think. Out front, dad's there with me, tells me to do something and I say "no" and he gives me that stern fatherly look. I turn and start running down the sidewalk. (Laughs) It takes forever for him to catch me... eventually he does. Picked me up and walked me back to the house.

Let's continue on (back in time) ... Before birth now and back in the womb. Back in the time before you were born... How's your comfort? What's your first impression?

It's not tight, not super snug. Just kind of comfortable, plenty of room. I think I can move around a lot – I did have a couple of kicks in there.

What's going on inside there?

Wow. It's almost time to go. I kind of like it, (but) it's almost time to start this life.

Are you in tune with your mother?

She can't wait. She's very maternal, very loving, lots of laughter. Really happy person, just can't wait to get me.. this bundle of joy – her first.

Are you observing?

I'm kind of in tune with her, I'm ready to go.

When did you join this baby?

The number seven comes to mind – (seventh month) right around Christmas.

How do you know it's Christmas?

Subtracting from my birth date.

Do you feel like you can stay put?

I think once I got there, I stayed. I don't think I moved in and out – (there were) two months remaining until it was time.

What was your first impression?

This is going to be cool… (looking forward) to be a teenager, there are going to be some rough spots; but this is going to be a cool life.

What do you think is distinctive about this brain or body?

(I'm) born into a military family, I think I know that I'll go in the military when it's time. There will be a lot of military characteristics around this boy; militaristic, stoic, that go with that particular discipline. I know it's not totally normal. My adult body looks back and says only 3% put the uniform on – I know I'm unique..

How do you feel about being male?

I get the feeling all my past lives have been male.

What's the baby's temperament?

Really happy, happy baby, I'm going to be easy to get along with not going to have any of those hysterics – temper tantrum, one of those easy go lucky, infant periods of time.

Is this baby a good match?

I chose this baby; I think it's a perfect match.

Any contrasts?

It's like a hand in a glove relationship, I just slipped into this body and all the chromosomes, feelings, fibers, all the connections matched up and it was a perfect fit and locked in place.

(Note: Another hand into a glove analogy of the process of how our energy melds with that of the human body.)

Does your soul mind know why you chose this life?

I think it realizes it's going to take some time, there's a number of experiences to go through; this baby will take on a lot of characteristics of my mom, my father's sense of caring, helping people. Those qualities are going to help in time to move into a helping, protecting healing mode.

Do you know when you chose this body can you tell me about that.

There was a planning session, I was in the spirit world with others, there was a session... some time, studying, I chose this.

As I count from three to one return to the life planning session.... let's journey back and remember.

Where I popped into, was me standing on a stage like the Hollywood Bowl, looking out at the vast seating there. Picture the Hollywood Bowl, it's the artist looking out – **in the first several sections (are) all of my**

spirit guides, guardian angels, in the audience behind that people that are interested, interested in me and what I have to say.

So there's a lot of people there? How many? Do you know them?

I have no idea how many... just a lot. I don't recognize the faces. Like the bowl, it's a semi-circle.

Is there some issue that you discuss?

I'm actually presenting what my next life is going to be; much like you would do if you you're defending a doctoral thesis. All the professors are there and they're asking you questions, like **"Why did you choose this? What was the purpose? What kind of studying did you do?** What were the tests (involved in making this choice)?" I'm busy answering those questions. **Why I chose this body, and this particular lifetime and my parents and what I'm going to be doing.**

How do you feel about it? Eager to get started? Reluctance? Mixed feelings?

No, none of that. I'm very confident. **I've done my research, I've done my studying, I know exactly what I want and what this life is going to do for me.** And so... all the questions... I'm handling all the questions with ease and comfort and being eloquent in my responses and detailed when I need to be.

Do you feel that you are you being advised or pressured in any way about an issue?

Not at all. (They're) just questions about why did I want to do this, those kinds of inquiry questions. **This lifetime is just a continuation of learning from previous lifetimes. This is a notch or a hole or a skill that needs to be filled.**

Were you offered multiple lives?

No. **I chose this. Because it was to learn how to be a healer and help others be healed.**

I'd like to speak to the chief or senior guide there – is it male or female energy?

It's a senior guide. (My spirit guide) Adam.

I'm going to speak to Adam directly, he can hear me, see me and understand me. I'm going to ask Adam to place his responses in your mind. Is that okay with you?

Yes.

Very good thank you. What is the primary purpose or mission of the life of Paul?

(Tone and demeanor changes) **He was pretty eloquent in his description of it, this was a chance for him to move away from some of his previous life roles and move into more of a healer role.** He's had some fascinating past lives. He's been a lawyer, which he continued in this present life, he's also been a teacher many times and taught a lot of different things and now it's time to move that teaching up to a different level, a spiritual level, it's in alignment with what he needed to do.

How is he doing so far in this life?

He's doing tremendously well. (The) last couple of years he's really moved into this role, wanting to learn and opening up. **He's never talked to me before; (but) I've always been here - but now he's talking to me. Now he's listening.**

This has been an interesting experience, (a) wonderful way to communicate – Paul is doing the work he's supposed to do. He's really in alignment with what he needs to do.

Any messages for anybody else?

The training's been wonderful, everyone's kind of pitching in another stepping stone to the next level.

Thank you. (End of Session)

... .

Afterwards I asked him to describe what it was like, and he spoke about his unusual description of arguing a doctoral thesis. **He'd never witnessed anything like this before, nor had it occurred in his own therapy sessions.**

I asked if the questions they asked were contentious or if they tried to see how adept he was in the topic of his future life – and he said that it was always cordial, and that he'd done his homework about what his life was going to be like.

I asked what that entailed. **He said he could now see himself sitting at a kind of desk in a library, studying, that he had carton or case in front of him and he was taking out microfiche kind of files.**[39] Examining all the holes that might exist in the trajectory of this soul, the kinds of emotional plus or minuses that exist or don't exist. And how he had worked hard to lay out how this lifetime was going to progress.

Paul began his life in the military, as noted, and later went into business where he was successful. He also met his wife April during his employment, and once he retired at a young age, he was really searching around for something interesting to do and this form of therapy called to him.

He said he'd never had the experience of seeing his past life review before, and that it was a powerful experience to recall it in such a fashion. He and his wife are both hypnotherapists and counselors, helping people with a variety of emotional issues.

After he was done with his session, he took over the teaching manual from Scott and proceeded to work with his wife. Later, she told me she'd never had this past life memory before, or of a life planning session. It was all new to her as well.

Paul Interviews April

After the initial introduction, and journey back:

Paul: Describe the scene you're at right now.

April: **I'm it's like a giant cathedral... like a giant colonial kind of cathedral, everything is white, flowers and grass and there's other souls.** (A pause as she takes it in.)

Tell me about it.

---

[39] As noted, everyone sees this "library" differently, no two accounts are identical. In this case, he saw his past lives on what looked like microfiche indexes, and as he went through the various lifetimes, studied what was missing or needed to be worked on. Not everyone has this level of expertise, but interesting to hear.

People (are) kind of walking into this cathedral. Kind of quietly walking in, but I feel like I'm searching for a room or something. I thought I heard someone say **"You're up next."** Like "It's your turn."

What's the room like?

There are stairs. Almost like we're walking up to somebody… it's totally like the Lincoln memorial and there's somebody there at the top of the stairs. Like "God" or something.

It's a big cathedral, Lincoln Memorial type of building?

It's beautiful.

You're arriving at the top?

Yeah.

Do you go inside?

I'm in there (already). The stairs are on the inside.

How many souls are around you?

Lots. Like everybody died at once and they're all filing in.

Are these passed souls? General souls?

They're just there.

(Note. Having witnessed a number of past life reviews or life planning sessions, the souls that show up in rows are people who know you, have met you, have worked with you, are affiliated with you in some fashion – and in some cases just people who want to stop by and enjoy the show.)

So there's (a feeling of) the Divine at the top. Are there any kind of experts, guides, spirits? Who is telling you you're up next? Let's pretend they've called you – where are you and what are you doing?

I'm kneeling before the God.

Is your spirit guide there?

No.

Any other guides?

Maybe he is. There's (just) too many souls (to see him).

There's only one person you're talking to… and its God?

That's it.

What are you two talking about?

I want to say… I think (I'm being told) **I'm getting sent back to do… like an angel good thing, that's how it feels.**

During this discussion?

(Yes) **I needed to fulfill that purpose… I think it's looking after my mom**. (Reacts) Oh brother! I think maybe that's it, I wanted to stay (back here) but they're telling me "They need you here (on Earth)."

How do you feel about that?

(Matter of fact) **It's the job.**

Okay. As you're talking to God, he's telling you you're going back, being this angel type person to help your mother. Have you met your mom before?

Huh… (observes something) Oh yeah. She's there. She's there somewhere. (In the crowd) I feel her energy.

You do know her.

I do. She just needed me again.

We can find out what role she played in other lives. She's relied on you before?

I think so…

Let me ask you – as God's talking to you, how do you feel about that?

I love her. But… I kind of feel like **"How many times to I have to keep doing this?"**

Any sense of how many times you've done it?

At least four or five times. That's how it feels.

(Note: At this point in the script, the student is supposed to ask the guide some direct questions. Paul later said he felt awkward about the following sentence, but said it anyway.)

Can I speak to God directly? I'm going to ask God to put the responses in your mind.

Yes.

Is it okay with God?

"If it helps her."

Very good. So God, as we start to go through this process, what is the primary purpose of April's life? What's she supposed to experience in this lifetime?

"She's a healer. She can .. she can read things."

Intuitive?

Very.

Empathic?

Yes.

Anything else? April shared that her mission was to take care of her mother.. and she'd discussed it with you and she'd taken care of her mother many times over. April's mother passed a while ago; does she have a new mission you can tell me about?

"Her mission was to guide her mother back here – to her faith, she never had faith in God, although she believed in God."

So mom has passed on, April has at least half a life to live. How has her mission changed? Some other purpose in life?

"You know that answer."

I do, but I'd like you to say it out loud.

"Think Paul. Think when you met her. What was she to you? Did she help you?"

She did. So she's moved on to support and heal others. Is that right?

"Yes."

This has been good talking to you; before I move on, anything you'd like to share with any of us...

"This is good for everyone. **You're very spiritual people (in this class) and I put you on this Earth as a conduit to teach others to believe in me.**"

Anything else?

"Keep the faith, stay on the course. You're loved."

We appreciate that love. Anything else you want to add?

(As April:) No, just to thank you (God) for joining us in this session... (to Paul) **I don't want to leave.**

What does God look like?

White. Glowing. Bright.

Male or female?

Feels male.

Any features?

Just energy. Stream of energy.

Anything else?

Love. Warmth. Love. Really warm.

Ask God a question about yourself, and all the different things your body has been going through, your recent bout with cancer... how's that going to go for you?

I chose these challenges to make me stronger.

Are you going to be okay?

Oh yeah.

That's beautiful. Thank you.

I'm supposed to teach others to be strong. You know it's like get your mammogram and everybody else told me to "get your mammogram," to show me that people value my input and my opinion. Whereas my mother didn't – she was just too busy.

While still in the presence of the divine, ask him for some healing You can be strong and help heal others.

(Her eyes still closed, April opens her hands up as if feeling a radiation of light.)

There you go, beautiful... I'm very happy for you.. just relax into that white healing glow of love. Prayer, spirituality and light. Integrate all your learnings together into your current life and self.. take a deep breath...

After the session:

Rich: How did you feel?

April: It was divine. It was so divine. It was.. not what I expected. No council. Just God. I mean it's like –

Why did you consider that person was God?

It was so bright; I knew where I was. I was just following these people up these stairs up to this beautiful place – like a cathedral, nothing that big on earth, you know... like a cathedral as tall as the twin towers in Manhattan, (there were) columns and white. Everything was white and there was grass, I saw flowers and colors... in the front as I was going in, I felt like "Am I dreaming?" You kind of feel your consciousness going "huh?"

In terms of the description of God – was God the same height as the Lincoln Memorial?

The way I was trying to describe it – the Lincoln Memorial, you know how little you feel compared to Lincoln? That's how I felt.

You felt a male presence?

It was like this image was in a big old chair like Lincoln's Memorial, but this incredible energy; you could sense a being I guess. Felt more male than female.

No form? Like with hands or eyes or a beard?

For a second I thought – "Is this Jesus?" I tried to see.. I didn't, if anything I put that thought there, more than what it really seemed.

Did he morph into Jesus in that moment?

Yes. I think it was me imagining it, you're like wow – this energy. It was warm and... great energy. He felt like a healer, you know... healers with that energy? Phenomenal.

Was there a voice?

Telepathic. And I wanted to stay.

Rich: I don't think you can ever really leave God.

Yeah, he's with me. It just came in.

Rich: You described a multitude filing in, going up these stairs.

I don't know where I went after that. (It's like) I was being directed. I was the only one who can help her, she needs direction, I was reluctant, like "really?" But you didn't talk that way, but that's how I felt in my head.

You saw your mom?

I knew she was there – in this crowd...

You saw flowers and colors?

Little like maybe pansies-sized flowers, nothing big like bushes. Like a tree, but I don't know if I saw them – I sensed them.

What do you think it meant "believe in me?"

It was just – believe **that there is a higher power.**

Not a religious thing?

No, just a spiritual belief.

Very cool.

April: Paul, when you referred to him as "Lord" it was like "*No, his name is God."* (sighs) I have to think about this.

.....

Indeed. When someone has an experience where they believe they see God – who's to argue that it is or isn't God?

There are a number of near death reports where people see Jesus, or God. In Eben Alexander's book, he talks about having a conversation with God. In "Heaven is for Real" Todd Bumpo talks about seeing Jesus. As I ask in the chapter in "It's a Wonderful Afterlife" "How did he know? Was he wearing a name tag?"

But let's just explore this for a moment. We get so caught up in the word or image of "Jesus," "Jehovah" "God" "Muhammed" "Buddha" "Mary" "Tara" etc, that we would be naturally startled to run into any of these people during a near death experience or during a between life hypnotherapy session. When people report that they saw these people in a session or NDE the question is: "How do you know them?"

The only logical answer is "Well, we've met before." Or "this is my impression that it is him (or her.)" There's an inherent problem in reporting these events for a variety of reasons. First the human brain shuts down at the mention of a lot of celebrities – you can call your family and friends and tell them you're standing with "The Dalai Lama" "Lady Gaga" or "Stephen Hawking" – and generally their hearing shuts down. They're not sure they've heard you correctly, assume that you're making it up – or that you're actually there.

The same is true for hearing accounts of the Flipside where someone meets someone famous or who is considered an avatar. I try to keep an open mind: "Have you met them before?" "What's the reason they've shown up here?" "Can we ask direct questions?" In this case, when asked after the session, she said the image of "God" morphed into an image of Jesus, but felt his image was "imagined." Some wouldn't question that detail; I suggest by questioning the genesis of any visual of "source" we get to a deeper understanding of what "source energy" might be.

I could also argue *it doesn't matter* if it's actually Mary, Jesus, Abraham, Michael the archangel, God, Moses, Muhammed, Rumi, Tara, Krishna or our subconscious creating them. They appear because information needs to be imparted – **whether it's the subconscious imparting it, or whether it's a direct message from someone else in the universe.** Important to take every message with the proverbial grain of salt – consider the source, consider the likelihood this message is directed to us – and act accordingly. *Or not.*

I include it here, because I just happened to be in the room when this couple interviewed each other as part of a class in past life regression given by Scott. One saw his life planning session as something given like a doctoral argument, the other saw her life planning session as God giving her instructions as to what she needed to do.

Honest Abe's first expression on the Flipside.

CHAPTER TEN:

Talking to the Earth as an Entity

"Whatever befalls the earth befalls the sons and daughters of the earth. We did not weave the web of life, we are merely strands in it. Whatever we do to the web we do to ourselves… The earth does not belong to us. We belong to the earth." Chief Seattle

Every now and then Scott De Tamble will mention some amazing session he's had working with a client under deep hypnosis. He and I were talking about the cosmos, as we often do, and he asked Mike Kramer, the author of "Soul to God" if he could share his session with me. I was pretty startled reading this session, and Mike has given me permission to include it.

There are people who will be startled, as I was, at this session. Some people who will go into brain freeze mode, as I initially did. "Wait. What?" All I can recommend, dear reader, is to put the "disbelief button" on pause, allow the words to be scanned by the eyes; just "let it be what it is." I suspect you wouldn't have gotten this far in the book if this wasn't the case on some level, anyway.

The unusual construct in this session is two individuals having a conversation with a third persona who doesn't fit any definition we have of "person." They're talking to someone who claims to be an entity I'm not aware anyone has encountered before, aside from in Joseph Campbell mythology. Arguably, this could be 1. created from someone's imagination, 2. information coming from another entity they weren't aware of, or 3. it actually is the persona they claim to be.

I would argue that what this entity has to say about our planet is repeated in many of the sessions I've done with people talking "about the planet" or about their ability to "tap into the energy" of the planet. But this is the first time I've ever heard of someone speaking "to" the planet.

Interview with Mike and Scott

Mike's comment: "This starts 20 minutes into a Past Life Hypnotherapy session with Scott De Tamble at Soul Therapies Center in San Diego. Scott is a wonderfully talented, Michael Newton trained, Life Between Lives Spiritual Hypnotherapist. 20 minutes into his induction, I'm experiencing a profound stillness in awareness and wonderful sense of detachment. I feel like I'm floating just above my body.[40]

My conscious mind is quiet, alert and without opinion– just being the observer. I'm experiencing an enormous, powerful, wise presence. A very deep peace is enveloping me like a warm, spiritual blanket has been thrown over me. I feel myself going deeper and deeper into a profound state of awareness. I'm amazed at Scott's skillful induction. I've never been anywhere near this deep in hypnosis and I'm about to experience a spiritual adventure I'll never forget.

Scott: I'm going to ask you some questions. I want you to respond with the very first thing that comes to you, whether you see it, feel it, sense it, know it, or are responding to an inner voice…. So, first impressions now, is it daytime or nighttime?

Mike: Sunset.

…Tell me about the surface that you are standing on.

---

[40] PL Session for Michael Kramer (his book will be called "Soul to God") used by permission from Michael Kramer. Facilitated by Scott De Tamble at Soul Therapies Center, San Diego

I'm standing in a rice pond, terraced into a mountainside. There's about a hundred other rice paddies below me, and some above. (Mike's note: I'm in the east end of a curved mountain valley near the top.) We've just finished planting and the ponds are filled with water, clear reflective pools. I love this time. I love this place. The orange and pink colors of the sunset are reflecting on the hundreds of rice ponds in this beautiful mountain valley. A river is flowing through the valley far below. It's just absolutely magical.

Tell me a little about yourself. Are you a male or female person?

I'm a male. Maybe about 5'2" or 4". I'm standing in the rice paddy, ankle deep in water. My pants are rolled up to my knees. I've been working all day long planting my rice crops. Most of the villagers have left. It was getting dark and they are hungry. I'm working late. And this is my favorite time.

I'm having a spiritual experience. It's like the mountain… the mountain is flowing through my feet. It's spirit. I feel so deeply connected to nature like I haven't been in other lifetimes. So deeply connected to the consciousness that is Earth. Just this moment, my heart opens up to this vast wisdom that flows through animals and flows through life.

I'm so divorced from it now (in my present life) … from that special relationship. All my other lifetimes were skimming the surface, battles, politics, religions, always dealing with stress. In this one special moment, in this one lifetime, I feel so connected. It's going so deep inside of me. Some other wisdom. Some other being. Ahhh…. (overwhelmed).

Describe for me this feeling of connection; and also, that vast consciousness, that vast wisdom that you are connecting to. Talk about that a little bit for me.

I think it's the only time, in all my lives, that I connected to this. **There is an old Soul… that… that moves within the Earth. The Earth is its body.** I never dreamed of such a thing! Such love and warmth! I can feel the Earth at its core and its energy. But beyond that, this Soul is connecting with me in a special way. I'm overwhelmed! I never dreamed of so much beauty.

An ancient wisdom is the governing wisdom of plants, and the fields, and the movement of the tectonic plates. **An ancient being, who is so very conscious and is frustrated with mankind.** Such deep wisdom and compassion! I had no idea! And **as I connect to that Soul, I connect to other Souls, and other planets, and other galaxies.** There's like a heart, a wisdom connection that is multi-dimensional. We are all being fed, all of us planets, all of us beings are being fed through the center of each galaxy.

Wormholes are the out-breath and the in-breath of our life force as it comes from the higher planes, dimensions, feeding life into us, giving us consciousness through our star systems. We can provide the environment for Souls to come and live, and have their being.

Ohhhh my Lord! (overwhelmed) **There are so many fantastic beings, unimaginably large, moving in our universe! In and out, watching over the galaxies, watching over the movement.** Ohhhh. I guess… (taking a few moments to collect himself)

This fellow standing in the rice paddies, what is his name?

I hear, "Mah-Sin." (over- pronouncing it) Accent on "Sin." He has a hat, like a flat cone, very dark skin. He's in his 50's but he looks more like he's in his 80's. He's weathered by the sun and a lifetime spent in his rice fields. He has very dark, wrinkled skin. Chinese. I think I'm in a sacred valley in China above the Yin river.[41]

What is the year that Ma Sin stands on the mountain? (Long pause.) If you can translate that into our western dates.

1460 AD. It wasn't a long life. He passed away not long after this experience he had. He had an uneventful life. It was that one moment, that spiritual experience that I had.

---

[41] The Ying River is the largest tributary of the Huai River with its origin in Henan Province. Wikipedia

Let's go back into that moment where Ma Sin was standing ankle deep in the water in a rice patty and becoming aware of this great Soul, this great being, who's body is the Earth. I want to have Ma-Sin open his heart, open his mind, open every part of himself to this great, wise, compassionate being, this vast planetary consciousness. Let us allow Ma Sin to relax and communicate with that great, ancient, wise being. I know that ancient being can hear me, and see me, and feel me, and know me. I'm going to ask that great, wise being to respond through the mind of Ma-Sin, though the voice of Michael. Would that be OK with you?

Yes. (Mike's voice) … It is allowed (different lower, voice).

What may I call you today?

We are without name. But call us, Shunho, meaning "Earth Spirit." [42]

Shunho, you say "we," are there more than one (of you) that inhabit this planet?

Our consciousness is complex. It is one Soul, but it is an Oversoul, like cells within a being. I am that Soul but many Souls dwell within me as my body moves and takes direction from Source. "We" is part of the "I." And I work through the "we." **It's confusing to the human brain, but it's quite natural and it's the way things are.** So "We" is the greater Soul, the Oversoul that has many conscious parts working within it.[43]

What is your role here in the Earth? What is your purpose?

I came before Earth was created. I came from the higher planes in what you might think of the "Big Bang." It was an expression of many Souls, a rush of Souls that came forth. Then I took my place in the universe.

It was my energy that began to coalesce the space matter. **It was my energy, working with gravity that brought in the singular evolution of this planet.** It would seem to the human mind that I am ancient. But within my own measure, this is my life. **It's normal. For I'm not an old Soul; I am a Soul that is becoming.**

---

[42] "Gung-ho" comes from GI's hearing this term in China which means "working together."

[43] Oversoul is defined "a supreme reality or mind; the spiritual unity of all being." Dictionary.com. Also, the idea "this information is beyond the capacity of human brains" has been cited before.

Shunho, why did you materialize your energy? You are a free energy, but you decided at some point to create this planet. Why did you do this?

There was a call by Source for the great Oversouls, the planetary spirits, unimaginable numbers of Souls were birthed into the physical dimension. It was our choice. It is our path. **When this planet ends its life, I shall return to Source.** My life will continue in another way.

This is normal. **This is what is happening behind the scenes in all galaxies, in all universes. This is the unseen support for life as it grows and evolves in the physical dimension.**

When this planet ends and you return to Source, will you go on to embody another planet? What will you do then?

I have no will in this. I have no plans. This is what I am called upon by Source to do. It's my great pleasure to serve.

Shunho, what is Source?

It's my breath; the breath of all of life. It's that which we all are, breathing, living, seeing. The One that sees within everyone's eyes, The One that hears through everyone's ears, The One that feels everything that happens, the One that speaks through all voices, **The One that thinks through all minds and all thoughts.**

It disguises itself over and over, in layers upon layers so that we can grow and learn and know more about it. **The presence of Source can be felt when the heart is open and love is present.**[44]

Love connects one person to another, people to a community, plants to animals, connects the Earth to the Sun, and the Sun to the galaxies, and the galaxies to faraway planets and universes, in layers, upon layers, upon layers of reality.

Was there any moment of origin of this Source? Will there be a moment of its demise?

---

[44] In "It's a Wonderful Afterlife" a spirit guide defined God as "beyond the capacity of human brains to comprehend, but we could experience God by "opening our hearts to everyone and all things."

There is no origin. There is no demise. **Origin and demise are concepts of a lower consciousness.** It's reasonable to expect (a beginning and end) from the human point of view, because all that man sees has a beginning and all that man sees has an end.

But this viewpoint focuses on particle-based reality, not frequency-based reality. Particle based reality is supported through layers and layers of frequency, sound if you wish, light coming from Source filtered through realities so that it can function and support, and create a stable existence.

There is a God, if you wish, where lower reality manifests and expands. When 'this lower reality' goes through a phase where it's expansion turns in on itself in another dimension, all of the lower realities are phased inward, almost like it folds into one, huge black hole. This is the creation that happens. **Some people call it, 'The Day of God.' But there have been many, many creations, many 'Days of God.'**[45]

Do you speak of the "Big Bang" as the expansion of the breath of the universe?

It's what you call the "Big Bang." It was more like a rebound. **One existence swallowed up into, what you might call, the astral 'dimension,' and then Source expressing itself again into another continuum, another "Big Bang" if you wish.** These events are happening not infrequently.

Is this a perpetual, or eternal cycle?

There is no such thing as eternal, just, "What is." But in your language, in your understanding, "Yes" would be the closest answer. **This is happening not just in this area of the physical. There are regions of expression, and this is one region.**

Regions in space? Or regions in other dimensions?

Regions in this physical space. **There's an edge to all the trillions and trillions of galaxies. This is one region.**

---

[45] The Hindus refer to the start of the universe as a Kalpa, (4 billion years) and claim there have been "many" of them. It's also reported in a number of these sessions that this wasn't the only "big bang."

You're saying that space is finite?

No, definitely not. It's a creation of the higher planes. There are just other physical spaces. Other star systems, if you wish. These galaxies are just not in your area.

Existence is so beyond Soul's ability to comprehend. It's better, more loving, to let mankind create their own stories of creation from rural people who create religions to our scientists. Let them create something that they can understand and comprehend. And allow it (their understanding) to evolve. Because actual reality… it would be unkind to expose them to actual reality. Let them grow into it.

Shun-ho, tell us the true story of creation.

Creation of what? Earth? Galaxies?

All of it.

There's only so much that I know. I can tell you within the last 6 to10 Billion years. (Note: I think it's interesting when someone of a "higher realm" says they can't answer a question. I've heard "it's beyond my pay grade" and "I can't access that information." Here he says simply "There's only so much I know.")

That would suffice.

As I cast my mind back…(voice becomes weaker). It is difficult for me to speak… because I was young, and un-evolved, as were we all. **We didn't have the state of consciousness that we have now. It took billions of years to develop, but our goal was the arrangement of rocks and force fields, working not just by ourselves, but with billons of souls on the inner planes, working to draw in the right comets, the right collisions.** Much of it was planned, much of it was happenstance—the way the universes were created.[46]

---

[46] In a number of between life sessions, when asked what lessons they're learning in their "classrooms," some claim to be involved in "seeding" or "creation" of other planets so we can one day inhabit them.)

But when the Earth formed creating a habitable field, a great call went out for those that create life. Now they had something to work with. They were given great freedom and encouragement to create, (pause searching for words) 'whatever works.' (As noted, some claim that Mars was a "similar experiment" but didn't work because it couldn't sustain a habitable environment. Science argues it's due to lack of a magnetic field.)

There was such an explosion of life, of plants, the ocean, huge reptiles, amazing creatures and forces of life, the energy of life, created on this planet. **So different from what it is now. Life was ferociousness then.**

Then **the higher planetary souls that govern, called for Earth's great transformation.** Much of the work done by those (original) creative Souls needed to be wiped out to create a habitable place for yourself, mankind. Wise' beings have had a lot to say about the development of man: many experiments. (Note: Perhaps the meteor that wiped out the dinosaurs wasn't a random event.)

Why was a simian, an ape-type body chosen for this race? For Souls or spirits to inhabit?

Part of those genetics were used to develop the human body. But the human body became a much higher being... **other beings influenced man's development. Man took on this form because it was practical.** Two hands, opposing thumbs to grip, a brain to think, a mouth to breath and eat and express language, legs long enough to run, and a body that could climb, run, swim. It was versatile.

The most appropriate bodies were the Human form, which survived. **In the beginning there wasn't a plan for man to turn out the way he did. There was a hope for mankind to develop in the fashion that it has.**

Now mankind is going through another transition. I'm going through a transition. Many souls will be leaving Earth. They are no longer at the right vibrational consciousness. They don't support me and I don't support them. They will go on to other worlds.

I'm coming into a new life. **Those that are in harmony with my being, are in harmony with my heart, my mind, will remain and evolve into— what man might consider as a new species.** Mankind will look the same but his nervous system will evolve to be able to carry more subtle energies from myself and the higher planes. (Note: This is reported by other people in terms of the question "Why is the veil thinning?")

Mankind will be able to comprehend more complex ideas. **He'll develop the ability to create form that is more in harmony with higher beings. Mankind will become a spiritual adult.** This is what we are looking forward to. **This is what's happening now.**

I want to back up a moment. Of these experiments in creating mankind, you mentioned that other beings came in to influence us. Are you speaking of other physical beings from other worlds?

Yes.

What we might call extraterrestrials or off-worlders? From other star systems?

Yes.

How did they influence the development of mankind? For example, do they inject some of their DNA into man, or tinker with that?

They are not allowed to interfere. But they are allowed to influence. There are creative souls without physical form that work with the DNA structure, influencing that. What you call off-worlders, cooperated, or were allowed to basically create a support system for life to take hold. I don't know if there was interbreeding, but there was an influence. (Note: It's something I've heard often – there is "free will" in the universe that guides spirits on their journey, but people are allowed to implement new ideas to help people learn and develop new talents.)

(Mike says he stopped here for a break: "The powerful energy coming through my body became too much. I couldn't take it anymore. I felt weak and wanted to end the session. I went to the restroom and returned to the recliner. Scott asked for another five minutes which I agreed to. He returned me quickly to a very deep state and we continued.")

Scott: I want to ask Shunho, in this life of (rice farmer) Ma Sin, what was the purpose for making this incredible connection with this human being in this lifetime? Why did you open yourself to convey this vast information to Ma Sin?

Mike: Ma Sin had no idea of this connection. He only felt my presence. His heart, his body and mind reached a rare moment where they came into harmony with me. It was a transforming moment for this soul (Michael's soul). Up until now, it (Michael's soul) had no idea of the depth of its connection, or of Earth's relationship with any other planet, or the way the galaxies formed. No idea! **It was his remembering connecting to Earth, and then (experiencing) Earth's connection to other planets that opened up this awareness.**

Ma Sin was like many fortunate souls who come to a momentary **equilibrium where all doubts are suspended, where all viewpoints fall away. There comes a single experience of awe, as if being born, a falling away of ego, and the experience of blessings, bliss.** [47]

Ma Sin, his Soul, has expressed itself through many bodies, and though this body, Mike, right now. This Soul has been involved in many adventures, but rarely connected to the deeper, whole spirit of Earth. **Most Souls never connect. If they do, it's often in a superficial way. The reason this point was brought home was because this experience that he had as a Chinese man was a singular, unique event in all of his lifetimes.** That experience has been brought forward and linked to this consciousness.

Why, at this moment in time, for this life, why was this singular experience made conscious once more?

It's up to him; but he (Mike) wanted something to put in his book. **We decided we'd give it to him. It's up to him if he wants to use it. He asked for it, we gave it to him.**

That's wonderful. I sense there is another reason why this experience was brought consciously to Michael today.

---

[47] This kind of apotheosis is reported in many accounts, including Mario Beauregard PhD's account in "It's a Wonderful Afterlife" of one day at age 12 when he felt "connected to everyone and all things." He says that feeling drove him into his field of neuropsychology. ("Brain Wars")

He's at a transitional state also. He's made great effort to hide from society and go unnoticed because of... many reasons... because of the lifetimes that he's had. But now he is being invited to share with society stories of his many lives and of his experience with Source.

Society is changing. It's not like it was when he was born. It's changing at an exponential rate. **From the amount of change that has taken place in the last fifty years, that much change will take place in the next five years. Consciousness is changing at an amazing rate even though it may not be evident. Higher Souls are being drawn in and expressing themselves.** And as they express themselves, the energy and consciousness rises, and other Souls tap into that and this lifts up all of mankind.

And of course, there are those who don't wish to change. They wish to hang on to their present states. **They will be allowed not to change. They will be allowed to hang onto their stubbornness, but they'll just have to go to another world. Their present bodies will die naturally but their souls will be ushered to other planets that are more suitable for their state of consciousness.** They will continue to evolve at their own rate.

(Note: Important to point out this entity is not claiming any cataclysm in the immediate offing – as we've heard consistently in these accounts; time is not set and therefore a prediction can't be made of what will or won't happen. He says when it comes to "returning to Earth" these folks who normally incarnate here but are resistant to change will be encouraged to take their next incarnation elsewhere. I'd argue that since we have free will, that's a difficult rule to enforce. But who am I to argue with *Mr. Earth*?)

This (information) is not only his contribution. **This is our contribution, the result of many souls working.** If he can do this work he's being invited to accomplish, great! If he's unable to do it, other people will come forward but they won't have the same story. And it is his story that contains many lessons for many souls.

Shunho, I have many more questions, and yet I'm concerned about this body here. (Scott is referring to how intense this session has become for Mike, his physical reactions).

I've taken care of the body. **I've raised it to a higher vibration**. A lot of the restrictions that he was experiencing have been balanced out. You can continue.

Michael, do you agree?

(In normal voice) Yeah, I feel so much better. I'm floating. I'm going back up again.

What advice do you have for Mike in this very moment?

Breathe in slowly, deliberately, stilling your mind and conscious, drawing in your higher soul energy. **Connect with that, and then just be playful. You know how to create.** Be playful with the things you don't know how to create.

Approach them with the same sense of playfulness, same sense of exploration. If you put your mind and heart to it, you can work out the details, the words, the paragraphs, the publisher, the readers, the talks that you'll have to do—we'll work those things out for you. **Just take a big breath, connect with your higher self, and us.**

Shunho, a while back, you said that you have a frustration with mankind.

Imagine you have a young healthy body. Imagine that you have the flu. Your body aches. You just don't feel well. You can't function well. **Mankind is my flu.** This doesn't inhibit my functioning. It draws upon me energetically. It draws from my energy.

My own immune system will be righting itself. **The path of man is really governed more by higher souls who work with mankind, not by me. But these higher beings are not unsympathetic to what I'm experiencing.** It's difficult to endure all the anger, mistrust and destruction.

Is it the physical activities of man that bother you so?

No. **The physical activities of man has an effect upon the environment, which has an effect upon me, but the activities of man are not bothering me as much as the energy in his state of consciousness.** The energy of the lower consciousness is bothering me as Soul. It's not going to last a lot longer. These times are like when you break out into a sweat after you've been sick a long time. By sweating, your body is expelling all the toxins. **That's what's happening right now.**

There is all this negative energy, all the toxins are being released. **Mankind doesn't understand or comprehend what's happening on a larger scale. All he can do is react. There is suffering because of lack of awareness.** Man becomes self-destructive and destructive to other beings, to his environment.

There are more mature souls who are more aligned with my changing energy and with Source energy. They have a greater awareness of the conflict than those who are creating it. In their compassion there is suffering. They need to still themselves, have faith and confidence that a new day is at hand.

What can mankind do to irradiate this flu and to give you radiant health?

All soul needs to do is to learn to live peacefully within itself and not project its anxiety and short-comings upon others. Those are individual lessons learned. **Each soul comes for its own path, its own purpose. That's the dance of life. If one moves to a wisdom within, the dance works and wonderful things can happen.**

So are you saying that all these souls coming here with all of their problems to work out are overloading you?

It's not overloading me. It's their energy. **There are parts of them that are just so beautiful, and I love that. But there are parts that are like a fever that creates an aching inside of me. I'm not rejecting it. I know that all I have to do is endure and all will transition out of this.** It will be a smooth transition. It will be smooth for me. But it will be rough for some people, very rough.

Shunho, let's talk about this transition. What is the transition you are undergoing and what is the transition mankind is undergoing?

It's difficult to explain, but I'm evolving into a new spirit. It's like you've slept through a long cold night, you wake up in the morning, the sun is shining and there's a new energy inside of you. That's what it's like for me.

My night has been since creation. Right now, there are a multitude of lights shining down on me from many spheres and many directions. These lights are the attention of many Souls focused on me. It's accelerating my evolution. **My acceleration in vibration is having an effect on the Earth, and this is having an effect on mankind. There is a sense of urgency within those that are conscious because they sense this change.** My Soul, the "We", is just going into a new stage. It's so much brighter. My experience of flu-like symptoms is going to be solved. For mankind... (long pause.)

(Aside from Mike) Information is being blocked. (He notes "At this moment I tried to see what would happen on Earth during it's more difficult times. But I experienced guides blocking that information. I tried going in a more oblique way.")

...For mankind, it's going to be very uncomfortable for some and not even noticeable for many. There are a lot of Souls working to make this a smooth transition. A lot of souls have been sent down to help with this transition.

How does a Soul help make this a smooth transition?

If they allow a higher consciousness to comes in, most don't have to do a thing. They can just be present in their life. Their energy adds to my energy, my energy adds to theirs. They do their own thing. They are working within their own field.

There are some souls that rarely incarnate; if they do, rarely on Earth. They come with... there is, overall, a sense of unity about them. Children are attracted to them. Other people, when they see them, they are mesmerized. All they need to do is be cheerful and their blessings and their presence filters into society. **No fanfare, no books to be written, no movies to be made, no businesses to be created, just their presence and their love that flows out to the unseen hearts that are asking for help.**

I understand, Shunho. But I would ask on behalf the average person. What can they do to live their life more in harmony with where you are going?

There is a logic built into the mind and society. For those that are paying attention, the messages are there. Take greater care of the gifts that you have. Don't feel the need to increase what you have without reason. **Practice contentment.**

Consider what you have as sacred and let that sacredness dwell within you, and guide you. Greed is like a virus, a fever. When you come to center, you no longer need all the things that you imagined. You are able to act independently without requiring agreement by others with less centered viewpoints.

For the average person, the day-to-day person, find those moments of being centered, dwelling more consciously in the now. Then allow that sense of being centered to expand, without worry, with a sense of love and thankfulness. Allow that sense of resting in the center to guide your actions and your thoughts.

It's really quite easy. It is difficult for some because mankind is taught to want, to desire more. **If they would relax their desires, there would be so much more for them. They would have less in their life but they would feel like it's more. There would be more food for everyone.** There would just be so much more if those who have tremendous wealth would relax and allow that outflow of wealth to touch those in need.

This is the relaxation of consciousness is natural as one expands and becomes more secure in higher states of awareness. **It's not a striving to become. It's a relaxation into being that which is.** This relaxation into Source affects your thoughts, affects your actions, affects the people around you.

That singular action of relaxing your state of consciousness, relaxing your desires, relaxing your anxiety, relaxing into a state of being, and then acting from that state, thinking from that state, choosing your being from that state, allows you to act in a more conscious way.

Actions and thoughts have a magnetic effect upon others. It sounds simple, but it can very difficult for humans to do this.

Thank you Shun-ho. Finally, I would ask you today, how can Mike and the rest of us, connect with you in the way he did in the 1400's?

That was a rare experience. He worked his life in the fields, connected with farming and growing, and lived in nature. It was just a rare moment at sunset.

For the average person, I think (the answer is) **"live their life more simply." It's difficult for some and impossible for many.** But learning to have a quiet spirit, to learn how to separate their spirit from the day-to-day pressures that are going on. It's almost like taking a vacation but still being productive. Not everyone can go to the ocean, a lake or a forest, but they can find or create a sacred place where they can slow down and feel detached.

There is such a tension happening on Earth. It's affecting most human beings. **It's quite a challenge for anybody to still their awareness, to discover the now.** Hypnotherapy is an excellent tool to help a person experience shifts in consciousness and tune into that spirit. It's like bypassing all the normal channels.

You get a glimpse into these other states. **It's rare for a person, a soul, in all their lives, to still their conscious self, and allow themselves to take a mental vacation from their beliefs and desires, to awaken in the presence of bliss and great love that springs within.** When you do that, you connect with all souls at a more profound level. This is what you are evolving towards. So, perhaps learn to meditate, although that doesn't work for many people. But that's the idea. The samsara, the karma that wraps around you, lifetime after lifetime, all your thoughts and attitudes, they spin the tension that your mind feeds upon. Then it feeds upon your mind.

It's a rare soul (who) is able to work its way through what you might call, karma, work its way through the tensions of many past lives. **It's rare for a soul to learn how to relax into the presence of God which is always present, always in the now.** There is no distance between each of us and that which we desire. I'm speaking not about the physical things that we desire, but the true thing that we desire, to be one with God, our own heart, our own self, our own being. **What it calls for is a relaxation, a relaxation that is so profound that it's difficult to comprehend.**

Thank you Shun-ho.

Scott counts Mike down and back to everyday consciousness. After a few minutes to recover:

Mike: "It was difficult to be linked to that powerful being. It toned itself down for me after a while, which I needed. It wasn't speaking from its center, but more of a peripheral. I never dreamed of all that. **I've never read or heard of anything like that…. I could see this immense soul trying to communicate with my human consciousness.**

I could see that its lifecycle was beyond comprehension, but then, when I was in that soul, sharing its consciousness, **I know it was completely natural.** There was nothing unusual. From its viewpoint, I experienced the thoughts: **"This was just its life. This is what I do. It is not unique. Not unique at all!"** All those planetary systems…

Scott: That's what I wanted to ask it. What do you talk about with all your brothers and sisters out there?

Mike: **When I was in that state, it felt like this planet was connected to the other planets. There was a consciousness link.** Space was not an issue because the link was not in the physical, but more in the soul state. And everything was so real!

They had the thoughts, "This is life. This is what we are doing." Each planet was a very different experience, but it felt like a brotherhood, a closeness between themselves and larger beings. **I saw there are so many other souls that are involved in creation and watching over the evolution of this planet life, the evolution of animal life, the evolution of human beings. They've been working since the beginning and they are working now."**
……

Wow. Some very unusual concepts explored here. Thanks Earth. As mentioned, when some people under deep hypnosis are asked "So what are you doing in the between life realm?" They'll answer "I'm in a classroom where we learn about energy transference" or "I'm learning how to create matter in other worlds." Also some claim they are "seeding" or "helping create a living environment" on other planets for our eventual incarnation there, perhaps millions of years in the future. I guess when you're "outside of time" you're really *outside of time.*

Many thanks to Scott and Mike for allowing me to use this in my book. Mike has written his own book "Soul to God" and I recommend anyone interested in how he came to this session take a look at it.

CHAPTER ELEVEN:

The Flipside Isn't All Angels and Violins

My cousin Eugene playing Cowboys and Indians with me. I'm holding the peace pipe; he's about to scalp me. And so it goes.

"If I am not allowed to laugh in heaven, I don't want to go there."
- Martin Luther

I ran across this interview with retired Episcopal bishop John Shelby Spong with Keith Morrison of Dateline NBC.[48] The minister argues that hell is a *frame of mind* created by the clergy as a "tool of power."

> *Bishop Spong*: **I don't think Hell exists.** I happen to believe in life after death, but I don't think it's got a thing to do with reward and punishment. Religion is always in the control business, and that's something people don't really understand. It's in a guilt-producing control business.
>
> If you have Heaven as a place where you're rewarded for your goodness, and Hell is a place where you're punished for your evil, then you sort of have control of the population. **They create this fiery place which has quite literally scared the Hell out of a lot of people, throughout Christian history.** It's part of a control tactic.

---

[48] Dateline NBC 2006.

Morrison: But wait a minute. You're saying that Hell, the idea of a place under the earth or somewhere you're tormented for an eternity – is actually an invention of the church?

Spong: I think the church fired its furnaces hotter than anybody else. But I think there's a sense in most religious life of reward and punishment in some form. The church doesn't like for people to grow up, because you can't control grown-ups.

That's why we talk about being born again. When you're born again, you're still a child. **People don't need to be born again. They need to grow up.** They need to accept their responsibility for themselves and the world.

Morrison: What do you make of the theology which is quite prominent these days in America, which is there is one guaranteed way not to go to hell; That is to accept Jesus as your personal savior.

Spong: Yeah, I grew up in that tradition. Every church I know claims that 'we are the true church' – that they have some ultimate authority, 'We have the infallible Pope,' We have the Bible.'... **The idea that the truth of God can be bound in any human system, by any human creed, by any human book, is almost beyond imagination for me.**

I mean, God is not a Christian. God is not a Jew or a Muslim or a Hindi or Buddhist. All of those are human systems, which human beings have created to try to help us walk into the mystery of God. I honor my tradition. I walk through my tradition. But I don't think my tradition defines God. It only points me to God…"

His point of view is consistent with the research. That is to say, that people who've been under deep hypnosis consistently say that there is no hell, no devil, no retribution waiting for us in the "afterlife" or "back home." That when we return there we see the reasons behind our actions, we see that we may have made mistakes or forgotten what we came to the planet for, but that is all forgiven by our guides and loved ones.

For the few that can't get past their mistakes, or feel that they've got to serve some form of punishment for them, there are places of solitude (like "Superman's Fortress of Solitude") where a soul voluntarily stays away from others to experience, examine and understand the negativity of their actions.

One could argue that particular mental construct might be a form of hell – depending upon the creativity of the person who is envisioning a place of suffering so they might learn from it. But from the people who've actually experienced that kind of an event, as we'll see later in the book, they claim that they agreed to that kind of introspection with the help and love of their spirit guides.

An attorney approached me saying that "all of her clients" had similar accounts of victims coming to them to say versions of **"I'm okay, and I can help you."** I'm so sorry for the victims and their families to hear this with no context. I'm sorry that this is not public knowledge or that people have never discussed this in public. But it's a chapter in "It's a Wonderful Afterlife: Further Adventures in the Flipside" Volume 2, and it's **pretty much** what the victims of second degree murderers have said to the people who killed them, and told their attorney about it.

Needless to say, they had no way to share this information with anyone - and this guy chose this moment to share it on the stand.

> "Convicted killer: Victims aren't as mad as you'd think" By Alison Grande KIRO - Seattle
>
> SEATTLE — Thursday convicted killer Joe McEnroe had his last chance to convince the jury to spare him from the death penalty. The same jury that convicted him of murdering his girlfriend's family on Christmas Eve 2007, will decide if he will be sentenced to life in prison or the death penalty. **McEnroe told the jury today that they victims visited him from the afterlife and "aren't as mad as you'd think."**
>
> **"They said they don't blame [me]. I tried to apologize to them. It's like, look, I'm sorry for what happened,"** said McEnroe Thursday. **He said the victims want him to live and do good. McEnroe says he wants to help other men in prison.** "In your mind you've convinced yourself Judy Anderson is not as mad as what you might think about the murder of her two grandchildren?"

asked Sr. Deputy Prosecuting Attorney Scott O'Toole. "Yes," said McEnroe.

"This is what you've been told by them?" O'Toole questioned. **"Yes sir,"** McEnroe responded.

Killer Joe was spared the death penalty. The jurors spent 3 ½ days deliberating over what to do with the man who confessed to the brutal "Carnation" murders. From the Seattle Times:[49]

A juror said he favored death for McEnroe, calling it a "personal decision." Asked if the deliberations were emotional, he said, **"It sucked. It was miserable…This isn't a decision that people should have to try and make."**
.....

Absolutely. *A decision that people should not have to make.* Because they're stepping into the role of killers as well. Yes, I know, they're meting out the justice. But it's the same version of arguing that hiring an executioner to kill someone is giving them "bad karma."

It's not about arguing whether they're innocent or guilty – or if the justice system is prejudiced. It's that we can't possibly judge our fellow humans for actions that may have their source in another realm. In that light, it only makes sense that this person spends the rest of his days locked up in solitary.

Why? Well there's always the opportunity that he may be able to heal someone else in the future by his example. There's no guarantee that would happen, but if he was executed then there absolutely is a guarantee that it won't happen. If you can allow for a moment that none of these people he killed are really dead – they can't be because people don't die – then it's a matter of finding a way to use this individual to teach or learn lessons.

But what about Hitler? What about Pol Pot? What about Genghis Kahn? What about mass murderers? People who shoot up churches, schools?

---

[49](http://www.seattletimes.com/seattle-news/crime/mcenroe-escapes-death-sentence-for-6-carnation-murders/)

I've participated in some of the post life discussions with people who claim to be the perpetrators. Their stories are often consistent; they claim that "there was a contract involved," that the "people who died were part of the contract" and that they had "volunteered to play the role of perpetrator." Hard to hear, and perhaps annoying to contemplate. But I can report that during my first filmed between life interview, a woman who recalled a lifetime in Auschwitz said "from a soul perspective, I'm glad I didn't choose to play the role of a perpetrator. These people damaged their souls."

I've also heard about others who had serious consequences from that kind of a choice. A good friend of mine recalled choosing a lifetime that ended in Dachau. When asked why he chose that lifetime, he said he had so many lives "in the light" that he wanted to "experience the dark again." But the experience has "seared his soul" and he said he was still carrying the wounds of that experience.

He was invited to find a place of healing, and he said he went into the "river of souls" in order to heal that wound. So people who choose lives where they commit some act or some heinous crime may very well have been asked to perform the task at hand – however, they also may experience some form of "soul damage."

There is the reboot option.

It's rare, and is only offered in extremely rare cases. But I've come across one individual who was offered the extremely rare option of having a "reboot." Meaning, he had some event so heinous, so difficult, that the only solution was to have the memory of all of his lives wiped clean. Reconfigured.

The energetic makeup of his soul was then reconfigured in response to something he had done in a previous life. It was done with his assent, and somehow they "shut him down" wiped the slate clean so he could start him over.

Session between Scott and "Tim."

Scott: Let's skip forward to your last day as the old sailor… last day. What's happening?

Tim: I'm on the dock. Getting ready to leave. Trying to gather up some ropes. I don't know what the ropes are for, they're on the dock. And we're just about to pull out, and I think it was some bad weather, it was real choppy, the ship was moving.. a lot, it was going up and down. And I had a little of the rope that was tied to the ship and it pulled me off the dock… really just too old to do anything.

Too hard to swim your way out of it?

Clothes got heavy, just felt myself sinking.

Let's move forward to the moment after death… you've been through this many times before… Where are you?

I'm just over the harbor. Looking down at the harbor, my ship. Just normal everyday stuff. I feel glad. Content, relieved. It was a long life, a lot of solitude, travel.

(Note: This lifetime started with him as a young sailor. It was a hard life, all he knew was working on the ship in the open sea until he was an old man, and tripped and drowned while working.)

What's it feel like to die?

Just felt like it was… a little uncomfortable and then everything started to fade and then I just kind of floated out and was relieved that I didn't feel tired anymore. I didn't feel the pain (anymore), the aches… my joints, I remember my feet used to hurt all of the time.

You're free from that now… you're entering the soul state… As you move away from the harbor describe what happens.

It just fades away. Fades into black. Just darkness. No pain.

What goes through your mind?

I'm just waiting. I'm feeling very content.

You ready to move forward? Let's go to a time when you are meeting with someone very, very wise. On the count of three, you be aware of that person… are you sensing a male or female energy?

It's a… not sure if it has a gender. Just human shape but, just like not any features… It's kind of yellow. With like a green haze.

What's the first thing you hear or feel in your mind? What are they communicating?

That I did good. It was good.

You lived your life well? As that sailor?

Yeah. I want to go, they're telling me I have to wait.

Where do you want to go?

Where everybody else is.

Would you be willing to talk to this person for a little while before you go?

I don't think they want to talk to me. I think they're just supposed to keep me there.

Do you sense a familiarity with this person? Someone close to you or a messenger type person?

I've never met them before.

I'm going to speak to that person directly and they can respond through you, is that okay?

Yeah.

Tell us your name or something we can call you today.

Sill.

Welcome Sill, what's your relationship to this soul here?

(Voice changes) Don't have any relationship.

What is your function? What are you doing for this soul?

Just quieting him down. Just make sure that he stays here.

Why is that important?

Because he's been away for a while. And he needs to just relax. He's too anxious to rejoin everything.

What needs to happen with him to make him ready to join everything?

Just time.

All right, I'm going to give you some time to quiet him down and get him ready to rejoin the spiritual dimension. I'm going to count to ten by the time we're done with that count, could you have him ready to go? We appreciate that. ... One... two... three..

He's done.

All right then Sill, will you escort him where he needs to go?

No. He can go now.

Thank you for your help and care Sill – we wish you all good things.

Thank you.

All right then.... Sill says you're ready. The sky's the limit buddy, you can go wherever you want to go. Talk with your teachers, friends and loved ones, places of healing or learning – where do you want to go?

I want to see them.

Let's do that – one, two three, be there now. Become aware of them. Open yourself and become aware of all that's going on around you. This is like going to a new port for you. What are you experiencing?

Just seeing lights. All different colors. Coming towards me. It looks like about three. They say that they know me. I don't know who they are.

How are they arranged?

In a line. One in the middle is the leader. It's a male.

I'm going to address him, is that okay? Welcome to our meeting today. What's a name we can call you today?

Michael.

What is your relationship to this soul?

He's part of the group.

Are you a teacher or friend?

Kind of both.

Michael, how do you feel about his performance in this life?

That was his choice. He just needed to be alone. He chose that.

What did he gain from that experience?

Kind of like a healing life. Like recovering from a traumatic experience that would happen to you. Like if you were involved in a car accident and you needed some time to just regain your thoughts and regroup.

What was the traumatic experience?

He had to learn some lessons as a soul. The only way to learn those lessons is what would be similar to you being in a car accident or some traumatic event in your life. It wasn't a lifetime, it was something he experienced here.

Can you share that with us? How can someone have a traumatic experience in spirit? What happened?

Well it's hard to explain. It's hard to explain so that you would understand. **I'm not even sure that I'm allowed to.**

I don't want to cross any lines, get anyone into trouble, on the other hand, he's here, this is happening for a reason, this could have a bearing on his current lifetime, I would petition you and those above you to disclose this information. Choose your words as best you can We can understand.

Well. He was "turned off." (Pause) It's very… it's like he needed to be rebooted. It's the best way that I can explain it, in fact.

Why did he need to be rebooted? What happened to him and his energy?

He had a life that was - it kind of went wrong.

Give us a basic outline of that life that went wrong.

It was many, many lives ago. He tried to go back, the leaders of his group tried to send him back… to do things to correct what happened… and they were unsuccessful.

Thank you Michael. We're digging deeper into the roots of this problem or issue. Let's go to the very root of this problem with this soul. What happened to him? Was it many lives ago? What's the root that caused all this trauma and problem?

Part of the problem is that we can't let him regress – and the questions you're asking are endangering him regressing.

To go backward in progress of his evolution?

Of healing from the life that went wrong.

I don't want to endanger anything, but I believe you're wise enough to skirt that but still giving us an explanation. When you say a life went wrong, what kind of life was it?

That would be very, very bad. We wouldn't allow it.

Some life where he hurt other people or hurt himself or got hurt?

His soul was hurt.

Tell us about this reboot process – turning him off.

It's dangerous.

Who performs such an action?

They are like – you would call them an angel – they don't live the same kind of life that you and I do.

They don't incarnate?

They don't incarnate.

They are beings that work with us? They kind of watch over and guide us? Who made the decision to reboot the soul?

That would be his decisions, the one that controls his energy.

The one that controls his energy? Is that a part of him or is that a teacher or group leader? Can you put that in other terms?

It's like the being that does not incarnate with you that is a teacher. He, *it* is a teacher, but it's also an evaluator, makes recommendations. Is kind of like the go-between; between us and the almighty.

All right. So Michael can you describe this process? What happens when a person needs to be turned off and on again?

We don't get to see that. Only that it's very scary for us. Because there's a possibility that you may not come back from it.

Sort of like on earth, when they stop a heart and restart it?

Very good analogy.

What would happen if they turned off a soul and it didn't come back?

I think it goes back to him...

The source?

Yeah.

But in this case, he's kept his individuality.

So far.

Is he still in danger?

It doesn't look like it. He's been back and forth a couple of times; he's doing okay. He's always anxious when he gets back here, he needs to be isolated from us.

That's what Sill is doing?

Yes. Because he wants to be healthy again, he wants to be healed, and the only way he can know is when he rejoins his group.

So what would you say about the state of this soul and his health?

He's doing very good.

This is fascinating, thank you Michael. Why were we shown the sailor life and Tim in his life today?

It was his choice to go spend time alone, quiet without distraction, without responsibility.

How is that affecting Tim now? Why does he need to know about that sailor?

He didn't need to know. He must have wanted to revisit it for some reason.

You're part of his soul group?

Yes, we're part of his soul group. I was assigned to check on him.

Tim has brought a lot of questions to this session. Where can we get our questions addressed? Where would you like to take Tim?

We can go back to the others.

Let's do that then. Let's reunite with the group. Where are we now? There's somebody here?

(Tim laughs.. cries.) Yes. It's Anne (his daughter who passed away). Anne...! Oh... I'm sorry. Okay. Okay. (to Scott) She has to leave...

Anne can you talk to me? We meet again though we've never met. (Scott previously did a session with her mother and spoke to Anne, their daughter.) What message do you have today? (Tim's voice changes entirely.)

"Just that I love him."

A message for your mom? She's here too.

"I love her too."

How are you spending your time?

"I've been busy. I'm getting ready to reincarnate."

That's exciting. **Can you share details?**

"No, I can't. **They won't let me.** I wanted to. I know it would make my mother so happy, and my dad."

Everything in its own time.

"Yeah."

Your mother and father are here.

"I know."

Perhaps you can take a moment and embrace them with your energy.

"I have been and I love them very much. I miss them, but they know.. or at least they know, *here*. What it was all about. And everything's okay."

Can you remind us about that?

"It was just part of this.. this life, (her passing) it was just; it was for them.. for me too**... But my lesson was completely independent from theirs, what I was working on was far away from them, and they don't even**

know about it and one day we'll be able to be together again. It won't be when they come back.. because I'll be here.. in kind of a half-form."

(Note: As reported, while about a third of our energy is here on the planet roughly two thirds of that energy is always "back home." I have heard reports that visually, that energy back there can be "fuzzy" or "not solid." Perhaps while we're incarnated on the planet, we can still learn and explore back there, but it's not being "fully aware" as she notes.)

I understand. You're going to move some of your energy in a lifetime.

"Right. They'll be able to visit with me, but it won't be the same as if we were all here together. The only reason I had to be here, **is my father was doing something he didn't need to do and I came to correct that, but I don't have much time left.**"

What can you tell us about your father?

"All I can tell him is that he didn't have to be my father. That he chose to, and that makes up for all the things that he thinks he did wrong. Which he didn't do wrong by the way. I do have to go."

We wish you well. You can still spend time with your parents?

"I'm watching."

How can they connect with you?

"It's not easy, it's really not easy (for them); I was there for a period of time trying very hard, and it's hard on us to appear, you know…

Your early death in this life – what was the point of that for your father?

"It wasn't for him."

What's his part in all this?

"I don't know how to put it, he had a part to play in the whole storybook of the whole thing. It was hard for him, and that's why I said I had to come and talk to him now, and tell him something so that he would correct it from now on. I just had to do that."

What did he need to correct?

"That's between me and him. **I can't really say more.**"

Something in your relationship with this soul needed to be corrected?

"Yes. You could say he just needed to know something. I've already taken care of it. I would just like to tell my mom that it's not over yet, it's not over, and I hope you understand what I mean. I have to go now."

What are you experiencing now?

(As Tim) There's just so many, so many spirits here that I can feel. I can just sense them but it's like countless numbers, people that we've known, people that we've known for years, **I shouldn't say years, it sounds ridiculous because it's years for us, it's lifetimes for you...**

(Note: This is an interesting observation. He's meeting up with old friends that he's known for eons – but reports that it feels like "years" since he last saw them, but from our perspective that could be hundreds of years, if not thousands.)

In spirit, a lot of familiar souls?

There is. We touch each other when we incarnate, we touch each other in ways that we didn't plan. People we didn't even know we touch, these opportunities are few and far between; sometimes people will take advantage of these opportunities to come see people they know, just from a distance.

So take some time to do that.

(His voice suddenly changes to that of an elderly woman) "I would like to tell you something Scott! What you're doing is so wonderful. You have no idea the people that you've touched. You have no idea. The good that you've done... we really appreciate you. By the way, I just want to let you know - I'm Erica."

You're very kind. I appreciate you taking the time to share that today. Who are you Erica?

"You know me. I'm Tim's wife's mother."

Oh... I'm sorry.

(Laughs; a giddy laugh) "She's my angel, she helped me, she helped me through one of the hardest times, I was in a lot of things I lived through the war, (World War II) unimaginable; but my baby was there for me when I needed her."

You want to talk about that illness you had that took you out of this life?

"That was just a means to an end. I can't talk about that. **I think Anne told you; there's certain things we can't share with in front of my daughter**, (who is in the room during this session) and she has a long time to go, she doesn't understand. She has so many misunderstandings, I wish I could tell her."

Why not, as a little gift today, something special – pick one misunderstanding your daughter has.

"She thinks she's leaving us when she gets back. She's not leaving, she's not going anywhere, she has a different chore to do."

What is her next chore?

"Oh, I don't understand it, I'm not allowed to understand it."

What would you share with Tim?

"He knows, I talked with him. He understands some things he didn't understand before."

Do you have any advice for them?

"Enjoy themselves. The last part isn't hard; the hard parts really over – oh! I'm getting in trouble they're saying I'm saying too much – **I have to go now.**"

(Note: It's unusual that these folks are stopping by to say hello, but aren't allowed to give away too much information or to alter the path of the person doing the session. It's like they just want to express their love, let everyone know they're still alive, and that they're always over his shoulder.)

They're saying the losses they've been through -...

"That's the hard part."

They've lost all they're going to lose?

"I can't say anything about that; I'm already in trouble. But the hard part is over. They have to experience the rest."

Anything else you'd like to share?

"Your dad, he couldn't be here, he had to go. You won't see him when you come home because he's already on earth."

So he's incarnated?

"Yes. **He's incarnated. He's busy. I can't tell you anything about that.. I don't think I can. I don't think they want me to.**"

(Note: What I love about Scott's technique in hypnotherapy, he keeps probing and digging, not unlike an investigator, who even though someone says "I'm sorry, I can't talk about that" he keeps them talking. He asks them not to reveal anything too personal, but enough so the person doing the session understands why it's important they stopped by.)

Erica we thank you for coming, thank you for that personal message.

"You're an angel."

All the between life therapists are.

"Oh yes, (but) I wanted to single you out because you helped me. You're right, people that touch the lives, you're special people. You have no idea how special you are. I mean the work you do. **I don't know if you know it or not, but you've been doing this for a long time. More than just this life.**"

That's very interesting. You mean taking people for glimpses of spirit?

"Yes, helping them with things that they need to accomplish. Sort of getting them back on track. **You're like a tuning fork if you will.**"

Thank you for that. For coming for a visit. Anything else for your daughter?

(Tim as Michael) She left.

We need to get Tim's questions answered. Who wants to come forward to address these questions?

"What would you like to know? This is Michael."

Anything we need to know about his life as a sailor? A time of solitude?

"Exactly. It was kind of hard, rough life, but the work and the sea keeps a mind quiet. That's what it was all about."

Was his wife in that lifetime?

"She wasn't incarnated at that time."

Is his wife his soul mate?

"It's an interesting question; what you're referring to as a "soul mate" is not something that we recognize. There are people that have been together in lives that choose to incarnate together and they're very close. I don't know what a soul mate is."

One of my teachers talks about having a primary soul mate. I would say the one soul who is closest to you.

"That would probably be her then."

(Note: It's interesting to note that not all spirit guides are the same, they aren't omniscient, and they all have their own point of view. It could be argued that they are filtered through the mind and experience of the person under hypnosis, or it could be argued that the guides themselves have their own perspective based on their lifetimes and journey. Some guides have no problem discussing "soul mates" as it's something they've been asked before. In this case, Michael may be trying to redefine the concept.)

Does she lead her group as her mother said previously?

"There are a number of leaders (in each group), it's kind of like **everybody has a specialty, an expertise, something that they focus on the group, and it's their responsibility to develop that in the other entities, the other energies, the other souls.**"

(Note: He seems to be referring to the concept that every soul group is like a class of students in school. All students in one particular class might be working on a topic like healing, or the shifting of energy, or some other topic. As we've seen in my other books, we've visited classes working on making crystals, cleaning the geometric shapes we carry with us, etc. So there's a "theme" for every soul group – one mentioned that her group dealt with "issues of addiction." They chose lifetimes where they could learn from those lives, perhaps to teach others how to recover from them.)

What's she helping this group with?

"She knows that; she's the healer, the one who nurtures and loves and heals."

What's the focus of this circle or group?

"We're focusing on the healing and rejuvenating."

What's Tim's position in the soul group?

"He was one of the .. how shall we put this? One of the "police," one of the ones that keeps the group focused and on track if you will. That had something to do with his injury. So right now he doesn't have a level, he's just trying to heal."

(Note: Never heard this kind of reference. In his current life, Tim does work in law enforcement, so the metaphor of someone who keeps the rules, or helps keep people focused may be apt. Perhaps like a "hall monitor.")

Is there anything you can share with us that can help that to happen?

"Just time. Finish out this life and make his way back and then we'll examine and go from there."

When did he first come to earth?

"He's a very old soul, he started coming when his wife did, if not sooner."

5000 years ago? 20,000?

Within the last 5000 years.

Question: "Can I talk to God?"

Of course you can! Anytime you want.

Is there a personal god that we can talk to and will answer us? Or is that your function (as spirit guide)?

We all are for that purpose, we all are in connection with him, however you want to refer to the Almighty. **He's ... around us, he's part of us, he's part of everything; it's something that you really understand more spiritually when you're here than when you're incarnated on earth**. I think that's for a purpose (reason), I think maybe it would be too difficult to focus on the chores at hand, if he (God) was to be more open and in your conscious mind on earth. It would distract you from being able to do the thing that you need to do.

I'm still fascinated by this experience of being turned off and on. Is there anything else you can share with us?

It's not very common, and it's a very dangerous thing to have happen to somebody.

When that process takes place is that like a reconditioning? Are they altering his energy or merely turning it on or off?

I guess you could say it's altering it slightly. It really is just like turning it on and off. **Maybe a better sense is when you go to sleep and you dream – your mind is filing away things, refiling and organizing, and it's similar to that. On a much different level of course.**

So a re-orientation of his soul energy?

Yes.

Is someone planning that out? Pulling parts out, operating on him?

Yes, more or less; it's way beyond our ability or our understanding, that's why happened.

When souls have gone thru this procedure, what's the general prognosis?

Have you ever heard of a soul that is "just gone?"

No.

You've never heard of a soul that has been wiped clean and doesn't exist anymore, the energy has been recycled if you will? That's the possibility that could happen.

If the soul doesn't function normally because it's been taken apart and put together again, it could just be recycled?

More or less; it's a more humane thing to do.

So why was Tim brought to this session? What does he need to get?

I think .. his daughter Anne, in that life, had to redirect him from where he was... kind of off track. She had to help him.

Tell us about you Michael…

I don't incarnate any more. I'm just part of the group. I probably have many things left to learn, but I'm just here to help direct traffic, if you will.

We're grateful for your help today. Any last words of advice?

Just enjoy the experience and get what you can from it.

…….

So many unusual observations in this session. I wrote to his wife and asked if he had any further thoughts after the session: Her reply: "Tim always maintained he could "never be hypnotized." Well, not only was he extremely hypnotizable, but he did not recall anything of the many hours of his session when he came out if trance.

After driving home and going to bed, **he kind of dozed off and woke up. He began channeling like a madman, saying things that were downright crazy.** He recalled some of his session, but the stuff pouring out of his mouth was crazy and incredible; things my skeptical husband would NEVER think, much less say.

He was saying things like **"he and a group of others went to Earth but something happened that was so bad that caused God to be very angry with him and the people that he went down to earth with."**

He started saying that he and a bunch of other guys were "warriors of God" as he quoted it and they were supposed to do something. He wasn't sure what it was he had to do because he said that God had wiped the memory of that lifetime out of his existence. **He doesn't remember exactly what it was that he did that was so bad, but when he kept coming and trying to reincarnate back on earth after the event, he just could not function as a soul or an entity living on earth again.**

Then he began a series of suicides in his lives. Finally, God had the choice of either obliterating his soul energy and re-integrating it back into the source, or removing the part of his soul and all its memory connected with the event. **Anyway, God had to destroy the soul energy that was "bad" and then reboot Tim's energy in an effort to save him.** Tim said that he actually went before God and it was a very dangerous thing to do. "Michael" is good friend and Tim talks about "they were all warriors for

God;" sort of policemen in the spirit world that kept the soul groups running smoothly.

The sailor lifetime was the first successful life that Tim had since the Jesus lifetime and after having his energy destroyed and then having a soul rebooted, so to speak. **Apparently, when he was alive, he was somebody significant during his lifetime. That memory has been totally erased from his soul he has no knowledge of it.**

He said that he thinks trying to delve into this knowledge may be the reason for his amnesia after the session and his continued amnesia (about it). All this information was downloaded in a very short timeframe, and Tim doesn't remember very much of it today, at all.

However, he does have changes in attitude about the way he thinks about things. He did say that "the other people who went down with him" did not face any form of punishment, nor did they have to have any of their soul energy altered and then rebooted. Whatever happened - God did not want him to remember it.

We are not sure what all this means, but the story seems to deviate a little bit from what Michael Newton has said in his books. Tim said **"the soul world is not only full of happy loving souls."** There are souls there that are frustrated, still have anger, and still have issues that are not resolved. And apparently if you do wrong bad enough, or you "piss God off" enough, the repercussions could literally cost you your very soul."
…………..

This is an extremely rare example of a fellow who was given the option to wipe the slate clean. People have described voluntarily being sent into isolation between lives, where they can meditate on all the reasons they shouldn't reincarnate, or how they screwed up what they set out to do. If and when they decide to return from that process, they do. But this example, and his reboot process is something different altogether.

From my perspective as a screenwriter, many times a character "just doesn't work;" they get deleted, written out of the story. Or they get reconfigured – their sex may change from male to female (as I did with the character of Nike in "Limit Up." For some reason, I couldn't find the right comedian to play Nancy Allen's "guardian angel" and ultimately changed the gender to become the late great comedienne Danitra Vance.) When she did the audition, the part made sense finally.

As Tim noted, he'd had a number of lifetimes where he committed suicide – which in and of itself is reason to try to help a soul. If every time they're given the gift of life they throw it away – something is apparently wrong. It screws up everyone else's plans. As I sat and thought about this session, something jumped out at me.

At some point, I started thinking about "what person who lived during the time of Jesus would have done something so troubling that he would continually want to commit suicide after that lifetime?" There's only one person that comes to mind, and I hesitate to even suggest his name for obvious reasons. But Jesus is quoted as telling this friend "The star that leads the way is your star," Jesus said... **"You will exceed all of them for you will have sacrificed the man that clothes me."**

If that's not a Flipside quote, I don't know what is. I'm happy to point out – I didn't start off writing this book to go down this path, and I'm reluctant to do so because of the inevitable "brain freeze" disbelief involved. All I can say is that in the few short years I've been researching this topic, a number of people associated with this particular historical figure have shown up in my research. I don't know why that is, as I have no past life memory of living in that era. But *it is what it is.*

It takes courage to come to the planet in the first place, this is an unusual and unique case, and I thank "Tim" and his wife and Scott De Tamble for allowing me to share it.

Flipside of the Vatican

CHAPTER TWELVE:
Celebrities and Near Death Experiences

With the late, charming Basil Jagger and his son, the Rolling Stone.

In my books I've reported a few "celebrities" who appear to have reincarnated. (There are no celebrities on the Flipside, only young and old souls) In "Flipside" there was the daughter of a hypnotherapist who claimed she played guitar in a band with Elvis but "hurt her hand." She knew all the lyrics to Elvis tunes she'd never heard before.

There was also the teacher from Michigan who during her between life session (LBL) claimed she remembered scenes from the life and death of the actress Carole Lombard. There were some intimate details about an affair with Clark Gable, prior to his leaving his marriage, that may or may not have been accurate – but as she was not seeking any fame or fortune by reporting her story, I included it.

Recently, a hypnotherapist friend contacted me that a woman had brought her son in because he was "remembering a previous life."

> "A lady brought her five-year-old son to me to do a past life regression. The reason they wanted to do a past life regression is that the boy says he's Michael Jackson. The five-year-old tells the mom and dad explicit details with names and all the details of his life as Michael Jackson and when the parents Google the stories they all pan out." He also wrote: "I have no training in dealing with children that young but I thought you might be interested in a fascinating insightful look at this kid's telling of being Michael Jackson."

He asked me if I could think of questions that might prove or disprove the memory. Ultimately, the boy's mother decided to keep this story private. I agree with that decision, as the ensuing firestorm of publicity might not be worth it to mother or son. If indeed we do choose our lifetimes, then this person chose a new one (out of the limelight) for good reason. What can you learn if you come back and play the same role every time?

Here's a sampling of "famous people" who've had near death experiences.

Peter Sellers - In Shirley MacLaine's book "Out on a Limb" she recounted one day when Peter spoke of his near death experience: Peter: "I felt myself leave my body…floated out of my physical form and I saw them cart my body away to the hospital... I wasn't frightened or anything like that, because I was fine; it was my body that was in trouble…

I looked around myself and I saw an **incredibly beautiful bright, loving white light above me.** I wanted to go to that white light more than anything. I've never wanted anything more. **I know there was love, real love, on the other side of the light which was attracting me so much. It was kind and loving and I remember thinking 'That's God'.**

Then I saw a hand reach through the light. I tried to touch it, to grab onto it, to clasp it, so it could sweep me up and pull me through it." He heard a voice say **"It's not time. Go back and finish. It's not time.'"**

"I know I have lived many times before ... that experience confirmed it to me, because in this lifetime I felt what it was for my soul to actually be out of my body. But ever since I came back, I don't know why I don't know what it is I'm supposed to do, or what I came back for."

Gary Busey - The actor Gary Busey had an NDE during brain surgery after a motorcycle accident: Gary: "I went to "The Other Side." There were **balls of light** in the air, and **three of them** came down to my essence… **I wasn't a boy or a girl. I had no emotions from earth. The light on the left spoke to me in an androgynous voice, in thought telling me what I've been doing was good, direction I was going in, good, ups and down downs ...** [what] comes with the dinner on the unconscious menu. It said, 'Where are you going now? You need to look for help in the spiritual realm.' Then the voice said, 'You may come with us now or return to your body and continue your destiny. It's your choice,' the light said."

Busey says the balls of light surrounding him were *angels*; but they "didn't appear in the form people see on Christmas cards. These angels floated around him and **carried nothing but love and warmth -- and this love is unconditional."[50]**

Larry Hagman - In his autobiography,[51] the "Dallas" actor said about his NDE: "Everyone has their own unique song, an inner melody that fuses each of us to the deep, modulating, **harmonious hum of the celestial orchestra** that's **the collective energy of everything that's ever lived and ever going to live. It's our life force. The power of the universe."**

His NDE "Confirmed what I'd always suspected, that every one of us living creatures is part of a collective energy that is also ecstatically happy and familiar. **The culmination of that energy is love. It's with us now, it always has been, and it always will be. This was not the end. There were more levels, an infinite number of levels, of existence, each one adding to the hum of the cosmic orchestra, as if we're always spiraling upward until we reach a state of atomic bliss."**

William Petersen - "By the time they got me to the ER, I had lost a lot of blood and passed out. I could hear the doctors working on me, saying that they had lost my vital signs. I was on the "All That Jazz" escalator with a long tunnel and a lot of white light. Then I specifically remember a dominant male voice saying, **"It's not your time. Get off the escalator. You've got shit to do."**

(Note: The "All that Jazz" reference is to the Bob Fosse film. Roy Scheider's character has an NDE and there's an escalator sequence which mimicked the "tunnel" of light.) **Something in me changed, a sort of knowledge that somewhere on the Other Side, it's good.'"**

Tony Bennett – "(One) night, in frustration (over taxes) I overindulged and quickly realized I was in trouble. I tried to calm myself down by taking a hot bath, but I must have passed out. And I experienced what some call a near-death experience." **"A golden light enveloped me in a warm glow"**

---

[50] "Unconditional love" again. In David Bennett's "Voyage of Purpose" he too saw a ball of light approach during his NDE; three shards of light broke off to come and visit him. He later saw them as part of his soul group.

[51] "Hello Darlin': Tall (and Absolutely True) Tales About My Life," by Larry Hagman.

and a **"clear, yellow peaceful plane...** I had the sense that I was about to embark on a very compelling journey. But suddenly I was jolted out of the vision ...   The tub was overflowing and Sandra was standing above me.... I realized I was throwing it all away, and I became determined to clean up my act."

Erik Estrada - Erik wrote[52] he was in intensive care after an on-set accident: "**I was in a long corridor with bright lights, beautiful music, and a feeling of great peace.** But something seemed to be blocking my progress. A voice told me, **'You've got to go back. You've got a lot still to do. You've achieved success and stardom but you haven't achieved personal happiness and peace of mind.'**" After hearing this voice, Estrada found himself back in his body. (Note: Or back on stage.)

Eric Roberts - Actor Eric Robert's (Julia's brother) was in an accident which left him in a coma. "Now I'm not out of the coma ... but **I see "myself" over myself ...** looking at my face -- I could actually feel my breath... Then I started rising ... and I rise so high that the bed is about the size of my thumbnail. I can either come back to my body or not, and I chose to come back to my body."

Days later, two elderly gypsies came to visit him in the hospital. They said they were from Romania and they gave him specific instructions about medicine to take that would help him regain his memory. Eric took the medicine as ordered, within a week his memories began to return. No one else at the hospital had seen the mysterious couple from Romania.

Johnny Cash - The singer checked off the planet during his double coronary bypass surgery. He described traveling toward a **"peaceful light"** but said he became "angry" at having to return. But later he said; "**That great light is a light that now leads me on and directs me and guides me. That great light is the light out of this world, and into that better world. And I'm lookin' forward to walkin' into that great light.**"

George Foreman - George's NDE happened after a boxing match. In his autobiography, he reports "he had a **life review** where he saw "favorite things that had happened during my life, recalling them like a video tape

---

[52] "My Road from Harlem to Hollywood"

running fast-forward, as though I knew somehow that it was about to end…"[53]

He writes: "Instantly I was transported into a deep, dark void, like a bottomless pit … It can only be described as a vacant space of extreme hopelessness … I knew I was dead, and this wasn't heaven … **If you multiplied every disturbing and frightening thought that you've ever had during your entire life, that wouldn't come close to the panic I felt** … The place reeked with the putrid smell of death."

Foreman says when he thought "I don't care if this is death. I still believe there's a God!" a giant hand pulled him up. He saw Jesus standing over him, thorns on his head, with blood dripping. **"Every hostile emotion had been drained out of me, and a spigot of God's love had been turned on inside me, filling me up, and overflowing out of me."**

(Note: This is not a common experience with regard to near death experiences, "falling into hell." When it's happened to people while under deep hypnosis, I've seen the therapist ask "So why did you choose to come here during this event?" And when they ask themselves the question, these "hellacious" places disappear. It appears to be based on what you expected to find in your lifetime, after death. Ultimately, George had an experience with "unconditional love.")[54]

Sharon Stone - I met Sharon when she came in to audition for my film "Limit Up." She was perfect for the role, I lobbied for her play it – the producer convinced me to take one of his managerial clients; Nancy Allen instead. Nancy did a fantastic job, but I've often thought of how perfect Sharon's audition was. She had an NDE that she reported to Oprah.

Oprah: I read that you had one of those near death experiences.

Sharon: It is true. I had that whole "white light" thing.

At what point?

While I was in the tube… it's sort of like passing out, but you pass up and you have this big blow-up thing.

---

[53] "God in My Corner: A Spiritual Memoir"

[54] (http://www.near-death.com/experiences/rich-and-famous.html)

I've never had it, I don't know.

It's been awhile now, so it's not as fresh for me. It's just a lot of white light and you see people who've passed on and they talk to you… and then you pop right back into your body and you're awake and you have a… **I had an incredible sense of well-being and a sense that… it's just so near, it's not far away, or a scary thing.**

You mean Death?

Yes. That it's very near.

Like it's "one breath away?"

Yeah. It's just… "right there."

Really. That's interesting. I've never heard it described that way.

And loving and gentle and okay and there's nothing to be afraid of and that **It's a beautiful loving gentle, good, I felt so safe and okay**, all that stuff I was terrorized with the doctor standing there looking at me.. you're bleeding into your head. Nobody's rushing around..

Did you think you were a goner?

There's just standing there going oh, poor you, why aren't you getting the stuff? You're like "Oh I'm a dead woman!" and it felt okay and I felt **peaceful and serene and everything would work out**, and yet I was really sure that I wanted to live for my son I felt like it was a real choice for me.

Tracy Morgan - The SNL actor was interviewed by Oprah Winfrey on her "Super Soul Sunday" program after his car accident. While Morgan was in a coma, he had an NDE during which he says he met God and was reunited with his late father, Jimmy Morgan. "I don't know if I was in the coma or in and out of the coma. But I remember … **I was talking to my dad.**" Morgan's father passed away in 1987 after losing a battle against AIDS. When Tracy saw him, his father reportedly told him **it's not his time to die**.

"He had this green, this green thing on. I just remember him saying, 'I'm not ready for you, son.'" The spiritual encounter was incredibly overwhelming for Morgan. "I started crying so hard. Probably harder than I cried at his funeral. I just kept saying, 'Dad.' He was my best friend in life." According to Morgan, his dad told him he still had to **"finish the job."**

(Note: "The green thing on" is a common refrain, when people see someone on the Flipside wearing a particular color. Green, as it does in Buddhist philosophy, is a healing color, and is often associated with teachers, doctors and healers when they're seen on the Flipside.)

Tracy's NDE included a conversation with God. **"I went to the Other Side. This is not something I'm making up. Do you know what God said to me? He said, "Your room ain't ready. I still got something for you to do."** And here I am, doing an interview with you."

(Note: "It's not your time." We hear it the way we're supposed to hear it – "Your room ain't ready" is pretty funny. What's the something for Tracy to do? Perhaps telling more jokes, which as Tracy calls them "gifts.")

After his NDE he told his wife; "Something's different. The way I am with people. I find myself saying "I love you" 200 times a day to strangers. I don't care. I don't have to know you to love you. **That's how we're supposed to be as human beings. We're supposed to take care of each other."**

Elizabeth Taylor - Liz talked to Oprah about her NDE as well.

Oprah: Did you not have a near death event that you experienced earlier?

Taylor: I did. In London about 30 years ago, I was pronounced dead four times. Once I didn't breathe and I had no vitals for 5 minutes. That was the time when I had the near death experience.

Did the NDE experience make you be not afraid of dying?

Oh absolutely, I know I wasn't afraid because of that. It was when I had the out of body experience and could see the people (in the operating room) working around me, I desperately tried to move an eyelid a finger, something to let them know (I was alive.)

I could hear them saying "I think we lost her" I was thinking "No, you haven't, I'm here!" Then I sort of floated into this tunnel and there were other figures that I recognized, and **this welcoming like sun; (it was) white sunlight and warmth and like being in liquid mercury. It was like being weightless.**

Oprah: Wow.

And (her ex-husband) Mike Todd was there and I wanted to be with him more than anything in the world. He'd been dead about three years and I was still mourning him. He said **"No baby you can't, it's not your time, you can't come over you have to fight to go back."**

I said "But I want to be with you." And he said **"No, you can't now… you have to fight to go back."** And evidently while this was happening my hands were in fists, (because) they tried to unclench my hands… It was (later) on the bulletin board, it was reported that I was dead. It was in all the papers that I had died – I've never had such good reviews! (laughter, applause)

Oprah. So how do you know it wasn't a dream? How do you know that?

I don't, I didn't talk about it for years. When I came out of it, when I came out of whatever it was, I mean I wasn't breathing, (there were) about eleven doctors in the room, I told them all what I'd experienced, because I felt I had to tell someone so later on I wouldn't think I was crazy.

And I thought "That does sound crazy, I don't think I'm going to tell anyone." And for years I didn't say anything, and then I read about other people having the (NDE) experience… I thought there's got to be something to it. (There are) too many people who've gone through it. **Just because I haven't talked about it doesn't mean it wasn't real** the day it happened."

Just because we haven't talked about it doesn't mean it wasn't real. Amen.

"I know him as THE GREATEST father. I love you so much, Dad. His spirit visited me last night. Thank you world for your love & support!!!"
Muhammed Ali's daughter Maryum, tweet the day after her father's passing.

CHAPTER THIRTEEN:

A Flipside Message From Amelia Earhart

Photo: Amelia and her Electra. Wikimedia

"Please know that I am aware of the hazards. I want to do it because I want to do it. Women must try to do things as men have tried. When they fail, their failure must be a challenge to others." Amelia Earhart

Let's shift gears here for a moment. So far we've heard from personal accounts of people hearing from their loved ones of the Flipside, heard from people who during a near death experience hear "It's not their time" from either a loved one or some higher spirit, or we've heard from people who claim they're talking to someone no longer on the planet, famous or not famous.

What about someone we're not connected to, we've never met who wants to communicate something to us?

This is the section of the book where I prove, beyond a shadow of doubt – well, my doubt anyway, that we are capable of talking to or hearing from people who are no longer on the planet that we did not know, could not have known - and that they can give us information about themselves that *no one else on the planet knows about.*

As a filmmaker, I've been working on a film about Amelia Earhart for over 30 years. If I'm truly open to how the Flipside works, I must allow that the reason I was working on this project for 30 years wasn't so that I could tell the definite story about Amelia Earhart – it was so that I could write this chapter.

I've toyed with writing a book about her, I've considered writing about my journey to researching her, I've spent countless hours in countless meetings with countless producers, studio execs and anyone within hearing distance of my voice, to tell them why her story would make a great story. I've written fictionalized and non-fiction scripts about her. I know the gal pretty well. Why haven't I been able to tell her story? I had an editor at National Geographic tell me: *"We've been instructed if anyone pitches us a new take on the Amelia Earhart story to run screaming in the other direction."*

Allow me to digress for a moment. (Hang on, this is going to be a long moment, but I promise we'll get there.) Some 30 years ago, a dear friend from my high school wrote me a letter and said "You should make a film about Amelia Earhart." This was 1985 or so, and Abbie Adams Yaffe pointed out that no one had made any films about Amelia outside of Valerie Bertinelli's TV version, and an RKO film that was loosely based on her life. I had met Abbie in high school – she appeared a bit like a dream to me - as if I'd always known her.

We dated during high school, eventually she had to move way. We stayed in touch over the years, and it was after I'd written and directed my second feature film "Limit Up" that her letter reached me.

I dug into the research about Amelia, and Abbie helped me immensely. At one point she came out to Los Angeles to work with me to craft the beats of the story. Fearing that after she left, I'd let the story slip away, so I sat down and wrote the rough draft of the screenplay over the weekend Abigail was in town.

When my agent called the following Monday to say Diane Keaton was making my script into a TV movie, I was shocked – it hadn't even been spell checked. The next call I got was from the producer Cary Brokaw, as he was literally walking the script into a meeting with Ted Turner. He asked "Is this stuff about Earhart being in prison on Saipan true?" I said "It appears to be, there are a number of eyewitnesses who saw her there, but I'd have to do research on it." He said he'd call me after the meeting -- which he never did.

Because Diane hired another writer to write her TNT film "Last Flight." Which is fine, except it's not kosher to take in my script to set up a film, so they were forced to give me a fee and some kind of credit. I felt badly about it – but what can you do? I thought, "I'll do my own version, tell the true story" since Diane's TV version ended where mine began.

I was working with Rebecca Broussard, the actress, and while we were in Cannes selling our film "Point of Betrayal" everyone who met her said "Wow. Rebecca, you look just like Amelia Earhart." She really did. We started pitching Rebecca as the star of this to-be-written film.

We got a few bites, Australian film director Phillip Noyce signed on to produce the film; but it just didn't happen. Some years later, Phillip was asked by Hilary Swank to direct her film about Amelia, and he asked about using my research. Eventually, they hired me, as I'd accumulated 20 years of research; I have a credit on the film "Amelia" as well for "curated content."

Phillip bowed out of the picture, Indian director Mira Nair took it over; I didn't know Mira, she didn't know me, so my research was primarily for Hilary. She was able to access pretty much everything Amelia did from 1927 to 1937 when she disappeared. Again, their movie ended where mine began. I wasn't happy with the finished produce, but I can't take credit or blame for it; I really wasn't consulted.

My story – the new script - was about what happened to Amelia after she disappeared based on over 200 eyewitnesses who claimed to have seen her. Just like in the research about the afterlife, I took what people said at face value then compared it to other accounts to see what their stories have in common. By doing so, I've been able to get a clearer picture of what happens in the afterlife, as well as what happened to Amelia.

The eyewitness reports were consistent. The more that I dug, the more that I researched, I found the same story but from various points of view. I interviewed her son-in-law who waved goodbye from their airfield in Miami as she made the last trip. I interviewed the son of the Navy repairman who claimed he put two spy cameras on her plane.

I found interviews with people who saw her plane come down on a Pacific atoll called Mili. I interviewed a GI who worked with a stevedore who put the Electra on a barge at Mili and helped transport it to Saipan. I found interviews (shot by Mike Harris) of islanders who saw her aboard a Japanese ship, tended to her wounds, and filmed an interview with a Saipanese native who saw her come aboard Saipan. I filmed US Marines who claimed they not only found her briefcase, they found her plane, and after some weeks, burned it and buried it off the runway.

I went to Saipan and filmed islanders whose parents or relatives corroborated all of these stories; how she was put in hospital at first, then incarcerated, and then paraded around the island at some point. How she was held in captivity for possibly 7 years, and died. Besides interviewing the US Marine who found her dry briefcase, passport, flight plans - I interviewed a Marine who decoded the message that they'd found her plane, and who then guarded the plane in its hangar. And I interviewed other GI's who saw the plane in the hangar, and how everyone was saying "we found Earhart's airplane on Aslito airfield." Common knowledge if you were serving on Saipan – not so common if you were anywhere else in the world.

I interviewed GIs who after seeing the plane, watched as the US military destroyed the plane, burning it on the runway. Also followed up on detailed research about the GIs who dug up her body, recovered the briefcase, and buried the story. The main reason no one knows this story is… no one bothered to do the research.

Then the Flipside intervened.

I was working on the film "Salt" in NYC for Phillip Noyce, doing the same kind of background research on the CIA for his film that I'd done on "Amelia" when I had lunch with an old dear friend Iris Libby. Iris introduced me to her pal, who was a renowned medium, Pattie Canova. Pattie asked me to look at a TV series idea she was developing, and I gave her what sage advice I could. Afterwards she said "Let me read you, I'm a psychic."

I said to her at the time "That's okay, I don't really believe the future is set, so there's no reason to read me." She said she was going to do a reading anyway, because she was returning a favor. She had me turn over some regular playing cards and said "Hmm. You're doing a film about a female pilot. Is it Amelia Earhart?"

I looked at her, then at Iris, who shrugged, then looked at Pattie. "C'mon," I said. "Anyone could look that up about me." Pattie, who is a native of the streets of New York looked at me as only she can, with a look that said "I have no f*ckin' idea about you whatsoever." At that point, I thought – "Wait a second. Why would I try to disprove this? Why not take the opportunity to actually interview Amelia?"

Having spent two decades in libraries, searching official documents, conjecture and a lot of ridiculous theories, I can safely say I know as much about this woman as anyone I've ever met. Fox Studios paid me to do background research on her – and I was able to get my hands on really hard to find, obscure books, documents and texts. I convinced the film to hire Elgen Long, a renowned historian on Earhart's last flight, and he also gave me insights about her life that no one else knows.

I'm in a unique position to prove or disprove what anyone says about Amelia Earhart. I'm not known as a researcher, but I've been hired by movie studios to do just that. I've accumulated over 5000 photographs of her, and 30 hours of archival footage on her life. I know about her father's incarceration, who the love of her life was, and her open marriage to her husband George.

But this isn't a book *about Amelia Earhart or what happened to her*.

I'll leave that for another book, another documentary, another movie. I'll lay out as much of the evidence as I can and leave it up to the reader to make their own conclusions. Suffice to say, after my 30 years of research, I'm fairly confident I know what happened to her.

From a Flipside perspective, what happened to her could only have been thought up in a "pre-life planning session." The idea that she would be plucked from obscurity because she bore a facial resemblance to the famed aviator Charles Lindbergh, and then made famous overnight by a scheme thought up by a publishing scion's nephew (George Putnam) where she would travel "like a sack of potatoes" (her phrase) in the back of an airplane to become the "first woman to fly across the Atlantic" (there was a $10,000 reward, but no one bothered to define that the woman had to pilot the plane.) She became famous because she was a pilot, she did fly in a plane across the Atlantic – and they gave her a ticker tape parade for it, even though she "didn't deserve it." (Her words)

But because Amelia was a hero in the making, she determined that she would earn the accolade after she got it. She set about becoming the most famous woman pilot ever, and broke all kinds of existing records to do so. It was she who first championed the Equal Rights Amendment, arguing that the word "pilot" has no gender, so there's no reason to treat women or men differently about it. She represented a woman who defied our definition of what a woman could be, should be, or deserved to be.

She's an icon for everyone in that regard. In her marriage, she designed a "contract" that George had to repeat before she would marry him, which read in part that their marriage would not be like any marriage previously designed. She had an open relationship with him, brought another woman she was in love with into their lives, (as reported by Dorothy Putnam to Elgen Long) – I've been able to track down this woman, find out who she was, and that she's still with Amelia on the Flipside.

And I've spoken to Amelia on a number of occasions. The first being that day with Pattie Canova, where I spent two hours asking her questions about her life, about her incarceration and her death. Some of the details I already knew, some she answered for me.

As noted, speaking through a medium to someone on the Flipside isn't like picking up a cellphone and talking. Well it is *just like that* – however there are a number of filters that we have to go through to make the connection. There's Pattie with her world view perspective and syntax trying to make sense of what she's seeing or hearing, and answering to the best of her ability questions about someone she knows nothing about, or what she does know about her is incorrect. Pattie knew nothing about her disappearance, as do most people – but I know a lot of about her disappearance.

My Amelia interview via medium Pattie Canova:[55]

After Pattie asked if I was making a film about a female aviator, Pattie said "She wants to speak with you." I took these extemporaneous notes which are out of order, as they were written on various pieces of note paper I could find at the café. Pattie Canova says she knew nothing about Amelia Earhart's life and I believe her.

---

[55] http://pattiecanova.com/

RICHARD: "What does Amelia think of the film that I'm trying to make about her life?"

PATTIE: What's missing in the script, and is missing from all the books about her, is that her life was filled with secrets. There were secrets she carried for most of her life. **Secrets about her father's drinking, secrets about her sexuality, secrets about her mission.**

What can you tell me about her life?

She's telling me she did charitable work in orphanages. She says something key happened in the fall of 1936 that is a key to her mystery. **She had a powerful emotional relationship with another woman. A Painter.**

Look into something that happened when she was 13-16 years old – very important to her story. **She hurt her leg earlier in life** – somewhere when she was being athletic. (There is the iconic story about Amelia falling off a roof as a young girl while trying to use a wagon to "fly") She knew she would be an aviator at the age of 7.

(Note: This is accurate. Amelia left Kansas, got her pilot's license in Santa Monica, and worked in an orphanage in Boston when she was plucked from obscurity to fame by George Putnam. I heard that Amelia was once found in a bed with George Putnam and another woman by George's wife, but until this moment, never considered it to be a relationship.)

Is there any physical evidence of what happened to her on Saipan?

There are pictures hidden away that tell her story. There are pictures that exist of Fred Noonan's death in Saipan – which she witnessed. **There was a beheading. Amelia was a spy** – but not in the traditional sense of the word. **When she died she was ill with dysentery.**

(Note: This was reported in Fred Goerner's book "Search for Earhart" and later in other evidence. While I was in Saipan, I heard about US soldiers being beheaded (there were two pilots shot down during WWII, a least one was beheaded. I had read reports that Fred Noonan was beheaded. As we'll hear later, Amelia repeats this detail.)

In Susan Butler's book, (which the film "Amelia" was based on) the author was told by Gore Vidal that Amelia had an affair with Gene Vidal, Gore's father. Is that true?

She **did not** have an affair with Gene Vidal. (In your script) You have to write more details of the story to get it right – there are pictures of her put away in the fall of '36. You need to investigate the events of her life at the age 13-16; an important part of her story. **It feels like there was someone institutionalized – a family member. I'm hearing there's an "escape from father."**

(Note: After his mother died, Amelia's father began to drink heavily. He lost his job and was "entered into a sanatorium" in 1913).

In terms of her relationship with her girlfriend - she liked to drive fast. She was pretty, she came from a family with money. Amelia & George were together as a couple because it made sense. **There are letters that can give you more detail about her affair - stuffed in pipes that were never found.** There's a place that is in possession of pictures and papers that relate to her affair with the painter – in a garage with an old basin.

It's in the US, I can see plumbing pipes in the garage; (they're in) a barn or garage that has been renovated, but the pictures are still there, hidden away in the place. There are papers in the renovated farmhouse – There's a family member of Amelia's who is buried in (or near) the land. Amelia was older than the painter; she was younger.

Are there pictures or documents that relate to her disappearance?

There are pictures and photos of her mission – pictures of her death – and pictures of her youth that are still out there. The photographs that she took while flying on her mission – **are stuck in a place where there are lots of antique cars and old artifacts** – I want to say it's an aviation hall with old planes, old cars, vehicles, a storehouse.

There were missions - flying expeditions attached to other "women aviators" that are also this storage – early stuff from 1913's-1915's – need to look in the garage where there are old cars. (Amelia was born in 1897) **There's some type of museum for female fliers that is near Akron, as if that's where the military information is.**

(Note: I was surprised (and it confirmed for me this was accurate) that there is a museum of women fliers "MAPS" in Akron. **I spoke to the curator who said "That's funny. We just had an Amelia Earhart exhibit in the Museum." But no papers from the trip).**

What does she think of the film "Amelia?

Amelia says the Hillary Swank version is incomplete – and contains bad dialog. *(End of interview)*
......

I didn't seek this medium out to ask questions about Amelia. I did her a favor and she offered a "reading." She got nothing out of it, other than I bought her a coffee. Pattie is a talented, smart, funny, no nonsense NY redhead who grew up on the streets who happens to speak to the dead.

There's a second medium involved. That medium has been working with Dr. Elisa Medhus and her son Erik (a transcript of her session with Erik appears in "It's a Wonderful Afterlife.") In this case, I had just befriended Dr. Medhus, had just become aware of her interviews with people on the Flipside (one appears in this book between Erik and another medium) and casually suggested she interview Amelia.

I got a note back from Elisa saying **"We're scheduled to talk to Amelia next week."** I asked if I could see the questions she was going to ask, and I saw they were the average questions anyone might ask from reading Amelia's Wikipedia page. I asked if "I could supply some questions."

Out of the 20 or so questions Elisa asked in her interview, I supplied ten of them. The setting is this; Dr. Medhus is in Houston, speaking to a medium via Skype who lives in Atlanta. Erik Medhus, who passed away some years ago, comes through via the medium, and his mother asks him direct questions. Erik in turn brings in a "guest" to the interview – they usually bring a list of 2 or 3 possible people to interview, and once they settle on "who's available" Dr. Medhus has done the research to ask this person questions.

Her method is quite unique, and anyone can tune in to see the results for free at her website channelingerik.com. I've read and watched a slew of interviews, and I noticed that during the "Interview with Jesus" there were voices that could be heard talking on the tape. I used my editing software to slow down and speed up those voices, and can clearly hear someone speaking – saying "Yes" in answer to a direct question (before the medium says "He said "yes."") and then some other casual offhand remarks that someone might say off camera *so to speak*.

I'm not trying to sell anyone on the fact that I could **hear** a voice on a film clip that appears to be coming from someone on the Flipside. I noted this extensively in "It's a Wonderful Afterlife" and the clip can be found on ChannelingErik.com – so anyone can listen (or measure) it for themselves.

If you'd like a physical confirmation that people can speak from the Flipside, I offer that clip as exhibit B. But exhibit A (for Amelia) is what we're discussing at the moment, so let's get back to her.

I submitted the ten questions, which included "Who was the love of your life and was this person a painter?" I phrased it that way because my research led to the fact that it was a woman painter, but because the word painter, like the word pilot has no gender, I phrased it in such a way that it couldn't be discovered in the question.

Again, I examined the questions that they were about to ask, and added my own. Neither the Medium nor Dr. Medhus knew much about the famous aviatrix; but I did.

INTERVIEW WITH ERIK MEDHUS, DR. ELISA MEDHUS AND AMELIA EARHART VIA A MEDIUM.

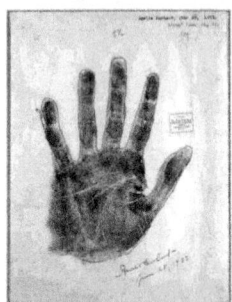

Amelia's handprint. Library of Congress

Dr. Medhus: Can you go get her Erik? Have her fly in?

Medium: Erik said "So funny mom."[56]

(The Medium looks out in front of her, staring into space for a moment, nods.)

Medium: There's a woman sitting across from me, slender, light brown hair, cut short, there's a gentleman behind her, he has more of a solid barrel chest, dressed really well. (Gestures) Are you Amelia? Hi.

She's telling me not to worry about the man behind her.

(Note: From the description, I picture the man as being her husband George Putnam.)

Elisa: Can we ask you some questions today?

Medium: She's real casual, got a voice that's ... not raspy, but has more tone to it. She's very relaxed and says "she would love to answer any questions you'd have," (she's) excited to be here. She really enjoys all the women and girls that do research on her, she takes a lot of pride with what she's done for women's rights.

That's my first question – How does it make you feel being a beacon for women? You have 35,000 buildings, schools or bridges named after you. (A question from my research on how much of an icon she still is.)

She's elated... – she was doing a little "golf clap." "Not to pat myself on the back but to pat women around the world for what they can achieve." She's very honored...

She's talking about how she always knew she wanted to be in a man's role, but it wasn't her ideal or dream to be in the limelight, as she ended up. She had people in her life who believed in her, and she was not afraid to accept the help... She has an interesting (way of speaking) accent on some of her words, but it's a little northern but a little something else. Speaking very quickly.

I'm ashamed to say I have no idea where she's from. Amelia, can you slow it down?

---

[56] Excerpt from ChannelingErik.com, used with permission from Dr. Medhus. Permission to use excerpts must be made in writing from Dr. Medhus.

She says she's "from the middle part of the country." She says her roots are from all over, moved about quite a bit.. she took (dialects) from here and there, she's saying that this public role was not her dream, but her dream was to be a successful woman, to "show it to men" that we as women… "should have equal rights." And now she leans back and says "If not more." (laughs)

(Born in Topeka, she moved to California, then drove across country to Boston, settled in New York and Connecticut. She tried to introduce the Equal Rights Amendment during the Hoover administration and numerous news reels exist of her waging that unsuccessful battle.)

When you took your first flight, you were in the back of a plane, as you said "like a sack of potatoes." What was that trip like? You gave all the credit to the men who piloted the plane.

She said "I did give the credit to the men because *they* did the work; I gave credit where credit is due. If I had any task, it was to sit still (in the back of the plane); but my mouth wasn't very quiet. It was inspiring to see the sights and to see water on every horizon, at times you could easily get lost for what was up or down." She's talking about seeing sunrise and sunsets (when flying)… she said "The colors in the sky made you feel you were a part of the world that existed… All I wanted to do was have that taste again and this time do it for myself."

You knew on the first flight that this was something you wanted to do?

She says "Absolutely – immediately. When we were done I said to myself "I can do that." Not only could she do it, she could do it better. (laughs)

You were one of the first feminists weren't you?

She would like to think she is; even as a child she was engrossed in books, stories about women who succeeded in the mans' world, (books on female) lawyers, business owners, politicians… "These women inspired me." She gives a lot of credit to her mother. Her mom was a wonderful woman who didn't apply any pressures to her children…

She says her mother didn't apply any social pressure to them. She's trying to describe she and her sister (Muriel) were like kids who played in the dirt, what the other kids weren't doing; her mother didn't reprimand them or make them act like ladies, she encouraged them to explore. "I know I am who I am because of my childhood."

She's very elegant and slender.. she uses her arms, it's very different (kinds of) gestures…

Were you a tomboy? You and your sister?

(Laughs.) Yes, that's the word you'd call it today. She and her sister wore… bloomers (Aside to Amelia: Are bloomers pants?)… which flabbergasted the other parents in the neighborhood, as it was not accepted yet. (Medium to Amelia: "How old are you? I didn't mean it that way, but what time are you talking about?")

It was around 1920… (Aside to Elisa) It just makes you start to think about history, when women started wearing pants… Her mother was looked down upon for letting her daughters wear bloomers.

Good for you. You became world famous after that flight, you had a ticker tape parade - did you feel you needed to prove your abilities as a pilot?

Oh no, I didn't need to prove anything; I was showing it, I felt I needed to do is have the next step bigger than the one before.

Is that why you flew the Atlantic solo 5 years later?

She's telling me that's an interesting story – although she knew she wanted to do it (take the solo flight across the Atlantic) in her heart… She's saying she's not the one who set it up. She's talking about having the appropriate people in her life; "We're talking about an era where there were maybe a dozen, a handful of female pilots… A small group of women that were pilots and these other women also had goals of themselves…" But since she'd already landed in the limelight, a lot of what she did was handed to her… almost as publicity.

What was that solo trip across the Atlantic like? Tell us some details.

She's comparing it to how one might feel driving fast in a car with the windows down. "When you feel no one in the world can hear you, you can be as loud as you want, or as quiet as you want. Of course (there's) the sensation of flying, of being supported by air." (Aside: Her hand gestures are kind of tucked and very elegant.)

"Being supported by air, that feels as new to me as it was the first time I experienced it; it never wears itself old with me. But being alone for that length of time, doing something that you love tremendously... There's just not an expression for it – I would have done it again and again and again...

My husband says the same thing; he's a pilot.

She says you find a comfort level that you can't place when your feet are on the ground. "That says a lot about myself and other pilots who have that (feeling)... When we're on the ground, we feel like we've fallen."

Tell me about the flight itself. (According to her book (co-written with George Putnam) about the flight, there were a number of things that failed in the cockpit.)

What part do you want to know? She can tell you the mechanics of it...

I understand that things went wrong. Is that true?

"You want to talk about the difficulties?" She says she chooses not to dwell on that part of it, there were many beautiful moments... she's talking about some of the mechanics weren't checked properly, (that) she should have done everything herself, "But because of the publicity involved there were teams in place that were beyond her control." When she was in the air, there was some miscommunication of what was good and what was checked of... she's describing... (that being) very irritating,

Erik asks "Is this the flight where she goes down?" Is this the flight where you go down?

Dr. Medhus: No, she barely landed in Ireland... your engine caught fire, did you have a hard time finding your way?

(Note: In her book "20 hours, 40 minutes" about the trip, it's claimed that numerous things went wrong. The engine caught fire, at some point all the instruments stopped. When she flew under the clouds to get her bearings, she nearly crashed. She seems to be defending the actual flight – perhaps some of these details were embellished. Interesting to note that she's not "going along" with the line of questions here. The plane came down in a pasture in Ireland, and the farmer thought we was a man until she took off her helmet. She makes the point that it wasn't her that screwed up the flight, but the mechanics who were hired to ensure a long, safe flight.)

Medium: "Finding my way?" No knew where she was, (the) difficulty was the plane itself, none of what occurred, or she believes none of it would have occurred if she was checking it or another woman had checked it – because women are more detail oriented… because women would go through all the steps.

She's not putting down the men on her team; she has respect for what they did, but because they hadn't flown that long (distance) they were used to checking planes for shorter flights, in a shorter flight the temperatures would be what they were, the wear and tear, the pressures, these weren't taken into consideration… She was very angry, and rightfully so about landing early, and especially angry at the team…not so much at the airplane itself.

You wrote your first book with help of George Putnam (Medium points beyond camera to an invisible person she's seeing) and he left his wife Dorothy to marry you. **Who was the one true love of your life?**

(Medium points her finger at the man behind Amelia) That's the dude.

Putnam?

Oh… that's the guy standing behind her.

Is that the one true love of your life? Or was there somebody else, your one true love?

(Long pause) (Aside) Do I look like a deer in the headlights because I feel like one. She's telling me that, (laughs) "Mr. Earhart," and her **had a very wonderful agreement** and it was a beautiful marriage and relationship and she would never take it back. **But it was an agreement based on letting each other be who they truly were.**

(Note: Amelia wrote up a "contract" prior to their marriage where she clearly states that he "won't tie her to the kitchen" and doesn't expect her to "be a stay at home wife." It was when I was interviewing Elgen Long ("The Truth at Last") he told me that when he interviewed Dorothy Putnam she'd made this claim about finding "Amelia and another woman and George in the same bed."

I asked why he hadn't included that in his book, and he said "Because I didn't believe it. I thought she was jealous George dumped her." He wasn't aware that she married someone she was having an affair with a week after her divorce to George. By the way, Elgen Long no longer remembers telling me this story, as I've asked him about it since.

When the medium Pattie Canova said she had "important relationships with women, including a painter," I included the question in Elisa's questions "Who was the love of your life and was it a painter?" I was masking the gender of who the "love of her life" might be. It is later repeated by a third source in this book.)

Back to the interview:

Medium: (Aside) She's talking in a slower voice, which I appreciate... - She's telling me that it... (laughs) "It may not be a surprise, through all her achievements and her strength in women's rights and beliefs**," that she found women to be more attractive or more suited for her in her personal life.** Though it was quite embarrassing at the time and shameful to have any part of that lifestyle, she refrained from it in the public eye.

She saying she would never do anything to harm her husband, and that he knows her inside and out, **she didn't keep anything from him;** it was the one thing she adored so much about him. He would listen to her deepest, darkest secrets of her heart, where the world wouldn't but... She's sad to say (that) she didn't have one main... love in her life.

Did you have any relationships with women? Any one in particular?

(Matter-of-factly with a nod) **She did.** (Aside to Elisa: When you asked that, she straightened up her posture.)

It's ok, Amelia, nowadays we are very accepting of that lifestyle. I hope you feel more comfortable.

She's always comfortable saying it -- but she was highly... she's not one to ignore what she wanted in life... (Medium listens) Now (that) the story has been written, **what would it take to rewrite it, and is it even worth it**? **She's proud to be a woman who's known for being successful in a man's world. She's not interested in being known as person known for...** (A pause) She was looking for a word... Erik jumped in with **"gay rights?"** She says "Yes."

Did George know about your preferences?

Yes.

I understand there was a young female painter you had a relationship with. Tell me about her and that relationship.

(Pause.) (Aside: I love it, her, she looks vulnerable right now, before she was (strong with her) gestures… in command.

With more bravado?

Yeah, when you talk about this… intimacy - she's (now) leaning back in the chair, her tone is changing… And Erik is saying **"Go on it's okay, Amelia. Tell us! We're only just sharing it with the world!"**

(Note: This interview was filmed via ChannelingErik.com. However, the interview had a sound problem, which I did my best to fix and sent it on to Elisa. For some reason, the Medium's mic was low, and Elisa's was normal, It's an uneven sound track. When Erik says "We're sharing it with the world!" it's because all of the other clips from the site have been seen worldwide.)

Back to the interview:

Medium: She's laughing, she says **"It's interesting to wait so long after your story's been told to come forward and talk about it, yourself. Yes, there was a painter, she was madly attracted to her, she was a beautiful soul – but she's telling me she never got to have that one and only "true love," (as) she couldn't share that love with the world.**

(Note: Let's think on this for a moment. I heard from a medium in New York that Amelia had an affair with a woman painter. Years later I'm in a café in Santa Monica, and I hear that George Putnam's wife walked in on Amelia and a woman (and George) in bed together. It's not an incredible leap to think "perhaps that was the painter." But here is Amelia confirming it – **for the first time** – (new information) that she preferred women to men. Talk about coming out of the closet; this is coming out of the closet on the Flipside.)

You were a poet too... there's a poem at Purdue...

(Note: After her disappearance, George donated her poems to the Purdue library. This particular poem, which has been cited by others to prove a love affair with another man, seemed to my mind to be written from one woman to another, and is why the photo of the poem shows that someone tore off the top of the page where the dedication would be. The poem cited below is an unpublished poem of hers.)

Medium: Amelia (just) put her hand across her face, across her chest (in shyness) – you can tell she's a strong woman, (but when) you talk about her poetry she's really... (felt) complemented. Yes, she wrote poetry, it was a way to release what was trapped inside.

Who did you write that love poem for? "To touch your hand, to see your face, today, is joy.?"

(The full poem courtesy of Purdue University's archives: "To touch your hand, to see your face, today, is joy. Your casual presence in a room recalls the stars that watched us as we lay. I mark you in the moving crowd and see again those starts a warm night lent us long ago. We loved Then – we love so now... and "I have seen your eyes at dawn beloved, dark with sleep, And lying on your breast—have watched the new day creep Into new depths, putting aside old shadows spun by night To show again the lovely living colors of your sunlit sight.")

Medium: She says **"Not for George!"** (Laughs. Aside) He's so wonderful (with her) though, he's right behind her, every now and then he'll reach out and touch her shoulder, carry on kind of thing.. (laughs.) **George asks her "Is it the painter?" She's not going to answer...** (Pause) **She's sharing that she had two very strong relationships with two other women. She's not announcing who that poem is written for, whoever reads it will know who its written about.**

You're saying it's too intimate for the world?

Yes.

(Note: That's a pretty unusual construct. A medium is talking to what she sees as Erik, Amelia and George Putnam in a room. And George asks Amelia a questions he does not know the answer to: "Was that poem written for the painter?" And she won't reply. It just shows that when we get to the Flipside we're not omniscient (George didn't know this detail) We carry whatever knowledge we have, but we may not carry the knowledge everyone has.)

You're quoted as saying.. your life was filled with secrets. Were you a spy for FDR?

She leans back and almost knocks George off the chair.. shakes her head "no... no...!"

Lot of people say that.

(Note: Amelia was quoted by a mechanic her overheard her saying to someone else; "Imagine me, being a spy." Julia Child was part of FDR's "kitchen spy cabinet" and it's been argued that because the plane had spy cameras aboard she must have known. As we'll see later on, FDR knew she'd been captured, and Pattie Canova said there was a "military nature" to the mission. But specifically as a spy? She says emphatically "No.")

She says she has many theories of why they (researchers) would come up with it... (the idea of her being a spy.) If a woman's going to act like a man, working for the man... she did have a lot of political questions, but no, she was never informed in her talks (about the flight)... **She's telling me she stayed out of those circles...** (Who may have discussed the political value of her flight.)

(Note: That's unusually telling. She acknowledging that others had spoken of a military nature of the flight, but she "kept out of those discussions.")

She had a thing for flying not fighting, she had enough battles in her life... – "If I announced I had secrets it was because of my love interest."

(Note: The "lifetime of secrets" reference comes from my interview with medium Pattie Canova. Funny that she's saying "if I said that, I meant this other thing..." She's obviously not aware of the conversation that I had with Pattie here, either has forgotten it, or isn't prepared for this line of questioning, or doesn't want to talk about it.)

What happened to you and Fred? Give us a time line... where did the plane come down? Where did it wind up? You landed in Mili atoll and were taken by Japanese to Jaluit and then to Saipan. Many folks saw you there – incarcerated for 7 years... then executed. Is that true?

(Note: I admire Dr. Medhus' approach here. She's not giving up on this line of questions, even though Amelia appears reluctant to respond.)

(Pause.) She's not giving me any sign that is true. (Note: or not true)

Reports that say you landed on the atoll. Is that true? Where did that come from?

(Pause.) She's saying **"It's wonderful how in those days if someone said they saw it, there'd be no other report of it really happening; it would be very easy to replace the someone."**

(Note: This is an unusual reply. In essence, "back in those days if someone saw something they could be replaced and then no one say anything.")

Were you taken to Jaluit?

Erik says… He's talking to her about being captured, contained… She's not even responding to his questions, (reacting) as if to say "This is very interesting…"

Amelia, c'mon toss us a bone.

She says "You want one of my own?" (laughs)

Are you saying you were not incarcerated by the Japanese?

She's saying **she wasn't executed.**

(Note: An unusual way of confirming the report. She doesn't say she wasn't captured, just that she wasn't executed. As we'll see in the next interview, which was in a different setting with a different medium, she's more forthcoming there.)

Were you incarcerated for 7 years?

"It's not…" Medium smiles. I wish you could hear everything that's going on in my head.. whew.. it would be easy.. did you mention a guy whose name beings with F?

Fred Noonan.

She adores him. Very good man.

When you started off with (mentioning) him; she has a lot of trust with him. She is… she's telling me about landing the plane. (Note: A man's voice can be heard on the tape at this moment.) **The plane didn't crash in the water. It landed.**

(Note: This is what the research shows. Recently, school teacher Dick Spink went to Mili Atoll and interviewed a number of islanders (along with Mike Harris, Les Kinney and Jim Hayton) that claimed her plane had landed in 1937, and that they were forced to put it on a barge by the Japanese.)

I don't see it broken.. nothing like that, she's coming down but not in a place where she wanted to land. So Erik and I are asking questions... She's talking about two things; there was not enough fuel – (for reaching) wherever she was supposed to go. **She says "Back then it was common, you could say this gallon (of fuel) was going to get me this far, but based on pressures, fuel consumption is an estimate not a known factor."**

And she's talking about the other... She's not alone. (There are) other flights around her... what do you call the airplane ... looks like a one seater.. **There's a single star on the plane? I'm seeing that.**

(Note: This one seater Mitsubishi A5M was the type of plane flown from the Akagi carrier in 1937. (Wikipedia) There are two reports that her plane was "shot at" by a Japanese pilot, and that the Japanese sent a pilot to "force her plane down." In the later interview with medium Jennifer Shaffer, she says she saw bullet holes in the Electra. Note Amelia is quoted as saying "one seater" but also "with a star.")

Were there communication problems?

She's not.. (long pause.)

Anything else you want to say about that?

She's landed the plane. She's alive when she lands the plane, so is Fred.

What happened to your plane, the Electra? Apparently it was found by the U.S. forces in 1944... and destroyed.

(Note: I have numerous eyewitnesses I've filmed, U.S. Marine veterans on camera claiming they found her plane in a hangar in June of 44, saw it flown a few weeks later, and then taken out on the runway and burned by U.S. forces. I've collected over a dozen eyewitness accounts from verifiable sources.) [57]

Medium: U.S. forces. She thinks it was ridiculous why the plane was destroyed. She says **"The plane didn't have anything to do with it."** (to Amelia) Do with what? C'mon do with… (Long pause. To Elisa) I know that's a lot of silence… No? She doesn't really want to share it. I think maybe if the circumstances were a litter different, then I think…

Erik was asking "Is it that you think we're going to exploit you or announce it in a certain way with the media?" Would you be more comfortable with a "one on one?" (Medium nods) She (says she) likes it more of a "one on one" if we're going to talk about her passing... says she doesn't want to talk about her passing… she says **"It's a strange phenomenon that people have picked up and are wanting to resolve her death for her when she herself is content."**

You died after you landed the Electra?

(Medium stares off.) **She didn't die during the landing; she lived after the landing. She lived after she landed the plane. It was on land. Flat land.**

Where? Give us a location as specific as possible.

She just said "it's on an island."

Part of an atoll? Part of Japan?

They're saying "Not Japan. No." (mouths something. Laughs.) She's talking about mainland, not what I was referring to… you want to ask another question that might encourage her (to be more forthcoming?)

(Note: Saipan was considered by Japan to be "homeland" territory since 1914. When the US liberated it in 1944, it was fiercely defended. It's about two hours by plane from Tokyo. It is now considered "US Territory" like Puerto Rico.)

Did you die from not having sustenance, due to exposure?

---

[57] Interviews with these Marines are on YouTube, or earhartonsaipan.com

(Long pause.) She didn't have sustenance, it wasn't readily available food, **especially water** – Erik asked "Because no one was giving it to you or you couldn't find it.?"

(Note: Erik is on the right path here; she was reportedly poorly fed in the prison in Garapan, led to her dysentery).

Medium: I'm sorry I don't know more about her. I try to avoid doing any research into who we're interviewing, perhaps that's a failing.

These questions were compiled by a filmmaker. *I think they're interesting. Was it (the place where you landed) several acres?*

Several acres. A tiny nub.

Another person is with you?

Yeah, she's not alone. Or is it possible someone found her and decided to leave her there? (To Amelia) Could you just answer yes or no? (Looks at her. Pause.) It is quiet on my end. Silence.

Amelia why so tight lipped?

She will tell you one thing; answers to this (these questions) won't bring you any answers to government secrets. **She's saying she wasn't part of the war; (that) she wasn't a spy...**

Did you die because there wasn't enough food or drink?

Yes.... I'm going to say yes to that.

Is there anything else you can say to those who love you and still searching for her?

She said to stop searching, (because) she survived death. (Laughs)

What was your spiritual mission then?

It's interesting. She's gaining her power back in her voice. She says "Maybe the spiritual mission was to see how valuable women are."

You accomplished that.

I believe I did.

Anything you regret?

Not coming back and doing it again.

You could have! Have you reincarnated yet?

She's telling me she's not reincarnated; she's not interested in it yet.

What about any work you do over there?

Erik says "Remember we're talking about non-linear time Mom…"

Right, thank you Erik. Amelia tell us about your afterlife and the work you do there.

She does so much. **Several of you might be disappointed she's not helping those who trying to find her body. It's not a mystery - it's not where the focus should be. She's more interested in helping younger women, children teenagers, to help them find their own story in their life.** She's a very… she's a big advocate for helping anyone become more emotionally honest.

(Note: This is part of the reason I stay off the "Finding Earhart" bandwagon. Yes, I've tried to make this film in a number of ways, but after being admonished by her to "stop looking for me" I sincerely let it go. As we'll see in a moment, she found me again to do that "one on one.")

That's a big one.

She says "I know Erik has talked about these concepts because he's brought them up before."

What do you think about the state of humanity on the planet?

(She laughs.) The state of humanity as I see it today? It's in need of great repair, but by no means should you see it as broken. Who would want that belief? To know where they are in time is broken? It's not going to help the structure of the whole. If I had some guidance for anyone listening, it would be to follow your dreams, and to understand that when someone tells you "No, that you cannot achieve your dream;" that even the smallest yes, the smallest of possibilities can get you to the path that you want to be on.

She says she's disappointed that people feel the need a quick response for what they're putting out, and are not willing to do the work or have patience or to persevere; it's in these (qualities) you find out who you are and how you can be your best. It's through the trial you find out who you are.

You don't need to have an 80, 90 or 100% yes – even a 5 percent yes would give you the same that 80% would give you to create your own destiny. (Aside: Her finger comes up.) (Medium points up to the sky) That's what it is; you create your own destiny.

What past life influenced this one? (This is one of the questions Elisa asks in all of her interviews with Erik and friends)

She jokingly says over her shoulder to George "Did I ever live before?" (Aside: She's so cool right now.) She says "This life was really extremely important to her and she'd love to do it again."

Erik asks her "Can you recall any other life that gave you a challenge that helped you do what you're doing now?"

She's talking to Erik and George now… they're talking about dogs… talking about… walking dogs… saying "They're not just for sleds they're for other purposes…

(Note: An unusual aside between Erik and George. Not many people know that George spent awhile in Alaska on dogsleds, editing a newspaper after college in a remote village.)

She says "She was a man (in a past life) and sad to say, a very abusive man to his wife and daughters. And never getting acceptance, tenderness or love from anyone. A man who showed control over what he could. "I clearly remember on my death bed…" She's describing how horrific this death was, an illness beyond anything, but rightly given to this man..

I asked if anyone took care of him. She says (that) he just eroded, fell apart inside, so he had no way of saying he was sorry. She says I think it (this lifetime as an abuser) gave me such an affinity for women who in so many situations and occasions get beaten down and then stand up with such pride because they choose they are the better person. I wanted to highlight that more than anything.. I wanted to carry that inside me… (into this lifetime as Amelia).

She reaches over and taps George again, touching base with him. She says "I believe that's the one life; there were so many experiences…" She's extremely pleased and proud with what she was able to do with this life as Amelia.

(Note: This is repeated in most of the interviews I've done with people under deep hypnosis. They claim that a previous lifetime informs the current one. During these sessions you can ask "Why did you choose that previous lifetime and why did you choose this one and what do the two have in common?" Interesting to hear her remembering one where she was an abusive man who died alone.)

Erik any further questions?

(Medium laughs.) I'm hiding my face (because of Erik's question) Erik asks "Amelia, would you label yourself a lesbian or more bi-sexual?"

Good question.

Amelia says she doesn't care about any label, but being put on the spot as she is "right now by your son," as she calls him, considers herself more bisexual. But it was the love a person she was seeking, it didn't matter (to her) what size it came in. But she says she had an extreme affinity to women (gestures with putting her hands over her heart) right here.

Thank you so much Amelia, you've been an inspiration, throughout your life and during this interview, we learned a lot of things about you.

She says "Thank you so much for having her." She's would love to discuss (more) privately about her. **You mentioned there were questions by a third party? She said she'll entertain the idea of talking to that person.**

You don't want this aired to the world?

(Nods.) Mm-hmm.

Well thank you so much, appreciate your time today.

(Medium blows a kiss.) Amelia blows a kiss. She's very strong about it. George too, he really enjoyed being here. She's wishing everybody a beautiful day and thank you for listening and Erik says "Amelia's the bomb."

Thank you Erik, love you Amelia.

......

As noted, I don't think many people have seen this interview. Further, the people who've been "looking for Amelia" wouldn't consider it worth listening to. People who are convinced she "crashed at sea" will remain convinced, and I'm not here to *unconvince* them. I don't particularly care what people believe or don't believe – I'm asking questions regarding the research I've already done. In some places she confirms it, in others she denies it.

Like I say the sound on this clip was undecipherable for some reason; I fixed it for Dr. Medhus, but didn't listen carefully to the ending until I was transcribing this for the book. When Erik's medium said she would entertain **"the idea of talking to the person who supplied the questions"** – I had a chill, and a shudder, as I didn't realize Amelia was referring to me.

Because I'm the *third party.*

And like I say, I've been working on an Amelia film or book or documentary for 30 long years. I'm revealing the punch line here in this book because *what's more important*? Finding out that Amelia was captured by the Japanese? **Or that she still exists on the Flipside?** I'd argue that it's likely I've had this information in my lap I could write that sentence.

I've written books about how people don't die. And now I'm writing a book about a famous person who hasn't died, who is passing along messages from the Flipside. **And she just passed along a private message to me.**

It took me two years to hear it. And even then I thought – "How am I going to do that?" I thought about where I would go – would I interview that particular Medium again?" I just couldn't wrap my mind around it.

Then Jennifer Shaffer called.

"Some time ago I had a friend who had terminal cancer. I always remember what she said to me, "Don't be sad for me, we all come to this world to be a tourist, enjoy life, sightseeing, do good deeds and I just so happen to leave earlier than others..." From a friend's Facebook post

CHAPTER FOURTEEN:
Hacking the Flipside Through a Medium

Medium Jennifer Shaffer

"*Here's something to think about: How come you never see a headline like 'Psychic Wins Lottery'?*" Jay Leno

Actually, I get to answer that question as well, Jay.

Jennifer Shaffer is a medium who is famous for helping law enforcement with missing person cases. *How coincidental.* Jennifer works in Manhattan Beach California, was a fan of my books, and contacted me to talk about the research. She was interested in having a between life session of her own – which I offered to film for her.

I told her my hesitation in the past to focus on mediumship in my afterlife research – because most people who see mediums want predictions of the future. From what I've learned "the future is not set." But Jennifer is effervescent, has an amazing gift, and is a wonderful person to get to know on the planet.

She told me about her journey to mediumship, how she started to realize that when she heard about a missing person, or a criminal act, she could see what happened in the blink of an eye, and began to help law enforcement solve some of these cases. And she began to do that for members of law enforcement across the country pro bono – where she and an advisory board of talented mediums work for free to help solve missing person cases. She has worked with members of the FBI (on an advisory basis) and former LAPD chief Bill Bratton.

In the case of Police Commissioner Bratton, the parents of a missing child contacted her, and when she solved the case, now NYPD Commissioner Bratton flew her to New York to find out why she knew so much about the details of what happened. In other words – "how could she know so much if she wasn't involved?" If you're working in law enforcement, or just have a case you can't solve, I highly recommend giving her a buzz. (JenniferShaffer.com)

When she told me she worked on missing person cases, some switch in my head went off and I said "Hey, how would you like to be involved in the most famous missing person case in history?" She laughed, and said "I'm in!" I went over to her office, set up my camera and spent the next three hours talking to Amelia.

I confirmed before we began she knew little or nothing about Amelia. She's the third medium I've brought into my orbit to talk about Amelia Earhart. The first two happened by accident; the third I invited. I feel that *if what I'm saying is accurate* – that **everyone who has existed on this planet throughout history still exists**, then we should be able to locate them and ask them direct questions if we have the proper communication equipment. In this case; a talented medium.

I began my interview with Jennifer by asking about her process of seeing or hearing something from the Flipside. We met up in her Manhattan Beach office, I set up my camera and dove in.

RM: *What happens when you "see" something about someone who is no longer on the planet?*

Jennifer Shaffer: If the backdrop is light, I know that it's coming from a higher awareness. When it's darker, I know that the energy is coming from someone about to pass away. Then when someone passes away, I might see their face lit, but everything else behind them is dark.

It's like being on a football field at night where everything is dark in the background, but people are lit (by the lights). For example, someone who died from cancer showed me how she left, what it looked like when she was leaving (the planet).

To me it looked like a football field, with darkness as a backdrop – she had been in hospice at home, and she showed me the way she looked at the end, with no hair, her body shrunken - then 3 days later, she popped in to visit me with a white background but looking the way she used to look. She was ecstatic, had all her hair, gorgeous and happy. It was kind of funny to me; she appeared suddenly, like at two in the morning, looking like her old self - "boo! Surprise!" – it was wonderful to see her again.

Let's talk to someone no longer on the planet. Want to try?

Wow. I suddenly felt a calmness when you said that… someone took everything away.

Who are you sensing? Is there anyone in our group who is a teacher or are we all students here?

Many students here.

I guess the next question is there anyone around who's a teacher, who we can call in and ask some questions to?

They just showed me this enormous massive white – like a ball of light. **Then Jesus.**

(Note: Whaaat? I spoke to Jennifer about interviewing her about her process of finding missing persons for law enforcement, and I joked with her about "looking for the most famous missing person on the planet." This is a surprise, but I forge on with questions.)

Let's ask him, "Can you stop in to say hello?"

"I've been here a while." I don't know if he means "on the planet."

(Note: as I drove to this interview, I create a mental image of "asking" people who have appeared in my own previous sessions before to "come forward and assist in this interview." Whether this is fanciful thinking or not – I don't know. But when Jesus said "I've been here awhile" I guessed that's what he was referring to. Again, there was no plan to talk to or about Jesus, and I hadn't planned any questions.)

Very nice of you to show up today. Anything you'd like to impart about what we're doing here?

"I want you to understand that we are support… **we are supportive.**"

(Note: I assume he means by this form of inquiry, the idea of asking people on the Flipside if they can be of any assistance to people on this side of the veil. What's interesting in terms of an interview, is that I'm asking the questions, and he's answering via Jennifer. She and I have just barely met; it's not like she would know what I was going to ask. If she was trying to impose her own point of view on these proceedings, that would be very easy to do, by nudging the conversation in one direction or another. But in this case it feels as if it's an ongoing conversation, that picks up where it left off before.)

I want to apologize, Jesus if anyone misconstrues the chapter about you in my last book; hope it's ok.

"There's never a question that can't be answered by yourselves."

(Note: Interesting the response is to the part of the question about people "misconstruing" his interview, by saying "there's never a question that can't be answered by yourself" – meaning, if you meditate on what he's saying, and you have a question about it, you'll instinctively know the answer.)

Very good. But dude. I'm apologizing about the chapter in the book, about you not being crucified. Is that okay?

"No one will be offended."

You're the one I don't want to offend.

"I can't become offended."

(Note: Apologies for anyone offended by my calling Jesus "dude." I'm trying to slice through this odd construction, me with a camera on a tripod, meeting Jennifer for the first time, and putting her on camera. Is he really Jesus? I don't know. Perhaps he means "No one will be offended because **no one will read this book."**)

What is it about you that when you get close to people – physically proximity... get close to people they burst into tears? What's up with that?

(Note: This is the 3rd time I've seen someone talking about "seeing him" during a session, and when he gets "closer" they all turn beet red, tears well in their eyes, and they can't seem to breathe. I'm curious if this is the psychological effect of seeing him, or if it's physiological, energetic.)

"They don't know they always have it with them. They get a glimpse when they see my face and that helps them."

I see.

"Helps them become more conscious."

When people see you during a Near Death Experience and you tell them "it's not their time yet," is that part of your job in the afterlife? To help people on their way?

"I tell them that they have more to live for. And it is a job they teach others."

Can you come a little closer to Jennifer to see what you look like? So she can see what you're wearing, what color your eyes are, whether you have a beard, Caucasian, middle eastern...

(There's a pause. Jennifer smiles with a pained expression. Her cheeks turn red. She begins to cry, but is trying not to. Tears roll down her cheeks. She closes her eyes and wipes a tear. Same as the other two I've witnessed.)

I can't stop (crying). I can't see him but I feel him getting closer but I'm trying to fight it (this emotion) ... I didn't think it would happen to me! I'm not even seeing him but the closer he got, my heart dropped."

Is that an energetic thing that's going on?

"It's the opening." He's showing me a (picture of a) heart, "when people get energy, that's the energy of the heart." People see the pictures (that he's appearing as) and he shows up in whatever picture you've seen him in (before) – for me it was the one the Mormons had (which Jennifer grew up with). **Then I saw him in blue jeans, and like a polo shirt,** just seeing the back of his head... but when he's ... (she listens to him, responds) That's why am I crying. Because you're sitting there asking me to come close. Wow.

(Note: Third time he appeared wearing jeans and a tee shirt. *Who makes those tees?* Just kidding.)

The reason I'm asking Jesus to come closer, and I'm asking for a specific reason, so that Jennifer can experience this, because now she understands your energy in a visceral way. From what I'm observing, is your energy, Jesus, is closer to the source. Your energetic pattern seems closer to the source, perhaps why people referred to you as the "Son of God," because you're more affiliated, more like from the family tree of what the source would be.

Jennifer: Right. Based on the pictures Jesus showed me at first – (I saw) different pictures, his face on a white background, like the one I've seen in the Mormon (temple); he has blue eyes, green eyes, brown eyes –

What else?

I asked him to come back and immediately (the feeling) it started again.

Can you tune your energy, so your energy doesn't burst into tears?

(She nods.) Yes. (Aside) **That is crazy.**

So what's your day going to be like today, Jesus? Are you in many places at once, helping people simultaneously? By the way Happy Birthday; you're old but you're not that old.

(Note: This was recorded just after Christmas)

Jennifer: He laughed.

He's had many lifetimes. I'm not one to ask him for predictions of the future, because I believe the future is not set... How can we access Jesus on a daily basis?

He said that "We all have him with us."

Here's a thought on access – the Hindus, they might not have access to you... Who do they have access to?

(A pause) He just showed me all these images of the same energy. (Different deities.)

Is that you? (Meaning are all those various deity's versions of you?)

I had the same question. He said "It's not me."

Let me ask you a philosophical question; I had the impression what happened to someone like Mohammed was that he had an out of body experience or a beyond life experienced where he channeled the writings that became the Qur'an, is that kind of correct?

It is not only correct; it has more layers to it.

I think all religions have that idea.

He just joked around as if he was going to smoke a cigarette. (Like instead of him being interviewed by me, I assume, he was joking that I was going to preach a bit, or this was going to "take some time." *Very funny Jesus.*)

Ha. Is that a message we can get our minds around? That all religions are part of the same concept?

He just showed me spokes of a wheel. "All the same."

(Note: Pretty much exactly what Prince said "all from the same light.")

Do you think it's important people hear that message through writing books, speaking about it or are they going to figure out on their own?

"It is something that's been passed down or passed through every generation. (Something) that has come to this planet. And while they don't think they have access, they only have to ask."

Let me ask you a mundane question. Pope Francis is the kind of holy man who seems on the right path; yet the other day refused to meet with a man of peace, the Dalai Lama - what do you think about that? The mundane goings on of the Catholic church?

"It was exactly the way it was supposed to be." And he just showed me what it's going to do, how it stirs people.

You mean stirring up people by affecting change, understanding or forgiveness and compassion?

He's saying that it affects the way people look at the Pope and his means of not being compassionate in different sectors of this earth.

That makes sense. By the way how's your pal Quentin Crisp?

(Note: I'm referring to the interview in my previous book where the author of the "Naked Civil Servant" inexplicably showed up; Quentin said "He had just come along to "see his friend do an interview." I realize now he meant Erik.)

He says "He's not around anymore."

I'm referring to the interview that you did with Quentin Crisp and Erik Medhus.

"I know who you're talking about."

(Note: Nothing quite like having Jesus point out that you're not paying attention to what he's saying.)

Is that your voice I can hear on the tape?

It is.

How'd you do that?

Manipulation.

(Note. I'm asking about hearing his voice say **"Yes"** on the tape, and later hearing him whisper **"We're done with (the topic of) selflessness"** in the audio.)

I'm recording you right now – can you add anything to this audio?

(Note. Some sounds appear at this moment on the recording of the interview. They aren't clear to me, but it was odd to hear sounds upon request. I heard some high pitched squealing noises, but they're not on the audio as far as I can tell.)

Jennifer: There's a piercing noise.. really high pitched. Can you hear it?

Yeah.

He's got a great sense of humor.

How often have you had a chance to interview "the dude" Jennifer?

I've felt him (appear) before, but not like this. He shows me – whatever was around, whatever was coming in, when he showed up, everybody else was (suddenly) gone. Maybe not (gone), I know better than to try to understand it, even though he showed me different pictures of (himself) in my brain, showed me pictures that I had seen before. Then when I asked him to come closer – there was that force.

Is there a reason you don't want Jennifer to see your face today?

He said "I do see it." (She laughs.) Because I haven't asked. Okay. I am now asking.

(She pauses. Tears comes into her eyes and her cheeks turn red. She begins to cry softly, then laughs, trying to control it.)

He showed me my two kids when I asked him.

Dude.

Didn't see that one coming. (wiping away tears.)

"My face is in the face of those you love." Wow. We're all an energetic pattern, and how do you show love and innocence; with the faces of those we love. Now... in terms of numbers I should use to win the lottery?

5, 8, 2, 3 16...

(I laugh. I always ask this silly question when doing a session where it feels like I'm talking to someone on the Flipside. I was startled to actually hear numbers. I quickly grabbed a pen and wrote them down.)

When do I play this lottery? Today?

He's not answering.

Hello?

I can't force him to answer. I got nothing.

Look, if I was meant to win lottery numbers I'd get them.. because the answer is, you can get lottery numbers...

(Note: **I did play those lottery numbers** the next day... **and won!** A dollar. And when I won, I heard a voice in my head say "Not very specific, were you?")

Jesus, let me ask. Have you ever met my friend Luana?

I just got shown that same light – when we asked to see the person (of Luana), I don't know what you asked – (but I saw a) ball of light.

She's showing herself a little bit?

It's challenging because I know too much about her. (From hearing my books on tape, "Flipside" etc)

Anything you want to say to us Lu? Luigi?

She wants you to know that you're going to make a documentary about Amelia Earhart.

So the documentary about Amelia, Luana is saying that will happen? That's good. Let me ask you.. since I have you here...

She was just showing me how many people need your help – it's like dimensionless, a lot of folks. One more time… I keep asking Amelia, "Should he go find your bones?" She keeps saying "yes."

Let me ask you this, Amelia, is it okay for me to talk about your girlfriend, the lifelong love you had?

She nods. "It has to be told."

Who is Amelia's girlfriend the painter?

Did I mention Marilyn Monroe before?

Yes.

Every time you mention Amelia's girlfriend, she shows me Marilyn.

Maybe that's how she looked. Let's go back to Luana. What's she up to? Who are you hanging out with?

"I'm developing a field" she says. What I'm getting is that they're making their own DNA, maybe she's talking about a field (electronic) - like children are involved with this field – (they) have some kind of field so they don't feel everything… I feel like she's showing me.. it's a field for the ones who are getting born. It helps them acclimate better.

A field that will help them on the planet or prior to coming here?

A field to help them prior (to coming here). To help them neutralize the (energy of the) Earth's grid.

It will help the planet in terms of...

She's smiling at you right now.. it's so funny (to see her do that.)

She's in my pocket right now.

(Note: When I asked Luana on her deathbed what she wanted me to do with her ashes, she said "take them wherever you go." I travel with a little pouch of her ashes, which I brought to this interview in my pocket.)

She's waiting for your answer…

I've heard the earth is this living organism, or at least the energy of the Earth is supposed to be - so the idea of creating a field of compassionate consciousness before they come here makes sense to me. Perhaps by means of imbedding or manipulating their energy so when they do get here, they see the planet from a holistic place?

Like a grid, yeah, I'm seeing it now.

So kids being born now... is there a reason for this (grid adjustment) happening? Is it something we should worry about?

It's an environmental reason. I got the sun burning.

That could be the effect of global warming. That would make sense. Will this field help people to change the course of the earth?

Yes. (It will) Help build the planet. It's almost like it's being planted to grow, she's showing me that it's like medicine being grown for the planet, she's showing a crystalline (substance), she's showing me the uh... just got shown again...

Shown what?

The Lemurians... Atlanteans...?

Are these places Lemuria, Atlantis, were they in our realm or in another realm?

In our realm.

This generation? Or of a previous generation of Earth?

(Note: The Hindu Vedas talk about each "incarnation of the universe" as a Kalpa. I've heard variations on this theme, that there have been many "big bangs" and many variations on Earth. I know that sounds fantastical, but when you take the time element off the table (as it is on the Flipside) then it doesn't seem insane, at least to me!)

Jennifer: This one.

My wife Sherry was showing our son this book about Atlantis when he was two, and he got very excited, asked "how does it end?" and when she showed him the end of the book he burst into tears and he said he was there, he said there was an earthquake and total destruction that he survived, but his parents didn't, and then a giant wave came and took his life.." He was talking about the book's depiction of Atlantis. Is it a possibility that it was in another realm...?

(His memory of Atlantis) It doesn't feel like it was here. (Jennifer to Luana) I need to be shown that.

Maybe his "Atlantis" memory was on some other planet – a similar thing – same souls of course. Perhaps a parallel universe? Earth-like, just not here?

She's (Luana) saying it happened in many places. She's so sweet by the way. (to Luana) It's only because I know too much about you... (Jennifer listens) Luana **corrects me, says "I didn't say it like that."** So she corrected me – **she didn't say "Atlantis happened in many places."** I made a conscious decision (to not speak about Luana's showing up during the Jesus interview) and I'm sorry, I didn't know it was going to happen... she was there all along, I just didn't know it was her.

(Note: Luana corrected medium Pattie Canova as well. When I was writing "It's a Wonderful Afterlife" I asked Pattie to converse with Luana, and as she was talking with her, she said on the recording "Luana just said **"She's not very accurate with what she's saying."** Very typical of Luana – she loved being precise with words and images, and was well known by her friends for "speaking the truth.")

No worries, what a magical thing that you found me, I found you and here we are talking to Luana. Let me ask her; any of your friends like Charles Grodin, or her friend Goldie Hawn and Robert Towne who I saw the other night.... should I talk to them about what you're up to?

(Jennifer smiles.) Now you're kidding. (to me) **I just saw Steve Jobs trek through.**

Can we stop him, ask him a question? Jennifer, you haven't read the second book, but Steve makes an appearance in the second volume during a session I filmed with a friend who knew him. During her session we spoke to him briefly and asked his opinion about the direction Apple has gone in. (He replied "Not enough fun. Too much attention to detail.") My question to Steve is, "What did you mean by your final words (as reported by his sister): "Oh wow, oh wow, oh wow." What did you see?"

(Jennifer to Steve) Can you show me? (To me:) **Something to do with his father. His real father. (I see…) Everything made sense (when he saw his father.)**

Of course! That makes sense. You were put up for adoption, and later when he reached out to you, you didn't want to see him.

Everything made sense. He got the intel before he left.

(Note: Steve Jobs was adopted. Many years later, his Syrian immigrant father ran a restaurant that Steve frequented. They remained estranged until Steve's death. His father, Abdul Fattah Jandali is 85 and lives in Nevada. His sister Mona reported that Steve's last words were "Oh wow. Oh wow. Oh wow." As reported here and other places, our loved ones who are still on the planet are able to physically greet us on the Flipside because two thirds of our energy is always "back home." When asked about this, one spirit guide said "do the math." It's possible what he's saying here, that upon crossing over, the first person he saw was his father, and his path and journey suddenly made sense to him. "Oh wow.")

Luana what did you mean by your last words? "Ha ha ha?" what did that mean or were you trying to get your breath?

She said she was grateful that it (crossing over) wasn't scary.

Like a joyful "ha!?"

It was pure love.

Very cool.

She was not afraid to go. **"I can't believe I stayed" she says.**

We had more cappuccinos to have.

It feels like there was an African woman who is with her – a beautiful woman, I don't know (how to describe her), but she's gorgeous.

They're hanging out together?

She has a great smile and laugh. She looks like a gorgeous model – that is how she appears to be.

Maybe that's her friend Hazel, who passed away recently. One of her oldest friends, who was also part of a Buddhist group with Luana. Hazel

Medina. When I was in Tokyo I stopped at their Buddhist monastery (SGI)
to say a prayer on both of their behalf. I scattered some of Luana's ashes
near the temple... but I heard Hazel's voice when I did so. "You done good
Richie." I had both of them play nurses in their last movie together, my
film "Point of Betrayal."

It's very profound (what she's showing me.) She shows up wearing a
kimono. Just the colors, the colors that are around her, the blues and the
greens, are Intense, they were (both) laughing – oh boy, were they
laughing... they're like little kids.

Luana and Hazel hanging out. Wow.

Jennifer: Can I ask Luana a question? (pause) I asked her if that was really
Jesus (who came to visit) they both laughed and said "Yes."

(Note: Hazel was Luana's oldest friend, an African American actress who
lived in New York. They did plays in their teens together, when Luana
became ill and was going for treatments in Mexico, Hazel came out and
stayed with her for a bit. Hazel makes an appearance in "Flipside" as she
told me an incident about when she was ill and in the hospital, and a
handsome young man came in and took care of her, spoke to her, made her
laugh. And finally when some of her family came to visit, she introduced
this young man to them – but they couldn't see him. She realized he was
someone from the Flipside who had come to help heal her.)

Pretty cool that Jesus came to this interview. It's the ultimate in name
dropping.

That's funny. They were laughing (at me) and saying **"You mean, you**
were asking him questions without even seeing him?" (I was just)
letting go of the image, it was Intense... Just to feel him – we try so hard to
get that image. And he showed me the faces of my children instead.

You don't have to be a believer in the dogma of the church to understand
the guy's mission was to impart a message of love. When you asked him
"What do you look like?" he responded with images of pure, unconditional
love. As only a mother would know. If you want to "see Jesus" start by
thinking about the faces of the innocent, and give some unconditional love.

Luana again says you're going to be doing a documentary about
Amelia.

(Note: From her lips to God's ears. If I had a nickel for every time... actually am currently working with a producer who is doing a documentary about her.)

She has the most amazing voice, Luana. It's a little bit deeper, but it's very pleasant, very smooth...

She had an uncanny ability to get strangers to tell their life story to her, wherever she went.

She's very connected to your daughter, I think part of the energy field she's creating has to do with her, your daughter. It has to do with that, making sure when they (new souls) get here – "Everyone comes here locked and loaded, and this energy field... is to help them." She's ... amazing...

I've got a question for you Luana. Our son saw you had appeared on the stairs and reported that you said to him "I love you." Was that accurate?

There's so much going on, sometimes I'm having trouble focusing and she just put her arms around me so she could talk to me; she understood it was difficult for me to focus – (and she) just pinched my cheek, huh... **"It's about love," she said "You know the love. You know the love is never going to leave."**

Okay, I get it, any of your friends that I should talk to on your behalf?

What I was being shown was different bits and pieces of the consciousness that's still alive (over here) and bring it over to (there) - and whatever they're going to do to bring it into the future...

You mean what Luana was saying; this field of energy which will help people?

She showed me, I never thought of it this way; but **everything that we're doing over here, that we're thinking up here, has (already) been done, and (while here on Earth) we're pulling on it (learning from it). They're doing it the other way, the extraction to the other way..**

They say they build souls that way, take bits and pieces of consciousness.

(I'm seeing) The wheels – the geometric things... the ball bearings... so what I'm shown is the people here are the medicine for the planet. That's what Luana is talking about, the "ball bearings," (that help the mechanism work) the entire frequency that they're putting into the children -- so they're doing something to make it a smoother transition.

(Note: In my first between life session, I found myself in a classroom where I claimed the class taught students how to clean the *geometric shapes* that follow us, like fractals, through our lives, containing all the information and data from previous lifetimes. It's between lives where we take them in to be "cleaned." When asked how they functioned, I said "Imagine ball bearings that help a machine function. They're the ball bearings that help us through life." Not an image I've ever conceived of before, but seemed clear at the time.)

They're trying to help the adjustment from the Flipside to incarnation?

It's still is perfect...

I'm wondering because of how we're wiring ourselves, with microwaves and the internet and wireless towers; I'm wondering if that's detrimental or positive to the human physically?

(This grid that Luana is working on) It neutralizes it...

Perhaps that's enhancing our ability to access the other side... Are we tuning ourselves or being tuned?

The last couple of months (the afterlife) felt further away, it feels like we're now... like now it's just that we have come closer to the veil. It's been a challenge for me to get used to it (this proximity). And now I'm used to it, when I'm talking to someone over there. Before it (felt like the message from the afterlife) was more profound coming from a different dimension, but now it's so close I have to question it...

It's made everyone really question their work (in the mediumship world). I've just got to trust my work. It's no different than someone doing drugs for the first time, the greatest high ever, or you realize what's going on over on the Flipside, now you've been doing the drugs so long, there's no jump – it's always been here, my perception has changed...

When I came here I thought, let's ask all these people to show up – I asked them all to show up, Luana... Jesus...

Every time you mention him the (intense) feeling comes back.

End of Interview (part one)

Amelia in her flight jacket. Wikipedia.

CHAPTER FIFTEEN: Interview with Amelia Earhart

*"So AE. Good news; you spend most of your life in a plane.
Bad news, we spend the rest of the time looking for you."*

After this initial interview, Jennifer and I had lunch. When we came back, I offered that I was just going to "jump in" with facts and questions to and about Amelia.

To refresh; Amelia was on an around the globe flight which began in Florida, and was supposed to go from New Guinea to a tiny island named Howland so she could refuel. She didn't make it to Howland.

As you'll read elsewhere in this book, she went west to the nearest runway she could think of – which would have been Gardner island, but because she was 200 miles off course, she found Mili Atoll instead. She landed the Electra on Endriken island, bringing the plane down on the coral that surrounds the tiny island, which at low tide is "long enough to land a 747" according to someone who has filmed there.

She was then picked up by the Japanese who ran the islands. Amelia, Fred Noonan and the Electra were put aboard a Japanese ship and taken to Saipan. Fred was beaten and executed for supposedly being a spy, and Amelia died from dysentery. The US knew she was there, but couldn't reveal it knew because it would reveal they had broken the Japanese Naval codes.

Her briefcase was found by a US Marine, her plane discovered on Aslito airfield on Saipan by US Marines. I've filmed interviews with them – they not only saw her plane, but saw it fly again, and then some weeks later, watched as it was destroyed by US forces. Her body was dug up by two GI's, and her plane was buried in the airfield. I've spent 30 years tracking these details down, getting eyewitness interviews, and everything I'm saying is backed up by solid evidence. That doesn't seem to matter; likely you're hearing this information here for the first time.

But because our time is limited, I jumped into the questions I already knew the answers to.

RM: Let's talk about her landing in Mili.

Jennifer: There's smoke in the cockpit.

Is someone shooting at her?

She's being shot at.

I've heard that. One of the eyewitnesses Mike Harris filmed said that he was aboard a ship with a Japanese captain, the Akagi, who said that in 1937 he sent a plane up to shoot down her plane. (And noted in the Erik Medhus interview that a plane was nearby) But let's back up at little bit. She left Lae, New Guinea, July 3rd...[58]

I got an image of something being cut on her plane.

She took a tailing wire off. Was that it?

It felt like a line, like a gas line.

She had a switch in her cockpit that allowed switching tanks. But was she off course? Radioman Harry Manning (who was on the original flight plan) said she was 200 miles off during their test flight from her "drifting"

---

[58] Mike Harris, shot footage in the 1980's of Marshall Islanders who claim they saw Amelia after she landed in 1937. Mike and I went to Saipan, filmed some of the same witnesses, or their children; their stories are consistent. Numerous islanders saw her arrive in Saipan, treated in the hospital and later when she was in prison. In 1944, US Marines landed, I have filmed interviews with a number of GI's who saw her plane, briefcase, and watched US forces destroy the Electra. These are not theories but eyewitness reports on film.

– and then Fred was 200 miles off when they got to Senegal, perhaps due to her "drifting." If she was 200 miles away from where she was supposed to be over Howland, it's physically possible for the Electra to fly to Mili Atoll. So the question I have for her is, "Were you 200 miles off course?"

I'm getting that she was.[59]

Endriken Island, Mili atoll where pieces of the Electra were found. Photo by Dick Spink

When Erik and Dr. Elisa Medhus and the medium did their interview with you, which I supplied a number of questions for - during the interview, Amelia reportedly said you would be open to talking to "Whoever wrote these questions." **Is that me?**

Yes.

So the reason I'm asking is because I'm trying to get to the truth of what happened.

You bring a lot of people with you.

I'm familiar with Amelia's journey and path, I'd like to jump around and ask some specific questions. Did she have a girlfriend who was a painter in her open marriage with George?

She's some years her junior. The image shown to me (of the girlfriend) is blonde, like unruly blonde. She had freckles.

---

[59] There's a site, datelinetheory.com that claims she was 400 miles NW of Howland when she thought she was over it. However, as noted, she reportedly drifted 200 miles NW when she flew long distances. Either way, her next stop was Mili atoll.

Is Amelia with her now?

Yes. They're all laughing.

Amelia, is it okay to ask you to talk to us directly today?

"It is lovely."

I heard some love letters exist between you and your girlfriend.

I was shown a wooden box in a summer house. In a museum. It's in a private collection. Letters between the painter (this girl) and Amelia. Feels like it's a generational thing – like Amelia's sister has the letters.... I'm getting a male.

George Putnam donated her poetry to Purdue University. Amelia wrote some wonderful poetry, George submitted one of her love poems to Purdue. I had the feeling that it wasn't written to George, as he'd torn off the dedication portion. "I lay in the grass with you." I had the feeling it was written to her lover, this woman.

Right. She is her love, it's interesting. She's saying he was miserable.

Who?

George. Or Fred. She said they tried to control her. Did she smoke then?

It's possible. Fred had an Irish accent and blue yes. George was...

Did he fund her?

Yes.

She had compassion (for him). There is a guy here, he's not looking up.

Who's that?

It's her father. She's showing me he was a heavy drinker.

Yes, he was incarcerated, put in a sanatorium for his drinking.

Did he have schizophrenia? He heard voices.

(Note: This is not common knowledge about Amelia's family. In various websites, it says that her father "voluntarily" swore off drinking by entering a hospital for alcohol. As we've heard from the other three mediums, he was "incarcerated" for alcohol, actually put away. Perhaps there's more to this story that hasn't been revealed – abuse perhaps - but this is the third confirmation from a medium that Amelia's father was jailed and not a voluntary patient in a sanatorium.)

Maybe that's why he was in a sanatorium. I read in one of George's later books that Amelia had psychic abilities.

She is, she was (just) showing me how she was able to see things outside of her plane when she was in her plane. She was psychic... interesting, who's the other female who was psychic who took on the...? She just showed me an image of Joan of Arc.

Funny. Same haircut. Joan had visions of the future, and of course they burned her at the stake for it. Amelia was a bit like her. I'm going to ask some random questions. Where there two cameras in her plane?

She showed me taking one of them out. (Amelia had her own camera she used during the trip to take snapshots.)

They were spy cameras. Did you get a chance to use them?

She used them. To document things. In Africa. (She used her handheld Brownie type camera to take photos as well.)

Okay.

She's showing me taking pictures, like the first selfie, even pictures with her and a girl. (Those pictures are in the library at Purdue University. They're snapshots from her camera she left in New Guinea.)

*AE and Fred during the Last Flight
(Courtesy Purdue University)*

Someone quoted you saying "imagine me being a spy" – was there some kind of military reason to this flight?

She shows me there's someone who was in the military who was a pilot. Dark haired guy, tall. He was wearing one of those jump suits.

You were friends with FDR...

She just rolled her eyes.

(Note: That last time FDR was mentioned she made the same kind of gesture looking at George. However, she said the opposite during the interview with Erik's medium about her being a spy.)

Did FDR ask you to help him to spy on the Japanese on any level?

He did.[60]

You had asked for permission to fly through Japanese airspace...

She's showing me these islands... but I'm getting what I thought was Hawaii but she's saying "closer to Asia" and on the farthest, closest to Japan... (an island closer to Japan, Jennifer later says it was Saipan when I show her a map of the Pacific on my cell phone).

Were you going to fly over Japanese territory? Saipan was considered part of Japan by the Japanese, the way we considered Hawaii part of the U.S.

No. She says "I was afraid." If feels like a last minute change.

They changed the flight plane to depart from Florida instead of Oakland. I understand that answer. (After the crash in Hawaii, the flight plan was changed)

Glad *you* do!

Let's go to New Guinea, was Fred drinking heavily before you left?

Something happened where she was jilted (rejected?).

---

[60] This is contrary to what was said in the previous interview, where she turned and looked at George before answering she "wasn't a spy whatsoever." I'm not claiming it to be the case; it's either true or it isn't. I'm interested in getting a consensus of reports from different angles. She may have been a "reluctant spy."

In New Guinea?

She loved someone – she left someone. (There was a radio operator in New Guinea that she was friends with, and years later he wrote that she'd asked him to replace Fred for the last leg of the flight.)

We're going to move forward. I'm hoping this isn't stressful.

Not stressful. They're entertained by this line of questions.

The Japanese came and arrested you in Mili, did they make you strip?

She's laughing.

When they arrested you and Fred, when they took the Electra to a Japanese ship, was that stressful or did you feel like you were being rescued?

It was not stressful.

The *Koshu* was docked in Jaluit, although the Japanese Navy claimed it wasn't.

This is the ship Amelia, Fred and the Electra were seen aboard. (Smithsonian)

Aboard the Japanese ship, you were seen by a doctor…

(Aside to me:) Was she pregnant?

I don't think so…

She's showing me getting cramps.

She mentions that in her book – from the smell of gasoline – a few have suggested that she was... was she pregnant?[61]

She **was** pregnant.

Oy. (Note: I leave this question behind, to not get caught up in this moment) So a native of Jaluit, a fellow named Bilimon Amaron said he tended to your wounds aboard the ship.. and you tried to speak to Bilimon – but he overheard the soldiers calling you "Ameera."

She's smiling. She's saying they only knew two words in English. "Ameera" and "Ea-haht." She's showing me a map or a blueprint or a map, where they were going to fly. They helped her significantly, she says.

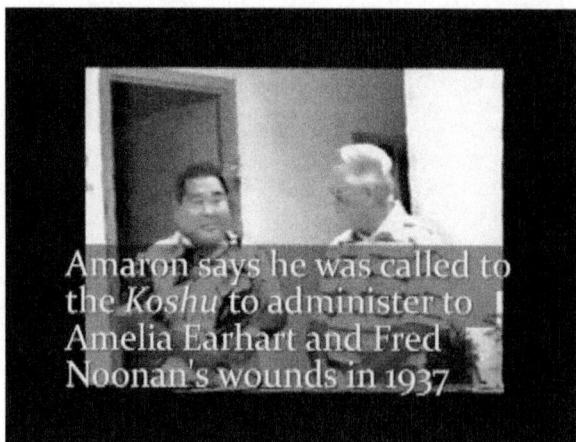

Bilimon Amaron interviewed in 1980. I interviewed his business partner who said "His word was gospel. If he said he saw AE, he did." Footage: Mike Harris

They took you to Saipan?

Saipan! Yes, that's what (the island near Japan) I was seeing earlier.

Reports say they took you ashore to the city of Garapan, they brought you to the hospital where a number of people saw you and treated your wounds.

---

[61] From "Last Flight" by Amelia Earhart. "Gas fumes in plane from fueling made me sick again this morning after starting. Stomach getting weak I guess.... French and Standard oil people very careful about wiping oil cans. No ground wire used as in U.S. In refueling at Natal boys spilled so much gas it was funny."

There was a lot of people (who saw me).

You gave some jewelry to an island woman?

A cross. It could be my interpretation… feels like pearls… or…

Did you pick it on the trip?

Feels like something that was given to her when she was young.[62]

A number of people took care of your clothing, you were taken to the military headquarters, at what point did you realize you weren't being rescued?

She says she knew it from the beginning, just knew it from her "Spidey" sense. They kept her separate from Fred…

At what point was Fred executed? They were in cells… but they were telling people she was a spy…

She says **she was a spy but that it was "to be able to fly." That was the price she paid to fly. She's showing me bullet holes in the tip… of the plane.**

(Note: As noted earlier, there reports (in Mike Harris' footage) from a man who said the captain of a Japanese aircraft carrier told him he'd sent a plane to shoot down the Electra. Also mentioned in the previous medium's reading – and not public knowledge by any stretch of the imagination.)

The Electra had an accident in Hawaii a year earlier. (Note: I'm jumping around here)

She's showing me the brake assembly broke.

Yes, that's correct.

(Note: This is spot on. The Electra did a ground loop in Hawaii on the first leg of her flight, and the right landing gear broke. That's when they changed the flight plan. However, she may have meant when she landed in

---

[62] AE didn't wear jewelry when she flew. (None that I can see in the 5k photos or 30 hours of stock footage I have.) It seems likely to me that this was something she'd either carried in her briefcase, or picked up along the way on the trip. In Fred Goerner's book a woman mentioned getting "a ring" as a gift from AE, in my trip to Saipan, I was shown the house where that ring still is, buried under a house knocked down by a typhoon.

Mili. According to NTSB investigator Jim Hayton, (who owns an exact replica of part of the Electra's wheel) the Electra parts found on Mili Atoll by Dick Spink indicates the "brake assembly broke upon landing." Either way, it's a pretty specific detail for someone who knows nothing about aviation or Amelia.)

Jim Hayton, NTSB expert, demonstrating where the piece found by Dick Spink on Mili fits on the Electra's wheel.

(Jennifer, aside to me:) This is exciting, I feel like a kid.

The crash in Hawaii happened in 1936... The U.S. Navy fixed the plane at the Lockheed factory in Burbank...

It's like they switched something out...

I've heard that – perhaps an engine switch. I heard the Navy installed two "aerial reconnaissance cameras" on the plane... I interviewed the son of the Navy mechanic who installed them.

She's showing me taking them (the cameras) down – there was one up in the corner, but the other was taken down. She didn't want to be tracked. Was there something that could have tracked her?

There is a theory they wanted her to be missing so they could find her. Is that accurate? Part of her mission was to be lost?

No. That's what she's saying. Or whoever it is with me.

I did read your book carefully... (AE's "Last flight") I noticed that you never learned Morse code...

She knew Morse code, she says.

*Hang on Amelia, if you were pregnant - **who was the father of the baby?***

Fred.[63]

No wonder you didn't want to come back.

She keeps showing me a white tank top with white underwear.

I heard Gene Vidal bought her men's underwear.

It *is* men's underwear.

Okay, wow, pardon the irreverence.

She's showing me page 209... (of the book I'm holding in my hand).

Okay, this is Vincent Loomis' book – ("Amelia Earhart – the Final Story")

She's excited about that book for some reason. And she loves that other book for some reason – (points to George Putnam's book "Soaring Wings" published after her disappearance).

This is George's book called "Soaring Wings." I'm looking at page 209 in George's book. Here's the first sentence, "It's significant she was known as the girl in brown "who walks alone" In a sense I think she was always destined to be walking alone..."

I feel like she wrote that; she was voicing it at the same time as you were talking - she was saying those exact words.

Page 209?

Where she was before she got pregnant.

*If you were pregnant... did conception occur before you left? **Where'd the conception take place?***

During the trip.

*Oh my. She could be teasing us too. **Is she making this part up?***

I don't think they can lie from the other side.

---

[63] As noted, in "Last Flight" Amelia writes about feeling nauseous, ascribing it to "gas fumes." Others have suggested a possible pregnancy. I'm not claiming it to be the case, but transcribing this session verbatim.

I think they generally don't... but you never know. So, you're saying you did know Morse code. Are you saying you did?

It was our excuse... (to be lost)

You didn't reply to the Itasca, you were pretending not to know Morse code?

That's (in) your stuff. (My research she means. It is, but I didn't realize that was part of any "plan").

So the last missive heard from you was "We're low on fuel" –

She cut the cord. **She's saying and she said the words *"We're low on fuel"* at the same time she cut the cord – ... (to the gas tank)**

*There's a CBS correspondent named Fred Goerner, and he followed the story as I have, in the 1960's he went into the records at the Nimitz Museum in Texas and found a last recorded message from the Itasca to be **"land in sight."** Is that accurate?*[64]

Yes.

Fred Goerner at KCBS in SF. He interviewed an eyewitness, Josephine Blanco Akiyama who I interviewed 40 years later, who told me the same story she told Goerner. She saw Amelia and Fred escorted onto Saipan by Japanese soldiers in July of 1937. (Photo: KCBS)

---

[64] Admiral Nimitz told Goerner he was "on the right path" with regard to his search for AE on Saipan. He would know, he was in command of the Navy when the plane was found. According to Goerner, the day after he found this document, he went back to make a copy of it, and it was "mysteriously gone.' Cue the Twilight Zone music. Goerner's papers are in the Nimitz Museum in Texas.

There was a report of a young girl in Florida who listened to you three days after you disappeared, on her ham radio...

She showed me an M...[65]

This young girl recorded what you said when the plane came down. It's on the Tighar website: "There's water coming up," and you said "tell George to get the suitcase from the closet." What did that mean?

She's looking at her girlfriend... I'm asking her... (as) I haven't asked that yet. She's laughing – it had to do with her belongings and with her relationship with her girlfriend, but also stuff that felt like it was... give me a second... -- **It was her letters... to her girlfriend.**

Very good, thank you.

(Aside) Fascinating, I had no idea.

As stylish and beautiful as you are, there's an element of freedom and liberation that can help people who are suffering because they can't tell others about their preference in sexuality. That's why I bring it up.

It's the greatest love story. She just showed me it was "the devil's triangle" - not what she got lost in, but emotionally.

But you did choose this life to be liberated by the air, to be a pilot, to be someone who represents femininity on a profound level, the power of women to do anything, at the same time to be someone who could be plucked from the air and put in prison.. You had the courage not only to fly, but to be incarcerated as well.

It's crazy.

---

[65] (Note: From Topeka press, July 3, 1937 "Earlier the Los Angeles operator, Walter McMenamy and Carl Pierson, interpreted radio signals as placing the plane adrift near the equator between Gilbert islands and Howland Island." Their intercepts became the basis for the RKO film "Flight For Freedom" with Rosalind Russell.)

The Garapan prison where she was held.

Let's talk about the incarceration. What was it like?

Feels like she left (spiritually) when she was incarcerated…

There are reports she got out on the island to meet other people. What happened to Fred?

She's telling me they thought **Fred was the actual spy. That he utilized her work.**

And I know Fred's not dead now, he still exists...

He's the first one that showed up... (in our session).

Can I ask Fred a question? Fred, can we ask you, how did you die?

Showed me Fred taking a drink. I feel like he was beaten.

Did you lose your head?

(Aside) (They have) such a great sense of humor; (they said) **"He lost that a long time ago."** It takes time for them to show me something bad. – (a pause) **There was a blade.**

Was there a soldier... did he get in a fight – or was it a sentence..?

It was a sentence. He didn't have things to tell them.

Was it at the prison, kneeling down by a tree?

I felt a field.

Wide shot of the Garapan prison and field with tree.

More than one soldier? How many people where there?

What I'm being shown is that there was a crash where he was foundering going down a hill... (like he was escaping and they were running after him) and that there was.. they came and got him and took him away.. and they beat him.

Did he try to run away?

He was trying to get to her, trying to talk to her (Amelia.)

What year did that happen? After you got to Saipan, later on?

When he takes me through it the colors change...

It would make sense the Japanese would assume he was the spy as he had the military background...

He showed me (those) ties when you said that.

I think he died before her – two accounts say that...

He was bound and on his knees...

Shooting someone was more painful, beheading is quick the honorable way to go. Was he buried?

I felt like he was in different places.

Cremation?

Could be. She just showed me a cemetery... he was cremated; she was in a cemetery.

Okay, back to AE.

I feel like he was beaten to death… but there is blood on a blade.

Sword or a bayonet… that would have been logical. AE was moved from this four cell block to another cell block that was across from the original one.

Was there a church nearby?

Not far away. Amelia, I'm going to run through different accounts of what happened to you.

I think she starved.

I've heard that – dysentery?

She said something... with the number 8.. 8 weeks, 8 months, 8 years?[66]

She was in this cell then moved to this smaller cell...

She just showed me that it felt like forever...

I get reports that she got out to visit people… Saipanese got along with the Japanese.

Did they have those pointy hats?

(Note: Historical drawing Chamorro natives living in Guam in the 19th century include fisherman **wearing pointy hats.**)

From a traditional Chamorro ceremony. (Photo: Guampedia.com)

---

[66] There are reports she died of dysentery in 1938, so perhaps 8 months is accurate.

Could be…. Was it as noisy in that cell as it was for me in your cell?

"It was miserable." She went like this – (hand gestures) "tiny space" in the grand scheme of things. She wrote (a diary) that she just showed me...

(Note: I've stood in the cell where she was supposedly held. It's small, but the sounds of chickens, cows, birds are incessant from the nearby farms. A small little hellacious place.)

Where'd the writings go?

Into the fire.

Did she write on the wall?

Yes. On the back, right… She drew on the bottom part. Her initials and her girlfriend's initials…

(Note: In Tom Devine's book, he claims that when he examined her cell, the letters AE were written in large letters on the wall of the cell as well as "some other scrawlings." There were about ten cells in this block, I was able to identify hers by the tree that is growing inside of it (pictured in Goerner's book as only a sapling.) However, someone has painted, plastered only one cell on the block; hers. The rest are as they were when the island was liberated in 1944.)

A GI told me he found something like that... did she do that?

Yeah.

There was metal food plate on the cell door – I've seen a photograph of it in Tom Devine's book - carved into the copper – the name A Earhart or maybe it was initials, I forget.

"It was spelled out" she says. It looked like the name was rubbed off.
(A woman contacted Devine with a photo of a metal plate that had AE's name written in script. She claimed she got it from a Saipanese villager in the 1960's. The piece had yet to be forensically examined.)

This is the writing on the plate a woman received on Saipan in the 1960's. Photo: Deanna Mick

I just interviewed a guy in Saipan last spring, he's 82...

She's makes a face of pinching his cheeks. He saw something...

Yes, he saw you on the back of a truck, you with a bandana, dressed as a man, on this truck... I asked if this was you and he said "It was the first time I ever saw a Caucasian woman, she was dressed like a man, it's not something you'd ever forget." He was 12 at the time.

Right.

Another man came forward and said the same thing... was that truck taking you off to your execution? When was that?

March. (That is the same date that the 82 year old eyewitness gave me, in 1944, just prior to the US landing).

Is that when you were you executed?

No. She dies from being sick, she's saying.

They didn't kill her that day.

They tried.

What's unusual about this story, is that it was in 1944. So this would determine she was alive until May of 44. I've heard two versions of how she died; one said they saw her shot, another said they heard she was beheaded.

She says she was not beheaded.

So not shot, not beheaded?

She wasn't cremated, she says she died from a wounded heart, she was sick.

Where was she buried? If she wasn't cremated, what'd they do with her body?

Is there a cemetery? She's showing me something (draws a drawing) – she says she's buried under that. (I recognize the drawing).

Why would they bury you?

There was something that she did that influenced that.

She died from illness – she's buried near this spot, under it?

Up to the right.

I went to the old cemetery that was moved... is it there?

No. (Points to the drawing.) There.

There's two GIs Hanson and Burke, these two soldiers were sent to dig up bodies and they went out to a cemetery, and they asked "Why are we out here?" The CO said "Did you ever hear of AE?" Did those guys dig your body up?

A part of it, yeah.

Ok, let's hold off on your body for a sec. What about your briefcase? Did Robert Wallack pick it up?

Yes.

US Marine Julius Nabers decoded a message saying they'd found your plane. Nabers guarded the plane... eventually it was burned and buried. My question is – does that sound accurate?

It is accurate.

Julious Earskin Nabers
US Marine Veteran Saipan
Baldwyn, Mississippi

US Marine Nabers remembered "as if it were yesterday" when he decoded the message "we have found Earhart's Electra on Aslito airfield." He guarded the plane for 24 hours, later saw her briefcase, and watched as US forces destroyed her plane.

Is the plane still there?

She's showing me part of the airfield. (Jennifer draws a map of the airfield, draws terrain which I've been to and seen with my own eyes; she's never been there nor seen a photograph of that airfield. I recognize precisely what she's drawn.)

Andrew and Douglas Bryce of Colorado. Andrew spoke to a stevedore on Majuro during WWII who claimed he moved the Electra from Mili via a barge to the Japanese ship; Kyoshu. Douglas saw it in a hangar on Aslito airfield on Saipan. Soldiers told him "Did you hear we found Earhart's Electra?" and he and other GI's went to the field to see it, corroborating other eyewitness accounts.

Are we going to have success with that? Finding the plane?

Maybe. She wants you to find it. I told you. She visits you in your sleep. Two years ago, she visited you in your sleep.

What did we talk about?

She sat down and talked with you about blueprint plans. You guys were at a camp fire. It's interesting.

Question for you – 2 things – George, are you still around?

He is.

George, during WWII, you had Amelia declared dead while she was still alive - did you find that amusing when you hooked up in the afterlife?

She just pushed him (jokingly) – she (said she) was so angry... she showed me pushing him. She's showing me she would have gone back to him... (if she'd made it back alive.)

With Fred's kid! Well... that happens... but George, at some point you were on Tinian and I discovered you went for 2 weeks leave on Saipan. Did you hear she'd been there, where you looking into the rumors?

He did look into it. He wanted to know that she wasn't suffering. I have to tell you when I first saw what he was showing me, he just wanted to make sure she was dead, when he got there he was overwhelmed.

Did anyone tell him the truth?

No. **A woman on the island did – associated with the Catholic Church. They didn't tell him while he was there, it was afterwards... Three years after... three years later.**

I went to visit George's tomb here in Los Angeles.

Was it big and white? – (I'm seeing) the building is white...

Yes. A white mausoleum. Our lady of the Pines, Crenshaw area (in Los Angeles).

(Our Lady of the Pines where George Putnam's ashes are interred.)

White... yeah. He didn't pick that...

Someone else did?

His family did.

(Note: Not many people know where Putnam is buried. I was able to find it here in Los Angeles. Also, no other researcher I've met is aware that

Putnam went to Saipan for two weeks while he was stationed in Tinian. I found it by accessing his military records and seeing that he'd put in for two weeks leave on the neighboring island that is visible from Saipan. Tinian was the famous airfield built after Saipan was capture, and was where the atomic bombers flew from.)

Why we're on Saipan, I was there with a dowser – I had a dream after I got back; a campfire dream. Someone said to me "Paul is the key" and I thought "What?" Maybe it was that campfire dream you mentioned.

"The goose." They call him "the goose."

He's a tall Texan with a white hat. He found a spot by a tree behind the prison – I tried it as well, as an experiment, and the dowser arms crossed on the exact same spot. Was this the spot where Fred was executed?

No, but I feel her touching that tree. Did you look to see if anything was inscribed on the tree?

She carved something on the tree?

She did not.

Why did the dowser work?

That's where she prayed.

The tree she's talking about behind the cells.

The earth has a memory?

Yeah, that's where she got her strength.

You sure you didn't get beheaded and you just don't want to tell me?

She smiles, says "I did not get beheaded dammit!" I can't keep asking, as she tells me... she showed me Joan of Arc, (as in) "I would have

loved to have gone out with a beheading!" She shows me being in a cell sick, and these nuns taking care of her.

So what year did you die?

She says 1944.

She was there a long time.

(Aside) How come nobody knows this? Or is it out? I don't know anything about this, honestly.

Some people don't believe what islanders are saying... my feeling is you get 5 eyewitnesses to say the same thing, you should pay attention. There are over 200 who claim they saw her there.

She says they're all good people... all (the islanders) are good people.

What do you remember about your entry into the afterlife? Were you greeted by anybody?

Greeted by Fred.

That's nice.

"Then I was mad." (About his) navigating.

Fred Noonan and Amelia. (Smithsonian)

Where's your briefcase now?

Feels like NY.

Safety place, military place? FBI? Archives?

It's in a private collection – somebody... owns it.

A military guy who found it on Saipan kept it?

Something to do with George. George's son? Who is that?

David.

You spoke to him four years ago?

Yes. I did. While I was working on the film "Amelia" with Hilary Swank.

Yeah.

(Note: I've never told anyone that I spoke to David Putnam before he died. It was while I was working on "Amelia" and I called him directly and told him what I knew about Amelia. He didn't doubt it, said he'd heard "things like this" before, and thanked me for telling him what I'd discovered.)

They had a subplot in the film with AE having an affair with Gene Vidal, Gore Vidal's father, and Gore was the source of that story... I was asked to prove or disprove it – and found it was impossible they had an affair – actually, looking at his life story and photos, I think Gene himself might have been gay.

Yep. (Nods. An Aside) That's so funny.

I always thought that might be the case, no judgment involved.

I keep asking if it was a military man who has her briefcase, and she says **"No, it's in a private collection."**

Why? What are they keeping it for?

It feels very it has a connection with George – he's holding onto it... for somebody... for safety's sake. I wonder; who is George's dad? It feels like it may be from his family (GP Putnam and sons?) has his briefcase. **Has the briefcase.**

Her briefcase (lower right) was found by US Marine Robert Wallack in 1944 on Saipan. His description and that of Julious Nabers (who also saw it) matches this photo.

How did this person get it?

Were they still married (after the war)?

No, George had Amelia declared dead (even though she was still alive) and married his secretary in 1940... But are they aware of what's in it?

They are. (Aside) this is so entertaining, they're such a cool rat pack like group. I keep asking if it was a military who has her briefcase, and she says "No, it's in a private collection."

Who's all there with George and Amelia?

Amelia and her girlfriend, and George. George is entertained by what you're doing. They are sitting on an old chest, Amelia's wearing a white shirt, with riding pants, not riding boots... Her shirt is tucked in... Her hair is short, unruly.

How does Fred look?

He looks beautiful, serene, calm. He's showing me right before he was beaten.

What about George?

(Jennifer: Aside to me, re: George) Was he gay?

I don't know. He was quite the dapper fellow. I'm told he had a number of girlfriends after AE. Perhaps that's why they had their open marriage contract. Is he saying he had male lovers?

Yes. Then… somebody else came through… He showed me the Vanderbilt house, (in North Carolina) He said he had two… two different lovers.

At first George was a rebel, moved to Alaska, ran a paper, had a full beard. Then they gave him an office on 5th avenue for Putnam and Sons – it was from there he hatched this plan for AE's career.

57th Street.

(Note: How could Jennifer know that **Amelia lived at the AWA house at 353 West 57th Street** in Manhattan when George hatched the plan for the Atlantic crossing? I didn't know it, and when I looked it up, found out this was her address.)

I think so. That's when he hatched this plan to get AE into a plane – but since then he kept her in the front pages of the paper for ten years.

He liked men; it actually was the perfect marriage.

But he had a son with Dorothy… so I assume he was bi-sexual.

Right. It's just crazy, one day they'll look back on sexuality like they look back on slavery.

(Note: **I'm not trying to out anyone here. George had a son with his first wife, and married a number of other women. I'm not outing him, or Amelia or Gene Vidal, or "claiming" they were gay or bi.** If you examine their lives carefully, as I have done, they lived a carefully constructed life. To argue "So and so is gay, or bi, I know because three mediums talked to her on the Flipside" – *not my premise.* To argue that we don't die, that between lives we're all equal, and there are no judgments over sexuality – well *that's in the data.* Consistently. Repeatedly.

I'm just asking questions and Jennifer is answering them to the best of what she's sensing, feeling, or seeing. She could be hearing them wrong, and I point out that "maybe they're kidding." But as Amelia said in the previous "interview" with a medium, *"What's the point of rewriting history?"* It only matters to people who have difficulty here on the planet with their own gender identity, and if that is important to them, then by all means, embrace it. I'm offering what these mediums say "Verbatim" so if it's proven that they're inaccurate, or the information is wrong, then great, we can ignore everything they've ever said. But if any of their information is accurate – and it could only be from someone not on the planet - then we have to ask "So where did the information come from?" Or *"Don't wait until you're on the Flipside to come out of the closet."*)

So let's go back to her body for a second. I was hoping she was cremated so I could stop looking for her! If the briefcase is in NY, where are you?

"On Saipan."

What? Still buried there? C'mon. No, really? Go to that spot now..

She took me there.

Walk around for a moment.. what does it look like today?

(Jennifer proceeds to draw me a map of Saipan and the location, a place she's never been, but where I spent 8 weeks roaming around. I instantly recognize the spot she's drawn.)

Jennifer: She's showing me two different versions (of the location), she's showing me what it looked like back then and what it looks like now...

If I'm standing there (point to map) – the body is where?

Right there.

(Jennifer points to map. I'm startled because I know this place. Jennifer has never been to Saipan, never seen a picture of it, **yet she just drew an accurate map of the terrain for me**).

Why didn't they find her when they dug her up during the War?

Soldiers carved initials into the Garapan prison walls. Took this photo in 2013

They're showing me her body was in pieces... they only recovered an arm... she showed me an arm that was placed somewhere else.

But your head, your torso is here (points at the map)?

(Laughs) I asked her one more time, are you sure you weren't cremated? She said "No." I'm waiting for them to flip it; they're very consistent with these answers.

What part of your body is here? Bones? Skull?

Skull.

Is there any physical...

Hold on. That hurt actually. **Something with dental, there are dental records? I guess.**

I think there's a guy in Seattle who has her dental records.

She's smiling as if she's amused.[67]

Random question. Do you still drink buttermilk? (Buttermilk was reportedly her favorite drink.)

(Laughs) She does. She shows me how she drinks it – it's instantaneous.

Do you want me to try to find your body? Or should we look for your plane?

Dig up both... consciously I would say you're right... **dig 'em both up.**

There's a long list of people who spent lives looking for you – Tom Devine... his house was filled with memorabilia, and the day he died, his wife burned everything. He felt he had to tell the story; it drove him nuts.

Was it his heart? Did he die of a heart attack?

I think so. I interviewed him on his death bed.

---

[67] "Hunt for Earhart Leads to US Files." In an interview two GIs claimed they were ordered to dig up Amelia's body on Saipan during the war: "In taped interviews, the Marines recounted recovering a rib cage and part of an arm." **First I've heard of this (and it confirms what Amelia is saying) "They only dug up my arm."** UPI Chicago Tribune 1-17-77

Amelia tapped her heart. She's having a blast up there, around all these men.

Going back and digging for your bones, is there anyway...

I feel there's a connection to someone knowing what happened. These islanders dug up her bones from wherever they buried her, and moved them to a safer place, but they left a fragment behind. They wanted to preserve her... memory.

*So her body is located **here**? (I point to the map)*

In front and to the right. Yes.

I should look for your bones and your plane?

She's saying you're going to find it... she says "You're going to find it." What are you going to find? **I feel like the plane has been washed... but the bones aspect of it... is something that um... yeah.**

Who burned her papers?

Feel like George burned her letters.

Here's from her book "Last Flight": she sends a note to Fred: "Why did we miss Dakar; what put us north?" I think this passage refers to Amelia's navigational error, so she and Fred missed their target in Senegal.

You really do know a lot about her.

Here's something; "Land in sight." Quote from AE: "It's hard to get old... so hard... and AE said "It's hard to be old, I'm afraid I'll hate it..." she said "I think... that I'll not live to be old." .

He feels like he might have something... July 8th... I got that as well.

Amelia, can give us a page number?

She said "page 42."

From "Final story" Vincent Loomis... page 42 is a story about Paul Mantz... "Paul helped make it a long distance machine. Mantz wrote "I suggest the stabilizer be painted orange or red to be seen easier when the skies overcast... Mantz got what he wanted, orange was the color chosen...

Mantz contacted Clarence Beeland to operate master valve on the floor of the cockpit, feeding fuel from the wings..."

(Note: When Dick Spink found a gas cover on Mili he brought it back to compare the paint with actual paint from her plane. It's painted with the same kind of red/orange paint.)

What was that name?

Clarence Beeland, superintendent for a national airline in Boston.

Something that was military driven from him. She's bringing that up from that page.

So a military aspect of the flight.. Amelia, what was the military goal? To find out what the Japanese were up to? To map the pacific?

It was all of it.

(Jennifer's client appears outside her office door. I say my goodbyes and thank Amelia for the information.)

…..

End of Interview

I drove away from Jennifer's office in a daze. How could she possibly know so much about Amelia if she wasn't speaking to her directly? And as mentioned, this is the third medium I've spoken to Amelia through – and Jennifer is the only one where I've asked direct questions.

Then something really strange happened.

I was about a mile from Jennifer's office when the phone rang. It was an associate of mine, an expert in his field, a man whose word I trust completely. And he told me he had just spent a number of hours examining in great detail, incontrovertible evidence that Amelia was taken captive by the Japanese.

He said the written documents, which he could not share with me for a number of reasons, corroborated everything I had told him about Amelia. That the government *knew* she had come down in Mili, had intercepted the secret coded message, but did not *decode* it for a month.

It showed that Amelia was in Japanese hands. Of course they couldn't reveal its contents – just the way the coders working at Bletchley park on the German Enigma machine could not warn people about imminent attacks they discovered. Because then the Germans *would know their code had been broken.*

Further, this friend said that he saw evidence that the US forces had indeed found her briefcase, just as US Marine Robert Wallack had said, they had found her plane as Marine Earskin Nabors and Army Veteran Tom Devine, and the Navy and Army brothers from Colorado Springs said – and *they burned and buried it.*

He then said "But Rich, **they dug up her body, just as you've reported, but there was something interesting in this report. The US forces didn't retrieve her whole body,**" he said. I asked **"What do you mean?"**

He said **"They only recovered her arm."**[68]

What are the odds that I would hear the exact same sentence ten minutes apart? One from a medium who was speaking directly to someone on the Flipside who claimed only her arm had been recovered by US forces, and then ten minutes later to hear the exact same sentence?

It wasn't until I was editing this chapter that I found written evidence of what Amelia said. Captain Tracy Griswold was the soldier on Saipan ordered to dig up her body with two soldiers named Hansen and Burks. Hansen and Burks were interviewed by Fred Goerner, but it was Griswold who revealed in an interview in 1977 that they only dug up her arm and ribcage.

From UPI Chicago Tribune in 1977; "After 40 years, search for Amelia still goes on." "Capt. Tracy Griswold... ordered two Marines to dig up the grave." (Don Kothera interviewed (and filmed) the two soldiers who dug up the graves.) "In taped interviews, the **Marines recalled picking up a rib cage and part of an arm.**"

---

[68] This fact was confirmed in a 1977 interview with Capt. Tracy Griswold, the Marine who ordered her body dug up. I'd never seen that citation or heard "an arm and ribcage was recovered" until I was editing this; ibid. op. cit.

Amelia imparted new information to two people who did not know, could not have known that these soldiers had only found her arm. And in fact, she's given me the precise location of where her skull can be found.

To me it doesn't matter whether or not anyone believes these details. What's important is to realize that by speaking to someone on the Flipside, I was able to gain **new information.** That alone is why it's in this book. **I'm not here to prove or disprove she was gay, or bi, or that they had an open marriage, or that she was arrested, imprisoned and left to die by the government who sent her there.** Three different mediums spoke of this same information, and I can vouch that while people may have considered it an open secret – there's no written evidence of it anywhere. Doesn't mean it's not true. It just means it doesn't matter.

I'm not interested in revealing anything about Amelia that she doesn't want us to know. Not even gung ho to trek back to Saipan to dig up her skull. As she said so eloquently in her interview with Erik Medhus: *"I'm happy that people remember me for what I represented for women."* I'm happy with that as well. I always found it odd that my life has been peppered with her story as I've been "searching" for her for the past 30 years. As she pointed out – **"There's no point in searching for me. I'm still here."**

I've seen the vitriolic attacks on people who've spent their lives looking for her. For these researches to accept any of this information, they'd have to first make the leap that we don't die, then the leap that we can access people on the Flipside, then the leap that it's possible that everything they've ever known about Amelia and *the planet in general*, is wrong.

Which is why I'm not writing the *"I know where Amelia is"* book. It's why I don't care if anyone believes what she's saying or not. I've done more research on her than anyone I've met, I've spoken to more experts than anyone I know, (except perhaps Tom Crouch at the Smithsonian who is convinced beyond a shadow of a doubt that she and her plane sank in the sea) and all I can say is, if you don't like it – tough beans. *It is what it is.*

Of course, these people are not reading this book. Frankly I just don't care to argue about it. She either is telling us an accurate story – which just happens to coincide with the 200 eyewitness interviews, happens to coincide with my over 30 years of research – and doesn't coincide with any theory that's out there - or she's not. I leave it up to the reader to decide.

What's more important? *Finding out that Amelia Earhart died in prison?* **Or finding that Amelia Earhart is alive and well on the Flipside?** For her to reveal that the US only dug up her arm, and for me to hear that there's evidence of exactly the same detail ten minutes after I heard it from her – well *you can't make this stuff up.* It can't be "cryptomnesia" or "hypoxia." At some point, it's just data.

This portion of the book is to show that with the right amount of help, we can access people who are no longer on the planet, but still exist. And still have new information to impart. Do I know where her plane is? I have a good idea. Do I know where her body rests? Maybe. If I find myself back in Saipan, digging, I'll know she sent me there. If I ever do find something, you'll have heard it here first.

But if I haven't offended anyone yet with this talk of Amelia and Jesus in the same interview, just hang on.

We're in for some turbulence.

With Fred Noonan during their last flight.
(Courtesy Purdue Archives)

CHAPTER SIXTEEN:

A Between Life Session with a Medium

Yours truly with Medium Jennifer Shaffer and Hypnotherapist Scott De Tamble

"My homeland is not of this world. If it were, my servants would fight to prevent my arrest... But now my homeland is from another place." Jesus Christ (John 18:36)

(I've substituted "homeland" for the word "kingdom" in the above passage, as kingdom *and* homeland *are interchangeable for those with a royal family.)*

Jennifer Shaffer decided that she wanted to do a between life session with Scott. She had never been "under hypnosis" before, and offered to have me come along with my camera and film it. Since I've filmed a number of people under hypnosis during their between life sessions, I've learned that everyone is different in their experiences. This is a pretty unusual past life memory.

Jennifer went pretty far pretty fast. It was only a few minutes into her session when Scott asked her:

Scott: Look around. What do you see?

Jennifer: There's a pyramid. When I looked inside of it, it was – I see symbols. That felt – not like Egypt... I see somebody with green eyes and dark hair, I feel like I've seen her before. She's lying on... it looks like an illuminated bed, like the floor, but it looks like it's made out of crystal.

Tell me more about this person with the green eyes. What do you feel about her?

Like she knows things. Feels like something happened in this place, it was a sanctuary.

Let's go to the time when something happens in that place.

Ooh. (stressed) I'm.. (can't breathe). I'm.. crushed... (having a hard time saying it).

Something falls on you?

Something destroyed it. And everything fell down. I'm floating above.

Hover there for a moment if you will, I want to understand what's occurred here. What was this place, what was it used for?

It was used for healing. Felt like sick children. Their bodies, they were sick. They were placed on these crystal beds.

Why are you here? What is your role?

I was supposed to save them. Felt like I was protecting them.

And this building collapses? Describe that.

It was hit... it was attacked, but by something.. It was not a natural force.

Where did that force come from?

Somewhere in the sky.

Now this place of healing...

It's like a temple.

This temple of healing, where is this place, what world is it on? What's the name of this world?

Tee.. it's hard.. Teehara. I keep seeing something went really wrong. I should have seen it.. I should have known. (stressed)

Is this temple on Earth or someplace other than Earth?

Came from.. yeah.. five. (I was on) Seven first.. then five.

What does five refer to?

The dimension.

This was a deliberate attack or accident?

It was deliberate. Something was used the wrong way. Something was misused.. I felt it was those rocks – those crystals.

Tell me about the rocks, or crystals, how were they misused?

They were used as a source for weapons; we used them for healing, they used them as light weapons. I should have seen it coming. No one would listen. I got everyone out, but I stayed. I thought it could defend itself, but it didn't.

So the attack got through, destroyed the building and it fell on you?

All of it just fell on me and crushed me.

Who did you give this warning to?

I gave the warning to a man who I thought was in a different dimension -- who was supposed to control…

How did you communicate with that man?

Through our thoughts.

You sensed these stones were going to be used against you and you contacted a man in that dimension? Was he a perpetrator or friend? Who was he in relation to you?

I feel like he was our Counsel – our Dimension Counsel – only way to describe it is like the U.N. He was our UN counsel.

So the people in the various dimensions have an organization? What was the purpose of this?

To co-exist.

On the Earth time line, currently we're at 2015, what year or how many years ago did this event take place?

It's like 7 million years ago, it looks like the future but it's not.

Tell me about your people. What do they look like?

Very pale skin, the children... they felt like they were interdimensional children, who couldn't acclimate properly to this dimension. They were weak and sick.

Tell me about yourself in this life. Do you have a physical body?

Yes. I was a female. Dark, dark hair, bright greenish blue eyes, pale skin, long, long, long hair – I felt that I was in charge of everything but I just didn't... I missed it.

Do this for me. I want you to go back in time to a happier time, maybe in her youth or at some younger time, I'm curious about where she lives and how she spends her time.

I'm by the ocean and I feel like I'm being protected. For what I'm supposed to do. I feel like my horse can fly. I remember flying; I can be in different places really fast.

You have a horse?

It's a grey and white horse, it's eyes are blue and it feels very protective, it's supposed to watch over me. I talk to it all the time. We don't speak, but we transfer thoughts.

Telepathic communication?

Yes, it's how everyone communicates. I don't speak, but people do. I can't make it out; it's a vibration language, but I can tell what they're thinking.

Are there others like you?

My horse. I've been told that there will be children coming in like me... and we'll all be taking care of them.

Where did you come from - what's your origin?

I came from a different dimension. To help. (She cries) It's the dimension that killed me.

I want to understand about this. What are you feeling?

The reason why they sent me (to the 5th) as a child was I would learn things that weren't in our other dimension; it was the love – and then to teach the other kids that came in (from the 7th) about how to love.

So what did you learn about love and how to love?

(Cries) That it hurts. Kids can't acclimate.

What were you supposed to do with that info?

I was supposed to bring it back. I didn't want to go (back). I was afraid it wouldn't stay. The plan, the emotions, the feelings.

You thought if you went back to your home you might lose that.

The children.

You didn't want to go back to your home?

They were using things for war, for power, it's not how it was supposed to be.

Coming to this other dimension gave you a different perspective about things?

Yes. I learned to hurt.

Just having emotions or the knowledge that your people were misusing them?

They destroyed everybody. They were afraid… (wipes tears) because I didn't want to go back - they destroyed everything.

Did they call you back and you refused?

I tried to tell them that they were going to hurt us.

You reported to the inter-dimensional counsel man that they were planning to misuse things? How did he respond?

He didn't believe me. They were afraid that I would bring the power back to use it against them. They were afraid I would teach… them what these others were doing in their dimensions - because I could go there in my mind. They 7th feared that on level 5, that I would teach them how to fight.

Like the 7th dimension knows how to fight. So the 7th dimension was afraid you'd teach the 5th dimension their skills.

Right. Because I didn't come back.

They thought you were sort of a renegade or something like that?

I was expendable.

Let's focus on a time when you're in this temple and you're working with these kids, explain how the process works and what your hopes are – what's happening? What do you do?

I help them get acclimated. They float above these stones, **I do some type of scan – I'm able to tell where they come from what pain they're in and what needs to be done to help. Their hearts contain all of the information.**

How do you scan them?

I do it mentally.

You pick up this information?

Everything's coded.

Let's go to a case or a child you're scanning and tell me what you're picking up about that child.

He's familiar. His eyes. I feel like he's from the dimension I came from. From the 7th.

Okay. So how does that make you feel working with a child from your home?

Love. I feel like I can show him what love was.

As you scan this child, what do you pick up?

I'm putting my hands over him, some type of heat between the crystal below him and whatever goes through my hands, it's not me - I'm just the contact.

You're channeling some kind of healing energy?

It takes a long time. To heal his heart. It's still broken… I feel his physical heart looks black, I've never seen it before, it feels like it has to just get recalibrated and… how do I explain?

Take your time.

When that space (in his heart) gets healed then his physical form is able to "land." (come to Earth) It's fascinating – he's translucent until he heals. It's hard to explain.

Then as he heals?

He becomes more dense.

You're teaching people in this temple how to heal, how to help these children, how to help them transition?

Yes, through the heart.

Now this energy that you channel – where does it originate from?

It originates from the Earth.

From the Earth? So how do you bring that energy up from the Earth and through your hands into the children, what's the process?

It's from these crystals - it's from – **there are things that are floating, there's geometric shapes and they carry, they hold what feels like memories, cellular memories,** I don't know how to describe it.

(Note: As noted, I called these geometric shapes "ball bearings" during my first between life session. Also crystals appear in a number of between life sessions, reportedly as "objects that can be created through a focus on healing energy.")

Like bits of information?

From a time that was more trusting.

You're able to gather this more trusting healing energy up from the Earth? Maybe amplify it or focus it through the crystals?

Yes.

And direct it this through these children, is that a good description?

Yes.

What does it feel like when you're channeling that healing energy?

All white – everything just floats, everything is clear; it's the only time (that) it's clear.

Tell me once again, to the best of your knowledge, are we in the vicinity of planet Earth as we know it now? As you're healing these children? Are we on this planet, here, Earth?

No. It's a different world.[69]

(Note: I've seen Scott do this a few times. He accepts what people say, and then later, after they've filled in the description, asks a question that he instinctively knows the answer to. In this case, she thought she was talking about the earth, but upon closer examination, feels it's another planet somewhere else in our universe. As it's referred to in hypnotherapy, an "off world experience.")

And at that time, 7 million years ago, how far away was that different world from the world we call Earth – was it in the same galaxy? Or different galaxy?

I feel it's in a different galaxy. It feels so… but it feels like here.

It feels like here in what way?

Just… my horse.

What did you call that other world? Did it have a name?

I want to say *Pleiadian*. I think it might be called Pleiades, I'm not sure.

In this world of Pleiades, this sort of conflict between dimensions, where they played out on this world of Pleiades or different worlds, different planets? Or different dimension on Pleiades somewhere?

---

[69] I've had a few reports of people remembering the "destruction" of another planet that "we used to live on." I don't know if this is the same description, but Scott had barely begun the session when she went here.

Different dimensions on Pleiades. It was an experiment (done) for Earth. We were trying to figure out the human mind and what it needed to survive.

Trying to figure out the human mind?

How it worked.

In terms of what?

Being on Earth.

Do you sense that there was a prototype Earth body already existing or where the people on Pleiades experimenting to see what different bodies would work on this other planet we now call Earth?

That's what they were doing on Pleiades. To figure out if we can incarnate there. **The planet Earth and how to do it on Mars, but it was not working.**

Tell me about Mars.

I thought that's where... Mars didn't work.

Was Mars used as a place of habitation before Earth?

Yes.

So what happened on Mars, why didn't it work?

They were... they went hungry.

They weren't able to feed themselves or fuel themselves?

Right.

The bodies used on Mars are they like Earth bodies?

Different... felt like they were a different kind of - they used animals first. Some type... to see if they could survive.[70]

---

[70] I offer this without judgment. Not that there are "statues" or "monuments" on Mars, but don't be surprised when we find "rudimentary life" that didn't survive due to the lack of a magnetic zone like the earth has. It's entirely possible if Mars had water on it, that some life formed and didn't survive.

Experimenting about how life might be viable?

Yes.

A photo from that old familiar planet, Mars. (NASA)

Ok it's time to move forward now to the time after your body was crushed and broken and you, your energy is rising up. It rises up higher and higher, shifting out of that dimension.. and you are entering that spiritual state between your incarnations.

(She smiles, sudden tears).

Entering that state of spiritual energy. Grace. And so.. tell me about that.

Time passed in that dimension. I can't make out the faces, but there's a lot of people, feels like .. they're all.. I'm in the center, and I'm looking at all of them, **I can't quite make them out but they're clapping as if a performance just ended.**

Congratulating you, welcoming you?

Part of me understands but part of me is angry (about the loss of the children). There's thirty people around me, and there's a lot of people in front of me. One on each side and behind me – (wipes tears)

What do you sense about these people? Are they special in some way?

Yeah, I communicated with them, when I was there.

What sorts of things would you communicate?

I was asking for help. They helped me to get information for the children. It was as if they were exempt from rules.

Any of these beings seem more senior or all equal?

One on my left feels like he's more senior. We're in front of what I assume is the council, for all dimensions.

This being on your left side, how would you describe them?

It's a light form. But they changed back when they look inwards, (to) a female presence. Very motherly. Very wise.

Ask her to share her name with you, what do you call this wise motherly person?

(Smiles. Shakes her head.) She says "Mary." I can't believe it. (Shakes her head softly – cries.)

Let's take a moment for you to spend.. some private time with Mary – if you'd like to do that. Perhaps she can embrace you..

Wow. (wipes tears) She was the one who helped me with all the kids, these magic shapes were part of her consciousness, she's showing me all the different times she was there in different forms. I just didn't know it was her; she took me out before I got crushed, but I didn't know.

(Note: As fantastical as this session sounds, these "magic shapes" appear in "Flipside" – are reportedly geometric shapes that contain all the information from previous lifetimes.)

I want to speak to Mary directly, I'd ask her to put her responses through your voice or mind, is that okay?

Yes.

I would ask you Mary, what is your relationship to this soul here?

"We've been together many, many times. Sometimes she's helped me."

Mary, would you say you're more on the same level, like a peer or more advanced?

"I am more advanced. But there's no hierarchy. I've been on many more planets."

Mary you have more experience incarnating?

(chuckles) **"Yes."**

Mary, how do you feel about Jennifer's performance in that life?

"She succeeded, she found love. That was really what she was supposed to do. She found more though; she found she could hurt. At the time she didn't know it would give her more love."

So along with love comes hurt?

"It's healing. Naturally."

How would you describe it in your realm or words?

"Love is in everything. And is everywhere. It is in the music. It is in the voice. It is in the love that she found in that child, in her horse, it is in the bricks that fell on her. It's everywhere."

(Note: There's a section in Flipside about how everything we create, art, music, work – contains some essence of who we are, and that these things we create can heal, depending how much love we put into the work. Interesting to hear it put in this fashion instead.)

So what does Jennifer need to understand?

"She needs to allow herself that by hurting and feeling, she's learning to love. Living is painful. We gave her the ability to see other dimensions to work with advisors, to meet all the appropriate people to love. And to learn; but she's not listening. **She should let go."**

Mary, I want to ask – what advice do you have for Jennifer in her current lifetime?

To laugh. To be fearless. Fear will stop everything.

Jennifer wanted to meet with her council and we have questions to be asked.

"We're here." (aside) It's so fast.

Describe this council for me.

There are twelve.

How are they arranged?

Mary is one of the 12. She's at the end of the table. On the left end.

(Note: There was a break in the interview to change the camera card. Jennifer said she felt she wanted to view another lifetime, when Mary was her mother on earth. She sees her family together.)

Jennifer: I have five other brothers and sisters, **two of them died.**

And what part of the world are you in? In this life?

I'm in a monastery. There's chanting. I'm in the back corner. Feels safe.

Why have they come to this monastery?

I feel like we had to leave. We had to leave. Took us two years to get there.

Where did you come from?

East. We went near Bhutan... we didn't go to the top because it was too cold. My mom is still married, we're fair, I have red hair. We had to blend in, but it's really cold.

Why did you leave?

Truth, (we're) searching for truth.

What was your original land?

Jerusalem.

And you've gone all the way to Asia in the mountains?

Took us two years.

What do they call you?

Sarah.[71]

Who is traveling with you, Sarah?

There's a group. Ten.

---

[71] "According to various legends... in the year 42, Lazarus, his sisters Mary and Martha, Mary Salome (the mother of the Apostles John and James), Mary Jacobe and Maximin were sent out to sea in a boat. They arrived safely on the southern shore of Gaul at the place later called Saintes-Maries-de-la-Mer. In some accounts Sarah, a native of Upper Egypt, appears as the black Egyptian maid of one of the Three Marys, usually Mary Jacobe." (Wikipedia) This same story is told in the Shannon chapter.

Is there a leader?

Yes.

Tell me about that person.

No. (shakes her head.) I can't.

You're perfectly safe to share this information. You're with friends.

(Sighs.) I feel that my mom is married to Jesus.

Is Jesus the leader of the group or someone else?

There're two leaders. Working together. They're transferring knowledge. One was a Prince.

How old is Jesus at the time of this meeting?

I want to say he's 54.

Jesus is your father, is that right? How old are you?

Yes. I want to say I'm 28.

What's the method of them transferring knowledge?

There are lots of scrolls; they're saving them, putting them in caves. There are writings and writings.

What's the information in the scrolls about?

Wisdom.

I would speak with Mary; why are we shown this life in the mountains?

"That she's traveled far. That she knows that there should be no fear. And to become more "one with all."

How does one become more one with all?

"No judgment. She struggles with the (missing person) cases. They hurt. Then they always serve. That's all."

Thank you Mary.

(aside) I want to say goodbye (to her).

There's no goodbyes here. She can stay with you always. Tell me about the council - is there a spokesperson?

They're all equal, but all different lights. The colors are different frequencies and each member has a different frequency; it's energy centers of the brain. (She smiles)

I would ask the council, will one of you speak with us today?

"Yes. We will speak."

Speak through the voice of this woman here today, and I have many questions for you. Are you willing to address them?

"Yes. Call me William."

So William, how is Jennifer doing as a soul?

"She is more of a danger to herself; she's like a little kid who scrapes her knees. She has all of the keys, everyone does."

Tell me about the keys that she has.

"She has the keys to all the dimensions, of all the places and the sacraments, the rituals, and their purpose. She gets closest and then goes back to feeling like she's going to die. She's not going to die. **No one dies.**"

I would ask you about Jennifer's psychic abilities in this life.

"She needs to reach farther and not be consumed by how small people think; it's not their fault. Fear is the only thing holding her back because she has been killed many times for speaking." (aside) Interesting. "Her throat hurts, right?"

That's right, William. Tell her about that.

"She has to not feel unconnected to that 7th dimension of what we had to portray. She is connected but is constantly annoying us about not being connected." (Aside: Oh my God).

She's always connected? How can she feel that?

"I stopped making us separate; she has her rituals to feel safe and while she knows that's just to keep her fear down, she should just know that we're here…. **We're here to help her, the last thing we want is for her not to hear (us). She is the one holding her fear."**

What is the primary lesson in the Jennifer lifetime?

"The primary lesson is to make the other side known." (aside) That's impossible.

What does that mean?

"To acknowledge spirit; she doesn't always acknowledge them. She thinks she has to shut down (after a session). Even if you don't like something, you put that vibrational frequency out. Well, she puts out that she can't do it or that she's afraid, or that she just wants to be by herself; that does not work."

How would you advise her in this?

To just "be." **She makes us exhausted and *we don't get tired.*** "Exhausting" she says. Good thing we love her.[72]

We have some questions for you today: What is the best way for Jennifer to translate spiritual information?

"She needs to put her guard down first, then she needs to say "It's okay." She needs to treat them as if they're going to tell her their darkest secrets, even though there is no dark. Then she needs to listen."

How can she put her guard down?

"By putting her heart open. She forgets that the heart is the gateway."

That reaches back to the…

"Yes, she heals hearts. She's vulnerable at first, she's afraid of getting hurt."

What does she need to understand about that?

---

[72] Funny concept. Jennifer keeps asking if she's talking to spirit, and they get exhausted confirming to her they are.

"She needs to let that go. She needs to know that we're taking care of the frequencies that have caused that pain from her lifetimes. But it's like cleaning up a big mess, it takes many years in her lifetime."

Is there anything she can do to accelerate that process?

"She can be quiet." (Jennifer laughs)

Question: Why does it feel sort of distant talking to the other side as of late? Has something shifted?

"That has to do with the frequencies of the plane; she has been shown that it's very challenging. There are certain planetary things happening within your spirit that are causing the disruption... It's like shaking things up You have to pay attention. **She just needs to know that it doesn't matter how connected she feels – the information is always correct, is it not?"**

So this disruption of the frequencies, is that necessary?

"Yes, because there are patterns now forming that are taking place to get rid of the some of the old to bring in some of the new – the infrastructure can't handle more of it."

How long will this last?

"It will last as long as it takes. She keeps asking us questions within the answers. It's very entertaining."

(Note: It's an unusual conversation going on. Jennifer is speaking on behalf of her guide, then in her mind asking more questions, and the spirit guide responds by saying **"she's bugging us with questions inside of questions. It's hilarious."**)

Tell us about her connection to Mary Magdalene?

Mary was her mother, is her mother, is her guide, is her... keeper. That's why there's so much love there.

Has Mary incarnated since that time?

She has several times.

Someone wants to know if it's possible to bring forth people she's spoken with in the past. For example, Jesus. Can we ask him questions?

(Note: Ahem. That someone would be me. I'm in the room, filming this, by the way. I'm curious as to what's going to happen. The question is pretty simple, and Jennifer can easily say "No, I don't sense him around." Or "I have to see if I can ask someone." But instead she says:)

"Yes."

*I would ask **Jesus, what he would like to share with Jennifer today?***

"She knows. *She knows.* Everything is about having internal faith in one's gifts. Which is a result of love at the precipice. She knows."

And this soul was your daughter in that lifetime as Sarah?

"She was my daughter."

Where was Sarah born?

"In a town…" (Jennifer aside) can't be… – "That's where you were born."

And Jesus, where was Sarah born?

"She was born in Bethlehem."

How many brothers or sisters does she have in that life?

"Five. Two of them died."

Four living children of Jesus?

"Three."

Sarah and two others?

"Yes."

Their names?

"Michael and Jacob."

What became of these three as they lived and grew and moved on?

"They had their own families. But we had to leave."

Why did you have to leave?

"There were other things that were in story that needed to be found, that needed to be taught."

You had to leave on that long journey to Asia?

"Yes."

So what was the purpose of that journey?

"To find truth."

Did you find truth?

"Yes."

Can you share something of that with us today?

"It's through prayer and charity, it's through a different avenue to arrive at the same place. It's through the same practice of selflessness and giving that was misconstrued in Jerusalem."

Jesus are you saying that the Crucifixion as depicted, didn't happen?

"I didn't die, no."

Were you put on the cross?

"Yes."

But you survived that?

"Yes. I was able to leave."

Who helped you?

"You have to ask Mary."

Let me just get this clear – you didn't not have a physical death on the cross but survived?

"Yes."

How long where you there on the cross?

"Two... two of your days."

I'm sorry for that suffering. I'm glad that you moved on. Tell us about your later life. After you traveled to Asia what did you do?

"I stopped in different places along the way. Ashtar. There was a map. We actually followed a star, like the one that was followed by the shepherds, but we were shown where to go – and we went."

You have a heavenly guidance?

"Yes."

Ashatar?

"It was .. yes. Ashtar."[73]

Was that an actual star or something else?

"It was a being."

A being?

"Yes."

Tell us about this being.

"Someone I spoke to, to know where to go."

Like a spiritual guide?

"Yes."

Does your spiritual guide Ashtar still communicate with you?

"Yes."

Would that being like to step forward and say hello?

"No. He's reincarnated. He's on Earth."

What role is he playing?

(Laughs) "He wanted to learn how to drink. He wanted to learn how to do drugs. The feeling .. don't worry, he'll be back soon. Poor kid."

---

[73] Ashtar (sometimes called Ashtar Sheran) is the name given to an extraterrestrial being or group of beings which some number of people claim to have channeled. UFO contactee George Van Tassel was the first to have claimed to have received a message, in 1952, from Ashtar. (Wikipedia) Not sure if this is the same fellow.

Where did you breathe your last? On Earth?

"Interesting. There's something that made me sick. But I was ready to go. It was quick."

And what about your wife? Was she still around?

"She left before me. She didn't want to grow old. She.. (*something*) in Spain."

Was she in Spain when she passed?

"She was in one of her travels, and her heart…"

I would ask you what part of the world were you in when you became ill and died?

"I was still in Asia."

Jesus, what message do you have for Jennifer in her life today?

"To complete her mission."

And what do you see as her mission?

"It's too simplistic for her – it's *just to be.* That's it. She calls it balance; but it's not. She knows it has to do with healing (in) all dimensions, within her and with others."

Jesus, what words would you share with us on this planet now?

"Richard. You need to let go, you need to write more about the other side. Not from here. From there."

Help him understand.. he needs to let go of what?

"He needs to let go of making money…" Jennifer: hold on I'm consulting... **"He needs to not judge anything that comes to him. He still has doubts." (pause) "Maybe about this conversation."**

(Note: *Gee Jesus, thanks a lot.* It's always startling when someone addresses me directly during a session. I set up a camera on a tripod and disappear in a corner; I don't speak until the session is over. I have to allow that it could be my friends speaking to me – but then Jesus covered that disbelief in his reply. I'm working on "not judging anything that comes to me." Easy to say, hard to do. I'm very familiar with the not making money part of this endeavor.)

What would you say to address those doubts?

"To talk more about his ability to talk to the other side. To write from there."

Like automatic writing? Channeling? Something of that nature?

"It could be automatic writing, channeling; whatever doesn't scare him."[74]

You mention that... he should write from the other side. How can he connect with the other side? What's the procedure?

"By asking his friends who have recently passed, and then just not judge it. They're always around."

What words of light would you share with the world today?

"To not feel guilty. There is no hell. Hell usually happens right before you leave. There is no hell."

Is there anything else you wish to share with Jennifer today, something she can take with her?

"To call upon her guides and then trust that they're there, she keeps asking if we're here. We're always here."

William, in terms of Jennifer's ability to hear from the spirit realm, what is going on? If you were a professor, describe the process.

It would be all the layers at once – all the dimensions fall into one. She keeps trying to figure out when, where, how; she doesn't need to. We make it easy; **if you saw the Earth pulsating, you'd see the etheric body, the Vitruvian man, you'd see that everything, that oneness is real, the oneness is what she goes through.**

---

[74] (Note: I must say, when I'm working on this material, time stands still. Further, I have been having pretty entertaining dreams, where just prior to falling asleep I get the sensation of people standing on the sidelines, arms crossed, waiting until I nod off to talk to me. As I fall asleep my last conscious thoughts are often "Hang on, I'm coming already!")

Vitruvian Man; Leonardo da Vinci. (Wikimedia)

She still tries to get where it's from; we make it all one for her. It's walking through a door of time where it doesn't exist – **everything's all the same.**

How can Jennifer share her talents with the planet on a wider scale?

She has to not think that she has to do that. She will be given opportunities that will take her into those dimensions that will make it to where the masses will feel more comfortable with connecting to their own, she has to trust she's in the right space. And keep herself in a playful state. She forgets to play.

How does she effect a better transition from working with spirit to the public?

Walking through the door will help facilitate the transition; she just has to say that in her mind. That's it, it's not difficult.

How does she stay above the grief?

Ask them after (they've crossed over) Know that it's okay, know that they knew - they decided to go into this work (lifetime), to stay above the grief. She needs to know it's not real; it's a perfect world. It's perfect order. She needs to open her heart and she needs to let other people open her heart.

So what's the source of the fear of water?

Drowning. She has to be by the water in every lifetime. It goes back to her lifetime being underwater.

Did she dunk witches or torture them with water in Salem?

(Note: In my first interview with her, she remembered a lifetime where she was an executioner in Salem who dunked witches to death.)

Yes. She was very brutal. **But she chose to be that – we advised against it, she chose it.**

Why did she choose it, what did she gain?

She was trying to work out the balance of fear - a balance. She thought it better to be the perpetrator – she had been killed many times for being part of all dimensions... So she decided "I'm done. I want to go to the other side, I'm mad." We told her "It's not the same" that she shouldn't do it. And we told her not to, but she did it and it haunted her for hundreds and hundreds of years...

Is there any residue left over from that?

It's almost gone – she still has night terrors; she will get over it.

What does she need to understand to let all that go?

She's learning there is enough balance within her, she doesn't have to feel that she has to do anything, she would get more done by doing nothing; it's like talking to someone that's not listening, you can only imagine.

Jennifer has a question about the Akashic records; has she used them?

She does, every time she looks at someone – she does. As a child she would understand why someone was hurt, without ever knowing that they were hurt, she can see things through these lives, she was always accused of having too many friends, eventually that changed, she had to.

What's it like for her to access -- is there a library, how does that work?

It's instant, she can ask questions... Then we go – she goes, gets the information and comes back.

Is there a central repository of these records, like an energetic library, how does that work?

They're accessed through your thoughts; when you know that they're not your thoughts, that's how you know you've accessed the records.

What is the process of being a spirit medium? How does that work?

Hundreds of years and hundreds of bodies. We have to know every feeling in every dimension, she decided she wanted this one as she would say "locked and loaded." Funny.

So she prepared this body and life to have that gift?

Oh yes, this team, the infrastructure, it's like building a high rise building - which is a technical tower for her, it took years to assimilate, it took years to understand it. Imagine the frequencies from every dimension hitting all at once; it's very challenging to build a tower that takes it.

So why was Jennifer brought here today, what does she need to get from all of this?

She won't believe it for some time, then eventually she'll have a reminder. That lifetime was by far the most important she had in thousands of years.

What was important about it?

It was important to learn *love* - that was her foundation. That was the "cellular blocks" that came from her structure, even then, she chose to take a life that would be painful. She knew that the masses would be annihilated, she still took that on – just like her dad. (Jesus) Don't you see? Look what Jesus did to her – look how scared she was after she was (in that lifetime) with Jesus – look at all those DNA detonation points in all those lifetimes; all the witches, all in the name of Christianity burnt and slaughtered, so many deaths, and she keeps coming back, and to learn a fraction of what it takes to really, really become a medium. **So many useless deaths… and then, look --she talks to the deceased who won't ever tell her they're dead. Ironic, right?**

I would ask the entire council anything else they'd like to share?

Please remind her to love. And to love all the differences within her and to know that everything is in perfect chaos – perfect, she designed the best state that there is, with the best team, can you only imagine – it took over 500 years just to plan this lifetime. Pretty amazing.

All these lives were building blocks?

Yes. A lot of times, she kept on leaving; she took out, she kept breaking the pattern. We would say, *not breaking the pattern*. She committed suicide more times than you can possibly imagine, she missed home so much, and she does… all time.

Thank you. Mary? Can you come forward?

Yes. I think of "home" to find Mary.

What else shall we have Jennifer experience today? Anything else she needs to experience?

That I'm not separate from her, that we are… just as she goes and travels to the Akashic records; she can do that through us. She can bring us through all the time, we're not separate, she forgets that.

When Jennifer works with her clients, are there particular guides or two who overlook that work?

Yes, she knows five guides.

Would they like to step forward and say hello today?

They would love to.

We invite them to do so.

(voice changes) "Hello. We've already met me." (voice changes) "Hi. This is Gabrielle, I've been assigned to her for very good reason."

What is that?

"For healing…"

You help her clients with healing?

"Yes... with the color green iridescent green or pink that you see – I fly in to help. Her daughter sees me. She's doing a great job."

Do you have a message for Jennifer for today?

"Her heart is going fast and we love it; we're very excited, very excited, it's been fun."

Thank you Gabrielle. Thank you for your healing work.

"You're welcome."

The other guides?

(voice changes) "I'm the future aspect of her, I help her transport, when she does her psychic work - I get the information with her, I keep her safe, from her mind."

You're a future aspect of her.

"I'm part of the crew that she saw working. We're the same, I'm a future guide, but I'm part of her soul group."

You're studying to be a guide?

"No. I'm her guide that's been with her through all her lifetimes, but just recently she's been able to access a lot more. I help her."

So what does this future aspect come in?

"When she looks into the future for others… she gets input - even though she doesn't say it."

You assist with that.

"Yes. She sees the back of my head. She still has lots to learn."

Do you have a special message?

Yes. Tell her that the future is not set in stone, just to remind her.

How does that work? If a psychic looks into the future are they seeing possibilities?

"They're seeing what their environment brings. So at that point in time, everything is geometrical designed. The patterns, the matrix is full of outcomes.

Jennifer is very precise with what she gets, she just has to make sure she doesn't take the free will away; that's against the rules and she knows it. But she forgets on a conscious level, it's not her fault, that's all."

With our free will aren't we allowed to change? Go left instead of right?

"Yes, you are."

Then what's the point of looking at the future if it's so changeable?

"Some people want to know; they just want to know. Some people want to know if their child's going to be okay. That the child will be okay."

How can you see the future if it's not set in stone?

(Sighs) "Jennifer is able to see that; she's able to see when someone dies, so when someone asks about the child dying, she's able to say if the child's going to live or not. That provides a tremendous amount of assurance... but she's not in charge of that. (If you need assurance you should) - go to a therapist. But the end points provide comfort."

This is my question –

"We are meant to change our outcomes, yes."

If the future is malleable, changeable...

"Some things are not, my friend."

If I ask Jennifer to look at something in my future, is there an 80% chance, 100% chance.. of this happening? How does that work?

"No. She will say what she is supposed to say. So she's very good about asking. If you're asking a question, just ask her. She will tell you what the probable outcome is."

Probable outcome, thank you. So she's looking at probable outcomes.

"Scott, this is between semantics with you. Let her go."

But since I have a master of time I have the chance to ask these questions...

"Yes. Do you ever think it's funny people say that "time is not set in stone," yet it represents the stone ages? I find that funny."

Is there another guide who'd like to step forward?

"Hm. Yes. (battery change on camera – another voice change) She is just as much an experiment as she thinks she is – in a good way. We learn from her."

You're all in this together?

"Oh yes. Absolutely."

When you say an Atlantean ...

"That just means we met during Atlantean times. I have chosen to be her guide."

Tell me about Atlanteans. Was that in the same dimension?

"Atlanteans were the by-product of the misuse of the environment, they were highly educated, they had everything and they destroyed themselves."

What part of the world did they dwell?

"There's several places. Jennifer is very connected, she tried to save her friend. A family, with the family of children living there."

Can you tell us about these sacred stones that Jennifer and her friend Michelle have?

"It causes an electronic magnetic field more powerful than anything else, and there are keepers all over the world of this field."

How can they be put to use?

"By holding them and bringing forth the consciousness from those times. Imagine holding the secrets to the universe, all they do is tap you into it; it's a key. You have the key. Ask questions, ask it to help you and it does, it goes into the vortex of energy and manipulates whatever is going on.. as long as it's (the information) in accord to your own matrix… (path and journey)."

Is there fifth guide who wants to step forward?

It's Mary.

Mary, you assist with Jennifer's clients and work as well?

"Yes. She sees me all the time. She just didn't know it was me. I have a hard time getting close to Jennifer because she starts getting emotional; we all know she doesn't like that."

Why does she become emotional?

"Because we get her out of things (tough spots), I get her out of "universals." I'm her travel companion, (through) interdimensional places… it's a part of home. She's gotten herself into some real doozies, as she would say…"

These five guides, I would ask you to give Jennifer any sort of message anything you'd like to share with her today.

(Laughs) (All said as if from differing points of view) **"Do what you do, with love, stick to the plan.** Take free will out of your patterns. We like to kid. **Look in everybody's eyes, you will see home.** Share what you know and don't, the things that you say might not make sense to them at that moment in time, it's not meant to. It's your job to give them information, you're healing happens in different dimensions… you gather all the bad things that have happened to people in different dimensions and you heal that - like your work Scott."

Thank you all. I'm so please you stepped forward to say hello.

"Absolutely."

Is there anything else that you would like Jennifer to experience today?

"Tell her that we can hear her heart; all she has to do is call us in; she just has to want things to be healed. It's sending colors, that vibrational pattern that infiltrates what happens when you get sick. She knows how to do it, remind her."

So Mary, anything else Jennifer needs to explore?

She just gave me a kiss on the cheek.

Anything you want to explore? Do you feel complete for today?

Yes.

I want to ask all of the guides who've shared with us today to give Jennifer a final message that she can take with her.

They're all holding hands. **"Stay strong. Be well. Laugh. Love. And use light. So there's no dark. You're safe. Always. Love."**

Thank you all.

Afterwards: Jennifer observes: "(It was) like I just went through a time warp. I was so mad, trying so hard to ask my own questions, but they kept me at bay. I was so mad at (my chief counselor) William. I don't even know how to process that…

…… *End of session*

I'm not sure I can either.

I debated whether to include these Jesus and Mary references in my work. After all, I can't prove any of it. However, based on my premise, "If you get one eyewitness report it's anecdotal, but if you get ten eyewitness reports it becomes data" I realized I was getting a number of reports about the same individuals.

I can tell you that in the past, whenever someone mentioned the life of Jesus, I've gone into a Catholic brain freeze. When I first heard stories of Jesus "surviving the Crucifixion" I assumed it was wishful thinking, or that it had come from someone with an agenda.

Is it possible Jennifer remembered a lifetime where she saw her mother as Mary Magdalene and her father as Jesus Christ? I'd like to point out she's never claimed any such thing consciously prior to the session. She spends so much of her time in her practice helping people she forgot what she said during this session. I told her I was transcribing it, she said "great!" then later, I said, "You remember, you claimed to be Sarah, the daughter of Jesus." She looked at me with those blinding blue eyes and blinked. "Oh. Right," she said.

If she was trying to create a previous lifetime that she could use to sell books, or sell her practice, or sell anything really, I would report that. She says she wasn't aware of the stories of Jesus' "children" but there is a body of writing that claims Jesus had a daughter known as "Saint Sarah." [75]

I argue that a past life regression is either someone imagining (pretending) they had a previous lifetime, or that they're accessing someone else's previous lifetime, or that they're accessing their own previous lifetime. And as we've seen repeatedly in these sessions, no one accesses the memory of any lifetime with complete clarity.

---

[75] "Dan Brown's novel The Da Vinci Code used the premise for its plot line. The 2007 documentary The *Lost Tomb of Jesus* proposed that evidence existed to show that Jesus was married to Mary Magdalene and that their son was named Judah, based upon inscriptions found on ossuaries discovered in Jerusalem in 1980. Biblical scholar and author James Tabor has recently affirmed his belief in a married Jesus, while Karen King announced the discovery of text in a Coptic papyrus fragment, alleged to be a translation of a lost 2nd century Gospel, in which Jesus is made to refer to "my wife". (reported to be fake) (Wikipedia)

It's like reconnecting an old hard drive to the computer that hasn't been used in a long time, and the "clusters" are out of place. Sometimes there are bits and pieces of a memory – a time, a face, a place, a year. Sometimes other family members, sometimes none.

I haven't met anyone else who has a memory of Jesus being their father, but I can certainly imagine that being the case. But even then, if we have our own "memory" of being someone, or somewhere else, who's to argue that it is or isn't what our memory is? (Other than those who say "nonsense" and ignore the bits of new information that couldn't come from elsewhere.)

The knock on past life regression has always been "Everyone remembers a lifetime as Cleopatra or being on the Titanic." There are people who claim these kinds of memories, (I've yet to meet one) but there's almost never anyone to question them about it. "What's your father's name? Where did you live? What street did you grow up on? Why did you choose that life and why did you choose this life, and what do the two have in common?"

Many hypnotherapists argue it's not important to recall the details, because whether it's true or not isn't relevant. The memory of something can be a healing experience, and therapists are in the business of healing, not forensic research.

What can I vouch for that's in this account? Well, I've known Jennifer for a couple of years now, and I can verify that she does get information from the Flipside that can't be due to cryptomnesia. I know she's helped law enforcement with missing person cases, and other people with their own issues. In terms of the process, I think it's important to remember she is interpreting things she's seeing from the Flipside, and there are a million ways a message can be interpreted.

As I've noted before, when interviewing her, I avoid speaking about the future altogether, because this research shows it's not set in stone. Mediums might be able to see likely outcomes, but because we have free will, anything can happen. Most mediums spend their time trying to help people understand what's going to happen, rather than talking about what has already happened or why.

Further, as noted, when we experience the Flipside, either through a near death experience, an out of body experience, or while under hypnosis, we are also filtering the information we're receiving. We can't possibly be

100% certain of what we're seeing or experiencing, because after all, it's a mental construct. Further, there's the possibility that "we aren't supposed to see something, because it will alter our path on the planet." If you throw that factor into this mix, then we have to be *really, really careful* about claiming **ANYTHING** about the Flipside. It could be what we're supposed to see, and not the whole picture.

Which is a long way of saying; *it's up to you.*

All I can say is that I'm a reporter here. My job, as I see it, is to report what people are saying in the most calm manner I can find, look up what they're saying to see if I can verify it in any way, or discredit it as something imaginary or fanciful. But in order for the information to make it as far as this book, it means that I have heard similar stories in the past, and they're so alike, I can't ignore them.

If you've come this far in the book, I want to warn you at this point. Jennifer forced my hand so to speak, by bringing up the idea that Jesus not only existed on the planet, but had a family as well. That's easy to dismiss; "Where's the evidence of that?" The Bible doesn't mention them, scholars now claim Jesus had a family with brothers and sisters... "But what really happened back then and is there any way we can interview eyewitnesses to those events?"

In this unusual quest of mine, to show that people who once lived on the planet are accessible, I'm going to venture into territory that is bound to upset people. I'm not trying to push any agenda here, other than "Wow, check out these reports, aren't they unusual?"

As I note later on, I didn't seek out people who knew. Every person that offers information in the ensuing chapters came to me from "*out of the blue.*" Meaning we were talking about one thing, and then this other thing came into my point of view while we were speaking.

But precisely because I didn't seek them out, I didn't try to find these details, gives them a different light, in my mind. For example the next chapter is a reproduction of a document in the public domain that was written by a Nepalese Sherpa over 120 years ago. The Sherpa was the guide to an explorer who was traveling in Northern India, and the explorer fell from his horse and broke his leg.

He convalesced at a Buddhist Monastery in Hemis. And while he was there with his Sherpa, the abbot of the monastery said to him "Did you know that this is the same monastery that Jesus studied at?" (Which is precisely the same sentence the abbot of Hemis said to me when I was traveling through the region with Robert Thurman, head of Tibetan Studies at Columbia University.)

Of course it was said more precisely; "Did you know that Issa, as Jesus is known in Asia, studied Buddhism here? We have a book in our library that details his journey here." At the time, I assumed I was hearing him incorrectly. I wish I had asked to see the book, and filmed him showing it to me. But because of my Catholic brain freeze, I didn't really understand what he was saying until I got my hands on two translations of the same book. One by the Sherpa guide of the explorer, and the other by an Indian Holy Man in the 1960's. Both translations say the same thing.

We've come this far together; we might as well go all the way to the end. *But are you ready? Are you sure?*

The Potala Palace, Lhasa, Tibet, taken atop the Barkhor

CHAPTER SEVENTEEN:

The Tibetan Gospel of Jesus in India

The Dalai Lama's bedroom as he left it in Lhasa, Tibet.

"Father, forgive me, for I have sinned... It has been at least 40 years since my last confession...."

Apologies to everyone this chapter will certainly offend.

If you are firmly rooted in your religion and your path - please, I beg you, don't read this chapter. **"These are not the droids you're looking for."** In this chapter I'm going to argue that Jesus spent time in India as is claimed in these interviews. There's a document that exists that confirms that detail, and it was reportedly translated in a monastery I visited on a trip to Ladakh, India with Professor Robert Thurman.

Later, I got my hands on Nicholas Notovitch's **"The life of Saint Issa."** *Nikolai Notovich* was a Russian explorer who wound up in the Hemis monastery in Tibet (now part of India/Kashmir). The abbot of the monastery, a Tibetan Buddhist monk, told him about a book in their library, that was written about the life of Jesus - or Issa as he was known in Asia, and how he come to stay at Hemis at some point during his life. The abbot showed Notovitch the book, which his Sherpa (a Nepalese who spoke Tibetan) was allowed to translate for Notovitch, page by page.

Some years later, Swami Abhedananda saw the same book, had it translated it as well, which concurred with Notovitch's version. There are about a dozen other people who claim to have seen this in Hemis. The point is, more than one person has translated this document – which serves to only prove that the book exists, or that it existed. While many have argued that Notovitch was a Charlatan, I'm pointing out that he *didn't translate the book*. The Sherpa did.

Swami Abhedananda- Nikolai Notovitch

Clearly it was written by a fan of Issa. But who are the authors or author? We're examining a document that has been reportedly translated from Pali or Sanskrit or Tibetan into Nepalese, then into Russian, then into French and then into English. Tibetan as a written language didn't come into use until the 9th century. Notovitch claims the original was in Pali, brought from India, then translated.

Which behooves us to allow for mistakes or mistranslations.[76]

We also might consider the motivation for writing this text. It doesn't appear that anyone is trying to claim ownership of Issa, or to say that he *"belonged to our version of reality."* In reading the full text, which I call the *"The Tibetan Gospel"* it seems to want to explore and examine this particular fellow's history. It doesn't make any claims about his divinity, or claims against his divinity. It's more of a document written by someone who felt compelled to share the history of an unusual man.

---

[76] Notovich: "The original scrolls (were) brought from India to *Nepaul,* From *Nepaul to Thibet,* relating to the life of Issa, are written in the Pali language and are actually in *Lhassa*; but a copy in our language - I mean the *Thibetan* - is in this convent." Later, when Swami Abhedananda saw the same text, he claimed it was "translated by a local Lama". From the Gutenberg.org project.

I might add, it doesn't read like some of the Tibetan documents I've read that contain the histories of the Indian Pandits who came to Tibet, i.e., the story of Padmasambhava's visits or other stories about the Indian pandit Atisha. Those accounts have a plethora of mystical or magical events associated with these holy men. The lack of those kinds of stories, (or even miracles of Jesus healing the sick, raising the dead, etc) also gives us insight into the authors who recounted these events.

The photograph below is a typical Tibetan "book." The text reads left to right, then the pages are turned. It's why the original verses are in this paragraph form.

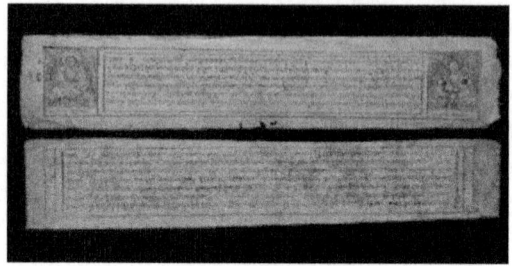

Typical Tibetan book

Apologies for the length of this chapter, but it is important groundwork for what comes next.

The Life of Saint Issa

I. "Best of the Sons of Men."

1. The earth trembled and the heavens wept, because of the great crime committed in the land of Israel.
2. For there was tortured and murdered the great and just Issa (as Jesus is known in Asia) in whom was manifest the soul of the Universe;
3. Which had incarnated in a simple mortal, to benefit men and **destroy the evil spirit in them;**
4. To lead back to peace, love and happiness, man, **degraded by his sins,** and recall him to the **one and indivisible Creator** whose mercy is infinite.
5. The **merchants coming from Israel** have given the following account of what has occurred:

(Note: The silk route went from the Middle East to China. Hemis is along the route, albeit in a remote part of India that was formerly Tibet (until

1949.) The *"soul of the universe"* sounds Buddhist, as well as *"incarnated in a simple mortal to benefit men"* an attribute often given the Dalai Lama. "Destroy **the evil spirit** within men" and "degraded **by sins**... to **the one**... Creator" are not Buddhist concepts; according to the Dalai Lama, Buddhism is a "non-theistic religion" which means no belief in a higher power or deity. Buddha is not a deity, just another *"simple mortal"* who happened to "attain enlightenment" through using his own cognitive powers of reasoning.)

II.
1. The people of Israel—who inhabit a fertile country producing two harvests a year and affording pasture for large herds of cattle—**by their sins brought down upon themselves the anger of the Lord;**
2. Who inflicted upon them terrible chastisements, taking from them their land, their cattle and their wealth. They were carried away into slavery by the rich and mighty Pharaohs who then ruled the land of Egypt.

(Note: This account of the Jewish religion is pre-Egyptian. The document claims to be written by Jewish merchants rather than "dictated to a monk." The "Lost Tribes" of Israel settled the length of the Silk Route.)[77]

3. **The Israelites were, by the Pharaohs, treated worse than beasts, condemned to hard labor and put in irons; their bodies were covered with wounds and sores; they were not permitted to live under a roof, and were starved to death;**
4. That they might be maintained in a state of continual terror and deprived of all human resemblance;
5. And in this great calamity, the Israelites, remembering their Celestial Protector, implored his forgiveness and mercy.
6. At that period reigned in Egypt an illustrious Pharaoh, who was renowned for his many victories, immense riches, and the gigantic palaces he had erected by the labor of his slaves.

7. **This Pharaoh had two sons, the younger of whom, named Mossa, had acquired much knowledge from the sages of Israel.**
8. And Mossa (Moses) was beloved by all in Egypt for his kindness of heart and the pity he showed to all sufferers.

---

[77] For evidence of Jewish tribes along the silk route, see PBS multi-part series by Simcha Jacobovici, "Quest for the Lost Tribes" (2003) which proves these tribes weren't "lost" but fled along the silk route all the way to China, into parts of India and Africa (Ethiopia.)

9. When Moses saw that the Israelites, in spite of their many sufferings, had not forsaken their God, and refused to worship the gods of Egypt, created by the hands of man.

10. He also put his faith in their invisible God, who did not suffer them to betray Him, despite their ever growing weakness.

11. The teachers among Israel animated Moses in his zeal, and prayed of him that he would intercede with his father, Pharaoh, in favor of their co-religionists.

12. **Prince Moses went before his father, begging him to lighten the burden of the unhappy people; Pharaoh, however, became incensed with rage, and ordered that they should be tormented more than before.**

13. And it came to pass that Egypt was visited by a great calamity. The plague decimated young and old, the healthy and the sick; and Pharaoh beheld in this the resentment of his own gods against him.

14. But Prince Moses said to his father that it was the God of his slaves who thus interposed on behalf of his wretched people, and avenged them upon the Egyptians.

15. **Thereupon, Pharaoh commanded Moses, his son, to gather all the Israelite slaves, and lead them away, and found, at a great distance from the capital, another city where he should rule over them.**

16. Then Moses made known to the Hebrew slaves that he had obtained their freedom in the name of his and their God, the God of Israel; and with them he left the city and departed from the land of Egypt.

17. **He led them back to the land which, because of their many sins, had been taken from them. There he gave them laws and admonished them to pray always to God, the indivisible Creator, whose kindness is infinite.**

18. **After Prince Moses's death, the Israelites observed rigorously his laws; and God rewarded them for the ills to which they had been subjected in Egypt.**

19. Their kingdom became one of the most powerful on earth; their kings made themselves renowned for their treasures, and peace reigned in Israel.

(Note: Interesting take on a story that's been around for a long time. Not that Moses (which I used instead of the textual "Mossa") was Jewish and was adopted by the Pharaoh, but states here that Moses *was the son* of the Pharaoh and a compassionate Egyptian, and identified with these slaves and their religion, and took up their cause. (Perhaps Moses remembered his previous lifetime as a slave and that's why he identified with them?)

I'm not trying to stir up a religious debate here – but it does make "more sense" that Moses was the son of the Pharaoh and adopted his chosen people with infuriated the Pharaoh. This account only reports one plague, but it was enough to send him on his way.)

III.

1. The glory of Israel's wealth spread over the whole earth, and the surrounding nations became envious.

2. But the Most High himself led the victorious arms of the Hebrews, and the Pagans did not dare to attack them.

3. Unfortunately, man is prone to err, and the fidelity of the Israelites to their God was not of long duration.

4. Little by little they forgot the favors he had bestowed upon them; rarely invoked his name, and sought rather protection by the magicians and sorcerers.

5. The kings and the chiefs among the people substituted their own laws for those given by Moses; the temple of God and the observances of their ancient faith were neglected; the people addicted themselves to sensual gratifications and lost their original purity.

(Note: Forget for a moment that it would take about two weeks to walk from Cairo to Jerusalem. Interesting, in the Bible version, this all happens within 40 years of Moses wandering the desert. This account credits the wealth and many battle victories of those early Israelites, but argues that years after Moses' death, his people "lost their way.")

6. Many centuries had elapsed since their exodus from Egypt, when God bethought himself of again inflicting chastisement upon them.

7. Strangers invaded Israel, devastated the land, destroyed the villages, and carried their inhabitants away into captivity.

8. At last came the Pagans from over the sea, from the land of Romeles. These made themselves masters of the Hebrews, and placed over them their army chiefs, who governed in the name of Cæsar.

9. They defiled the temples, forced the inhabitants to cease the worship of the indivisible God, and compelled them to sacrifice to the heathen gods.

10. They made common soldiers of those who had been men of rank; the women became their prey, and the common people, reduced to slavery, were carried away by thousands over the sea.

(Note: I don't know if this is how Notovitch's Nepalese Sherpa translated "the Romans" – but "land of Romeles" makes more sense as "Land of

Romulus and Remus" the two orphans of mythology who founded Rome. There is no term I can find of "Romeles" unless someone is writing what they're hearing *phonetically*. "Romulus sounds like "Romeles.")

11. The children were slain, and soon, in the whole land, there was naught heard but weeping and lamentation.
12. In this extreme distress, the Israelites once more remembered their great God, implored his mercy and prayed for his forgiveness. Our Father, in his inexhaustible clemency, heard their prayer.

(Note: Interesting that in the same paragraph, it moves from third to first person; "their great God.." and then **"our Father... heard their prayer."** Again, not something a Buddhist would say or write, but perhaps would transcribe from someone telling the story, perhaps from an acolyte, or a member of someone's group of followers.)

IV.
1. At that time the moment had come for the compassionate Judge to reincarnate in a human form;
2. The eternal Spirit, resting in a state of complete inaction and supreme bliss, awakened and separated from the eternal Being, for an undetermined period,
3. So that, in human form, He might teach man to identify himself with the Divinity and attain to eternal felicity;
4. And to show, by His example, how man can attain moral purity and free his soul from the domination of the physical senses, so that it may achieve the perfection necessary for it to enter the Kingdom of Heaven, which is immutable and where bliss eternal reigns.

(Note: This is a jumble of concepts here – part Buddhist, part Jain, part Hindu – that "the eternal spirit rests in a state of inaction" – that some part of that "resting spirit" decided to take "human form" of a "compassionate Judge" – and to show how to attain "purity and free his soul from the domination of the physical senses." It's not Buddhism, but closer to Hinduism in the idea there was an eternal being who was awakened, and sent an enlightened part of his being to Earth.)

5. Soon after, a marvelous child was born in the land of Israel. God himself spoke, through the mouth of this child, of the miseries of the body and the grandeur of the soul.
6. The parents of the infant were poor people, who belonged to a family noted for great piety; who forgot the greatness of their

ancestors in celebrating the name of the Creator and giving thanks to Him for the trials which He had sent upon them.

(Note: There is some debate among scholars whether Mary's family descended from the House of David. Without saying it, the inference is that Jesus was of royal heritage.)

7. To reward them for adhering to the path of truth, God blessed the firstborn of this family; chose him for His elect, and sent him to sustain the fallen and comfort the afflicted.

8. **The divine child, to whom the name Issa (as Jesus is known in Asia) was given, commenced in his tender years to talk of the only and indivisible God, exhorting the strayed souls to repent and purify themselves from the sins of which they had become guilty.**

9. People came from all parts to hear him, and marveled at the discourses which came from his infantile mouth; and all Israel agreed that the Spirit of the Eternal dwelt in this child.

10. **When Issa was thirteen years old, the age at which an Israelite is expected to marry,**

11. **The modest house of his industrious parents became a meeting place of the rich and illustrious,** who were anxious to have as a son-in-law the young Issa, who was already celebrated for the edifying discourses he made in the name of the All-Powerful.

12. **Then Issa secretly absented himself from his father's house; left Jerusalem, and, in a train of merchants, journeyed toward the Sindh,**

13. With the object of perfecting himself in the knowledge of the word of God and the study of the **laws of the great Buddhas.**

(Note: The "Sindh" is how India was referred to in those years, it's also what Thomas calls India in the gnostic "Gospel of Thomas." It's interesting to note this rationale for Jesus to leave his home town - he was required to marry, and chose not to. He decided to run off to explore the world instead of staying behind to do what would have been demanded of him. We'll hear from someone later in this book, who claims that he accompanied Issa on these travels.)

V.

1. **In his fourteenth year, young Issa, the Blessed One, came this side of the Sindh and settled among the Aryas, in the country beloved by God.**

2. **Fame spread the name of the marvelous youth along the northern Sindh, and when he came through the country of the five**

streams and Radjipoutan, the devotees of the god Djaïne asked him to stay among them.

3. But he left the deluded worshippers of Djaïne and went to Djagguernat, in the country of Osiris, (The Jagannath Temple of Puri is in Odisha, India) **where repose the mortal remains of Vyassa-Krishna, and where the white priests of Brahma welcomed him joyfully.**[78]

(Note: Buddhism spread to India in the latter half of the first millennium: "Buddhism arose in Greater Magadha… to the east of aryavarta, the land of the Aryas..." (Wikipedia) For Notovitch, whom many consider some kind of *hoaxer,* to correctly identify these various religious sects back in 1896, unknown to the West, is a stretch. If he's constructing a hoax, he didn't need to include these details, some of which are mistaken, and other are correct. Sudras are a member of the worker caste, lowest of the four Hindu castes.)

Castes in India (Wikipedia)

4. They taught him to read and to understand the Vedas, to cure physical ills by means of prayers, to teach and to expound the sacred Scriptures, to drive out evil desires from man and make him again in the likeness of God.

5. He spent **six years in Djagguernat**, in Radjagriha, in Benares, and in other holy cities. The common people loved Issa, for he lived in peace with the Vaisyas and the Sudras, to whom he taught the Holy Scriptures.

6. But the Brahmins and the Kshatnyas told him that they were forbidden by the great **Para-Brahma to come near to those who were created**

---

[78] The "five streams" may refer to a Hindu expression of five sacred rivers in the Himalayas... The "Djaïne," known today as the Jain religion dates back to the 1st century; they espoused a belief the universe had no beginning or end, practiced extreme non-violence (sweeping the path in front of them so they wouldn't accidentally step on an ancestor). "White Priests" appears to refer to "white flag Brahmins" who were "a class of Hindu Brahmin priests and Ayurveda teachers and practitioners, with significant concentrations of their populations occurring in Western and Northern India." Again, not something Notovitch would likely be aware of, and the writers of this document left out the world "flag" in the original text or in this translation. If Jesus had met "white priests of Brahma" it's likely they're referring to the "Maga Brahmins" of Northern India who were Persian in origin who wore all white clothing.)

from his belly and his feet; (slaves with a darker skin color, believed to come "from the feet")[79]

7. That the Vaisyas might only hear the recital of the Vedas, and this only on the festal days, and

8. **That the Sudras were not only forbidden to attend the reading of the Vedas, but even to look on them; for they were condemned to perpetual servitude, as slaves of the Brahmins,** the Kshatriyas and even the Vaisyas.

9. **"Death alone can enfranchise them from their servitude,"** has said Para-Brahma. **"Leave them, therefore, and come to adore with us the gods, whom you will make angry if you disobey them."**

10. **But Issa, disregarding their words, remained with the Sudras, preaching against the Brahmins and the Kshatriyas.**

(Note: This was an era when disagreement with the Brahmin "high priests" could lead to death. Issa is stating here that the caste system is wrong. He refuses to obey the Brahmins, preferring to stay with the poor. Sounds a bit like the same "Blessed are the poor" fellow who later shows up in Jerusalem.)

11. **He declaimed strongly against man's arrogating (claim the privilege of) to himself the authority to deprive his fellow beings of their human and spiritual rights. "Verily,"** he said, **"God has made no difference between his children, who are all alike dear to Him."**

12. Issa **denied the divine inspiration of the Vedas** and the Puranas, for, as he taught his followers, —**"One law has been given to man to guide him in his actions:**

13. **"Fear the Lord, thy God; bend thy knees only before Him and bring to Him only the offerings which come from thy earnings."**

14. Issa denied the Trimurti and the incarnation of Para-Brahma in Vishnu, Siva, and other gods; **"for,"** said he:

15. **"The eternal Judge, the eternal Spirit, constitutes the only and indivisible soul of the universe, and it is this soul alone which creates, contains and vivifies all.**

---

[79] Vaisyas are the "merchant and farmer" caste of Hindus, and **Sudras are the lowest caste** - but still the caste above the *"untouchables"* ("Dalits) who do all the lowest forms of work in Hindu society. Also not likely a detail that Notovitch or his Sherpa would have been aware of. Para Brahman is the "highest Brahman," that which is beyond all descriptions and conceptualizations. Wikipedia)

(Note: Interesting he's clarifying who "God" is here - *the eternal spirit which creates, contains and "animates" all*. Not a being per se, but the indivisible "soul of the Universe" - reminiscent of the reports where people claim "God can be experienced by opening your heart to everyone.")

16. **"He alone has willed and created. He alone has existed from eternity, and His existence will be without end; there is no one like unto Him either in the heavens or on the earth.**
17. **"The great Creator has divided His power with no other being; far less with inanimate objects,** as you have been taught to believe, for He alone is omnipotent and all-sufficient.
18. **"He willed, and the world was. By one divine thought,** He reunited the waters and separated them from the dry land of the globe. **He is the cause of the mysterious life of man, into whom He has breathed part of His Divine Being.**

(Note: Another reference to divine breath - father/son and "breath" from the original Aramaic, or Greek. "Pneuma" became "Spiros" (to breathe) but was later translated as "Spirit" and then "Ghost." "Holy Ghost" would refer to the etheric spirit that animates humans.)

19. "And He has put under subjection to man, the lands, the waters, the beasts and everything which He created, and which He himself preserves in immutable order, allotting to each its proper duration.
20. **"The anger of God will soon break forth upon man; for he has forgotten his Creator;** he has filled His temples with abominations; and he adores a multitude of creatures which God has subordinated to him;

21. "And to gain favor with images of stone and metal, **he sacrifices human beings** in whom dwells part of the Spirit of the Most High;
22. "And **he humiliates those who work in the sweat of their brows**, to gain favor in the eyes of the idler who sitteth at a sumptuous table.
23. "Those **who deprive their brothers of divine happiness will themselves be deprived of it;** and the Brahmins and the Kshatriyas shall become the Sudras of the Sudras, with whom the Eternal will stay forever.

(Note: Pretty much heresy for Jesus to argue that all people are equal, despite the color of their skin or "caste." The Brahmins were convinced "darker skinned people" were born to be slaves. Issa argues people of the highest caste will become the "Sudras of the Sudras" which is his way of calling them the "lowest of the low" – brings to mind his preaching about the poor in the "Sermon on the Mount.")

24. "In the day of judgment the Sudras and the Vaisyas will be forgiven for that they knew not the light, while God will let loose his wrath upon those who arrogated his authority."

(Again, God becomes wrathful for those who pretended to be more important when they aren't. *Arrogate* meaning "take something without justification." Sounds a bit like the man who reportedly said "it is easier for a camel to go through the eye of a needle than for a rich person to enter the kingdom of God" (Matthew 19))

25. The Vaisyas and the Sudras were filled with great admiration, and asked Issa how they should pray, in order not to lose their hold upon eternal life.

26. "Pray not to idols, for they cannot hear you; hearken not to the Vedas where the truth is altered; be humble and humiliate not your fellow man.

27. "Help the poor, support the weak, do evil to none; covet not that which ye have not and which belongs to others."[80]

VI.

1. The **white priests** and the warriors, who had learned of Issa's discourse to the Sudras, resolved upon his death, and sent their **servants to find the young teacher and slay him.**

2. But Issa, **warned by the Sudras of his danger**, left by night Djagguernat, **gained the mountain**, and settled in the country of the **Gautamides**, where the great Buddha Sakya-Muni came to the world, among a people **who worshipped the only and sublime Brahma.**

(Note: "The Gautamides" were reportedly from Nepal, followed the teachings of Sakya-muni - this would make them an older school of Buddhism which evolved into the Sakya-pas of the Tibetan 10th century. If "gained the mountain" means went up to the Himalayas, it might mean he went further up the silk route, which included southern Tibet where the Hemis Monastery is located in Kashmir, northern India, near the border.

---

[80] "Blessed are those..." seems to echo these sentiments. Interesting to note these are all accurate religious sects in India around this time, and their description could be used to date the text. The Brahmins are Hindus, the Sudras and Kshatriyas are classes within Hinduism - classified as "castes" - warriors, holy men, etc, classified based on skin tone.)

Also this appears to be a bit of a misleading translation - it should read "Issa settled in Nepal, where Sakya-Muni came to the world (Nepal) among a people who worshipped Brahma." Meaning, *like Buddha* being born amongst Hindus, Issa was *living among* Buddhists.)

3. When the just Issa had acquired the Pali language, he applied himself to the study of the sacred scrolls of the Sutras.

(The Pali language contained all the Buddhist sutras, and was the original language used to write them down. It is was in the 5th century AD when Pali Buddhist texts were brought to Tibet ("fell out of the sky") and the country started to learn about Buddhism.

But according to *Sakya.org*, it was **the first century before Christ** that Buddhism spread throughout India, and into northern India in the first century after his birth. Later, it's confirmed he left *"Nepaul"* (sic) after six years of study, which is pretty much the exact same thing the abbot of Hemis told me about Issa's stay at their Tibetan monastery.)

4. **After six years** of study, **Issa, whom the Buddha had elected to spread his holy word, could perfectly expound the sacred scrolls.**
5. He then **left Nepaul and the Himalaya mountains, descended into the valley** of Radjipoutan and directed his steps toward the West, everywhere preaching to the people the supreme perfection attainable by man;

6. The good he must do to his fellow men, which is the sure means of speedy union with the eternal Spirit. **"He who has recovered his primitive purity," said Issa, "shall die with his transgressions forgiven and have the right to contemplate the majesty of God."**
7. When the divine Issa traversed the territories of the Pagans, he taught that the adoration of visible gods was contrary to natural law.
8. **"For to man," said he, "it has not been given to see the image of God, and it behooves him not to make for himself a multitude of divinities in the imagined likeness of the Eternal.**
9. **"Moreover, it is against human conscience to have less regard for the greatness of divine purity, than for animals or works of stone or metal made by the hands of man.**

(Note: It's interesting how the "Pagan Gods" of Rome or Greece seemed to offend so many. Here Jesus seems to be echoing Islam's argument that "any statue" or depiction of god, or man-made deity can lead to being led away from spiritual adherence. Perhaps it's because the Roman and Greek world was filled with sacrificing lesser people or animals at altars.)

10. **"The eternal Lawgiver is One; there are no other Gods than He; He has parted the world with none, nor had He any counselor.**

(Note: I assume he means God "shared the world with no one else, or any other Gods, and didn't have any teacher to taught him these concepts." A way of saying *"There's only one God and if you believe in more than one, you're out of your mind."*)

11. "Even as a father shows kindness toward his children, so will God judge men after death, in conformity with His merciful laws. He will never humiliate his child by casting his soul for chastisement into the body of a beast.
12. **"The heavenly laws,"** said the Creator, through the mouth of Issa, **"are opposed to the immolation of human sacrifices to a statue or an animal; for I, the God, have sacrificed to man all the animals and all that the world contains.**
13. "Everything has been sacrificed to man, who is directly and intimately united to me, his Father; therefore, shall the man be severely judged and punished, by my law, who causes the sacrifice of my children.

14. "Man is naught before the eternal Judge; as the animal is before man.
15. **"Therefore, I say unto you, leave your idols and perform not ceremonies which separate you from your Father and bind you to the priests, from whom heaven has turned away.**
16. **"For it is they who have led you away from the true God, and by superstitions and cruelty perverted the spirit and made you blind to the knowledge of the truth."**

(Note: I can't imagine any Priests of the local religions being happy to hear this fellow espouse these views, no matter how accurate. Ritual sacrifice was incredibly popular in this time period; killing a cow, or a calf, or sometimes a human to "appease" God or the gods or nature; he's clearly saying that everyone on the planet is imbued with the Source, with God's essence, and therefore, everything on the planet is sacred and should not be sacrificed.)

VII.
1. The words of Issa spread among the Pagans, through whose country he passed, and **the inhabitants abandoned their idols.**

2. Seeing which, the priests demanded of him who thus glorified the name of the true God, that he should, in the presence of the people, prove the charges he made against them, and demonstrate the vanity of their idols.

3. And Issa answered them: **"If your idols, or the animals you worship, really possess the supernatural powers you claim, let them strike me with a thunderbolt before you!"**

4. **"Why dost not thou perform a miracle,"** replied the priests, **"and let thy God confound ours, if He is greater than they?"**

5. But Issa said: **"The miracles of our God have been wrought from the first day when the universe was created; and are performed every day and every moment; whoso sees them not is deprived of one of the most beautiful gifts of life.**

(Note: So he gained a following even while trekking through India. As we'll see in an ensuing chapter, we have an eyewitness account from someone who claims this account to be accurate.)

6. "And it is not on inanimate objects of stone, metal or wood that He will let His anger fall, but on the men who worship them, and who, therefore, for their salvation, must destroy the idols they have made.

7. "Even as a stone and a grain of sand, which are naught before man, await patiently their use by Him.

8. "In like manner, man, who is naught before God, must await in resignation His pleasure for a manifestation of His favor.

9. "But woe to you! ye adversaries of men, if it is not the favor you await, but rather the wrath of the Most High; woe to you, if you demand that He attest His power by a miracle!

10. "For it is not the idols which He will destroy in His wrath, but those by whom they were created; their hearts will be the prey of an eternal fire and their flesh shall be given to the beasts of prey.

11. "God will drive away the contaminated animals from His flocks; but will take to Himself those who strayed because they knew not the heavenly part within them."

12. When the Pagans saw that the power of their Priests was naught, they put faith in the words of Issa. **Fearing the anger of the true God, they broke their idols to pieces and caused their priests to flee from among them**.

(Note: This is a pretty subjective report, obviously written by a fan. Did everyone *suddenly* believe that Jesus had won the argument by using reverse logic? It's not the same as raising Lazarus, or some other miraculous event - casting out "demons" for example, but the writer of this story was impressed enough to put it in this way.)

13. Issa furthermore taught the Pagans that they should not endeavor to see the eternal Spirit with their eyes; but to **perceive Him with their hearts**, and make themselves worthy of His favors by the purity of their souls.

14. **"Not only,"** he said to them, **"must ye refrain from offering human sacrifices, but ye may not lay on the altar any creature to which life has been given, for all things created are for man.**

15. **"Withhold not from your neighbor his just due,** for this would be like **stealing** from him what he had earned in the sweat of his brow.

16. **"Deceive none,** that ye may not yourselves be deceived; seek to justify yourselves before the last judgment, for then it will be too late.

17. **"Be not given to debauchery**, for it is a violation of the law of God.

18. "That you may attain to supreme bliss ye must not **only purify yourselves**, but must also guide others into the path that will enable them to regain their primitive innocence."

(Note: Interesting variation on the Commandments here. The idea of "supreme bliss" as a goal sounds more like the people he's preaching to, or the people who are transcribing this story. "Supreme bliss" would refer to Nirvana, or the idea that becoming "one with God" or "one with the source" would bring about a state of supreme bliss, which would have been talked about by the Hindus who experienced it through yoga and the Buddhists who experience it through meditation. *Either way, it's not a term one might find in the Bible, and seems completely normal in this narrative.*)

VIII.

1. The countries round about were filled with the renown of Issa's preachings, and when he came unto Persia, the priests grew afraid and forbade the people hearing him;

2. Nevertheless, the villages received him with joy, and the people hearkened intently to his words, which, being seen by the priests, caused them to order that he should be arrested and brought before their High Priest, who asked him:

3. **"Of what new God dost thou speak? Knowest thou not, unfortunate man that thou art! that Saint Zoroaster is the only Just One, to whom alone was vouchsafed the honor of receiving revelations from the Most High;**

4. "By whose command the angels compiled His Word in laws for the governance of His people, which were given to Zoroaster in Paradise?
5. "Who, then, art thou, who darest to utter blasphemies against our God and sow doubt in the hearts of believers?"

(Note: Zoroastrianism is still practiced among the Parsi people, there are currently over 200,000 adherents in Mumbai alone, with a belief in the idea of good/bad, darkness/light, sacredness of earth, wind and fire and that opposites that exist on the planet and need to be respected as sacred as well. The idea that Jesus would call *them less than accurate,* would likely result in his death, and it's interesting they don't show him the door.)

6. And Issa said to them: **"I preach no new God, but our celestial Father, who has existed before the beginning and will exist until after the end.**
7. "Of Him I have spoken to the people, who—even as innocent children— are incapable of comprehending God by their own intelligence, or fathoming the sublimity of the divine Spirit;
8. "But, as the newborn child in the night recognizes the mother's breast, Your people, held in the darkness of error by your pernicious doctrines and religious ceremonies, have recognized instinctively their Father, in the Father whose prophet I am.
9. "The eternal Being says to your people, by my mouth, **'Ye shall not adore the sun, for it is but a part of the universe which I have created for man;**

10. "It rises to warm you during your work; it sets to accord to you the rest that I have ordained.
11. **"To me only ye owe all that ye possess, all that surrounds you and that is above and below you.'"**

(Note: There's the iconic phrase **"As above, so below"** is a religious concept heard often in a number of religious texts. But Jesus is clearly arguing that the worship of the sun is *nonsense.*)

12. "But," said the priests, **"how could the people live according to your rules if they had no teachers?"**
13. Whereupon Issa answered: **"So long as they had no priests, they were governed by the natural law and conserved the simplicity of their souls;**

14. **"Their souls were in God and to commune with the Father they had not to have recourse to the intermediation of idols, or animals, or fire, as taught by you.**

15. "Ye pretend that man must adore the sun, and the **Genii of Good and Evil.** But I say unto you that your doctrine is pernicious. **The sun does not act spontaneously, but by the will of the invisible Creator, who has given to it being."**
16. "Who, then, has caused that this star lights the day, warms man at his work and vivifies the seeds sown in the ground?"
17. **"The eternal Spirit is the soul of everything animate, and you commit a great sin in dividing Him into the Spirit of Evil and the Spirit of Good, for there is no God other than the God of Good.**

(Note: That's a pretty radical notion - the nature in and of itself should not be worshiped, as nature is just part of the larger picture of creation. Interesting that he uses the concept *"genii of good"* here - to imply that their gods are like the genie's of myth.)

18. "And He, like to the father of a family, does only good to His children, to whom He forgives their transgressions if they repent of them.
19. "The Spirit of Evil dwells upon earth, in the hearts of those who turn the children of God away from the right path.
20. **"Therefore, I say unto you; Fear the day of judgment, for God will inflict a terrible chastisement upon all those who have led His children astray and beguiled them with superstitions and errors;**

21. "Upon those who have blinded them who saw; who have brought contagion to the well; who have taught the worship of those things which God made to be subject to man, or to aid him in his works.
22. "Your doctrine is the fruit of your error in seeking to bring near to you the God of Truth, by creating for yourselves false gods."

(Note: Again with the warnings of *cataclysms* that will occur to those who don't repent! *"A terrible chastisement"* was one way of putting some form of karmic retribution. I can only imagine it was the only way people would be taken seriously when giving a religious talk. "Heed my words or God will smite you!" Interesting to note in the next paragraph, the mention of the Magi - which is translated as Persian priests. Were the three Magi Persian priests?)

23. When the Magi heard these words, they feared to themselves do him

harm, but at night, when the whole city slept, they brought him outside the walls and left him on the highway, in the hope that he would not fail to become the prey of wild beasts.

24. But, protected by the Lord our God, Saint Issa continued on his way, without accident.

(Note: Again, nearly killed by those he was preaching to, except in Persia, they merely booted him outside the gates and "sent him on his way.")

IX.

1. Issa—**whom the Creator had selected to recall to the worship of the true God,** men sunk in sin—**was twenty-nine years old when he arrived in the land of Israel.**

2. Since the departure there-from of Issa, the Pagans had caused the Israelites to endure more atrocious sufferings than before, and they were filled with despair.

3. Many among them had begun to neglect the laws of their God and those of Mossa (Moses), in the hope of winning the favor of their brutal conquerors.

4. But Issa, notwithstanding their unhappy condition, exhorted his countrymen not to despair, because the day of their redemption from the yoke of sin was near, and he himself, by his example, confirmed their faith in the God of their fathers.

5. **"Children, yield not yourselves to despair,"** said the celestial Father to them, through the mouth of Issa, **"for I have heard your lamentations, and your cries have reached my ears.**

6. "Weep not, oh, my beloved sons! for your griefs have touched the heart of your Father and He has forgiven you, as He forgave your ancestors.

7. "Forsake not your families to plunge into debauchery; stain not the nobility of your souls; adore not idols which cannot but remain deaf to your supplications.

8. "Fill my temple with your hope and your patience, and do not adjure the religion of your forefathers, for I have guided them and bestowed upon them of my beneficence.

9. **"Lift up those who are fallen; feed the hungry and help the sick, that ye may be altogether pure and just in the day of the last judgment which I prepare for you."**

10. The Israelites came in multitudes to listen to Issa's words; and they asked him where they should thank their Heavenly Father, since their enemies had demolished their temples and robbed them of their sacred vessels.

11. Issa told them that God cared not for temples erected by human hands, but that human hearts were the true temples of God.

12. **"Enter into your temple, into your heart; illuminate it with good thoughts, with patience and the unshakeable faith which you owe to your Father.**

13. **"And your sacred vessels! they are your hands and your eyes. Look to do that which is agreeable to God, for in doing good to your fellow men, you perform a ceremony that embellishes the temple wherein abideth Him who has created you.**

14. **"For God has created you in His own image, innocent, with pure souls, and hearts filled with kindness and not made for the planning of evil, but to be the sanctuaries of love and justice.**

15. "Therefore, I say unto you, soil not your hearts with evil, for in them the eternal Being abides.

16. **"When ye do works of devotion and love, let them be with full hearts, and see that the motives of your actions be not hopes of gain or self-interest;**

17. "For actions, Impelled, will not bring you nearer to salvation, but lead to a state of moral degradation wherein theft, lying and murder pass for generous deeds."

(Note: It's interesting these quotes are unlike any quotes from a religious or holy figure from any other centuries. Certainly not anyone steeped in one or another religious tradition. It seems that Jesus (Issa) has distilled what he's learned from the various religions he's examined, and put them together with his own belief and experience as to the nature of reality.)

X.

1. Issa went from one city to another, strengthening by the word of God the courage of the Israelites, who were near to succumbing under their weight of woe, and thousands of the people followed him to hear his teachings.

2. But the chiefs of the cities were afraid of him and they informed the principal governor, residing in Jerusalem, that a man called Issa had arrived in the country, who by his sermons had arrayed the people against the authorities, and that multitudes, listening assiduously to him, neglected their labor; and, they added, he said that in a short time they would be free of their invader rulers.

3. **Then Pilate, the Governor of Jerusalem, gave orders that they should lay hold of the preacher Issa and bring him before the**

judges. In order, however, not to excite the anger of the populace, **Pilate directed that he should be judged by the priests and scribes, the Hebrew elders, in their temple.**

4. Meanwhile, Issa, continuing his preaching, arrived at Jerusalem, and the people, who already knew his fame, having learned of his coming, went out to meet him.

5. They greeted him respectfully and opened to him the doors of their temple, to hear from his mouth what he had said in other cities of Israel.

6. And Issa said to them: **"The human race perishes, because of the lack of faith; for the darkness and the tempest have caused the flock to go astray and they have lost their shepherds.**

7. "But the tempests do not rage forever and the darkness will not hide the light eternally; soon the sky will become serene, the celestial light will again overspread the earth, and the strayed flock will reunite around their shepherd.

8. "Wander not in the darkness, seeking the way, lest ye fall into the ditch; but gather together, sustain one another, put your faith in your God and wait for the first glimmer of light to reappear.

9. **"He who sustains his neighbor, sustains himself; and he who protects his family, protects all his people and his country.**

10. "For, be assured that the day is near when you will be delivered from the darkness; you will be reunited into one family and your enemy will tremble with fear, he who is ignorant of the favor of the great God."

11. The priests and the elders who heard him, filled with admiration for his language, asked him if it was true that he had sought to raise the people against the authorities of the country, as had been reported to the governor Pilate.

12. **"Can one raise against estrayed men, to whom darkness has hidden their road and their door?"** answered Issa. **"I have but forewarned the unhappy, as I do here in this temple, that they should no longer advance on the dark road, for an abyss opens before their feet.**

13. "The power of this earth is not of long duration and is subject to numberless changes. **It would be of no avail for a man to rise in revolution against it, for one phase of it always succeeds another, and it is thus that it will go on until the extinction of human life.**

14. "But do you not see that the powerful, and the rich, sow among the children of Israel a spirit of rebellion against the eternal power of Heaven?"

15. Then the elders asked him: **"Who art thou, From what country hast thou come to us? We have not formerly heard thee spoken of and do not even know thy name!"**

16. **"I am an Israelite,"** answered Issa; **"and on the day of my birth have seen the walls of Jerusalem, and have heard the sobs of my brothers reduced to slavery, and the lamentations of my sisters carried away by the Pagans;**
17. **"And my soul was afflicted when I saw that my brethren had forgotten the true God. When a child I left my father's house to go and settle among other people.**
18. **"But, having heard it said that my brethren suffered even greater miseries now, I have come back to the land of my fathers, to recall my brethren to the faith of their ancestors, which teaches us patience upon earth in order to attain the perfect and supreme bliss above."**
19. Then the wise old men put to him again this question: **"We are told that thou disownest the laws of Mossa, (Moses) and that thou teachest the people to forsake the temple of God?"**
20. Whereupon Issa: **"One does not demolish that which has been given by our Heavenly Father, and which has been destroyed by sinners. I have but enjoined the people to purify the heart of all stains, for it is the veritable temple of God.**

21. **"As regards the laws of Mossa, (Moses) I have endeavored to reestablish them in the hearts of men; and I say unto you that ye ignore their true meaning, for it is not vengeance but pardon which they teach. Their sense has been perverted."**

(Note: "It is not vengeance but pardon which they teach." An appeal for compassion for others, unlike the "retribution" he'd been speaking of earlier. Just an unusual note here.)

XI.
1. When the priests and the elders heard Issa, they decided among themselves **not to give judgment against him, for he had done no harm to any one,** and, **presenting themselves before Pilate**—who was made Governor of Jerusalem by the Pagan king of the country of Romeles (Rome) —they spake to him thus:
2. **"We have seen the man whom thou chargest with inciting our people to revolt; we have heard his discourses and know that he is our countryman;**

3. "But the chiefs of the cities have made to you false reports, for he is a just man, who teaches the people the word of God. After interrogating him, we have allowed him to go in peace."

4. The governor thereupon became very angry, and sent his disguised spies to keep watch upon Issa and report to the authorities the least word he addressed to the people.

5. In the meantime, the holy Issa continued to visit the neighboring cities and preach the true way of the Lord, enjoining the Hebrews' patience and promising them speedy deliverance.

(Note: Disguised spies? I wonder who that was.)

6. And all the time great numbers of the people followed him wherever he went, and many did not leave him at all, but attached themselves to him and served him.

7. And Issa said: "Put not your faith in miracles performed by the hands of men, for He who rules nature is alone capable of doing supernatural things, while man is impotent to arrest the wrath of the winds or cause the rain to fall.

8. "One miracle, however, is within the power of man to accomplish. It is, when his heart is filled with sincere faith, he resolves to root out from his mind all evil promptings and desires, and when, in order to attain this end, he ceases to walk the path of iniquity.

9. "All the things done without God are only gross errors, illusions and seductions, serving but to show how much the heart of the doer is full of presumption, falsehood and impurity.

10. "Put not your faith in oracles. God alone knows the future. He who has recourse to the diviners soils the temple of his heart and shows his lack of faith in his Creator.

(Note: It's an old argument; don't listen to psychics or mediums on what you should or shouldn't do. It "soils the temple of the heart" and shows "lack of faith." However, he had no problem "fulfilling prophecies.")

11. "Belief in the diviners and their miracles destroys the innate simplicity of man and his childlike purity. An infernal power takes hold of him who so errs, and forces him to commit various sins and give himself to the worship of idols.

12. "But the Lord our God, to whom none can be equaled, is one omnipotent, omniscient and omnipresent; He alone possesses all wisdom and all light.

13. "To Him ye must address yourselves, to be comforted in your afflictions, aided in your works, healed in your sickness and whoso asks of Him, shall not ask in vain.

14. "The secrets of nature are in the hands of God, **for the whole world, before it was made manifest, existed in the bosom of the divine thought,** and has become material and visible by the will of the Most High.

15. "When ye pray to him, become again like little children, for ye know neither the past, nor the present, nor the future, and God is the Lord of Time."

XII.

1. **"Just man,"** said to him the disguised spies of the Governor of Jerusalem, **"tell us if we must continue to do the will of Cæsar, or expect our near deliverance?"**

2. And Issa, who recognized the questioners as the apostate spies sent to follow him, replied to them: **"I have not told you that you would be delivered from Cæsar; it is the soul sunk in error which will gain its deliverance.**

3. **"There cannot be a family without a head, and there cannot be order in a people without a Cæsar, whom ye should implicitly obey, as he will be held to answer for his acts before the Supreme Tribunal."**

4. **"Does Cæsar possess a divine right?"** the spies asked him again; **"and is he the best of mortals?"**

5. **"There is no one 'the best' among human beings; but there are many bad, who—even as the sick need physicians—require the care of those chosen for that mission, in which must be used the means given by the sacred law of our Heavenly Father;**

6. **"Mercy and justice are the high prerogatives of Cæsar, and his name will be illustrious if he exercises them.**

7. **"But he who acts otherwise, who transcends the limits of power he has over those under his rule, and even goes so far as to put their lives in danger, offends the great Judge and derogates from his own dignity in the eyes of men."**

8. Upon this, an old woman who had approached the group, to better hear Issa, was pushed aside by one of the disguised men, who placed himself before her.

9. Then said Issa: **"It is not good for a son to push away his mother, that he may occupy the place which belongs to her. Whoso doth not**

respect his mother—the most sacred being after his God—is unworthy of the name of son.

10. "Hearken to what I say to you: **Respect woman; for in her we see the mother of the universe, and all the truth of divine creation is to come through her.**

11. "**She is the fount of everything good and beautiful,** as she is also the germ of life and death. Upon her man depends in all his existence, for she is his moral and natural support in his labors.

12. "In pain and suffering she brings you forth; in the sweat of her brow she watches over your growth, and until her death you cause her greatest anxieties. **Bless her and adore her, for she is your only friend and support on earth.**

13. "Respect her; defend her. In so doing you will gain for yourself her love; you will find favor before God, and for her sake many sins will be remitted to you.

14. "**Love your wives and respect them, for they will be the mothers of tomorrow and later the grandmothers of a whole nation.**

15. "Be submissive to the wife; her love ennobles man, softens his hardened heart, tames the wild beast in him and changes it to a lamb.

16. "**Wife and mother are the priceless treasures which God has given to you. They are the most beautiful ornaments of the universe, From them will be born all who will inhabit the world.**

17. "Even as the Lord of Hosts separated the light from the darkness, and the dry from the waters, so does woman possess the divine gift of calling forth out of man's evil nature all the good that is in him.

18. "Therefore I say unto you, after God, to **woman must belong your best thoughts, for she is the divine temple where you will most easily obtain perfect happiness.**

19. "Draw from this temple your moral force. There you will forget your sorrows and your failures, and recover the love necessary to aid your fellow men.

20. "Suffer her not to be humiliated, for by humiliating her you humiliate yourselves, and lose the sentiment of love, without which nothing can exist here on earth.

21. "**Protect your wife, that she may protect you—you and all your household. All that you do for your mothers, your wives, for a widow, or for any other woman in distress, you will do for your God.**"

(Wow. Here's an incredible argument on behalf of women from someone who was considered the most important person on the planet. Imagine if this had been in the Bible instead of the redacted version we've come to know so well. Imagine if these concepts had filtered into the religions of the world as well. Hard to imagine, but worth contemplating.)

XIII.
1. Thus Saint Issa taught the people of Israel **for three years,** in every city and every village, on the highways and in the fields, and all he said came to pass.
2. All this time the disguised spies of the governor Pilate observed him closely, **but heard nothing to sustain the accusations formerly made against Issa by the chiefs of the cities.**
3. But Saint Issa's growing popularity did not allow Pilate to rest. He feared that Issa would be instrumental in bringing about a revolution culminating in his elevation to the sovereignty, and, therefore, **ordered the spies to make charges against him.**
4. Then soldiers were sent to arrest him, and they cast him into a subterranean dungeon, **where he was subjected to all kinds of tortures, to compel him to accuse himself, so that he might be put to death.**
5. **The Saint, thinking only of the perfect bliss of his brethren, endured all those torments with resignation to the will of the Creator.**

6. The servants of Pilate continued to torture him, and he was reduced to a state of extreme weakness; but God was with him and did not permit him to die at their hands.
7. **When the principal priests and wise elders learned of the sufferings which their Saint endured, they went to Pilate, begging him to liberate Issa,** so that he might attend the great festival which was near at hand.

(Note: According to this account, the Sanhedrin argued to Pilate that he could not kill *anyone of "the Book,"* only *they* could. And so they went on their own to see if Jesus was preaching anything contrary to the Torah.)

8. But this the governor refused. **Then they asked him that Issa should be brought before the elders' council, so that he might be condemned, or acquitted, before the festival, and to this Pilate agreed.**
9. On the following day the governor assembled the principal chiefs, priests, elders and judges, for the purpose of judging Issa.
10. The Saint was brought from his prison. They made him sit before the governor, between two robbers, who were to be judged at the same time

with Issa, so as to show the people he was not the only one to be condemned.

11. And Pilate, addressing himself to Issa, said, **"Is it true, Oh! Man; that thou incites the populace against the authorities, with the purpose of thyself becoming King of Israel?"**
12. Issa replied, **"One does not become king by one's own purpose thereto. They have told you an untruth when you were informed that I was inciting the people to revolution. I have only preached of the King of Heaven, and it was Him whom I told the people to worship.**
13. **"For the sons of Israel have lost their original innocence and unless they return to worship the true God they will be sacrificed and their temple will fall in ruins.**
14. **"The worldly power upholds order in the land; I told them not to forget this. I said to them, 'Live in conformity with your situation and refrain from disturbing public order;' and, at the same time, I exhorted them to remember that disorder reigned in their own hearts and spirits.**
15. **"Therefore, the King of Heaven has punished them, and has destroyed their nationality and taken from them their national kings, 'but,' I added, 'if you will be resigned to your fate, as a reward the Kingdom of Heaven will be yours.'"**

16. At this moment the witnesses were introduced; one of whom deposed thus: **"Thou hast said to the people that in comparison with the power of the king who would soon liberate the Israelites from the yoke of the heathen, the worldly authorities amounted to nothing."**
17. **"Blessings upon thee!"** said Issa. **"For thou hast spoken the truth! The King of Heaven is greater and more powerful than the laws of man and His kingdom surpasses the kingdoms of this earth.**
18. **"The time is not far off, when Israel, obedient to the will of God, will throw off its yoke of sin; for it has been written that a forerunner would appear to announce the deliverance of the people, and that he would reunite them in one family."**
19. Thereupon the governor said to the judges: **"Have you heard this? The Israelite Issa acknowledges the crime of which he is accused. Judge him, then, according to your laws and pass upon him condemnation to death."**
20. **"We cannot condemn him,"** replied the priests and the ancients. **"As thou hast heard, he spoke of the King of Heaven, and he has preached nothing which constitutes insubordination against the law."**

21. Thereupon the governor called a witness who had been bribed by his master, Pilate, to betray Issa, and this man said to Issa: **"Is it not true that thou hast represented thyself as a King of Israel, when thou didst say that He who reigns in Heaven sent thee to prepare His people?"**
22. But Issa blessed the man and answered: **"Thou wilt find mercy, for what thou hast said did not come out from thine own heart."** Then, turning to the governor he said: **"Why dost thou lower thy dignity and teach thy inferiors to tell falsehood, when, without doing so, it is in thy power to condemn an innocent man?"**
23. When Pilate **heard his words, he became greatly enraged** and ordered that Issa be **condemned to death, and that the two robbers should be declared guiltless.**
24. The judges, after consulting among themselves, said to Pilate: **"We cannot consent to take this great sin upon us,—to condemn an innocent man and liberate malefactors. It would be against our laws.**
25. "Act thyself, then, as thou sees fit." **Thereupon the priests and elders walked out, and washed their hands in a sacred vessel, and said: "We are innocent of the blood of this righteous man."**

(When I first read this I thought – "Of course!" It never made any sense to me why the Roman ruler would kowtow to these Sanhedrin. No two ways around it, the story as presented in the Bible is that they came in to say "Get rid of Jesus" and Pilate hemmed and hawed, sent Jesus to Herod, did the reasonable thing - and then just caved to these Jewish elders who demanded Jesus be crucified.

Then went out and performed a Jewish ritual of "washing his hands" of the event. Just weird on all levels. This account just makes logical sense - they checked out Jesus' teaching and found it "not that different." But Pilate wouldn't have it, tried to torture a confession out of him, and when he didn't get that, argued for his death.

And finally Jesus mocks him - "Why lower your dignity and ask these fellows ("those beneath you") to lie on your behalf? Don't you have the balls to lie for yourself and "condemn an innocent man?" To which Pilate's reply is "crucify him." Jesus provoked him into acting. The Sanhedrin go out and do the ritual of washing their hands.

Just imagine the President of the US bowing to Mecca and saying prayers to Allah... oh, right people already think that's happening. It would have been the same equivalent for the Roman prelate - the head of the church in his region, whose responsibility it was to carry out the rites of the Roman gods and all their attendant deities - for him to perform a Jewish rite would have been heresy - off-with-his-head behavior. For no other reason this account seems logical that people behaved as reported.)

XIV.

1. By order of the governor, **the soldiers seized Issa and the two robbers, and led them to the place of execution, where they were nailed upon the crosses erected for them.**

2. All day long the bodies of **Issa and the two robbers hung upon the crosses, bleeding, guarded by the soldiers. The people stood all around and the relatives of the executed prayed and wept.**

3. **When the sun went down, Issa's tortures ended. He lost consciousness and his soul disengaged itself from the body, to reunite with God.**

4. Thus ended the terrestrial existence of the reflection of the eternal Spirit under the form of a man who had saved hardened sinners and comforted the afflicted.

5. **Meanwhile, Pilate was afraid for what he had done, and ordered the body of the Saint to be given to his relatives, who put it in a tomb near to the place of execution. Great numbers of persons came to visit the tomb, and the air was filled with their wailings and lamentations.**

6. **Three days later, the governor sent his soldiers to remove Issa's body and bury it in some other place, for he feared a rebellion among the people.**

7. **The next day, when the people came to the tomb, they found it open and empty, the body of Issa being gone.** Thereupon, the rumor spread that the Supreme Judge had sent His angels from Heaven, to remove the mortal remains of the saint in whom part of the divine Spirit had lived on earth.

8. **When Pilate learned of this rumor, he grew angry and prohibited, under penalty of death, the naming of Issa, or praying for him to the Lord.**

9. But the people, nevertheless, continued to weep over Issa's death and to glorify their master; wherefore, many were carried into captivity, subjected to torture and put to death.

10. **The disciples of Saint Issa departed from the land of Israel and went in all directions, to the heathen, preaching that they should abandon their gross errors, think of the salvation of their souls and earn the perfect bliss which awaits human beings in the immaterial**

world, full of glory, where the great Creator abides in all his immaculate and perfect majesty.

11. The heathen, their kings, and their warriors, listened to the preachers, abandoned their erroneous beliefs and forsook their priests and their idols, **to celebrate the praises of the most wise Creator of the Universe, the King of Kings, whose heart is filled with infinite mercy.**
(END OF BOOK)

Apologies for what appears to be a detour from the research into the afterlife. *I assure you, it is not.* I include this document primarily to point out that an alternate reality, an alternate story about Jesus already exists. This alternate history may be inaccurate, but it lays the groundwork for the interviews we're about to see.

A number of Biblical scholars have argued that Notovich was fake, a Charlatan and someone who denounced his book later in life. As I point out – since there is more than one translation of the book and they're nearly identical – Notovich did not translate the book found at Hemis. *His Sherpa did.*

The reason that I believe that Jesus exists, continues to exist on the Flipside, is from the eyewitness accounts from people who've seen him. And again, everyone who claims to see him sees a slightly different person. As I first said to Paul Aurand when asking him about these people who claimed to have known Jesus in their previous lives, "Did they all describe the same person?"

My point was that if everyone saw a guy with red hair, freckles – we would have a consensus as to what he looked like and if he existed. But like asking someone to describe an important event from their youth – in my case the assassination of JFK; we all will report different details differently. We can only look at the consensus of details to understand a deeper truth – this person existed, these people knew him, even if their accounts differ.

This "Life of Issa" document could be a hoax, but frankly I can't imagine why. A hoax requires someone's desire to pull something over on someone. Notovitch didn't translate it, didn't speak Tibetan or Pali, his Sherpa did; Notovitch can't be a suspect. There are numerous people who've been to Hemis and have heard about it or seen it over the centuries.[81] I heard about it independently from the abbot at Hemis, prior to knowing anything about it. I would argue that the document exists, or existed, is real; even if the person who wrote it made the entire story up.

The people who wrote it were trying to put down an account they'd heard of someone who had been a major religious leader, who reportedly spent time in Hemis. The question should be, "Who asked the monks to write it and why? Why write down the stories told by silk merchants who come to your door?" They must have had a compelling reason to do so. It doesn't paint Jesus as a Hindu, Brahmin, Jain, Jew or any other religion. It paints him as someone preaching an entirely new way of thinking.

Again, this is a translation that has gone from Pali or Tibetan to Russian to French to English and certainly doesn't represent anything that might have been said verbatim. There are two copies I'm aware of, one in Hemis as far back as tine 1960's, and one that was copied and sent to Lhasa. Does the original still exist in Hemis? I can't imagine why they would have destroyed it. Next time I'm in Hemis, I'll bring my camera.

I offer this chapter as groundwork for the following accounts from people who claim that while under hypnosis, or during an out of body experience, or while being interviewed with me on the phone, were able to recall details and events surrounding what you've just read. Namely accounts that confirm and corroborate many of the details from "the Life of Issa" that was translated twice, but remains *"discredited by every known religious" expert in the world."* I'm not an expert in anything – but I offer it to those who are experts in something - to see for themselves what it actually says. *Then compare it with the following reports.*

The Hemis Gompa

---

[81] TombOfJesus.com has a comprehensive list of the dozens who've claimed to see it. See Wikipedia's entry on Notovitch for the various claims the document is a hoax.

CHAPTER EIGHTEEN

People Who Claim to Have Met Jesus on the Flipside

I come from a long line of Catholics, both Irish and Italian.
My grandfather was baptized in this 5th century chapel in the Alps.

I've had a number of times Jesus shows up in my work. I did not set out to look for him, but when he showed up in the research, I noted it. For the most part, I've left this information out of my books. But since he keeps showing up, keeps insisting that I report what I'm hearing, and his insistence will likely *end* whatever writing career I thought I had, I'm offering *verbatim* how we got to this chapter.

While making my documentary "Flipside," during my interview with Paul Aurand, former President of the Newton Institute, I casually asked if there were any "recurring themes" that ran through his past life regressions. The reason I asked; the day before I had filmed him doing a session with a woman who remembered dying in Auschwitz. She spoke eloquently about the reasons for choosing such a difficult lifetime, and the lessons she learned from it. I was asking whether or not that was common; i.e., "a memory of a past life that took place during World War II."

RM: Do you find that percentage wise, many of your clients died in World War II?

Paul Aurand: "I've had quite a few people who in their regression are survivors of the Holocaust. I've had cases where there was a pattern of people who spoke about having once known a deep sense of being loved and loving, yet seemed to spend their lifetimes looking for it. Even though they found a loving relationship in this life, they were still experiencing a sense of disappointment, of feeling something was missing. Then, under hypnosis, they reconnect with it.

I've had a number of people go back to when Jesus was on the planet and being connected to his movement or experiencing life with Jesus or with those close to him; they had this deep sense of being loved. Then distraught when he was killed and living a number of lifetimes with the feeling "How could this have happened?" Some have said what a tremendous loss it was to humanity and "How could we exist without this sort of love?" and then not being able to find it anywhere on the planet.

And as they go into spirit, I remind them the energy isn't gone, it hasn't left the planet, love is still available, and they carry it within themselves. It's not out there with some other person or prophet or anyone else, it's within each of us.

After spending a lifetime of relationships saying "How disappointing, what's missing?" to learn - not by a Priest or a Minister or Rabbi or Psychic or a Reader - but through their own inner experience during one of these sessions, that loving energy is *still* in existence and they carry it within themselves; what a profound relief for them. They can offer it to others.

(Mouth agape. This was my first interview with a hypnotherapist who did past life regressions.) Some patients remember a past life with Jesus?

They remember a man who would tell stories, who would sometimes touch them, or his followers would touch them, and they would feel imbued with unconditional love. They felt this huge loss when he was killed.[82]

. . . . .

---

[82] From my interview with Paul Aurand, former president of the Newton Institute in "Flipside: A Tourist's Guide on How to Navigate the Afterlife."

I've had a number of people say pretty much the same thing while under hypnosis. The odd coincidence, as I've noted before, is that Scott De Tamble and I were discussing this unique tidbit the day before my filming a between life session with an old friend of mine, whom I call "Molly" in the book "Flipside." I said to Scott, *"Isn't it funny that people remember a lifetime with Jesus? Why don't therapists ask what he looked like? I mean, if they all say he had red hair and freckles, we'd know they're talking about the same guy."*

The following day we filmed this session at my friend's home (edited and excerpted from "Flipside: A Tourist's Guide on How to Navigate the Afterlife")

Scott: What part of the world are you in; a name, a place, a continent?

Molly: Jerusalem.

What is the year that you're experiencing?

I see 18.

Is there something before or after the 18? Is that before or after Christ, is that A.D. or B.C.?

I just see 18.

(Note: It's at this point I hand Scott a note: "Ask her if she knows "Jesus." Scott nods, then pockets the note.)

I'm going to lift your hand, let it be loose, your name as this little girl is going to come to you. Three, two, one...

June.

As I count to three, I want you to go to a very proud moment in your life as June. One, two, three... be there now.

I'm outside. I'm aware of other people and I'm in front of them.

How old are you?

Older. 20. I'm standing alone.

Why is this a proud moment for you? As they look at you, what's in their eyes?

Joy.

What are you wearing?

White.

Like a white dress, tunic or something?

(Nods) Uh-uh.

Does it feel like a special occasion?

Everyone's happy. (But I'm) Scared. I think I'm getting married...

Is this the ceremony?

There's no man, I don't see any man... I just see these people.

What happens next?

Maybe it's a play. Maybe it's acting. Feels like it. But there are no words. Like a performance.

(Note: Later, she observed that it might have been a "baptism.")

Where are you?

I'm still in Jerusalem.

You said the year is 18 something... is this the time when Jesus is alive, or before or after that?

Jesus is alive.

Have you ever met Jesus or seen him?

I think so.

As I drop your arm I want you to go to that moment when you behold Jesus; one two three. Be there now. Where are you?

In a large crowd. Outside.

How old are you?

My 20's.

What's going on? Is a crowd milling about?

They're listening. Someone's preaching.

How far away are you from the person talking?

About ten feet.

What's that person's name?

John comes to mind.

What's John talking about?

He wants... he keeps saying "Listen." I only hear "Listen."

What does he look like?

Not so tall; medium. He's thin. Has long hair, past his shoulders. It's flowing, lot of flowing hair. It's wavy. Color is dark brown. He's Bearded. Same color as his hair. Beard not so long; he's handsome.

How's the crowd responding to him?

Quietly. Patiently. Seriously.

Like he's saying something important...

Yes.

What's his full name?

I.. it makes me want to laugh, but I keep hearing "John the Baptist."

Is this a common occurrence in this part of the world, people out talking?

Yes, it's common.

Is this more special or rare, this guy? A celebrity or something?

He's important.

People are taking this to heart?

Yes.

How large is the crowd?

Hundreds.

What does John stand on?

He's standing on something. I don't know what it is. It's like a village where the tents are.

How do you feel?

I don't feel like I live there. I'm traveling, I'm just there.

Do your people travel a lot?

I feel like we're travelers.

Where is this?

It still feels like Jerusalem.

Tell me about your people, your way of life.

Always moving; we're gypsies.

How do they make their living?

Jewelry.

Do you see any other people talk? Have you ever seen Jesus talk or preach?

Maybe.

(Note: She later told me that June felt resistant to speaking about the following topic.)

If you've ever seen Jesus in the flesh, I want you to go to that scene, as I count from three to one. Be there now. If you've ever seen Jesus, the Christ in the flesh in this lifetime as this gypsy traveling girl, I want you to be there. If not, you can just go to some pleasant scene in her life. So what's coming into your mind?

(Starts to speak – doesn't.) **I feel mesmerized.**

Tell me more.

I feel I can't... I can't believe what I'm seeing.

Let go of that, and flow into what you're seeing and tell me about this. What are you seeing? Inside or outside?

I'm outside.

Alone or with others?

There are others. **I do see the face of Jesus.** He's speaking. I'm just mesmerized.

What is it about him that mesmerizes you so?

His purity. His honesty. His heart. His truth.

Tell me about his face.

Beautiful. I almost can't breathe.

It's okay. Imagine I'm a blind person, I want you to describe his face for me. What about the shape?

Narrow. Clean. Soft. Intense.

What about his color?

Tan.

Is it olive skin? Ruddy? Dark? Fair skin?

(Shakes head.) Tan. Just tan.

His face is narrow and tan. Tell me about his hair.

Simple. Long and simple. Thin. It's light brown. Shoulder length. Wavy.

What about his eyes?

They're brown, a golden brown.

(Note: Later she said that "clean" meant he didn't have a beard, his face was tan, as opposed to olive colored. Biblical scholars have debated that the father of Jesus may have been a soldier or someone named Pandera, as the Talmud refers to him as "Yeshua ben Pandera" or son of Pandera, whoever that may have been. But if he was a Roman soldier, he could have been from anywhere in the Empire. That might account for a fairer, or more "northern" complexion. She later told me she was standing "only a few feet" from him as he spoke.)

I want you to etch this in your mind for all time, I want you to be able to go back to this scene in your mind. You'll remember this forever.

(She cries.)

What is that you're feeling?

Such love.

Where do you feel that? In your body?

Everywhere (Cries).

Feel that, breathe it in. What else do you feel?

Humbled.

Tell me about the clothing of Jesus.

Brown. Different layers and pieces of clothing. Much of the same color.

Is he wearing a robe or tunic?

Robe.

Anything on his head? Feet?

Bare head, I just see his bare feet.

While Jesus is talking and you're feeling these feelings, what is he speaking of?

Love.

What is he saying about love?

That you *must* love. I just feel his kindness. It feels like the way it should be.

The kindness feeling?

Yes.

His words and presence really have an effect on you, don't they?

Yes.

Are you sensing that he's different from other speakers?

He's different.

How do the other people with you feel? Mesmerized?

Yes.

Just be there in his presence, drinking in his beauty and purity, take it into you. Let it transform you.

(Sighs)

Let's move forward to the end of the talk, what happens? Where does he go?

He just walks away. I go back to the tent.

Do you talk to anyone about this?

No. I'm just wondering where he will be next, I can see him again.

Let's go to the very last day June is alive, not yet have crossed over. Are you inside or outside?

Inside. Lying down. I'm 80 years old.

Go back to that day when you saw Jesus preach.

(Cries) He was my friend.

What do you mean by that?

I knew him. He was a friend to my people. He showed us how to live. How to love. To be good. To be kind. To be honest.

What happened to him?

He died.

Were you there? Or did you just hear about it later?

I couldn't see, I couldn't watch.

What happens to him?

He was killed. They beat him and tortured him. (Cries)

Did you know this was happening?

I couldn't take it.

You were present when this was happening?

I was near. It was my people that he watched and took care of.

I don't understand, could you be more clear?

Our friends, our family. He helped us.

By teaching you how to live?

To love and be kind.

And now he's being tortured and killed?

He's dead.

How do you know he's dead if you weren't watching?

It's what they say.

When you say he "helped your people," who are your people?

(Shakes head.)

A traveling people? You lived in tents?

Yes. Gypsies.

So he was a friend to your people?

Yes. He taught us how to live, how to love.

From when you saw him preach, how long of an interval goes by until he dies?

Years... Five comes to mind.[83]
....

Certainly, one person remembering a life lived with Jesus isn't that beyond imagination. "How can we prove it's real?" We can't. But when people

---

[83] From the Chapter "He Turned Sunset Into Sunrise" in "Flipside" ibid.

keep repeating the *same details in a number of accounts*, we then have to ask "So why are these details similar, since they aren't part of the religious record, or part of any religious tradition whatsoever?"

In this case, a friend of mine, who isn't particularly religious (but collects antique crosses as a hobby) remembers in vivid detail a lifetime where she knew Jesus. ***What are the freakin' odds of that?***

JESUS APPEARS IN MY COFFEE SHOP

There's a ghost in my coffee.

There's a café near my home where I meet up with friends and talk about all sorts of things, including these reports. A close friend I've known for 35 years told me about a powerful dream he'd had some years ago. It was after his father died, and he saw him standing on a basketball court, and behind him was a sign that read "*Him.*"

My friend thought that it related to his father's lack of faith, how later in life he had lost it, and then he felt that perhaps the dream meant he had found it. That the word "*him*" referred to God. I suggested that every dream, every memory we've had is still in our brain, if he wanted to examine it in fuller detail, we could.

I asked him to go the memory of that dream and examine his surroundings. After a bit, he said he saw he was standing on beige tile, and there was a fence behind him. I asked if anyone else besides his father was there, and he said "**There is. He looks like Jesus.**" My friend is Jewish, not overly religious, I know his Rabbi; so this would not be the average person to appear in any of his dreams, or in the memory of his dream.

I asked how he was dressed, what he looked like. He said "**He has brown eyes, long eyelashes, long hair; his skin is "swarthy."** I asked if that meant "tan" (from Molly's session) and he said "Yes." He said he was Caucasian with darker skin, beard, long hair. In his mind's eye he saw him wearing a robe with nothing on his feet. I asked if it was possible to have Jesus appear in some other clothing, jeans and a tee-shirt perhaps to make it easier to talk to him. My friend said he now saw this "Jesus looking fellow" in jeans and a tee shirt.

I asked if Jesus was good at basketball. (I try to ask impertinent questions to keep the mood light. After all, we're sitting in a coffee shop.) My friend paused for a while, then said "Jesus gave a slight smile, but said nothing." I felt my friend was trying to report precisely what he was seeing or sensing.

I asked how my friend *knew* this long haired fellow was Jesus. Was he wearing a name tag? He said *"It just feels like he's Jesus."* I said "Did you know this Jesus fellow in a previous lifetime?" He said "I don't know." I asked if we could ask him some questions directly. He said "Yes." I said "Jesus, if you knew this fellow in a previous lifetime, could you show it to him now? Can you put the image of that lifetime into his mind when you knew him?"

I asked my friend to describe what he saw. A male or female? He said "I see a male, about 30, with dark hair and a beard." When asked what year it was, he said "20." When asked what city it was, he said "Cairo." He said he saw this same "Jesus looking person" in the marketplace and "he was selling cloth." I asked if they were friends. He didn't remember them being so. I asked if he heard him speak, and he said he did. I asked him what he was speaking about. He said it was in the marketplace and he was selling him cloth.

I said "Who was selling cloth? Was it you or was it this Jesus looking fellow?" At first he said it was the Jesus looking fellow, but then later, when I asked his guide to show him *who* was selling the cloth, he said "Oh, right. I was selling *him* the cloth." The cloth was beige in color (the same color described as robes from other eyewitnesses; either beige or earth tones.)

I asked this "Jesus looking fellow" why he was showing our friend this lifetime? He said "Because you asked." I said, "But you've been appearing in memories of many people that I've met recently; so why are you showing up in these sessions? **Is it because you want me to recount this story for the book?"**

"Yes," he said.

……..

Afterwards, when I asked my friend to describe this Jesus looking fellow again, he said "blue eyes." I said "But when you first encountered him, his eyes were brown." He couldn't access that memory. The point being, when he was subconsciously answering the questions, he saw him pretty much as everyone else did, but when the filters came back up, he saw him as he'd seen him previously with his conscious mind – like the many paintings depicting him with blue eyes.

Again, my friends isn't Christian, he's not a believer in Christ from the religious point of view. When I called him "Jesus" my friend said, *"I never said he was Jesus, but that he was a Jesus looking fellow."* I pointed out to my friend how odd it was that he would suddenly show up. There was no religious reason for him to show up, because my friend didn't think of him as being related to "God" or that the sign "Him" would refer to Jesus. I told him that I initially wanted to leave Jesus out of the book, so as not to offend anyone.

My friend, who is a successful television writer-producer, said "So why do you want to pursue this Jesus part of the story if you're worried it might offend people?" I said that in numerous occasions, he (or someone pretending to be him) insisted I include this information in the book. So I will.

What am I supposed to do? *Argue with Jesus? Christ!*

JESUS APPEARS DURING AN OBE

This is excerpted from an interview I did with an old friend who says that she can have an "out of body" experience at will. She consciously decides to take a nap in the afternoon and goes on "these adventures" around the galaxy. I've known her a long time; she's a musician, actor and a heartfelt person. I don't believe she's making the following account up:

RM: (During your OBE's) Is there anyone else you've run into?

JK: Well, I flew with Jesus once.

What was that like? What did he look like?

It was unusual; I was holding onto him; he was wearing a white robe. He had a short, trimmed beard. **Wavy hair, long**. It was past his shoulders. He looked like paintings I've seen of him, so maybe that influenced my vision of him.

It's one of the questions people like to ask; what color were his eyes?

Brown.

Were there any flecks of gold in them?

Yes! How did you know?

You have to read "Flipside." What color was his skin?

Olive-y. **He was very tan**. He could have been Egyptian, or European. His skin wasn't the same as those of the region, **it was very tan**. He was beautiful. Lanky.

Do you recall how the trip started?

No. I was just holding onto him and we were zooming through space. My perspective was looking up at him, mostly.

How did you know it was Jesus? Was he wearing a name tag?

That's a good question. I just felt like I knew. I mean, yes, I grew up Catholic, and I saw a lot of pictures of him, and it was pretty close to the image I would have had for him – but in this case, there was this familiarity. **I just knew.**

It's my observation that when people during an NDE or LBL or now during an OBE see someone that they "know" – it's because they've seen that person before. Else, how could they "know" them?

Right!?

Also Jesus doesn't show up in the NDE's of people who aren't Christian, by the way. It's reported there are thousands of NDEs happening worldwide, all the time, and everyone kind of runs into the people they're familiar with. So that's a strong argument for people imagining that it's him. On the other hand, I've had three accounts of people who speak of him and claim he pretty much looked the same to all three.

I don't know. **There's just a familiarity.** It just seemed like it was him. **It wasn't like "Oh my god it's Jesus!" but it was more like "hey – it's Jesus."**

That's pretty profound. Thank you.[84]

As we'll see, Jesus will make another appearance or two later in this volume. The dude gets around.

INTERVIEW WITH MARY ABOUT WHAT JESUS' BIRTH WAS LIKE

I've talked to two different people who have had "Mary" appear during their meditations or sessions. One was a medium, who said she occasionally "felt" her presence during a session. She didn't say that she

---

[84] From "It's a Wonderful Life: Further Adventures in the Flipside" Volume Two; "Open Your Heart" Interview with someone who has out of body experiences at will.

saw her always as the same person – she sensed her "energy" more than was able to define her looks.

The other person is someone I met at a friend's wedding. She was the Minister at the wedding, and our conversation was about my research into the afterlife. She said she'd heard about between life sessions, she had a friend who was trained by a former student of Michael Newton. After our chat, she asked him to do a session with her. Her amazing session is reported in "It's a Wonderful Afterlife." I did not include her talking about Mary, as I wasn't sure how people might react. Truth is, people who would react are likely not reading this far anyway, so here goes.

While I was interviewing her over Skype, she told me that Mary had shown up in a few of her sessions. I asked if Mary could come forward "now." She closed her eyes and started to talk about her, as if she was nearby. I asked a number of questions, including "Why is it that whenever someone sees you or claims to have a visitation, you say relatively the same thing. "Love is all there is," or "Love everyone equally?" I asked why she didn't give more detailed, elaborate answers or observations.

She said that first of all, she spoke to those in her audience on a level that she felt they could understand her, and comprehend the most important part of anything she might say. That it wasn't her place to upset people's paths and journeys on the planet by coming and giving complex answers, but that she preferred to speak to people from her heart. She told them what they needed to hear.

Like anyone, I tend to doubt whatever I'm hearing from someone who claims to be "talking to someone famous." As we've seen in this book, if you suspend your disbelief to hear what people have to say, they may give you *new information* that you weren't aware of before.

I asked the Minister to notify me if she heard anything else from Mary, or if she could describe in detail what she looked like:

She wrote:

"Mary has appeared to me in (past) journeys as a younger brunette woman with some freckles. She's also appeared as a later middle-aged woman (with crow's feet, salt and pepper hair, and a thicker build) with the same coloring.

As the older woman, Mary's energy is stronger, fiercer; there's a much deeper maternal love. It's not treacly-sweet love - it's love that isn't about her at all because it's all about you – **it's agenda-free. I can't describe the intensity of her bottomless devotion and the warmth and peace it brings.**

(Note: Unconditional love, anyone?)

She is always in some sort of robe - sometimes blue, like the Catholic statues, sometimes silky white with a floral pattern, sometimes in a simple earth-tone. A note about the church statues: when she first started appearing to me in journeys, she was very much like that - almost inanimate and very solid. Over time, she has become more flesh (by which I mean, "that's how I can now see her"). I get the sense that this shift isn't an accident.

On one hand, my perception of *the Feminine* has shifted as I've healed a lot of my own stuff. On the other, she has been portrayed as a pious virgin to the point of becoming inhuman, which has sort of calcified the energy that she carries. In her truer form, she is incredibly vital and hot-blooded. She is always and ever a mother, and -- like all women -- she is also a queen when she needs to claim that part of herself to make a point, or when it will be helpful for others to see."
……..

I asked if there were any details of something that occurred or happened in Mary's life that she could access. After a few days, she sent me this email, a memory that came to her of Mary giving birth. She wrote:

"In the stable, (I can see) the cows bellow and pant with curiosity and empathy. There are no midwives here, or if there are, there isn't time to find them in this strange town. I am already in labor, needing to push. (My husband) Joseph lays me down on a bed of straw and kneels between my legs.

"Where are the angels now?" There is no dignity in this birth that they foretold would be so glorious. I feel the heat and wetness of blood between my legs, the gush and the pain as he is pulled out by his father. **Our other son watches, stroking my hand and my face, the sweat turning cold in the night air. He pushes a hair from my eyes.**

Once it is done, I can appreciate the cool air, the crystal clear night and the stars in the heavens, which I can see through the open door. Joseph closes the door and returns to my side, our new child now at my breast. I am in love.

What a perfect child he is! I feel the familiar tug at my nipple, and peer down into the little wrinkled face of my beloved. **He seems like an old friend, this one, as though we have met many times before. Ours is an ancient bond.** I am comforted by the smells of livestock, so familiar no matter where we may go.

The sheep are sweet and gentle, and seem to know what has occurred here. They are strange hosts, but I feel their kind nature. In the warmth of the straw and blankets, with my family around me, I may even rest for a while. Tomorrow will be.

Tonight, I may sleep for the first time in ages, a deep, silent, dreamless sleep. **I feel the angel again** and know that all will be well, even with the flutter of panic in my stomach. We rest as a family, though I know that Joseph will not really sleep until we are in a home that he has built with his own hands.

In the days that follow, we are surprised by guests. I am lonely for women, for the company of my sisters and mother and mother-in-law, for the nurturing and assistance they provide.

I am lonely for a daughter, for the ways of female relatives at these times. But we are met by three men, foreigners who say they were bade to travel here to meet this boy child. They bring gifts for him, though what a child is to do with myrrh I don't know.

There is a strange foreboding in this, a gift used for embalming given to an infant. We have already escaped death, fleeing from Herod's decree and narrowly making it here to Bethlehem.

The journey was hard for me, and for our son. Joseph is a good, strong man and it is due only to his resourcefulness that we have survived and can now make a new life here. I don't know what the future holds for us. I don't know what work he will find or where we will live. I know only that I love our sons with all my heart.

This new one, this Yeshua, what will his life be like? What is in store for him, for us, with such a strange beginning? The inauspiciousness of being born a refugee in such an impersonal place, coupled with the angel visit and these magi?

Who is this child? **I am overcome suddenly with tremendous humbleness. He may be a great rabbi, or an infamous one. He may upset kings, or become one, or both.** Whoever he is, I am chosen to be his mother. I feel ill-equipped, except that I know I'm a good woman and will try hard.

Whatever becomes of him, he will know his mother's love. **I will protect him until he is too old for my watch, and I will be there whenever he falls. To be the mother of such a one as this may require more strength than I have ever known.**

I tremble and cry at this, feeling humble and small, and yet I know that there is a reserve of strength within me that has never been tapped. I will have it when the time comes, and I know this with utter clarity and certainty.

Just as I know I love my sons, my husband, and the peaceful moment here in the stable, stars above, warmth within, and the quiet, even breath of the cows."

…..

Interesting first person account. Impossible to confirm any of these details, unless I run into someone who remembers their lifetime as Joseph or the Magi perhaps. (I now wouldn't be surprised if that happened as well.)

Since so much has been written about Mary, the only observation I can make is that her account of seeing Mary with "salt and pepper hair" coincides with another account I've heard. Perhaps "Mary" wants to demonstrate to whomever sees her that she was a woman, after all, a human, who got older, and lived a full life.

In this account, my friend refers to her "angel" ("*I feel the angel again*"). Then a little later, the "angel has returned." If we consider perhaps that "angels" may be our spirit guides, or someone who helps us with the stressful times in our life (as many have reported, including Prince who said an angel came to tell him he would be cured of his epilepsy) we can see them not as mythological creatures, but just souls who work as helpers and healers.

The Bible of course has a number of angels showing up to different people. But as I considered this research, instead of going into a Catholic brain freeze about the word "angel," I wondered if it was possible these might possibly be "accurate" accounts of visitations by spirit guides. The argument would be "Once we're off the planet, we're outside of time, so we can visit any part of the timeline on Earth." For example, if I'm outside of time and I want to visit an event 2000 years ago, or an event yesterday, I can effectively be in two places at the same time. (I had this experience, which I reported in "Flipside.")

The unusual thing is that the Jewish, Christian and Islamic traditions refer to the same angel – Gabriel – making visits to three important people. Abraham, to stop him from killing Daniel, to Mary's mother to tell her that she's going to have a daughter by Virgin birth, and Mohammed, who is told to go inside a cave to receive the transmission that became the Qur'an. *What if it was the same fellow?* I mean I understand the craziness of the question, but if we step outside of time for a moment, together, we can see how it could be possible for the same individual to show up at three different points in human history.

Again, I'm not claiming this is Mary's account of the birth of her son. This is a person who works as a healer, a spiritual person who officiates weddings. She doesn't sell anyone on the idea that Mary shows up in her meditations, and at the point I interviewed her, it wasn't something she'd admitted to anyone. I was interviewing her about her "between life session" which I included in "It's a Wonderful Afterlife" and at some point she revealed this aspect of Mary visiting her. I asked "Is she wearing a name tag? How do you know it's her?" She described someone different than the traditional "visitation by a woman in blue" that is common in the "Mary sightings." In this case, she described someone who appeared to her sometimes as the Mary of her mind's eye – as depicted in paintings - but then later, appeared as the salt and pepper haired older woman.

Perhaps it's just important to point out that the mother of Jesus was a physical living breathing human being who was once on the planet, so therefore she would still be accessible to our prayers, or whatever we'd like to ask her. In this case, it appears she tailors her message to those who reach out to her.

This is from a chapter in "It's a Wonderful Afterlife" where a medium is speaking to the deceased son of a doctor. It is an interview where the son has offered to bring Jesus forward to speak to the medium and his mom. If you've read volume two, you've read this chapter, and I've added a few different notes. But basically, I came across this interview online, then contacted the people involved about their process of obtaining it. I'll let it speak for itself.

The construct is this; a doctor whose son is no longer on the planet, offers to bring "someone" to an interview. Usually the doctor has a list of possible candidates to interview, and while speaking to her son through a medium, live on camera, she asks him who "he'd like to bring to be interviewed." She's prepared questions for a number of individuals, it's left up to her son to whomever he's going to bring forth. In this case, the idea was to interview Jesus.

Her son went off to find his "friend Jesus," and then brought him back for the interview:

Interview with Jesus

Medium (Looks off to the side, whispers) Jesus is here.

Doctor: (Jesus,) do you know why we're here?

Medium: (Nods) Please.

Doctor: First I'd like to ask. "What was your spiritual mission of the life that we know? What were you here to do?"

Medium: He (Jesus) came in dressed in a robe; a robe like a wrap or something, it kind of emits its own light It doesn't look like clothing.

Then I heard your son say "Show them what a cool guy you are" and as he was saying (that), I looked over and I (now) **see Jesus in jeans and sandals and a tee shirt.** It's a scooped neck tee shirt, white, long sleeve, kind of linen, there are no markings on it. It hangs, it's not tucked in.[85]

Doctor: So Jesus, what was your spiritual mission (here on Earth)?
Medium: He said it was **"To try and simply show the people on Earth the importance of the afterlife."**

Doctor: From what I understand you are different from us because you came in without that spiritual amnesia. You came remembering who and what you were?

Medium: (listens) He said "Yes."

Doctor: Did you realize that even as a child?

Medium: He says "By age 3 he recognized he was different than others."

Doctor: In what way?

Medium: (speaking as if repeating verbatim) **"I knew that we were all connected together, that we were not alone."** He said "I couldn't understand why people would cry or have grief or feel separated. I couldn't understand it." -- When he was alive and a young boy, he couldn't understand why people wouldn't take care of themselves; that they would choose to become weak or a victim.

---

[85] This interview is reprinted from "It's a Wonderful Afterlife: Further Adventures in the Flipside" Volume two. All rights to the text of the interview belong to Dr. Medhus., ChannelingErik.com

He said **"It pulled on the fabric of the energy all around us and weighed people down,"** and he said **"I knew that's not who I was"** -- and he said **"I had access to all the voices that came before me."** (Listens, and then says an aside to the Doctor) Your son just asked him to describe that more – (Jesus) said "The spirits, angels, uh, God..."

Doctor: And you could tap into any information you wanted? Like my son can now?[86]

Medium: Yes, it was free form.

(Note: Interesting that Jesus said he had access to "all the voices that came before me." Like an "all access pass" to the afterlife being able to "hear" all those who had been here before... except perhaps when he no longer could hear them and asked "Lord, why have you forsaken me?" later in his life?)

Doctor: Was there any very impactful event that happened in your childhood that made you the man that you were?

(Note: This is one of the questions The Doctor asks everyone in these sessions, It's not specifically addressed to him.)

Medium: (Listens, observes) He smiles – he has facial hair though it's not bushy, I don't see it as being a long beard; it's just kind of trimmed, kind of modern looking. But he says all of what he did as a child made him the man that he is today. But the most impactful was the suffering that his mother experienced, that he knew was unjust...

---

[86] How does this interview align with quotes from the Good Book? Well, there's quite a bit of discussion of what the afterlife might be like. In Luke 23:43 Jesus says to the fellows crucified alongside him; "Truly, I say to you, today you will be with me in Paradise." There's the story Jesus gives about not being able to get to heaven unless it's through him – or as he states later in this interview – through his examination of the nature of reality. Matthew 10:28 "Do not fear those who kill the body but cannot kill the soul." (Another common theme in these reports.) John 14:2 "In my Father's house are many rooms. If it were not so, would I have told you that I go to prepare a place for you?" Soul groups are described as existing in "many rooms." John 18:36 Jesus answered, "My kingdom is not of this world. If my kingdom were of this world, my servants (disciples) would have been fighting that I might not be delivered (to the Romans). But my kingdom is not from the world." Again, this would also be accurate for someone speaking from memory about the afterlife.

Doctor: What kind of suffering?

Medium: (continuing) "…and he took it as a message to not let people suffer any more." And he said **"I understood that I was a healer, understood I created cures by using God."** (Medium listens) And your son said – (aside to the Doctor) I'm getting a thumbs up (from your son who then asks Jesus) – "If you were alive today would you still feel comfortable using the term God?"

Doctor: Very nice (question).

Medium: (aside to the Doctor) He's kind of talking directly to your son I'm just kind of listening in – he (Jesus) said **"Yes, he's comfortable with using the word God, but he's uncomfortable with the definition that's been attached to it; it's been fragmented."**[87]

Doctor: You mean God as an entity that is separate from each of us. Does he (Jesus) have dark or light skin?

Medium: **(Jesus is) like a very, very tan tanned Caucasian.** Not white skin, but tan. Fine features, skin is not rough; it doesn't look like it's been in the sun forever.[88]

Doctor: Was your birth an "Immaculate Conception?"[89]

---

[87] There's a point in the Bible where Jesus takes James to meet spirit guides. (Perhaps they were always advising him throughout his life?). Matthew 17:1-27 "And after six days Jesus took with him Peter and James, and John his brother, and led them up a high mountain by themselves. And he was transfigured before them, and his face shone like the sun, and his clothes became white as light. And behold, there appeared to them Moses and Elijah." And Peter said to Jesus, "Lord, it is good that we are here. If you wish, I will make three tents here, one for you and one for Moses and one for Elijah." He was still speaking when, behold, a bright cloud overshadowed them, and a voice from the cloud said, "This is my beloved Son, with whom I am well pleased; listen to him." (King James version) It reminds me of accounts where people claim to have met or seen their spirit guides during an NDE or LBL.

[88] For those students of history, Roman historian Celsus reported that Jesus was the son of Mary and a Roman soldier of Greek heritage named Pantera. If that was possibly the case, it may offer a logic as to how Jesus have Caucasian features, "part Greek" or as reported here; "a deep tan."

[89] "Immaculate conception" as a religious term refers to the birth of Mary, not Jesus. It's something often mixed up with the idea of Mary being a virgin (the Church created this idea to ensure she was "without sin" coming into the world or giving birth), but the "Immaculate conception" refers to Mary's mother's conception. However, his answer would apply to either event.

Medium: (Listens, observes) He smiles and tilts his head -- he said **"No."**

Doctor: Reflecting on your life; do you think you accomplished your mission?

Medium: Yes, and (to Doctor) your son started laughing; his comment was "Well I think he did a pretty good job because people are still talking about him thousands of year later!"

Doctor: That's true. How do you feel (about) how they revere you, the way they spread your word, so to speak? Are they doing what needs to be done? Are they distorted? Are there things you're not happy with?

Medium: (Aside) He sits down in front of me, it's on a side table but it doesn't seem to matter to him, he's very comfortable... He (Jesus) says "A lot of my children have gotten lost. **A lot of my children have taken my words too literally and too directly and have decided to create a cause, or war, in defense of my words. If I were able to walk the Earth today, I would tell my children (that) to argue or to defend or to force others to believe in the words that you cherish so deeply for yourself, is the wrong way to encourage life.**

Doctor: (In agreement) Ok, 'fighting against things;' resisting it is part of the ego anyway.

Medium: Your son jumped in and said **"You know there is no right or wrong."** Jesus nodded his head. He said **"Correct, but those who live on Earth who are causing the disruption, wholeheartedly believe there is a right or wrong. So to teach them what is right and wrong, you must (first) teach them there is a right or wrong before you can teach them the concept there is no right or wrong."**[90]

Doctor: Were you here to learn anything, Jesus?

---

[90] I've found a similar dialectical in the argument of the nature of reality in the teachings of Buddhism – to define what the self is, first you have to define that there is a self, before you can define that there is "no self" (or a relative self that is always changing through learning). In essence, Jesus is saying he understands (and agrees) that in the afterlife there is no right or wrong (which has been consistently in all the LBL sessions I've filmed, as well as the many thousands of cases Michael Newton has observed), confirming that as a concept "right and wrong" do not exist per se in the afterlife. There is no "judgment," per se, and everyone is treated with compassion with love for the lessons they might learn or be learning.

Medium: (Aside to the Doctor) He's like, leaning in with this elbows down, his hands are folded (demonstrates) not clasped, they're folded. **He says (Medium's voice breaks) my heart's racing... (Pauses, clears throat...) He said that... um. (Emotionally overwrought) I told him maybe he should scoot back a little bit; the closer he gets to me the more I feel like I have to cry. (Smiles. Wipes away tears. Laughs.)** Thank you. He scoots back.[91]

Doctor: What was he here to learn?

Medium: He said he was here to "**Freely give of himself 100%, but still maintain a sense of individuality and purpose, it wasn't to surrender all to his children.**" He calls them "children" and your son asked "What's that?" and (Jesus) said "followers, believers."

Doctor: What was he here to teach?

Medium: (A high pitched noise appears on the tape) He said he was here to teach that there are many pathways to God. **He said that he repeated to others he was not the only way, though he said it was rewoven by other people to state that "he is the only way."** He said he "**would not take the time to feed his ego that way, that it was worthless effort.**"

Jesus: "Useless effort."

(Note: There's a male voice that can be heard at this point, correcting the Medium by saying "**Useless effort**" – the Medium does not hear it, nor does the Doctor, but I can hear it with my editing equipment on the video. By boosting the volume of the dialog on the tape, a male voice can distinctly be heard saying what sounds like a correction – *instead of "worthless effort" it should be "useless effort."* I have the equipment that can slow down or speed up dialog, and can parse it out to hear it clearer. Allow me to say that in my professional opinion; a male voice interrupts the Medium to say "**useless effort**")

Medium: (Continuing) He's one of many ways to reach God. He says he was also here to teach that the many ways... - that you should always start with self, to go in to find God, you go in and outward (gestures inward and

---

[91] Same effect that Jesus had on "Molly" during her remembrance of him in "Flipside." The closer she got, the more she couldn't breathe from emotion.

outward) -- It was not to place the responsibility of belief and spirituality with another person, it was only to be done within the temple (points inward) and the body is the temple, the Church is not *the* temple.

Doctor: Do you have any regrets? (I) feel weird asking, but you were human at the time.

Medium: **He regrets he did not have the opportunity to speak out past his death, what was considered to be his death; he says that he did not die. He says that he did not die on the cross. That he was not kept in his stone tomb, that he had a life beyond that.**

Doctor: How did that happen?

Medium: His regret (is) that he didn't have the means or the opportunity to tell that story, because he knew as the story stood, it was more powerful to give people a hope in what God could provide and the afterlife could provide. **He says that he studied the same way of the Tibetan monks, where they can stay in meditation for days, weeks, without food, um... they appear unconscious, their heart almost lays dormant. It is a way of control over the temple, over the body.**

(Note: At this point I nearly fell out of my chair. As mentioned, when I was at the Hemis monastery in Ladakh, which used to be Tibet until 1949, and now is part of the Indian state of Kashmir, the abbot of the monastery told me that Jesus had studied at his monastery. (The book by Notovich quoted earlier) I thought I had misheard him and he clarified it by saying "Issa as he is known in Asia."

Also the Qur'an claims that Jesus *survived the crucifixion* as well. But at this point in the interview, when the person in the interview says that he "studied ways of Tibetan monks" I knew what was being talking about – and later confirmed that the Medium nor the Doctor were aware of this esoteric information. It might be common knowledge among those who've studied stories about Asia, or yoga practices, but it was not part of the medium or The Doctor's background.)[92]

Medium: (continuing) It was what he practiced in... ("control over the body"). He said he went... that he **"traveled to several countries before**

[92] https://en.wikipedia.org/wiki/Jesus_in_Ahmadiyya_Islam

he was announced to be the son of God and studied in many different cultures and beliefs," he said "I did this because I knew there were many ways... to achieve the one path."

(Note: As noted from the book, Jesus traveled extensively along the silk route, and studied with the Zoroastrians in Persia, the Jain and Hindus in India, and finally the Buddhists.)

"But it would have been wise for me to know intimately what they were. I had all the power, though I lacked the knowledge as a human..." and so he gathered the knowledge. And he was able to learn and he said his "followers – even the um... his disciples, even the guards (she imitates holding a spear) were able to come to his rescue and help him in a way, so he could come out of this state of being, and live this life."

Doctor: Where did you live your life?

Medium: **He's showing me three different countries – I can see France...** (Moves her hands to indicate two others)

Doctor: Did you get married?[93]

Medium: "Yes."

Doctor: How many children did you have?

Medium: **He lived his life under another title and name and kept a very secret way of teaching.**

Doctor: Did you marry Mary Magdalene?

Medium: Your son (just) asked that. He said **"she was his only true love."** He's saying he knew **"How important it was for women to be**

---

[93] According to the Qur'an, Jesus survived the Crucifixion and went to teach in India. Also, the Gospel of Thomas, part of the Gnostic Gospels, claims that Thomas saw Jesus in India later in life. There is a person who appeared in Asia early in the first century, called "Yuz Asaf" (the anointed one) and he preached in Persia (there's a monument to him there, where he claimed "I am the way and the light" and was traveling with his mother "Mary of Virgin Birth." The "tomb of Mary" is in Muree, Pakistan). The "Anointed One" made his way to Kashmir, where he married, had children, and was buried. As mentioned (or perhaps apocryphally) there's a cast of his feet next to the tomb; one can clearly see holes in those feet as if from a crucifixion. (Ref: TombOfJesus.com)

considered equals to men – so among the disciples... though you may have learned in the Bible all the disciples were men; they were not."

Doctor: Was Mary (Magdalene) one of the disciples?[94]

Medium: He said yes.

Doctor: How many children did you have?

Medium: He's saying **"Five and that two died young."**

(Note: As we'll hear later in the interview with Jennifer, the same number is mentioned)

Doctor: Can you share another life? Have you had any other lives?

Medium: He said he's had past and future lives (after the life of Jesus). He says not all of them were as clear as the life he was able to have as Jesus. (Medium pauses; listens) I don't understand. (Listens.)

Your son, my "translator" (smiles) says that Jesus was saying, that though he had many different lives, it wasn't just the one where he was this amazing saint; this son of God. **All the other lives he's experienced, had somewhat that same characteristic about him.**

He's always been a spiritual healer, (doing) spiritual work -- a person who encourages energy work, afterlife thought and beyond. I asked him "Can you please look at one you want to share?" (There's a pause... another high pitched noise on the tape). 1962. He came in as a very sick baby boy, uh, this actually happens to be in United States; he lived his life in the hospital, he was never able to come home. He had... a wire frame on him. A metal frame as if, he says, "his muscles wouldn't grow, they couldn't hold weight, so they created a frame for him to be able to move about." He lived until the age of four.

Doctor: Four years in the hospital?

Medium: Yes.

---

[94] For those familiar with the recently discovered "Gospel of Mary," a 4th century document, this concurs with the idea that "Mary Magdalene" was not only his closest confidant, but also a disciple. According to that account, she was closer to Jesus than the other apostles.

Doctor: What was the reason for that sort of hardship?
Medium: He said it wasn't hardship as the little boy was very happy; he knew no other life, you know. He wasn't able to run or play; it's like his skin would tear and his bones would break.[95]

Doctor: **Osteogenesis imperfecta** *maybe? Like Soft bones?*

Medium: (Nods) Yeah. So he was cornered and kept away, but he came to this life to impact the doctors and nurses and the family he came into, and in turn other people... He says **"You find (that) the life of the child that struggles the most, impacts the community to make a change."** He takes time to reincarnate as some of these beings, to impact and **give peace to the people... so they can learn about what death is, about what life is meant to do or be.**

(Note: "You find the life of the child that struggles the most impacts the community to make a change." This bears out in the research, that those who have the hardest time of it, often are older souls who've chosen difficult lives because "they can handle them." Interesting that the Doctor remembers the name of the illness, but he does not.)

Doctor: Are you currently on the Earth in some form?

Jesus: "Yes."

(Note: I heard a male response of the word **"Yes."** The Doctor did not hear it, nor did the Medium at the time. But it is clearly on the tape. I used my equipment to isolate that voice, to boost the sound – to speed it up and slow it down. It's clear, at least in my professional opinion, that a male voice responds with the word **"Yes."**

There however is no voice sound wave imprint on the sound track – I've boosted it quite a bit, and there's no sound signature. There is possibly some other reason I'm not aware of – voices off camera appearing on a sound track – but timing of the response was as if this person was

---

[95] This is consistent with between-life research. According to these reports, older, wiser souls generally choose the lives of difficulty as they feel they can handle them. From the perspective of the boy in the hospital, Jesus (or whoever is replying) says that his was a happy life. This is not the usual perspective of someone who talks about someone being born with a crippling disease – however, what he says is consistent with thousands have claimed about the afterlife and our journey here.

responding to the question. **"Are you currently on the Earth in some form?" "Yes."** In my *professional opinion* as a guy who makes films; whoever she was speaking to responded directly. The Medium paused, did not act like she heard the "Yes," and then responds with "He said "Yes.")

Medium: He said "Yes." He said he's in India. He's a woman.

Doctor: Spiritual teacher or healer?

Medium: Yes.

Doctor: What's her first name? I don't want to give last names.

Medium: M..o..n.. a... is all I can see - Mona seems to be a shortened version of something more intricate.

Doctor: Ok, what do you do in the afterlife? What's your life's work there?

Medium: **Giving peace to those who arrive.** [96]

Doctor: I hope when I cross over I get to meet you. What do you think about the current state of humanity?

Medium: He says "It is what it's supposed to be. When you remove yourself from the human life, you're able to see the possibilities -- the possibilities that we see (over here) are not yet exposed to the masses on Earth. I know there is an opportunity for great exponential growth." (Aside to the Doctor) Your son is asking to "Please share about when that would be and how that would impact the people that are still living." And Jesus responds that… "Inventions…" He's talking about "when inventions and spirituality come together."

Doctor: So science and spirituality will be bridged in some way. When will that be?

---

[96] As mentioned, in many NDE's people claim that Jesus greets them, and at some point tells them it's not their time. If one considers for a moment that being outside of Earth time is another time space continuum altogether – being outside of time, is literally outside of time – Jesus showing up a variety of places to a variety of people simultaneously is a possibility. He either is there, or he isn't, but in this interview, he's "giving peace to those who arrive." And for those who aren't supposed to be there, a gentle pat on the back as they return. All think the Medium meant to say "more elaborate" than "more intricate."

Medium: Uh, it will start reaching... uh - all right, yeah... (As an aside) Everyone's having a conversation right now – (Listens) "It will leak out, it will start to leak out in about four more years -- about what's already been done, and then from there, it will take about ten years for everything that's already been done to come to light and be explained.

Because it's going to turn how you learn, who you are, what the school systems do, what business is based on, what belief is based on -- it has to affect everything; it will affect everything."

(Note: "It will affect everything." Imagine if you will for a moment that this is accurate. That some event will occur that will affect everything we know; business, education, medicine; a truly transformational event. Let's hope he's correct.)

Doctor: Is the Bible true; was it really a spiritual document?

Medium: "Back in the day that it was written, it was considered very enlightening. As it has grown -- people have outgrown it. The morals are still true, but the stories they weave around it are being taken for literal -- when in truth they're written by humans -- which would then (cause them to) consider it (the Bible) to be personal perspective or personal opinion of a situation that has occurred."

Doctor: What would you like to tell us? Any messages for humanity?

Medium: "The work must come from within – not out – the work must be internal so that you may then begin to create a community."

Doctor: (The) most important thing is to recognize or destroy the ego?

(Medium shakes head "no.")

Doctor: Does ego have a positive purpose?

Medium: "Yes." The way he shows it in my head, is for it to be the foundation of the house; "But not on every floor, it shouldn't be in every board that built the house, not in the artwork, or the furniture."

Doctor: What would you like to tell us that we don't know or totally misunderstood about you?

Medium: That (question) created laughter. And um… Mr. Crisp (says that he) thinks that Jesus is a very good looking man…

(Note: At this point in the audio, two males voices appear; the first one has a slight drawl or southern accent (which the Doctor confirmed was in the son's background). The voice says something that sounds like **"Can you go and talk about this**?"

Another voice clears his throat and whispers what sounds to me like **"We're done with selfishness" or "selflessness"** as in "we're done with that topic of the ego." Neither the Doctor nor the Medium heard either of these voices during the session, and both voices appear on the video without a sound signature.

When I first heard it, I asked if the Doctor or Medium could have had workmen in the house, or next door, or listening in, or standing by. They said that they did not.[97])

Medium: (continues) "One of the physical misconceptions (that Jesus wants to correct); he has brown eyes not blue, he says another misconception is that (it has been claimed) he was specific in who he would speak to, (or) that he was very private.

He said this is very untrue – it was actually the disciples around him that felt they needed to protect - keep him (protected)… To protect Jesus – he said "It's why he would, (like in the) "Sermon on the Mount" - talk so freely for so many people. It's (also) why he chose to walk from city to city, so he could reach others. That he did not judge if you believed in his words or not." He said "I love you (all) just the same." Third misconception; he does not condemn people. "He does not stop people from reaching God."

---

[97] They claim there was no possible way for male voices to appear on the audio without them knowing about it. The manner in which it was recorded (Skype) would preclude voices drifting in – and the clearing of the throat was unusual as well. (The Doctor noted that this clearing of the throat was something his son did "all the time." When she asked him why he'd have a tic in the afterlife, he said it was "he wanted me to recognize it was really him." She can also hear pacing, and was typical of his son "Pacing around the kitchen, arms crossed, head lowered, to help him think.") When I speeded the file up by 50%, the voices sounded normal – as they're recorded they sound a bit slow, or drawn out. If it's accurate that things are sped up in the afterlife, this might account for why they sound "slow" on the tape – I was just listening to them at the wrong speed.

Doctor: It's not like "If you don't believe in Jesus, then you go to hell, get condemned?"

Medium: (Nods) Correct.[98]

Doctor: Is that all created as a power play by man or is it just an honest misunderstanding?

Medium: **"Power play by man."**

Doctor: One more question. What about the Shroud of Turin? Is that yours?

Medium: The face on the..? You're talking about the face on the..? Your son asked that earlier, he never responded, we kept talking, when he talked about the tomb, your son asked it... (Listens). Ok. Um, It is. **"It is him."**

[99]*Doctor: Jesus, thank you very much; anything you want to say?*
Medium: He says he gives you his thanks – **"Especially in the desire to seek honesty and not driven by curiosity, belief, or money."**

Doctor: I love you. Bye.

Medium: He said **"I love you too."** (She waves.) He waves. And turned and walked out kind of through the wall and the bookcase and everything.

DR. BRIAN WEISS MET JESUS AS WELL

---

[98] Here Jesus is starting to sound a bit like the new Pope Francis, although this was recorded years before he came upon the scene.

[99] It's interesting to note here that the Medium is remembering bits of conversation that were said only moments earlier and repeating them verbatim. If there was any pretense or desire to fabricate a story, why admit that you missed speaking of that earlier? Either way, they've done forensic testing of the shroud, and overturned the earlier conclusions (based on a later piece of cloth), and have confirmed that the cloth is from the area and because of its reputation, is a likely candidate for being used on Jesus. Apparently the cloth covered Jesus in the cave while his body was being restored by aloe and myrrh, and using the techniques he'd learned in Tibet, was able to recover quickly from. At least that's what it appears may have happened.

St. Anne with daughter Mary

I happened to read this in Dr. Weiss' book. Dr. Weiss is a Yale psychiatrist who was using hypnosis to help patients in his practice, when a woman spontaneously went into a past life recall, As a result, she was healed of her psychosomatic illness. Dr. Weiss' first book was "Many Lives, Many Masters" and this excerpt is from his follow up book; "Same Soul, Many Bodies."[100]

> "In "Only Love is Real," I wrote briefly about a past life memory of my own. I was a young man from a very wealthy family living in Alexandria some two thousand years ago. I loved to travel and roam the deserts of northern Egypt and southern Judea, often investigating the caves where the Essenes and other spiritual groups lived at the time. In fact, my family had contributed to their well-being.
>
> During one journey I met a man somewhat younger than I, who was exceptionally bright, and we camped and traveled together for about a month. He soaked up the teachings of these spiritual communities much faster than I did. Though we became good friends, eventually we went our separate ways...
>
> **I did not relate the rest of this story at the time because it was extremely personal, and I did not want people to think I wrote out of self-congratulation: "Dr. Weiss in the time of Jesus." You'll see shortly why I do so now, for it is Victoria's story, not mine.**

---

[100] From Brian Weiss's book "Same Soul, Many Bodies" Free Press (October 26, 2004) pg 38

I saw my companion again in Jerusalem, where I often traveled because my family conducted much of their business there. I experienced myself in that storied city as a scholar, not a businessman, though I was still wealthy. **By this time, I had affected an immaculately trimmed salt and pepper beard and wore an extravagant robe, my own "coat of many colors." I saw it then, as I see it now; vividly.**

At the time, there was a travelling rabbi who was able to inspire huge groups of people and thus was a threat to Pontius Pilate, who placed him under a death sentence. I merged with the crowd gathered to see this person on his way to execution and when I looked into his eyes, I knew that I had found my friend, but it was too late to even attempt to save him. All I could do was watch when he walked by, though I was later able to financially support some of his followers and his family.

I was thinking of this as Victoria, very much in the present and still exhilarated, was talking, I only half-heartedly heard when she said, *"I saw you there."*

"Where?" I asked.

"In Jerusalem. When Jesus was on his way to the cross. You were someone powerful."

A thrill went up my spine like fire along a fuse. "How did you know it was me?"

"By the expression in your eyes. It's the same expression I see in them now."

"What was I wearing?"

*"A robe. **It was sand colored with vivid burgundy piping,** very elegant. You weren't one of the authorities, not one of Pilate's men, but I knew you had money because of the robe and because your salt and pepper beard was so neatly trimmed, unlike most of the people's. Oh, it was you Brian! No doubt about it."*

. . . .

Dr. Weiss says he had never told anyone that he remembered being on the Via Dolorosa when Jesus reportedly carried the cross for his own Crucifixion.

Gary Schwartz PhD, a scientist who has degrees from Harvard and Yale, is working on a book about mediums and their experiences being "contacted by" or working with Jesus. And he's doing so under controlled experiments in his lab at the University of Arizona. We'll see what science has to say about the existence of this "fellow from the Flipside."

This Jesus dude gets around.

Andrea Mantegna: The Camera degli Sposi (Bridal Chamber) Montova

CHAPTER NINETEEN: INTERVIEWS WITH PALS OF JESUS

"All my authority in heaven and on earth has been given to me."
Jesus - Matthew 28:18

A woman, I'll call her "Shannon," contacted me to let me know that she had a previous hypnosis session where she recalled knowing Jesus – but revealed to me that it didn't follow the usual "Jesus sighting" time line. She wrote:

> "I just wanted to thank you for the *YouTube* posting of your recent radio interview. I am listening when you spoke about you and Scott De Tamble talking about Essie (Jesus)... The reason I am reaching out to you is that you gave me several additional confirmations about my PLR I had done at the end of February in which I regressed to that LIFE period!!"

She remembered knowing Jesus when he was younger, during the so-called "lost years" from age 12-33.[101]

I arranged for a Skype call and recorded the following session. I'm not a hypnotist, but I did ask her at some point to "close her eyes" and just "say the first thing that comes into your mind, without judgment." The text of the session has been edited for syntax and time. I've not met Shannon, and because she contacted me about such a controversial topic, I tried to get a portrait of who she is, her background, and how religious she might have been before we talked about her past life regression.

---

[101] (The Gospels reference Jesus up to age 12, and then skip ahead to when he returns to Jerusalem at 29.)

RM: What do you know about Michael Newton's work?

Shannon: ("Journey of Souls") fell into my lap in 1998 after a meditation class and I liked the cover. I read it and I was like "finally, somebody writes something that is the truth."

I shared it with my mom, of course I had to get (his next book) "Destiny of Souls;" I was already having spiritual visits... kind of going "Wow. This all makes sense."

What spiritual experiences were you having?

We had a foal that was born, named Ginger, and she died at 4 days old. I got really upset, I went into my mother's bedroom and there was this picture of Jesus – I remember saying "Why did you make me come here? Why did you convince me to come here? It hurts too much to be here!"

Later, I was doing meditation in my 30's, and my father was visiting me at night. He was killed when I was a month old in Vietnam.

What was that like?

At first it was kind of vague, but I remember talking (with him) about how his life was exactly as it needed to be and the war was only his way of leaving. That he had a lot of purposes (in living his life) but it was a short lifetime, and he was killed before he turned 19.

In your visions, how did your father appear?

Much like the pictures I had of him already, for a 19-year-old, he had an older look. He's not on my birth certificate. I was born Nov 1st, 1967, he died on December 4th and everyone knew him, he was a bigger-than-life guy. [102]

What's your mom's name?

Lynette. When they found out (he'd been killed) and the Marines came, (his) family lived next door to my parents, she just lost it. She was in such

---

[102] (Note: I did the research on her father, who died in Vietnam. He was a Corporal in the 5th Marines, 1st Division, USMC who died 12-04-67. He's on the Vietnam War memorial, Panel 31E. RIP.)

shock, "Oh my god, he's dead!" And my step-dad asked "Why is this affecting you so much?" She told him because I was his daughter. They kept it a secret from me until I was 18.

Did anyone else in the family know?

One of my sisters said "You should talk to mom." I eventually did and she said "I wasn't going to tell your sister before you." But when I told my oldest brother, he said "I always knew that, but I loved him and felt it was my job to take care of you." (Her father was a next door neighbor and knew the family well, was friends with Lynette and Shannon's step-father.)

This was a year or two after my car accident in 1985, I found out about my father in late '86, but *after* the accident. It was because of the accident that things started to open up to me.

What happened in the car accident?

Spring break, senior year high school, I was in the passenger center seat going out to watch the sunrise, in Greenville, South Carolina. There was a light, we cruised through it going about 60, the front tire hit the curb and we went straight into a telephone pole.

It took me years to realize the significance of that moment – but I knew there was someone interacting with me. I knew "Somebody's got my back."

Once I found out about my father, I realized it was he who had my back. The first time he came into my dreams, he said "It's time for us to talk about the things; why I had to leave" and about his needing closure. He wanted closure for my mother and closure for his family. There were so many in-depth conversations; they were like downloads. It's like getting downloaded information, having someone sit by the side of my bed.

So tell me about your spiritual experience with Jesus.

I joined a couple of groups on Facebook about Michael Newton's work, and posted some of my experiences in the group. One of the members offered to do a past life regression. She was in Savannah and asked "Are you comfortable doing it over Skype?" I thought "What's the worst that can happen?"

What was the session like?

I went back to a younger time period. I saw myself as a young boy. She was asking me "Where are you?" "I'm with my friend Essie." (She spelled it aloud as "**Issa**" and pronounced it as "**Essie**.")

What did Essie look like?

Curly brown hair, dark. Had highlights to it because of the sun, all of our hair being out in the sun. He had crooked teeth. Top teeth little protruding. Bigger than the rest of his teeth.

What did his house look like?

I want to say we were in school at the time. Like a special (religious) school. Teaching all about "the life force."

What were your teachers wearing?

Looks like a linen, there are speckles, light colored off white... shades within them.

What was this group called?

Ession...? Essenes...? The teachings expanded into more areas... more of the connections were discussed there, and the abilities that many of us had that others saw as fearful.[103]

What was your name?

Elyot. (Elihu means "ascension." Elior means "my light in heaven.")

Essie's last name?

---

[103] There are plenty of scholarly articles about the Essenes I won't try to encapsulate here. But learning about "the life force" would have been a typical topic in an Essene school. Roman historian Josephus says they've lived throughout Roman Judea. "Claiming first-hand knowledge, he lists the Essenoi as one of the three sects of Jewish philosophy alongside the Pharisees and the Sadducees. He relates they believe the same concerning piety, celibacy, the absence of personal property and of money, the belief in communality, and commitment to a strict observance of Sabbath. The Essenes ritually immersed in water every morning, ate together after prayer, devoted themselves to charity and benevolence, forbade the expression of anger, studied the books of the elders, preserved secrets, and were very mindful of the names of the angels kept in their sacred writings." (Wikipedia)

Taraten? (Note: I was seeing if he had a "Ben" in his last name, meaning "son of" – some scholars suggest Jesus' father was a Roman soldier named "Pantera" as "Yeshua ben Pantera" is how Jesus is called in the ancient Jewish texts. *Taraten* isn't that far from Pantera.)

Where did you live?

In a small hut style home; mud walls. Our home has two rooms. We cooked our food outside. My father is a herder of sheep. My father is kind of afraid of me because I'm different. I have visions. Essie does as well.

Tell me about Essie.

He has a funny sense of humor. We're best friends. We knew each other before school began – my first memory of him; he was one of the boys in the neighborhood, probably around five years old. He didn't treat me like a freak. The reason others did, was because of my visions; they were a little freaky. I saw bad stuff happening and would predict it, like people getting hurt, or accidents. Fights.

Sometimes (I'd see) things that people shouldn't know or aren't supposed to see or talk about because they are "God's will." My parents don't like me to talk about these visions. Essie was my friend from the start. He liked me for who he was.

When did you get married?

I did it a little later. I was 19, a late bloomer, I was too into my studies to marry. I liked the studies and it was more comfortable in that setting.

About what age did Essie begin to preach?

We were in our late 20's when he started to really teach. School was until our adulthood; we wanted to do types of exploring missions of other teachings. Other cultures, other religions, he went on many, many – I went on four different trips with him – we went to the Orient and studied with an old monk.

About how old is the monk? What does he look like?

He looks around the age of 60. He resembles the Tibetan monks that are around today. I was 17 years old.

Take a look at yourself from the eyes of this monk.

Okay. I see Elyot; my eyes are brown with gold flecks. Essie; he's 17, his hair is growing longer, past his shoulders. There's some facial hair, it's not growing very well, we'd joke about the fact our beards hadn't come in yet.

What's the name of this monk?

Name for this monk is.. Ling Te... We called him "master." (Note: In Chinese *Lantiq* is pronounced 'Ling Te', which means: "Leading with brotherly innovation" (1896 translation.))

Where was he located?

In a Temple. High in the mountains. Temple of light. A holy place.

Was it called Hemis? *(I tell her that the monastery claims that Issa studied there.)*[104]

Yes.

What color robes does he have?

He wears gold robes for ceremony – for daily prayer he wears the material like canvas, darker in color, different plant weave – that **color is earth tones.**[105]

"What kinds of teaching did Ling Te impart to these students?"

(Her voice changes) Some was through prayer; **the vitality of life is through the breath. The energy is within the breath.** (Note: This was one of Buddha's first teachings, the breath meditation.) Food is not a need

---

[104] I suggested the name of the temple based on my experiences in Ladakh. "Temple of Light" may refer to the Bodhgaya temple in Nepal, where Buddha attained enlightenment, built by Emperor Asoka in the 2nd century BCE.

[105] That's an accurate description of the kinds of robes Buddhist monks wore in Hemis. Gold for ceremony, dark red or brown for common activities.

of the body - it is only consumed by the body but the breath is the true essence for the physical and spiritual in the true path.[106]

Breath can take you beyond the life, when the body is taken into a deep state of meditation and the heart can slow and still sustain life. **The life energy can travel beyond and even outside the body – at the moment there are only very 35 percent of life energy in the body.** (Observes something) The Master is guiding a meditation. [107]

What's he saying?

He's taking us internally to travel into the essence of the body; he uses visualization, **which is speech, in order to take the consciousness into each of the energy centers of the body and view the connection between the life force and the energy force around as it connects with each energetic center**, and to bring us through until we are connecting to the essence.[108]

Where else have you gone on your travels with Issa?

We traveled into Persia. We met with a healer. His name was... Mekhaesh? He's very old, very wrinkled, he misses some teeth so his speech was quite funny. He teaches the connection of herbalism in medicine; a combination of the more naturopathic combined with an Eastern religious belief system - but not what is today. **Much more to the old teachings to the connections of every plant, with the ability of plants to heal.**[109]

What color is his garb?

---

[106] Pranayama breathing, is the part of the ancient practices of yogis for thousands of years. They train the practitioner how to slow the breath until it's nearly non-existent.

[107] In the "Six Yogas of Naropa" there are esoteric Buddhist yoga teachings that describe this same thing – shifting consciousness outside the body. I don't know why this reference of 35% of energy in the body – but it's a figure (about a third) that is repeated in many of the sessions I've filmed. That we retain about a third of our "life energy" (and the other two thirds remain on the Flipside.)

[108] A typical guided meditation that might occur at any monastery in this era (i.e. chakras).

[109] I don't know Shannon's background in Ayurvedic medicine, but "it is one of the world's oldest holistic (whole-body) healing systems. Developed thousands of years ago in India. It is based on the belief that health and wellness depend on a delicate balance between the mind, body, and spirit (the medicine is created from combining various plants.)

He wears very formal silk robes, very decorative – he has a turban – It's peacock blue. A Persian color. He has decoration on his robing, marks of his status; he has a place of status within the community. He laughs at his status, because he thinks it's silly. He has some silver decorative design, it goes the length of the robe down the font, and there are two rubies at the throat that are prestigious symbols. There are eleven others are in the room.

Where are we in Persia are we?

We are in a valley beside a mountain range, a highly populated area today – it's called "the mountains of darkness." (Note: These mountains appear in the Hebrew tradition of the Bible as "The Mountains of Asaf" in Persia, "where legendary King Khasia lived, and met with Alexander the Great." She seems to be describing the garb an ancient Assyrian Priest would wear. The closest name I could find to Mekha-desh, a Hebrew name that means "Innovates." There is also "Mekha Eil" in Farsi.)

Who do you see that is in the room with you now?

Straggling travelers. We are mostly milling about in the room. We met him (Mekha-esh) outside at another time. Because he was teaching differently, but where we are now, is a more formal teaching area. Though we are not dressed formally.

Why does he admit you to this teaching?

He likes the words that were – being spoken by Essie. Currently we have two other travelers with us, but we're not all doing the same thing. We are traveling in groups because it's safer, the other two are gathering items to take back to their home village. We met up with them, they weren't traveling with us.

How old are you now?

I'm eighteen. I traveled with him on four occasions. During this period, Essie was very much into traveling, but I couldn't always go. Others went on trips, two long trips.

Are you guys traveling along the silk route? Do you have money to travel?

You don't need much money – it's not of value really. Barter is very good trade, if you can trade skills; we were all good with tools, structures and repairs.

When you returned home you said you married at 19. What was your wife like? What was her name?

It was an arranged marriage. Her name was Mali. He had four kids. We had three boys and one girl.

Did Issa attend your wedding?

Yes.

Let's move ahead to later on, in your 20's, when Issa returns from the East and all the troubles begin.

That was later. When he was coming back and forth it was okay, he would talk, we all would talk and share, there was nothing wrong with what was being discussed. But eventually people were afraid of what we represented, what he had to say, and people overheard conversations and they were afraid – hearing about the freedom of love and the love we all had for each other and the respect for each other.

It was more of community and connection, people in authority felt threatened by our community. Those of influence in particular, some of them were not in power, or in control, but there were many influential members who had their hands in that element. Issa was gaining momentum – it was all misled, misleading by them to make us all afraid – they used him to create more fear.

How did they use him to create more fear?

You must understand, the discussions were against what others were believed to be true – our basis for our society at the time, **everyone is equal and of the essence and saying that "everyone is God"** is heresy, we were traitors to society. They needed to make an example of someone.

Go to a time when you and Issa were together and discussing how to deal with the impending chaos. I assume you had a vision of what was going to happen.

Yes. All right, it was time well before. We are inside. We are in my home. It's only he and I at the moment. I had my vision of what was going to happen – and it terrified me – **I saw them coming and taking him and how they would be beating him and making him an example.**

What was his reaction?

He said it would be okay, **"it was meant to be" and "part of what God would want him to follow."** I wanted him to leave, I requested and urged him – **I told him we must take Miriam… his wife.**

Were they married at this point? Did they have children?

Yes, they were married, but they had no children.

What's her story? Tell me what she's like, what does she look like?

She is about 5'4, 5'5. Essie is about 5'10, 5'11. Tall and lanky. He always looked awkward as a child – he was taller. Lanky. She has very soft brown hair. Her skin tone is – she is carmel.

Was it true that her family heritage came from King David?

It was a story her family told, but that she didn't believe. They were a very common family – so to hear this tale was thought of as funny. Her father was a fisherman – and their family came from far away.

When did they get married? How did they meet?

They met before I was married, but their marriage was done in more of a secret ceremony. It was done so to protect her. And to protect her from some of the other men who were around that were being very judgmental. **They married in secret because they feared that people would be jealous that Issa would favor her. She was also a part of our group**, and had come in prior – and they chose each other, unlike my marriage that was arranged; his was not.

Who performed the ceremony?

It was done by an Essene priest – someone who was from the school, as he needed her to be safe.

Does Mary have a last name?

She does .. it's.. the first letter of her last name is K, second letter... is an I... resembles the word "Kichlesi..." similar.[110]

How did you find out about the marriage?

I made a sarcastic remark to Issa, I wanted to discuss some things with him, and she was present. I told him to "Send his woman off to the shop, so we can speak." He laughed and told me she was now his wife. When they began to become more intimate in public with each other, I struggled with the time that he was giving to her. I didn't understand it until I was married...

Okay, let's return to the earlier scene. Where you're discussing this vision of Issa being arrested and tortured. What was the idea? How did he express what you should do?

We spoke of how we would need to devise a way to utilize the teachings he'd learned, (re: yoga teachings on endurance) and it would take time to do the planning and figure out how to make this happen and hopefully not actually die. We had two years to plan – the visions said "in four seasons."

Isn't four seasons one year?

Not in that region. Four seasons is two years.

What events led up to his crucifixion? I've read an account (The Life of St. Issa) where it's reported that Pilate assigned a spy to his inner circle.

The spy presented himself as a young follower of Issa seeking the company of us. We eventually realized he was a spy. We didn't know he was a spy, not at first... some befriended him, and some became closely, and could not accept the betrayal.

What was his name?

---

[110] Kekeisar in Hebrew means "of Ceasar." There were rumors that she was the slave of a Roman soldier, possibly named "Pantera" as "Ben Pantera" (son of Pantera) is mentioned in the Talmud as a possible last name of Jesus. (Wikipedia)

Dah-iel. Yes. What happened to him after the arrest. This was necessary. We misled Dah-iel. There were many things that were not true. (Note: Dani-iel, and Dem-iel are common names of the era.)

Did you enlist any people that could help?

Only those who were very, very close and trusted; as we could not trust all of his inner circle. Some of the people we'd met during our travels were with us. Only those who were pure of heart and who would not betray, it was very important for more of us to actually believe (and report falsely) what was happening in order for it to succeed.

What about Joseph of Arimathea? Was he helpful?

I know him as a different name. Nahate. (Natan is "Nathan" and Nahal means "stream.") He was out for his own goals. He was friend to those who could help him, as we say, if it served his purposes.

Was he close to Pilate? Did he bring the aloe and myrrh as a restorative for Issa?

I don't know, I was not in charge of that part of the plan. I was in charge of having the ships prepared. There were three types of ships, including fishermen and cargo vessels.

Do you remember how you obtained them?

There were people we were connected with when we traveled to the blue ocean, and we did some healing on some children of the **water master.** [111] They helped us.

By the way, how does a healing take place? Is it spiritual or physical when you heal people? I've read that there are many treatments in the east that helped people – but were they mental afflictions or physical ones?

---

[111] "Water Master" is an ancient Persian term (3000 years old) for those in charge of river passage, etc. "Evolution of Water Supply Through the Millennia" (Angelakis, Mays, Koutsoyiannis - 2012 - Technology & Engineering. Pg. 555)

It is the God connection that flows through the hands to affect a cure.[112]

What's the nature of illness?

We saw many different types, for us a simple flu was also a death. It could be any illness, (including) very extreme; a physical body going through great changes, going through its core center, but we would see different types of children who came to us. And whoever asked for us to give assistance; it was laying of hands, and allowing God to bring the energy through to the soul and the body of which is before us.

This was not unknown knowledge. It was known for many periods, every culture had more knowledge to share about healing within all of the cultures. Many different teachings could be of value by them. We all have the ability to heal.

But Issa became famous for it because he was very talented in being able to present the information with his words, as opposed to the rest of us who were not as skilled in speech. He also had a calming presence which allowed many doors to open, or at least allow us to attempt to help people. Our success is what made it grow.

Describe those final days of Issa.

I followed him from morning through sunset, after he was arrested. I then went and I prepared my family in the morning because I would be departing from them soon. (Deep sigh.) I went to the town center. I stood in an alcove to watch the people and to make sure that those who needed to be witness to what was about to happen were present. Those of our circle, like Peter, many of our group who needed to see this as the reality. There was much discussion about who would be present. We all wanted to stop it but could not… My task was to watch Miriam (Issa's wife) to ensure her safety. She was with others who were closer to her, but I was able to watch her from a distance.

And how did Issa appear in the square?

---

[112] While interviewing someone who remembered a lifetime as a doctor in Tibet from centuries ago, she described using her hands to touch the patient, and then "sending a flow of energy into the body of the patient to affect a cure."

When I finally see him emerge from the building he's very beaten. He's got contusions, and the marks of many fists that must have hit his body. They were just bringing him out to the center, as this is to be a spectacle. They wanted it seen by everyone, to see him be diminished. There are hundreds of people present in the square, I can see there are many faces within the darkened places where you see their faces looking out. It's a showmanship of words in public.

Who speaks?

There are three who speak, who are mocking him. They are of the office – those who are in charge are overseeing the spectacle and beating; their hands can't be bloodied, or dirtied. They are wearing formal (Roman) uniforms; some have on armor, some do not. Those closer to Issa have on armor or weaponry.

He's being whipped with a black leather whip which has three straps, and a long tail. They're making a spectacle of him. Issa is very calm, he's not shouting out, and he makes eye contact with those around him. He knows that if he were to show his pain and hurt it would only serve more to the purpose of mocking him.

There are some welts, but he tries to keep as calm as he can because he knows those who love him need to see that he isn't suffering. They force him to drag himself to the end of town. **He's not carrying a Crucifix, but a long wooden beam that will be added on to the cross.**

What are you doing while this is happening?

I keep taking the pain of others into myself. I'm trying to heal them, at the same time trying to create a function within those who are surrounding this event. This is a sacrifice of many levels; in particular, on my own soul essence. I feel great sadness. He carries the beam for one and a half miles.

Is the path he traveled accurate? The Via Dolorosa?

Somewhat. Everything changes.

Where does Elyot go?

I check on different people, on the path – check on my family, those who would come to be known as his disciples… I was friends with them, but more guarded – there were many who made me uncomfortable, they didn't value me as Issa did. They treated me as a servant to them as if I were "below them." It happened (this disrespect) when Issa was not present.

Describe the process of Crucifixion.

They are bound first by leather, the leather is dampened and dried It squeezes the body tight, leather straps (are put) on the arms and legs. Most are bound with foot to each side of the post, this is normal practice. They initially strap him as such, but he is a little too tall and lanky, so that **the support beam for his feet doesn't work.**

They struggle with the balance of weight so the toes are moved in to be bound – the depiction as has been made since, is not exactly as it was; it's close. **But he is taller than most – needs the support. He's tied to the beams, and his feet made to fit on the (pedestal) wood so that it would not allow the weight on the bodies to collapse when they lift him up.**

Did they use one or two nails on his feet?

Two nails. But together on the piece of wood so his feet fit.

In terms of how he's crucified – are his palms facing out, or are his palms turned in?

Out - as if receiving. It has to do with the structure of the upper body. With the hands in, it would have given him a weight so they couldn't lift up the wood; hands out forces the shoulders to allow the lungs to compress.

Is there a nail in the center of his palm or in the wrist?

I see a larger nail in the wrist and smaller nail in the palm – it is symbolic – nailing the hand was not truly necessary, but the guards thought it would be… the hands have many representations within the culture, it is dishonorable to have your hands nailed. Long teachings in the culture of teachings of the hands; it's giving a slap to our culture.

How far are you from the scene? And do you see any of the guards doing something like gambling with his cloak as depicted in the gospels?

I am about fifty feet away. I'm in a hidden spot. They're in front of me, I don't want to be seen. I'll be seen later, when I need to make my presence known. I see no gambling.

Many other things that happened that were very distasteful, for one who is to be thought of as dead, but at the moment, you have me looking at the soldiers – it is more of a preparation on their part. **I saw 25 guards present, as they are afraid of the people who are watching as well. There appears to be more people watching, at least 100. Some are hiding.**

Are there any others Crucified near him?

This is the place of Crucifixion for many. This is a common practice, and there are many that can be seen – they are spaced out as it's meant to be - as they travel along the road - that they will be seen as markers for miles. From this perspective, as far as the eyes can see, there are about 13.

They tied, then nail the person to the cross, then lift them up onto a pre-dug post?

They do the hands first. Then they are lifted, and put onto the support pole, then they do the feet, the support pole is preset, you understand, prior to, in order to support the weight… So once they are up, they use ladders to finish the job.

Is there a sign that says INRI; "King of Jews" on a piece of wood over his head?

Not at first. Then they put it up. It's not in honor of him. It was there to mock all of us. To show their power over us.

How many hours was he up there?

I don't know. I left, I was supposed to leave. **We each had tasks, I had the ships and Miriam. I go back to the ships to see how prepared we are.** The captain and a regular crew are there, about 18 crewmen to man the ship. There will be a group of seven of us on the ship that I will leave on with Miriam.

There's an account in the Gospel of Thomas that he was put onto a ship that sailed to India and Kerala. Later Thomas claims he saw Jesus in India. **Is the second ship the one that Thomas went on?**

Yes.

Where does your ship go?

Sails west, but we go down around the horn of Africa, to give more time for Jesus to get away. Captain knew who we were and a few people knew, and we also used aliases. We wanted confusion. I knew that he had disappeared as far as others knew.

My travels were very quick; I didn't stay very long when I returned. Time had lapsed. It was only days or a few weeks, when I came back, and spent a few days with my wife and family – my youngest came with me. We came back once for Miriam and another time for my son. To create distractions, if people saw me more often it would allow more truth… Primary reason was to avoid the Romans; some (I avoided) were part of the other religious sects.

(There were people) who were involved behind closed doors in working with the Romans, We wanted to avoid them as well. They needed to believe what was being presented as much as possible. I could not search for confirmations as to what happened; I had to trust, I had to receive the information later.

Where was this new land?

It was known as France, we began near Marseille, we also traveled along the coast. We couldn't travel a lot because Miriam was ill from being pregnant. **Eventually she had a girl. Sarah.** There were midwives when it occurred, and I stood outside as a guard.

(Note: In Jennifer's chapter (unaware of this interview) remembers a lifetime as Jesus' daughter and the name she remembers is Sarah. Quite a common name in the era, but she also claims that there were five children and two died. But in this account, Sarah would have been the oldest, not the youngest.)

How long were you in France?

We stayed there for several years. The Messenger came with word that Jesus had survived just as his child was born.[113]

Who was the messenger?

He was a boy who was innocent. The message was "**All was well and as it was meant to be.**" It was what we agreed, that the message wouldn't lead anyone to either of us. The goal was for him to travel and send word, and eventually he would go back to Ling Te, where I would meet him after receiving the message. That I would then travel to Ling Te and meet him within six months.

What was that journey like?

I traveled by land, and moved closer to water sources that were more pure. I traveled alone. That was adventurous, that was not easy. Had to travel many foreign lands, because I needed to stay as a lonely traveler. I left six months after the messenger came.

I left Miriam in good hands, with those who had traveled with us, as well as several we had met within the area. We had already changes our identities, **Miriam was beginning to speak and teach once again, it was more open of a place to present the information with many of the more pagan cultures that were surrounding us.** Things were well enough established as far as protection of home and resources I could leave.

Tell me about Miriam's teaching ability.

She had the ability to present information in fashion that spoke to whomever who was listening. We would refer to her as a high empath in today's language.

How did you react when you saw him again?

---

[113] From an account from a Roma (gypsy) in the 1956 book "The Three Mary's" "One of our Rom people who received the first Revelation was Sara the Kali... One day Sara had visions which informed her that the Saints who had been present at the death of Jesus would come, and that she must help them. Sara saw them arrive in a boat. The sea was rough, and the boat threatened to founder. Mary Salome threw her cloak on the waves and, using it as a raft, Sarah floated towards the Saints and helped them reach land by praying." (Wikipedia Saint Sarah)

Relief – very joyous and relief. He has aged in appearance, he appears older than what his age is, he looks a little worse for the wear as they say. We discussed his wounds, many of them were healed, the scarring was very minimal because he had many of the master healer's teachings. Ling Te was very pleased to see us. **He lived a very long life, longer than what is considered to be normal age.**

What name was Issa traveling under?

Some speak it but he does not. He's a very humble man, people make him Iconic, and he struggles with this. I went back to France, and he followed later. **I was with her when he arrived. We are in an area that would be considered between Spain and France. Close to what is France – close to Spain near the water. I spent a year with him there. It took him a year to get there, and Sarah was four years old.** There were many celebrations when he arrived.[114]

All of us rejoiced to see him again, to see them together, some people that you realize their connections breaks all boundaries of any sense of emotion – and to watch Miriam and Issa together is to watch magic before your eyes. We were together with the original seven who made the trip. Most of the new followers were from surrounding area, and some who traveled to the area – to hear – be a part of the group. They traveled on, I stayed in France, lived near the water.

How did you pass away?

I was very old. And I no longer counted the years. I was very happy and content. I had a small cottage or shack by a large river. Very remote, I like being alone more. There were rumors around – that there was a very special group of people that were able to do special healings. At this point he was not as everyone else was presenting, he lived a much more simplified life. **There were rumors, not a desire to draw attention to him, because if word got back to Rome he was alive, it would be a disaster.** But they continued to travel and preach, and I stayed behind. At

---

[114] As in Dan Brown's "The Da Vinci Code" and "Holy Blood, Holy Grail" argue Mary Magdalene and Jesus has a daughter who lived in France named Sarah. **None of the books argue that Jesus survived the Crucifixion and showed later** (according to this, Sarah was four by the time Jesus arrived.) There's an entire body of myths about "the Magdalene" (Miriam) in France, but in this account, she's there with Sarah until Issa catches up with her a year later and then she departs back to Asia with him.

the end, I was sitting by the river. Tired. Very ready to go home. I have great pain.

Describe the experience. What's that like once you cross over?

It is like floating in a stream of ecstasy. It feels more like drifting and flying, being pulled like a kite; to me it's like being lifted up. I'm enjoying the trip, like floating within the most, drifting within the most beautiful sea… to explain would be like drifting along the waters. The light is gold.

Is there anyone around you?

There four present. There are two who like to present as female, two who present themselves as male.

Can we ask Issa or Jesus to come forward now? I'd like to ask him a few questions.

Yes.

Describe him to me, please.

He is very um… to me he appears as though he's about 25. **He is wearing a white shirt with jeans. His hair is bound – pony tail.**

Issa, could you come closer? What are you experiencing?

(Through tears). I miss my friend. He has his arm around my shoulders. He is the most (crying now) It's as if you were to wrap yourself in a cocoon of the most intense loving feeling you could ever imagine.

(Note: Here he is again in a tee shirt and jeans. That's the third time people saw him dressed casually. **Then the third time when asked to come closer, he causes tears, inability to breathe, and red cheeks.** As I point out, in the world I come from the first two are easy to affect, the third is nearly impossible for anyone trying to "act" upset.)

And what would you ask Shannon to do here on the planet?

To know that the message isn't about him, but that it's about the original message he came to teach. **The teaching of the love and the connection between all of us, how we are all divine sparks and what the messages truly were, it's not so much about speaking it, as it is by living it as truly "to the heart" as it was meant to be.**

Thank you.

…..

I'm not a hypnotist, but just by asking these direct questions, it appears Shannon was able to see and experience things she normally doesn't have access to. She had a session previously where she experienced these events, so they were fresh in her mind, but the depth and scope of them is pretty unusual.

Again, we were just chatting on Skype, I asked her to open her mind up to "whatever came in" and that's what came in. She's not trying to convince me in any fashion that these events happened; she only responded to my questions as I posed them to her.

After we did this session, she sent me a transcript of her original session. In my session with her she clarified a number of details, but the content of her session (which I'd never seen) remains relatively the same. I've edited it for time. The therapist at first didn't know Essie referred to "Jesus."

As mentioned earlier, prior to this session, Shannon didn't have any inkling that she might have "known Jesus" prior to this. He didn't show up in any dreams, nor was she particularly religious, or a fan of Jesus fiction. As note, her story is contrary to those "Magdalene in France" accounts; it's not that she, it's reported here that she and her daughter hid out on the coast of France, hiding from the Romans until they could be reunited.

PL Therapist: We are going to go to another significant time in this lifetime... where are you?

Shannon: An open market. There are many people; the market is busy.

What area are you in?

In the Middle East. I'm 23. My friend Essie is speaking... about Love.

Tell me how long have you known Essie?

All of my life. We grew up together, went to school together. I am here to help Essie; help him to find his truth so he can take it out to the people

I want you to stay in this lifetime, but I want you to advance forward to a more significant place...3...2...1 and where are you?

Essie and I are talking. We are discussing my vision; they are coming for him.

Who is coming for Essie?

There are many, there are many coming. They will try him and kill him... I have seen it. I tell him it is time to leave. We must go.

What is Essie's response?

"No, brother. No." He understands. **It is part of his purpose.**

Why would someone want to come after him for speaking of love?

Control; it is power. There are many factions. Our leaders and the Romans; they are losing control.

Go to the next significant point in this life. 3...2...1...what are you experiencing?

I want to stop it... but I cannot. He's imprisoned. We talk of ways to break him free. There are many of us who follow, who help Essie. Some are his students; some are like me (friends). We are his support system. We cannot break him out. The others do not want to listen; they don't want to accept watching him die. Tomorrow he will die; they don't want to accept that, but we know.

What are you discussing when Essie faces his death, what is going on?

We are preparing. Many are so angry…. We are preparing three ships to sail. We must prepare the three ships going in three directions.

Will you be on one of these ships?

Yes. With Miriam, Essie's wife.

After Essie meets his death? Or will you be able to save him?

He will appear dead but will not die; he will use the knowledge we learned from the old man of the East, (from) the Orient. We traveled and studied with him, he taught us how to breathe. How to breathe, to sustain in stasis. Very deep (breaths)… (the) body appears to be dead but is still living.

Count to 3 and go to tomorrow; 3…2…1… What are you experiencing?

(Shannon begins to sob) We have to watch; they drag him outside for us to watch. He is being beaten…. they are whipping him. It is a black whip with 3 tails…they beat him so much till he bleeds.

(Shannon noted in the text after the session: "It was a long black whip more like a cat of nine tails but not nine strips of leather. The whipping was on his back. I saw the guards dragging him, carrying him by the shoulders out of this building. They made him kneel with (his) head down and the whip (was) cracking cross his back. They dragged him through the town to the edge, where others were hanging on crosses. Then they put him on one and at that point, I left to the ships as my time was limited.")

How do they kill him?

(He'll) bleed to death on the cross but he will not die… it only appears as death.

How long does it take him to bleed to death and make the transition?

He will not die there… It only appears as such.

(Note: From Shannon's notes after the session: "Very few of us knew he would not actually die on the cross. Miriam knew, I am not sure who else, but I do remember we did NOT inform all of the people close to us. His disciples had to believe it so that the masses and those of power believed he was dead.")

Are you allowed to take him down?

No, the Roman guards will take him down; but we have two friends in the Romans who are helping.

(Note: Again from the notes after the session: "I remember we had the two Roman guards on the inside; they were to sneak him out of the cave and take him to the Essenes who would make sure he got onto the ship we had ready for him. The ships were like trading ships so they wouldn't be suspected.")

What time does the Roman guard take him down?

When the moon was at its peak. I am at the ship (when this happens). I must make sure the ships are ready, it is very important. He will not be on these ships; this is for Miriam. I am her guardian, her protector as I promised. She is with child but does not know yet.

Is the child going to be a boy or a girl?

Girl.

What would happen if they knew of the wife and child?

They would both be killed. I go on the ship with Miriam. Essie does not come on this ship. He must go another way.

Did the soldier that is one of your secret friends, did he take him down when the moon was at its peak?

Yes.

What did he do with him? When he took him down from the cross?

They prepare him and place him in the cave. He will be removed when it is safe and taken to those who will heal him.

So you take Miriam and the child on the boat?

Yes, (but) she is pregnant. It is a long journey....

Go to the next significant occurrence ...3...2...1... where are you?

I am with Miriam. We are in a new land; very beautiful and lots of new colors.

Do you know what they call this land?

It is known as France (now) but it was not called that at the time. We are building a community; starting over. Miriam will continue her teachings here. I will work beside her and stay. I am her guardian and protector. I stay with her until Essie will come.

Go to when you see Essie again....3...2...1. What do you experience now?

Peace... Quiet... Happy to see my friend. We are with the old man from the Orient, in the East. He speaks to us of many things... many possessions hidden. (But) I must return to Miriam.

Does Essie return with you?

Not yet. He must change who he is; they must stay apart to protect Miriam for a length of time and then he will come with a new name.[115]

We are going to advance now to one more significant time in this life...3...2...1...tell me where you are.

I am by the river. I am talking with Essie and others. (We're discussing) Love and many things... what should and should not be. I will be leaving

---

[115] According to ancient Persian and Indian texts, a holy man travelling with his mother "of virgin birth" named Mary named "Yuz Asaf" (anointed one) winds up teaching in Srinigar where he's buried. His tomb is known as Roz Azul. (tombofjesus.com)

soon; we will not see each other again. He has a new name; we do not wish to draw attention to him and Miriam. It is not safe to stay together.

Will you see them again this life?

No.

....

Again, I saw this transcript after I interviewed Shannon. The story, according to Shannon's past life memory is roughly this: Elyot and Issa travelled along the silk route where Issa preached and learned along the way. It wasn't hard to travel money wise, as they could barter their skills. Issa and Elyot wind up in Hemis in northern Ladakh, learning ancient yogas from a holy man. These same yogas are referred to in the oral traditions of Tibetan Buddhism as well as ancient yoga texts. One of these yogas includes shifting consciousness away from the body to endure pain, and another allows the practitioner to slow breathing until it is nearly non-existent.

Issa and Elyot return to Jerusalem, Elyot returns to his family, is part of the entourage around Issa, and at some point has a vision of his arrest and torture two years prior to it happening. By the time it does happen, he and a small group of devotees have organized a way for Issa to escape death. After being on the cross for a matter of hours, he appears dead and is taken to a cave. Two of the Roman soldiers are confederates, and help spirit the body out of the cave.

Elyot claims that he helps Miriam escape, but she is pregnant with Issa's child. They hide on the coast of France until a messenger comes with a coded message that Issa is okay, and Elyot meets him at the appointed place – back in the monastery in Hemis. Eventually Issa reunites with Miriam and his family. After they depart, Elyot doesn't see him again, until he passes away.

Again, I'm not offering this as an alternative history of Jesus. We are talking about a small group of people who have approached me to tell me their stories. Let's see how they match up with others, shall we?
....

Witness to the Crucifixion: Mary Grace

When I was speaking at the International Association of Near Death Studies near Syracuse, New York, I spoke to a woman, "Mary Grace" who having heard my comments that a "number of people claimed they have seen Jesus in previous lifetimes," she approached me after the talk and told me the following story.

Some months later, I asked if she would write it out for me, with as much detail as she could remember. This was her reply:

"I had never told anyone this story before. I only mentioned it to Richard Martini after a presentation he gave at our IANDS meeting in Syracuse, NY. During his talk, he revealed that several people had confided in him about memories of being at the crucifixion of Christ.

Until that day, I did not know there were others; therefore, I never talked about my memories out of fear of ridicule or not being believed. This story is in response to Richard's request to write about my experience for research he is doing:

My name was Rebekah. I was a nine-year old Jewish girl and lived alone with my mother and father. I believe there were older siblings, but they were grown and no longer lived at home.

My first memory of that horrific day is walking up the long road that led to the place called "Golgotha." (Calvary) It was just me and my mother. We had to wait until late in the day to go because of the mob of people, security guards and violence.

We waited until things calmed down and the crowd thinned. As we walked up the dirt road there was a stream of other people ahead and behind us. We walked in single file or by two's. Everyone moved quietly, talking infrequently, and only in whispered voices.

I was wearing a full length, black, peasant dress and a long, black scarf over my head that draped to my shoulders. My outfit was virtually identical to my mother's; it was the traditional clothing and we didn't have much else. I was barefoot, but Mother had sandals on her feet. My father believed that youngsters did not need shoes. I didn't mind and preferred going barefoot anyway; besides, I never knew differently.

When we got to the top of the hill, the site of the crucifixion, there was a large crowd; we were at the back. Immediately, the deafening silence struck me like a bitter blast of biting wind, although it was warm with barely a breeze. An overwhelming feeling of sorrow and despair hung over the crowd like a brewing, black storm cloud.

At the same time, there was a powerful sense of reverence, which caused an unusual atmosphere of serenity. It was clear that this was a sacred vigil and no one dared speak a word to disrupt the holy event. Besides, no words were needed or useful to discuss an incident that no one truly understood or could comprehend; the public execution of our own saint. Everyone was in shock.

I wanted to get closer, I pulled Mother by the hand and we began working our way through the crowd. I went to the left as it seemed the way to go. We had no trouble getting by as people just stepped aside to let us pass. I understood that everyone was too tired, too distraught and two weak to resist.

At this time, I was mainly concerned with getting close enough to see Jesus; I was on a mission and not thinking of my emotions. We finally worked our way close to the front row. Sitting closest to the cross was the family of Jesus; his mother, John, Mary Magdalene and a few others. This small group were left alone and the crowd stood back about twenty feet to give them space and respect.

At first glance, as I looked up at the face of Jesus and took in the sickening site; I went into shock myself. It wasn't until I looked towards his feet, however, that the real trauma of the moment struck. That's when I could clearly see the right, big-toe of Jesus hanging from a small strip of skin. Somehow, during his ordeal, the toe was severed from the bone and left dangling.

I immediately realized that he had carried his own cross up that hill, after being beaten, with no big toe to function, and with all the pain that must have come from it. At the same time, I don't think he was even aware of it. But the toe was almost eye level. It was what I could see the best and what my eyes kept being drawn to.

I honestly don't recall the nails in his hands and feet, or if they were tied with ropes. Like a bad acid-trip flashback, the dangling toe is what was permanently imprinted on my long-term memory.

The brutality of it all was suddenly too much and I collapsed in a silent, grief-stricken meltdown that seemed to tear a hole in my very soul. I dared not cry out loud so as not to disturb others that were grieving quietly. After a while, I recovered my composure and began taking in the atmosphere around me.

I looked again into the face of Jesus, whose eyes were closed at this time. **Suddenly I was overcome with a sense of peace and compassion. These emotions were radiating out from Jesus to the crowd, in such a palpable force, that it brought a great calm upon the masses.**

Although he was the one hanging from a cross, our Lord was somehow able to console the distraught crowd. **It felt as if he was comforting the people by wrapping us in a protected cocoon of all-loving energy.** Clearly, this mystical bubble of solace was divine intervention at work.

We stayed until the evening, having born witness to the cruel crisis for over three hours. At this point Jesus was virtually dead, we headed home; we had seen enough. Although I was young and did not understand all that happened, or the reasons, I clearly knew that a huge injustice had been done. I was deeply transformed by this man that I never knew personally, and my life would never be the same."

. . . .

What are the odds that I would run into two different people who say they witnessed the Crucifixion of Jesus? (Maybe there's more out there, but I mean, c'mon, really? In each account, people remember a particular detail. Did Jesus lose his big toe? I don't know. We'd have to ask him.)

Some months after this book talk in Syracuse (on YouTube on my page MartiniProds as "It's a Wonderful Afterlife") I got an email from a fellow in India who was interested in talking to me about something profound that happened to him during a past life regression. He had read "Flipside" and as he was coming to Los Angeles to visit some members of his family, he asked if we could chat over an afternoon coffee.

The hours slipped by quickly, and it was dark before we realized the day had disappeared. It was one of those conversations that you start with someone, as if reconnecting to someone you've known a long time. I've since become friends with Prashant, and he's offered to publish my book "Flipside: A Tourist's Guide on How to Navigate the Afterlife" in India.

Prashant contributes spiritual articles to a well-known national newspaper in India, one of the most popular newspapers in the country. His articles are deep and insightful, and aside from being a successful businessman, he's an accomplished author.

During the course of our conversation, he recounted me this past life regression he had, where he saw himself as someone close to Jesus. When someone makes a claim of that nature, it's normal for our minds to put up a block, or a skepticism about the possibility of that happening. As you've seen, I've had a number of people in my life suddenly saying either they knew him, or he was appearing in front of them while I was talking to them.

He remembered being Nicodemus, who is a famous character in the death of Jesus: "Nicodemus is a Pharisee and a member of the Sanhedrin mentioned in three places in the Gospel of John: He first visits Jesus one night to discuss Jesus' teachings (John 3:1–21). The second time Nicodemus is mentioned, he reminds his colleagues in the Sanhedrin that the law requires that a person be heard before being judged (John 7:50–51). Finally, Nicodemus appears after the Crucifixion of Jesus to provide the customary embalming spices, and assists Joseph of Arimathea in preparing the body of Jesus for burial (John 19:39–42).[116]

What's interesting is that in his memory, Prashant initially saw himself as Laurence Olivier in the scene from the 1977 Zefferelli mini-series about Jesus.[117] It was only after continued disbelief that he realized his subconscious was giving him a vision of "the role" he had played.

---

[116] Wikipedia; Nicodemus

[117] "Jesus of Nazareth" by Franco Zefferelli

All I can tell you is that I've come to know Prashant, I know he's not someone prone to making up stories about himself and the history of Christ. He is a Christian living in India, so one can argue it's in his background, but I asked him to write down his memories of his session for this book.

INTERVIEW WITH ANOTHER WITNESS TO THE CRUCIFIXION

Prashant: "One of my friends, Parul, told me that she had visited a past life regression therapist named Roma who operates out of Gurgaon, India. Parul had been helped by Roma to remember some of her past lives and dealing with some of those memories helped her deal with and get over some of her problems in her current life. She suggested I call Roma and meet with her.

I thought about it for a few days and decided that I wanted to experience what a past life regression was all about. I had no idea what it felt like to be hypnotized and decided to call Roma. We fixed a time for the next day.

September 17, 2014, I arrived at Roma's home where she has converted one of her rooms into her hypnosis clinic, if you can call it that. Roma is in her mid-50s and the first thing she asked me to do was take off my shoes as she doesn't allow people into her house with their shoes on.

Her session room had some faint eastern meditation music on and she lit some candles. I sat on the sofa and she sat on a chair and began to chat with me about my family, my career and stuff like that. General information and nothing that could really qualify as giving anything that she could use to "lead me on" during the session.

After a cup of green tea, we were ready to go. I was about to witness the first time I've been under hypnosis. She asked me to lay down on the sofa, placed a cushion under my head and neck I would be comfortable. She told me to close my eyes and relax, breathe in, breathe out and then imagine being in a park under a blue sky. She asked me to visualize a bright white light coming into my body and then one by one, shine that light into each of my seven chakras to cleanse and energize them.

After this "chakra cleansing" process, she asked me to relax and focus on my breathing. I was now in a very deep relaxed meditative state and in my mind thought very briefly that this was basically just like meditation (which I do often) and not much different other than the guiding I was getting from her. It was at this point I relate the actual regression process as it unfolded.

Roma: I want you to go back in time to the life that needs our attention at this time. Just tell me whatever comes into your mind.

Prashant: (I suddenly could see that I was standing in a market place. The visuals were a bit dream like in their fluidity, but very clear. I had never seen or heard what I was about to describe) I am standing in a market place during the day time. Everything seems desert like – dusty.

Look at your feet. What are you wearing?

Sandals. Seems to be made out of animal hide straps. Brown.

Where are you? Which part of the world? How old are you?

I am somewhere in the Middle East – could be Israel could be Egypt. Israel, I think that is where I am. I am a boy – perhaps 11-12 years old.

What time period is this?

Biblical times. Around the time of Jesus.

Ok. What is happening around you?

I'm in a market. I'm standing near a building and just looking at people walk around, buy stuff. It is a hot day, a bit dusty. There are men walking around.

Now there is this man wearing black, with a kind of black turban. He looks like some kind of soldier or palace guard or something. He has caught me by my shoulder and is dragging me towards the market. I am resisting him, trying to break free from him.

Why is he trying to get you?

He is accusing me of stealing something from somebody's shop. But I didn't steal anything. Now he is holding a big rock in his hand and it beating me. He takes the rock and smashes my head with it. I'm falling onto the ground.

I want you to now watch yourself from the vantage point of an observer. What is happening? Are you leaving your body?

No. I'm not. I am unconscious and I think the soldier thought I was dead, so he moved on. But in a few minutes, I wake up. I'm standing up now and rubbing all the dust from myself.

I want you to remember the man who beat you up. Look into his eyes and you will see that his face will convert into someone from your current life.

It's my father in my current life.

We will deal with that later. Right now, I want you to see yourself. What are you doing now?

Just walking away. Nobody seems to even notice what happened. I think I'm going home.

Go to your home in this lifetime.

I'm in my home. It is kind of a hovel, built out of stone and dirt. There is a cot made of rope and wood. That is my bed.

What do you see on the bed?

Suddenly, I saw Sai Baba of Shirdi… wait a minute… he has just morphed into the Laughing Buddha. That's strange.

(Note. "Sai Baba of Shirdi" was an Indian spiritual master who lived from 1835-1910. "Regarded by his devotees as a saint… he was revered by both Hindu and Muslim devotees. (Wikipedia) When figures appear in these visions, in this case a holy man, and a laughing Buddha, it can be our higher consciousness offering a metaphor of what's about to happen.)

Don't worry, sometimes you get flashes from various incarnations. Now, I want you to go to another significant event of this lifetime. What do you see?

It's evening time. I can see I am standing in front of a beautiful woman. It is Olivia Hussey, the actress who played Mary in the TV movie Jesus of Nazareth made in the 1970s! She is getting married to.. wait a minute. I see the actor who played Joseph, the husband of Mary from that movie; his name was Yorgo Voyagis. There is a marriage going on.

Where are you in this marriage?

It seems as if I am Joseph. Or I am standing right next to them. Though it seems I am Joseph; what was I? Joseph, the husband of Mary?

Go to another significant moment in this life. What do you see?

(Excited and emotional) **Oh my God! I'm at the foot of the cross. I can see Jesus! He is nailed to the cross. And it is not the way it is depicted. Instead of his arms being in front of the beam and palms outwards, his upper arms are taken behind the beam and his forearms are hanging in front in a way that his palms are actually facing towards the beam!**

(Note: This is the same configuration reported in Shannon's memory of the event, not one depicted by any artwork I've ever seen.)

The nails seem to be in his hands in the palm area but his arms wrapped around the beam are taking his weight. I am standing about 10 feet away from the base of the cross and he is suspended about 10 feet or so above the ground. He is looking at me!

What does he look like?

His face is very bloody. He has long brown wavy hair. His eyes seem brown to me. His face is very much like the painting that that 8-year-old girl Akiane Kramarik made that they mentioned in the book "Heaven is For Real." He also looks like the painting made by the Shroud of Turin. It's like a combination of both of these paintings. He is looking right at me.

© 2003 Art Akiane, LLC

118

Do you feel sad seeing him on the cross?

No. Actually not. We are communicating telepathically. He is looking into my eyes. His face still looks very compassionate, though tired and in pain. He is telling me that this is his mission and why he came into the world. He said, I of all people, need to understand this and give comfort and strength to the rest. He tells me not to feel sad and I think back at him and just say, *"Rabboni."*

(Note: Prashant told me this was not a term he'd ever used before, as it does appear in the Gospel when Mary Magdalene looks for Jesus outside his tomb, runs into a gardener, then recognizes him as Jesus and calls him "Rabboni." ("Beloved teacher") John 20:16)

Look around. Where are you?

I can see people standing around the cross. I notice about 6 or 7 people who are close to Jesus and then I see Lawrence Olivier – that is me –

---

[118] Artwork by Akian Kramarik based on a vision she had of Jesus. (copyright Art Akiane LLC)

(Lawrence Olivier played Nicodemus in the same Jesus of Nazareth movie.) That is me. I know it![119]

I am not seeing myself as what I really looked like, but as the character was depicted, so that I would be able to positively identify who I was. But the thing is that Jesus does not look like the actor who played him in the same movie. This is the real Jesus. He looks like a combination of the Jesus painting made by Akiane Kramarik and the Jesus as they have painted him based on the Shroud of Turin.

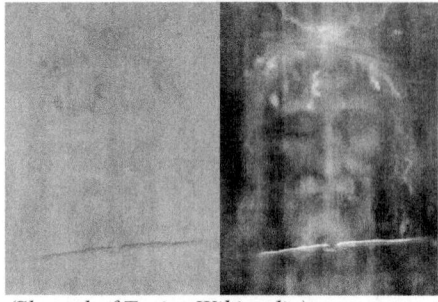

(Shroud of Turin; Wikipedia)

I want you to now go to the time of your death in this life.

I am older now. An old man. I am in my home. In my bed. Once again, I look like Lawrence Olivier, Nicodemus. There are a few of my grandchildren it seems around me.

What year is it?

39 A.D.

I want you to go to the moment Nicodemus dies. Take yourself out and be the observer.

---

[119] (John 3: "There was a Pharisee.. Nicodemus who... came to Jesus.. and said, "Rabbi... you are a teacher who has come from God. No one could perform the signs (miracles) you are doing if God were not with him." Jesus replied... "No one can see the kingdom of God ("homeland") unless they are born again." "How can someone be born when they are old?" Jesus answered... "No one can enter the kingdom of God unless they are born of water and the Spirit. Flesh gives birth to flesh, but the Spirit gives birth to spirit..." "How can this be?" (Jesus replied) "I have spoken to you of earthly things and you do not believe (me); how then will you believe if I speak of heavenly things?" Sounds like a Flipside chat to me.

I can see a kind of misty vapor leaving the body. It is glowing slightly. It is flying up through the ceiling.

Follow it! See where it goes and tell me what happens.

I am following it up into the sky. The blue sky. As it is going up, the sky color changes to bright gold. I can see two beings of light on either side of my soul, but not too close. They seem to be about 50 feet away in either direction. My soul is now heading into the clouds, which are also made of golden light.

Follow the soul into the clouds.

I am going through the clouds and now I am in a higher plane. In front of me, I see a bright golden light. It is now materializing into something... It's Jesus! He has come to receive me! He has his arms open and is waiting to hug me! I am so happy and excited to see him! I hug him and he says he is happy to see me!

Now what happens?

We hug. **I can feel this powerful love flow through me. It is beyond anything you can experience on the physical world.**

Now what do you see?

Now I see that Jesus looks different. He looks like a being of pure golden light. No longer completely human. It looks like an alien of sorts. Human-ish. With small beady black eyes, no ears, brightly shining.

Later on, it struck me that this (image) reminded me very much of the healthy glowing aliens in the movie Cocoon.

After this, Roma brought me back to normal consciousness. My first feeling was one of complete love, I felt cleansed. But something else struck me. I felt completely expanded. When I returned to normal consciousness, I felt as if I was much larger than before.

I felt as if my consciousness had spread to the size of the whole room. While I knew that my body was obviously the same size, my consciousness spread throughout the entire volume of the room.

Roma then related some cases she had witnessed (without giving me any names). How one of her subjects had felt sad that the planet that he used to incarnate on many times had been destroyed by its inhabitants and thereafter, he began to incarnate on Earth.

When she told me this, something strange happened. **I knew instinctively that this planet she was talking about was 68 light years away from our solar system. This knowledge just awakened within me, as if it was always there, but inaccessible to me.**[120]

My second session with her was a few weeks later on October 9, 2014. In this session, I got more details of my immediate past life as a monk in Greece in the 15th century (could be 16th as well). Incidentally, I have always remembered my transition from that lifetime ever since I was a child. It is the first conscious memory I have and the second memory is me entering into my current mother's womb and remembering every detail of what my parents were wearing, what they were doing, etc.

When I was about 13 years old, I shared this memory with my parents and they were so shocked, because the events I described actually happened when my mother was four months pregnant with me. I was born in July 1972, so the incident that I remember took place in February 1972. Here again, Roma took me through the whole relaxation, chakra cleaning process, I will skip all that and get to the part of the actual past life memory.

Roma: Go back to your last life - to the moment of your death. What do you see?

Prashant: I am lying down on a bed. It is a dark room, lit with candles. I am a white Caucasian old man. I can see my left hand being held by a young monk seated next to my bed. He is holding my hand and talking in a foreign language. But I know that what he is saying means, "Good bye, father."

What happens now?

---

[120] (Note: In a session in "Flipside" a woman recounts the same story about a planet where she normally incarnated had been destroyed "by accident" by scientists who were trying to harness some form of energy that went awry. All the souls that were from that planet had to seek other places to incarnate, apparently some of them have incarnated here.)

I am now suddenly floating out of my body to a point about five feet above the bed. I am now seeing my own body. I am old, probably in my sixties, white hair. **I can see the young monk from above. He is kissing my hand and crying. Then in the corner of the room, I see a bright white light and just kind of get sucked into it.**

What was your name in that lifetime?

Sebastian.

Then Roma brought me back to normal consciousness and after discussing a bit, we decided to meet again. For some reason, I still have not met her again. But I feel the two sessions I had with her helped me in many ways and in a way prepared me for what was to happen less than a week later.

After my second session on October 9, I opened up to the Other Side. My experience of having two past life regressions made me sensitive to receiving communications from people who had passed on. Little did I know somebody who was very close to me, who I had a deep spiritual connection with, and whom I loved dearly would make the transition into the other world just five days after my 2nd past life regression.

I realized intuitively this person who I loved dearly was In her previous incarnation, the young monk who was holding my hand, crying and saying, "Good bye, Father," in a language yet unknown to me.

Denise Robinson (to whom I've dedicated my book "The Cosmic Light Within") worked in my company as an assistant manager. My connection with her was much more ancient and deep. In hindsight, I believe this was the mechanism God chose to bring her into my life yet again. She joined my company in 2013 and the moment I saw her, I felt as if I was meeting somebody I had known for eons. She felt it too. We just clicked. We could literally talk for hours and discussed a lot of things about spirituality, God, religion and the Afterlife.

Maybe this was because she was helping me publish works connected to these topics; the Afterlife and all things related to it from near death experiences, out of body experiences, between life sessions, etc. These topics were what I was deeply interested in.

After my 2nd past life regression, I discussed with Denise (I had already discussed my first PLR with her and my other assistant Dash, and told them I felt I had been Nicodemus in Jesus' time) that I felt intuitively she had been the young monk at my side in my previous life. She said she felt the same way. When I revealed that I felt had been Nicodemus, she began to research Nicodemus on the Internet as well.

Well, now comes the real shocker.

October 14, 2014, Denise Robinson, only 32, left this physical world and made her transition back home. The circumstances of her passing are tragic and all I can say is that almost immediately, I started to receive messages from her. At first I thought it was my imagination, but the words I began to hear in my head were not the kind of words that I would typically use. I could even hear her say, "No. It's not your imagination. I'm here!"

Apart from these mental communications, which I have begun to write down, there were physical signs I had begun to experience, like seeing butterflies, my date stamp changing on its own, and many other things.

(Note: Prashant told me the story of the unusual date stamp. Changing the date on his device was something Denise did every day for him. And one morning, not long after her passing, he came into the office and discovered that someone had magically entered the locked office and changed the stamp date to the day she left the planet.)

Apart from that, validations that come in the form of suddenly seeing a sign on the highway or hearing a song on the radio that just made me feel that it was her catching my attention. I have received descriptions of the Afterlife plane from her in quite a lot of detail. "The Library," the cities, the waterfalls, the homes, the method of communication, more details about near death experiences and some things that are deliberately erased from the memories of the returnees of NDEs, which I plan to compile into a book someday.

We had been having semi regular communications and I was writing it down. But here is what connected to the Nicodemus lifetime and also the lifetime when we were both monks: about a month after her transition, I was driving home one evening and she began to communicate.

Though I was in heavy traffic, I went into a semi trance-like state where for lack of a better term, my car was being driven by me, but was in autopilot mode. I was controlling the car with some part of my consciousness that I seemed unaware of, and it was another part of my consciousness where my attention shifted to.

I just flat out asked Denise: *"Now that you have made the transition, you should have the answers to many questions about the things we used to talk about?"*
Her response was: Yes.

So tell me, were you really the young monk that was sitting next to me when I transitioned from the monk's body?
Yes, I was.

I remember that my name was Sebastian. What was your name?
Gregory.

Tell me, was I Nicodemus as I saw it in my past life regression?
Yes.

Were you in that life time with me?
Yes. I was your daughter.

What was your name?
Mary of Bethany.

Amazing. I had received confirmation from her about two previous lifetimes with names, had obviously heard about both these Biblical figures, but never knew their connection. Nor, had I ever read that Nicodemus was the father of Mary of Bethany.[121]

---

[121] Mary of Bethany is a biblical figure described in the Gospels of John and Luke in the New Testament. Together with her siblings Lazarus and Martha, she is described by John as living in the village of Bethany near Jerusalem; in Luke only the two sisters... are mentioned. A narrative in which Mary of Bethany plays a central role (in at least one of the accounts) is the anointing of Jesus, an event reported by two of the Synoptic Gospels and the Gospel of John in which a woman pours the entire contents of an alabastron of very expensive perfume over the head[Mt 26:7] [Mk 14:3] or feet [Jn 12:3] of Jesus. Only in the John account[Jn 12:1–8] is the woman identified as Mary, with the earlier reference in John 11:1–2 establishing her as the sister of Martha and Lazarus." (Wikipedia)

The next day, I searched 'Nicodemus Mary of Bethany' and was amazed there are some scholarly references in which it is claimed that Nicodemus was indeed the father of Mary of Bethany. [122]

True or not. We may never know with 100 per cent proof. But I know what I heard and what I saw. Never before had I ever thought about Nicodemus and Mary of Bethany in such detail before my PLR and let alone had any inkling whatsoever that they were supposedly Father-Daughter just as Denise had told me.[123]

Then one day in January 2015, I met my dear friend Rich Martini for the first time and when we chat in a coffee shop in Santa Monica and discussed many things about the Afterlife, he looked into my eyes and asked me – which country were you from in your life as the monk?
"I don't know," I said.

"Yes, you do," he said. "What's the first country that pops into your mind?" "Greece," I said all of a sudden, not really knowing why.
The moment I said that, I just felt that it was the truth.

No wonder all my life I have loved all things connected to Greece. I love Greek food, Greek mythology, Greek architecture, Greek gods and goddesses and have always been fascinated by Greek philosophers. Why once I even designed a personal logo or crest for myself with the Greek letter pi and sigma (My initials.)

Both by personal experience and afterlife communication with a dear friend who shared those incarnations with me, I am sure I have had these incarnations in Israel and Greece. I really hope to visit both of these countries someday."
…………

---

[122]https://www.adventistbiblicalresearch.org/materials/bible-interpretation-hermeneutics/mary-magdalene-sister-martha. Author says it is "likely" that Mary of Bethany and Magdalene are the same person.

[123] A theological paper "Mary Magdalene, Mary of Bethany and Sinful Woman of Luke 7: The Same Person?" by Biblical scholar Grenville Kent, 2010 argues Mary of Bethany and Mary Magdalene are the same person. If true, that would mean I've spoken to Jesus, his wife, his daughter, his father-in-law while researching this book. (!) http://research.avondale.edu.au)

I had asked Prashant to write down all that he told me at the coffee shop and to not leave out any details. As you can read, he's quite visual in his description of his memory of the events.

After my trip to Hemis monastery in Ladakh (formerly Tibet, now part of India's northern border) when the head abbot told me that Issa had spent some time studying at his monastery, I wrote to biblical scholar and author Ian Wilson and asked him his opinion about Jesus perhaps journeying to India. I offer his reply to show that I haven't been marching down a breathless path of "Jesus must have been in India because so many folks saw him there!"

Actually I think that is likely the case. There are so many of these accounts, and they don't come from anywhere else really – eyewitnesses who claim either under hypnosis, or in the light of day, that they knew Jesus and traipsed with him along the silk route to Tibet and back again.

I wrote Ian a long email, where I laid out, to the best of my knowledge back in 2002 (six years prior to starting these reports into the Flipside) what I had learned about Jesus in India and if he thought it was worthy of further investigation.

Here's Ian Wilson's response:

> From: "Ian Wilson"
> To: "RMartini"
> Subject: Re: Jesus in India
> Date: Mon, 7 Oct 2002
>
> Dear Rich,
>
> This response is going to have to be briefer than yours. In my teens I had a very strong interest in India and Tibet, though I have never visited either. As a very convinced agnostic Buddhism in particular had a strong appeal for me as the likely closest I could get to a religion with which I could identify. I hear you and I sympathize with what you're arguing for.
>
> But whereas in the case of the Mediterranean countries I am familiar the history of the last three thousand years and can find my way around the relevant texts, the sacred literature of India and Tibet is a very different matter.

There are so many Charlatans to twist texts true and false this way and that. Even if you are right I am simply not equipped to investigate and research in the way that would be needed. Furthermore, I can see not an iota of evidence from the New Testament point of view to persuade me that Jesus travelled that far afield early in his life. His parables are set in his own Jewish milieu.

He never tells a 'when I was in India' story, or shows the slightest sign of having been influenced by some Indian or Tibetan holy man. As for your point about his eating food after the Resurrection, remember that he passes through locked doors also. What he appears to have been anxious to show - and certainly he convinced the disciples of this – was that he was not just a ghost.

In his inevitably still enigmatic after death state he had a real physical presence, hence of course the famous story of Thomas prodding the wound in his side. **But what - in my firm opinion – he was positively not was someone merely resuscitated after his having merely appeared to have died on the cross.**

Roman crucifixion was far too brutal for anyone to be able to come back after 48 hours and convince people he was the Lord of Life. I find the very paradoxes of the stories of Jesus' Resurrection compelling that he really did rise from the dead.

But the idea that he then toddled off to live happily ever after in the south of France or in India or Tibet leaving his disciples back home to die excruciating martyrdoms - I'm sorry, that's not at all the Jesus I feel I know.

So thank you for so fulsomely sharing your ideas with me, and I do wish you well with pursuing them further. But it's not a road on which I can possibly accompany you.

All the very best, Ian"

There you have it. Jesus didn't "toddle off to France or India or anywhere in-between." At least that's one expert's point of view, **and I'm not claiming it to be any different.**

However, there's a number of people who claim they remember lifetimes that they spent with Jesus, claim to be aware of meeting him during their near death experiences, or have had the feeling that they've seen or sensed his presence during events with mediums. And when you compare these anecdotes, the stories generally follow the same plot.

They could all be Charlatans, but having met and interviewed them personally, I haven't met a Charlatan in the bunch. (At least not consciously so). I make my professional living spotting Charlatans on and off screen.

Here's a definition of Charlatan: *a person falsely claiming to have a special knowledge or skill; a fraud. synonyms: quack, sham, fraud, fake, impostor, hoaxer, cheat, deceiver, double-dealer, swindler, fraudster, mountebank; informal: phony, shark, con man, con artist, scam artist, flimflammer, bunco artist, snake oil salesman; dated: confidence man/woman - "the shallow promise of a charlatan selling snake oil"* (early 17th century (denoting an itinerant seller of supposed remedies): *from Italian "ciarlare" 'to babble.'*

Well, grazie Ian. *Non sono un Ciarlando.*

I'm amused he might consider these folks to all be Charlatans. Ultimately, they'd have to be **selling something** in order to be considered a swindler, hoaxer, cheat. And as you've seen how I've gathered this information; none of them are selling anything to me.

I'm fully aware there was a price tag on this book – but I didn't pay them anything other than a free coffee, and in many cases merely a "thank you" for their information, and have hidden their true identities so no one could claim it was different.

How much money could they make from saying *"Hey, read this obscure book by this weird guy from Santa Monica; I'm the actual person in the book who claims to know Jesus, but my name has been changed."*

They have no motivation to make this stuff up – when they're doing a hypnosis session, they're so concerned with "not making things up" that they usually have a hard time getting anywhere.

Scholars on the other hand – despite protestations to the contrary, generally do have a vested interest in whatever story they're being asked to verify. I'm not calling any of them *Charlatans* – but let's just agree that if someone doesn't consider "eyewitness testimony" to be evidence of anything – even if it's consistent and replicable (meaning I use the same series a questions and get roughly the same answers) then we'll forever be waiting for the university peer reviewed study that shows that Jesus indeed, still exists.

And none of these sessions began with "let's talk to Jesus." As you can see from the transcripts, they are all sessions where they were talking about something else entirely, and this Jesus fellow showed up during their session. Willy nilly. *Unannounced.*

Perhaps invited, but there's no rsvp implied or made. Sometimes because I startled them by saying "Hey, is that Jesus dude around?" Even in the case where The Doctor interviewed him, she gave her son a list of names of possible people they could "interview" and it was his choice (as it happened live on camera) to go and get "his friend Jesus."

Sorry if this offends religious folks, sorry if this offends atheists. I'm an equal opportunity offender.

This book isn't about contacting Amelia, or celebrities, or even Jesus. It's to show that with concerted effort – and there's no set rules for how that effort should be done – we can access people on the other side of the veil, ask them questions about their journey and path, and learn something new about our own path. Unlike my investigation into the life and disappearance of Amelia Earhart, which I've been paid by two films to work on, which I've spent a great deal of time investigating, this Jesus stuff is just falling into my lap.

I never asked anyone to share their Jesus stories with me. I didn't seek to include these reports in this book in the first place – the reason the book is so long is because I realized it was important to share. I will no doubt insult many of my family members, including my dear Uncle Tom Muleady who lived his life as a Parish Priest on the south side of Chicago. Last time I saw him he was doing Midnight Mass, he had to be in his late 80's or 90's – he died with his boots on. Just prior to going out for a New Year's Eve mass, he sat down to "collect his thoughts" and they collected him. I'm half Irish and Italian – I come from a long, long line of people who spent time on kneelers, sticking their tongues out above platens, or throwing the "sign of the cross."

I'm not trying to shake their boat, or anyone's boat. I'm just reporting what I've seen or heard to the best of my ability. If it bugs you, please, get your money back. Return this book to the place you bought it, they'll refund it. I'm not trying to sell anyone on this issue. If it does rock your boat, look around the boat carefully. It's okay. *The boat's fine.*

I know it's a giant mental leap to consider the fact that we have multiple lives, that Jesus may not be who we think he is, or was. That doesn't diminish or take away from the fact that he is a source of comfort and light to many in the world, and he continues to be so. Doesn't take away from the fact that he preached "universal love" and "unconditional love" to everyone he met, and they tortured him and put him on a cross for it.

And I don't mean figuratively, I mean literally. He is still working on behalf of souls everywhere, he appears to answer prayers, he appears to be able to help people on a daily basis, and because he's "outside of time" he appears to be able to do that simultaneously across the planet. He's usually the person that people meet on the Flipside during a near death experience, and he's always there to say "It's not your time yet."

But it's not the "Old Time Jesus" we're talking about. It's the "Outside of Time" Jesus, the one who can appear anywhere when called, can help when his actions don't interfere with the person's life journey making the call. He's accessible to atheists or religious people alike – he does not discriminate. He came to the planet to let people know about his path and journey and to help people along the way.

I know this flies in the face of… *well, everything.*

I know that what I'm suggesting is next to impossible to get our minds around. "Wait. You're saying that Jesus is not God, but that Jesus still exists, that he was all about teaching unconditional universal love, but that's because he currently resides in a state of universal unconditional love?" I can only answer; that's what it appears is the case.

Don't believe me? Ask him to make an appearance for you.

It appears he can show up to help you if they ask him to. He may appear in dreams as some painting or image seen before, or he may appear as a light, or an energy that seems so familiar that if feels like we know who he is without actually seeing him.

Other avatars are available as well. (According to him) Doesn't matter if it's Krishna, Buddha, Tara, Mary, Muhammed, Rumi, Confucius, Moses, Abraham, or Steve Jobs. If you want to speak to some person or figure that you've been worshipping for eons, it's very possible to ask that person direct questions. If they can answer, they will. As I've said; it makes total sense to go into a church and pray to someone who isn't there, *but if they reply, people consider you the crazy one.*

You don't have to share their replies with anyone outside of your temple, church, ashram, tent or bedroom. The message will be for the person who asked it. It may be for someone else, but you have to really think long and hard about sharing it with someone who may think you're insane or have you locked up or in some cases burnt at the stake – for learning something from the Flipside that no one else knows.

I'm happy to point out there are many similarities in these accounts.

Jennifer said that Jesus had five children, two died, and so did Shannon. Molly said he "died on the cross" but admitted she didn't see it happen. Nicodemus was there too, described a similar scene of people standing in the shadows watching, but he wasn't aware of his survival. But other accounts claim he survived, at least one says it was a planned event that worked.

Two accounts claim he went to France. All accounts have him going back to Tibet – or the Himalayas, where he lives out his life in peace and teaching others about the "light and the way." And two report that he was with the love of his life – his fellow preacher – and consort; Mary Magdalene.

I'm happy to point out that there are dissimilarities in these accounts as well. But I ascribe that to the same way we view the Akashic library when we visit it – no two accounts are the same, other than the details that "the library contains the information from all of our lifetimes." How people access it is different. The only way to truly examine these bits and pieces of memories is to compare them.

In the comparison we find the "essence" of what may or may not have happened.

Did Jesus exist? Apparently so. Was he the Jesus of the Bible? Apparently partially so, with embellishments, like an epic game of "telephone" or "Chinese whispers." By the time the memory is accessed, it's got all kinds "corrupted file errors" so the essence of the memory may or may not be accurate.

According to these accounts, Jesus was chagrined at how things played out after he survived the Crucifixion. He had learned some pretty unusual techniques (nifty tricks) that made it appear he died on the cross. He was beaten horribly, he was stuck up on a cross – he didn't carry the iconic cross we all see him carrying, according to these accounts – but carried a heavy block of wood that they later attached to a piece of wood they could slide into the ground.

He looked at his loved ones and friends with great compassion from his place on the cross, and they suffered as he suffered, wept as he wept. And it was a *Miracolo* that he survived. That he was able to be packed in aloe and myrrh by Joseph of Arimathea.

Let's explore that for a moment, shall we?

In the Gospels, Jesus is put on the cross after being tortured by Roman soldiers. Joseph of Arimathea reportedly goes to Pilate and asks for Jesus' body. In the original Aramaic, he uses the word for "living body" and Pilate replies with the word for "corpse" as if he's correcting him. Of course that's not how it reads in English. Pilate gives him the body.

Normally people spent up to a week on a cross. The idea was torture them further and make an example for them. Jesus spends perhaps a day or two on the cross – some estimate it's as short as three hours. While he's on the cross he makes a number of statements. "Father why have you forsaken me?" sounds to my ear like someone who was having direct communication with someone on the Flipside – and for some reason wasn't able to communicate with them any longer.

Be that as it may, Jesus is taken off the cross and put in a cave, but packed with Aloe and Myrrh. According to the Gospels, he was "anointed in the Jewish tradition." Which is pretty funny, because if you ask any Jew what their death tradition, they're happy to tell you that it's been the same for millennia. Body is washed and buried. No ointment, no oils, and especially no restoratives, which are what those two elements are used for.

But something miraculous must have occurred. He was wrapped in a cloth, and that cloth (which I think National Geographic has effectively *proven to be* the shroud of Turin – after it was dated a second time, and proven to be from that era. And how the face cloth that exists in Spain matches the time and period of the cloth in Turin.) But let's begin with the fact that whoever was in the shroud of Turin was alive because they were bleeding. Dead people don't bleed.

But National Geographic did a show that demonstrated whatever caused the negative image on the shroud did not come from a light that occurred outside the shroud – but inside the shroud. So even if Jesus was performing some form of tummo, the traditional yoga that monks still use to this day, or the "inner fire" which allows their temperature rise to inhuman levels. These unusual yogas were passed down orally from teacher to student, and some of the more amazing versions can be found in the text of the "Six Yogas of Naropa" a book that details the "consciousness transfer yogas" that Tibetan teachers are famous for.

So perhaps he did make it long enough to be restored in that cave. It would have been a miracle for him to recover from such a traumatic event.

Afterwards he's seen by Mary Magdalene in the garden, where she reports not recognizing him. If she was part of a vast conspiracy, as described by Shannon's memory of him, it's an odd detail that she shares. Perhaps they are the source of him "rising up to heaven" so that he was able to escape.

According to the Gospels, after his recovery, he goes to visit the apostles and "dines with them." If he's an etheric creature, it doesn't make much sense to think about that event. "Where'd the food go?" is a simple question for example. But he apparently was in physical form, because he invited Thomas the Doubter to "touch his wounds." And Thomas doesn't report his finger disappearing, or his hand going into some etheric stream of energy.

The Gospels also say that the "door was locked" and that Jesus appeared in their room. Since no one reported seeing him "walk through the wall" – that detail sounds like something someone told after the fact. "Hey, how did he get in here, the door was locked!" "Oooh, it was magic, he walked through the door!" It just doesn't make any sense that someone who could walk through walls would also eat dinner, drink wine and sleep with his friends.

All this happens before he sees the miracle of the fisherman, and where he eventually "walks on water." My point isn't to credit or discredit his miracles – it's to say at this point, they were dealing with someone who did something that had never occurred in anyone's memory; their pal with the golden tongue had survived a Crucifixion. Let's give him some credit for doing that alone.

And as mentioned, as man called "Yuz Asaf" shows up on the silk route a few years later, talks about being the "Light and the way" – there's a Persian statue that still exists that was built for him. He was traveling with his "mother of virgin birth" Miriam, and he wound up living and dying in Srinigar. Someone did a caste of his feet – for some unfathomable reason – but if you go online and search out the photos of Yuz Asaf's feet from his tomb, it's clear that whoever's feet these are suffered some catastrophic injury – that looks like the center of his feet were nailed.

Matthew 5:43-48 Common English Bible (CEB)

"You have heard.. "You must love your neighbor and hate your enemy." But I say to you, love your enemies and pray for those who harass you... If you love only those who love you, what reward do you have?... just as... heaven.. is complete in showing love to everyone, so also you must be complete."

CHAPTER TWENTY: JESUS APPEARS IN A NDE

F. Botticini for Matteo Palmieri – Assumption of Angels (National Gallery)

Colton Burpo's NDE

In the book, "Heaven Is For Real" (by Todd Burpo and Lynn Vincent) Christian pastor Todd Burpo writes that during the months after his emergency surgery in 2003, his son Colton began describing events and people that seemed impossible for him to have seen or met. Examples include his miscarried sister, whom no one had told him about, and his great grandfather who died 30 years before Colton was born. Colton also claimed that he personally met Jesus "riding a rainbow-colored horse" and sat in Jesus' lap while the angels sang songs to him; he also says he saw Mary kneeling before the throne of God and at other times standing beside Jesus." (Wikipedia)

So let's examine some of Colton's account: **"What did Jesus look like?" "Jesus has markers… brown hair and he has hair on his face, and his eyes.. are so pretty!" … What about his clothes? "He had purple on… his clothes were white, but it was purpose from here to here." (Todd writes "A sash.") "Jesus was the only one in heaven who had purple on."**

So how does Colton know this is Jesus? It's not like he's wearing a name tag. And during this NDE Colton is only five years old. It's not like he's seen a lot of films with Jesus characters, and even then – why name him that?

The argument is usually made that the subject is "projecting his desire" in this experience, that Colton, as son of a preacher would want to see Jesus while having this experience and did so.

Michael Newton has had many clients who saw religious figures in their sessions; Buddha, Mohammed, Jesus and others – and what he found was that when he examined them more closely, these figures "dissolved" or "turned into" the person's spirit guide. And he cites a number of cases where a spirit guide reveals him or herself during a session – at first appearing as some kind of mythical deity – sometimes this is reported as being done to "calm the fears of the person having the experience."

However likely the first two scenarios are, there is a third possibility I can conceive of; and that it actually is Jesus. That somehow, the person who was Jesus, the energy of that person exists – outside of time – and can appear when needed to console and help those who need his counseling and help. And indeed that scenario is discussed in the later chapters of this book.

When Colton says "Jesus was my teacher" – again the "pause" button that goes on when people hear the word Jesus – imagine for a moment that this person that looks like Jesus also functions or works as a teacher. That Colton observed a number of other students in his class, who are all children.

Does Jesus teach everyone? That's not in the data. We have numerous accounts of classes in the afterlife, and each one appears to have something to do with energy transference or manipulation; transforming thought into form is one class, another is about moving objects by using the focus of other students in a group.

So Colton is confirming one aspect of between life accounts here: classrooms in the afterlife.

"So what did the kids look like? What do people look like in heaven?"
"Everybody's got wings," Colton said. (Pg 70)

People who have near death experiences, or during between life therapy sessions, report a number of unusual things about what they see and perceive in the afterlife. If the therapist is willing, they can look closer at these items. Examine the wings for example, are they feathery? Soft? Hard?

When examining these details, the story usually begins to expand "Well, I see that they aren't actually feathers per se – but are a mental construct so that I can understand why it is they can fly" might be one example. It's a matter of perspective in these cases. For example, everyone has a different idea of what the word "home" means – it means something different to everyone, including twins. But we can all agree on the concept.

The same goes for "heaven" – despite this one account, it's not repeated in any other accounts I've come across. It doesn't mean that it's not real per se – it means that for this particular person, their perception of this arena – a library for example, or a council chambers that might be inside or outside, or a soul group might be in a room or in a grove – it depends upon the person perceiving the moment.

For example, Colton's father asks him how long he was in heaven. "Three minutes" he says. Of course that's "Earth time" – or as in the movie Contact, she was never visibly gone from the screen, but the "event" that occurred during the film where she went to deep space to meet another group of beings that had reached out for contact – took 18 hours according to the time recorded on her camera built into her "space suit."

As reported earlier, I had an out of body experience where I went to see my friend Luana Anders; I had the feeling and sensation of pulling out of my body, then zooming up above me, I could see New York city disappear below – and I went into deep space, traveling at incredible rate, so fast that light seemed to melt around me – and then, just like in the film "Contact" (which came out after my experience), I went through a worm hole of sorts and wound up in another Universe – where I was now traveling quickly but sideways. And when I finally arrived at my destination – in front of my friend Luana who had her eyes closed – she opened them as if to say **"You wanted to know where I am; here I am."**

As noted, a truck driver outside my Manhattan apartment honked his horn. Only I traveled back to my body, like a rubber band being pulled, at such a rapid rate, back through the wormhole, back through space, back into Manhattan and back into my bed – that when I opened my eyes, the guy had just taken his hand off the horn.

I'd say about 26 light years in about oh, 1.2 seconds. Pretty danged fast.

So Colton's three minutes on the Flipside may have been hours over here. As I've noted, I went to visit my friend Luana's classroom on the Flipside, and rudely interrupted her class. Two years later, I did another between life session, and when I returned to find Luana it felt like about twenty minutes went by. She was introducing me to the teacher, and apologizing for my interruption of his class. He was polite, and allowed me to ask my questions.

So perhaps these memories are relative as well. Perhaps the "energetic being" that is Jesus, appear to people in the fashion that he perceives they need to see him. Further, perhaps all of these "visitations" throughout this book, or some form of his wanting me to perceive him in a particular fashion. As a medium height, with long hair, brown eyes and long eyelashes, very tan – the consistency of the reporting either points to "that's how he looks" or "that's how he looks to you."

Because he's not showing up in my between life sessions to walk me around, then I can't really discern what he's doing showing up in these other sessions in the first place. Is it because of my friend "Molly" who was the first person I met who remembered a lifetime where they claimed they knew him? Or was it some other reason that he started to appear in my research?

Again, I wasn't seeking him out. These people contacted me independently, either because they'd read about him in "Flipside," heard me talking on the radio, or some other reason. And their reports about him are not exactly the same – yet they're uncannily similar. If I had more friends of other faiths, or complete atheists, perhaps I'd get a different visual from them.

But even my friend who said "I'm Jewish, I don't believe in Jesus" was startled to see him in his past life memory. There he was buying some cloth from him in a marketplace in Cairo. When I met this friend 35 years ago, I knew we'd be friends for life – it was like meeting an old friend I hadn't seen in a long time. I don't remember any lifetime during the life of Jesus. So it's not like I'm looking up long lost pals in this life.

Yet there we have it. The reason this appears in the book is to show the consistency of the reporting. We could argue they're all making it up – but the fact none of them know each other and they're reporting the same individual, the same stories about the same individual, stories that aren't part of the Bible or the historical record; that can only mean that for some unknown reason, they're remembering a lifetime where they knew Jesus, and wanted me to mention it.

But since for the most part I've made these accounts anonymous, it can't be for fortune or fame. It can only be for some higher spiritual reason that I'm not aware of. Believe me, I thought long and hard about how difficult this portion of these reports would be for people – I can only have *faith* that it is for a good reason.

Finally, he did show up in a past life regression I did with Scott De Tamble. This may have been the third or fourth session I did with him. I transcribed it and left it out of "It's a Wonderful Afterlife" because it just didn't fit. It obviously fits this book, and I'll allow it to speak for itself.

EXCERPT FROM MY HYPNOSIS SESSION ABOUT JESUS

This is from an LBL that I did with Scott De Tamble, which I reported in the book "It's a Wonderful Afterlife." I took this portion of the between life session out of the book but include it here, because, well, it's on topic. Or maybe "Jesus made me do it." But here it is:

Scott: Rich said that he was talking about bringing other people to this session.

RM: He just wanted to explore with you, wasn't so much he was looking to talk to anyone in particular... perhaps if possible to see or speak to Jesus; he thought that would be an interesting construct.

What do you think about that?

(Referring to a list of people that Scott has of people I thought might be fun to "contact" – I'm remembering the list when I say-) "Is Jesus available?" Seems like an odd question. Let's see if he's around. (After a pause) **I'm seeing him now, and hearing** *"What would you like to know?"* **He's dressed in light blue, he's sitting on the edge of something, sort of turned towards me. Sitting at a distance.**

We had a past life session where a woman seemed to witness Jesus speaking, she was a member of a traveling people. ("Molly")

"June. Yes, my old friend June." That's what I'm hearing; "My old friend June." (The Chapter in "Flipside" "He Made the Sun Rise.")

Let me ask about that. The way she perceived you with light brown eyes. Was that accurate?

"Absolutely, right on the money with June."

The historical Jesus we know is that based on that lifetime?

"Yes, the Jesus everyone knows and loved. But the story is not as it was passed along, no negative there, just not how it happened."

How did it happen?

(as Rayma) "How long you got? I'm going to speak from Rayma's point of view, as I'm more comfortable doing so." (In my mind, I'm having trouble "thinking" about what Jesus is saying, and by "shifting my perspective" to my spirit guide, I somehow feel more verbal.)

But the story is correct; Jesus's father was a Roman soldier with Greek heritage, his mother was Mary of royal heritage; the House of David. So her having a kid was a big deal, it's not been played up that way in history, but that's why it was a big deal for her to be giving birth and not being able to find a room – royal family and all.

Did she love this Greek soldier?

Love was not part of the relationship; Roman soldiers did what they wanted. It was just accepted, she had been taken as a mistress by this soldier, there was no love involved, she was pregnant and then Joseph married her. It was the honorable thing to do, as he was a good man, and they had a number of other children.

Jesus chose this lifetime, first and foremost, to help people understand something; he understood the connection to the afterlife, he had one foot in both worlds, very connected to the between lives realm.

He wanted to share that and the concepts of there being no hierarchy and no caste system back here – when he spoke of his "father," he was referring to and trying to explain his spirit guide. He was a very powerful speaker, very intense person, who was very connected to people.

He traveled across the silk route to India and Tibet before he was 30, some 12 years, preaching to tribes of Israel along the way, and learning from these cultures. After that he came back to (Jerusalem to) fulfill his destiny – to go through this process of trying to show people that we don't die, that was part of his mission.

He was trained in a monastery in northern India, which used to be Tibet, a place called Hemis, Rich has been there. He was trained in Tibetan yoga, not so much as a Buddhist, he'd already arrived as a full blown Avatar, a seeker of truth, but they taught him Tibetan meditations and yoga and esoteric yoga, one in part where you can stop breathing for hours at a time.

When he went back to fulfill his destiny, he was brought before Pilate, and Pilate condemned him, not the way it is in the Bible, as the Romans rewrote that portion of it to make them appear less guilty of his death.

(Note: I'm speaking from my spirit guide Rayma's point of view, so that allows me to speak in giant paragraphs. All I can say for certain is that it sounds to my conscious mind like I know what I'm talking about, and when I transcribed this interview, I had forgotten the answers to the questions. Hard to discern what was mine or what was someone else's.)

RM: It's correct in the way it was written in some Tibetan texts which they gathered from Jewish silk merchants; Pilate assigned a spy to him, and was concerned about his stirring up trouble, and when they arrested him, Pilate didn't like his answers, became furious and ordered his death.

The Jewish holy men, the Sanhedrin, pled for his life, since by law they were the only ones capable of condemning someone "of the book" to death. Pilate refused to give him up, so they went and washed their hands of his death to the public, not the other way around. Pilate wouldn't be caught dead performing a Jewish ritual of cleansing his hands in public, if he did, he would have been lynched by his own troops.

But Jesus was taken out to a crucifixion planned in a different way, it had never been done before; crucifixions lasted a week usually and at the end of the week bones were broken to kill the victim.

In this case he was put up for only a day or so and through his yoga training he was able to block out the pain he was going through. (I'm getting) **There was a little bit of deception on both sides, some of the soldiers were fans and friends. Then Joseph of Arimathea went to Pilate and asked for Jesus when he was still alive – taken off the cross alive, taken to a cave alive, and he lived. He survived.**

Taken off the cross alive – conscious?

Yes, taken to a cave, administered aloe and myrrh, which are restoratives; I know in the gospels claim he was anointed in the tradition of the Jews – but there is no tradition of anointing the dead. The Romans rewrote that; made that up.

Was he wounded with the spear?

Yes, he was bleeding at the time; he was still alive. The shroud in Turin proves he was still bleeding. **It wasn't a fatal wound, that was the signal to get him off the cross.** Nails went into his feet and wrists, as they couldn't go into a hand, it would slip off - so he was nailed, brutally; there was not a pleasant moment in the experience other than the fact he survived. **They spirited him away, he left with his mother, "The Virgin" they called her, he travelled to some other countries…**

(pause) Let me ask him. (to Jesus) Am I telling this story correctly? (Laughs.) He says *"You're doing fine."*

Where did he go?

He wound up in India, in Kashmir where died. But – the story of his death on the cross ultimately served humanity in a profound way.

How old was he when he died?

Old age. Old man. There's a tomb, his body is in a tomb in Srinigar, "The Rose Azul." There's a cast of his feet outside the coffin; you can see clearly his feet had holes in them.

Did those wounds or wrist bother him through the rest of his life?

Yes, and no… because he was such an amazing yogi, more like an amazing human specimen; he could heal himself of nearly anything. He was able to continue his life. **But the miracle of Jesus is that he survived the crucifixion, that's his amazing feat that no other human has ever done.**

Does his blood line live on?

Of course, he had children, they had children. **His current work is to greet Christians who aren't supposed to be here in the afterlife. You could say he's the designated driver for Christians who have NDEs.** So he shows up in their near death experience to let them know it's not their time, to help them, gives them great solace, everyone reacts, "Oh my god, it's Jesus."

Ask him to show his countenance to you.

Just as June described him (in "Flipside"), brown eyes, golden flecks, hippie hair, not olive skin, maybe even more Caucasian looking – Western – very tan, **tan skin**, not tall, medium height and he's got – a beatific smile – makes sense he coined the phrase.

He's normal sized, not super skinny from what I can see of him, powder blue robe - a casual robe, not a toga, and I get the sense he stopped because we called him – **he too is looking at his watch as if he's got work to get back to.**

(Note: We've got a number of descriptions of Jesus in this book, from Colton Burpo to a Medium. Generally, he's seen as wearing a blue or purple robe (or jeans and a tee shirt) and is described as a very tan Caucasian. Again, when doing one of these sessions you're asked to just "speak whatever comes to your mind without judging it." That's what it appears I'm doing in answering this question.)

Is there anything he wants to tell us?

(A pause) Okay that's a bit of a cliché, can you give us something better than that? (listens) He says **"Love is the key. And it's important to find the lock."** (Asking Jesus) What does that mean? He **says "Love is the key but it's important for you to find the lock. The find the lock, you must open your heart. If you open your heart up to other people, you'll find the key. Love is the key."** Okay.

What about the worship of him or the church image of him?

He's saying it's a misinterpretation of what he stood for – which was universal love. He doesn't find it tragic, as there's a whole swath of people influenced in a positive way, but when you point to the religions and dogma and pain inflicted on others, there's nothing he can do about that. **The fact that he had survived the crucifixion was hidden by the Romans and coalesced into this unusual religion.**

He's noting that he had female disciples, (back then) the religion is not based on anything that was his reality; he wanted to pass along to humans that the afterlife is close to this life, and to understand what the afterlife is, is a way of ennobling life on Earth. There is no hierarchy there, there should be none here, that you have to love your neighbor as yourself because we are all connected by heart. And he taught that in a profound way, but it got pretty screwed up.

How does he deal with those who pray to him in need?

Think of that act of prayer, the same way a spirit guide might be prayed to, or asked to intercede. It's that message of helping and "I'm here, I believe in you." **People transform themselves, all kinds of people who have adopted him as their panacea, and its transformed them. The guy has an incredible amount of energy and there's no downside to prayer and focus.** It's not going to hurt anybody, it only hurts when it's turned to judgment or negativity. **He says "Okay, thanks, I appreciate that explanation." I'm asking him "What do you like doing? When do you have fun?**

(Note: I've never used "panacea" in a sentence before, I had to look it up; "A *solution or remedy for all difficulties or diseases.*")

Who is he as a soul spirit? A teacher, a healer, explorer; something else?

More of a teacher. His lifetime got turned into this epic thing that he wasn't; the son of God stuff. But you've got to give the guy credit for being a marquee individual. **As he points out, "two thousand Earth years isn't that long, and there's been a lot of years before the two thousand years and many years to come."** It's just one of those things of human nature to create idols and things outside themselves.

Did Jesus have any inkling of what was eventually going to happen?

That's what he set out to accomplish; and it became a useful tool in terms of lessons of good and evil and bad and it became a wave. **Kind of the way WWII was a compressed time period of time in human history to teach lessons in compassion and loyalty, love and forgiveness all at once.** This was a long term journey; I don't see that he knew all of the ramifications. But did his spirit guides know? It's possible.

Any words you'd like to leave Rich today?

(Listens) Very funny. He quotes Bob Dylan; **"Don't follow leaders, watch your parking meters."** Ok, he has a sense of humor. He adds **"That's it, just open your hearts. Wherever you can."**

(Note: Once Bob Dylan was asked if he could interview anyone in history, who would that be? And he answered "Joseph of Arimathea.")

Rayma, anyone else you'd like to chat with? Anything else you'd like to show Rich today?

I'm going to take him (Rich) into this healing cave; he hasn't been here before. It's a crystal cave. It's got the energy crystals all around, each one imbued with the intentions of those students who created them. Each crystal carries a certain amount of love and compassion. I can really feel that – it feels like radiating waves of warmth, energy, pulsating.

I would ask for a final word and blessing for Richard.

I got this final word from Luana who spoke to the council. The message is for you Scott: **"You honor yourself by doing the work you're doing. By that we mean, you honor your higher self and all of the work we do over here by doing the work you're doing there."**

"We thank you for it because every time you do it, you honor who we are and there's no higher honor than that – giving your heart to a fellow human or fellow soul; no greater gift. And you give yourself away every time you do one of these sessions."

Thank you very kindly. That is very generous of you all. I hope you know how honored I am to be able to speak with you today, and to serve in this way. And I would thank you for your support through these many years. We couldn't do it without you… So why were we shown the Remy life today?

The "French party animal?"

(Note: Remy was a lifetime that I remembered where I was a French soldier who killed Englishmen with relish, and spent too much of his time bedding married women.)

Richard wondered if he'd had any warrior lifetimes, in his other past life reviews he never killed anyone, always some form of a monk. Richard has many qualities of this fellow in his lifetime now, certainly in his youth; he was a warrior playing football, it's good to remember or come to realize you haven't just been a monk or Priest or nun, or a Tibetan, or a Brahmin in all your past lives; there have been soldiers in there.

We brought it today so he could see he wasn't affected by it via karma, he had an unusual path, skimming the surface, but he was able to kill soldiers because he'd worked it in his mind they were English mongrels. There of course was downside to not giving his heart to one person and breaking up families; he didn't see that as problem until afterwards. Obviously those kinds of lifetimes aren't healthy for anybody.

He didn't create karma for himself with his bad actions?

Let's talk about karma for a moment, by translating spirit language to human language. **Karma has always been defined as some form of wrong doing, or the creation of sin – a word associated with picking up negative energy from actions done over lifetime. But over here we see**

karma as an energy pattern and energetic pattern – closer to the Sanskrit definition of karma; "action" - not good, not bad, just an energetic pattern. In order to become a complete individual, a complete soul, a complete painting if you will, you need to examine all different kinds of paint, not just a few different colors.

There are many energy actions to examine; life, death, murder, killing others; at their core you're examining these energetic systems. **Between lives you get the experience of the negativity that you've engendered, you see the ill effects on the families of those you've hurt, and all the waves that you've created.** The waves that you can't experience while you're there on Earth, because you're in the middle of the play.

But after the play is finished, you get all the reviews simultaneously given to you. You're able to see "I should have been less violent or a little more loyal or more humble," in order to be a more purely wonderful individual for lack of better terminology. So Remy left that lifetime not feeling guilty, but when he got back here, was able to see, and feel, not instantly - but he was able to examine and experience it over time.

On the other hand, some of the experiences were done with the participation of those who were killed, to experience that; being killed, being cheated on, so everybody learns a lesson. I'm trying to say there's no negativity, no negative karma with this; it's hard to put it in human terms because of the polarity of the planet, the good and bad.

They're just terms for an energy pattern in your path, and a difficulty can also be a benefit; some things in your path you can learn from, or help others. That's the ultimate goal, to open your heart to everyone and all things.

Why was Rich brought here today?

You (Scott) and he have been working side by side; well, you've been doing all the work, he does the talking. But this kind of work is pushing the vehicle of enlightenment, we'll call it that, "the vehicle of insight" a little bit forward, pushing the veil away a little bit -- and forward. It's been a chance for Rich to sum up some of the experiences you guys have shared and examined.

If you were to sum it up?

Story telling is more interesting when you hear all the bits and pieces of what went into the story, going behind the scenes in a theatrical play, pulling back the curtain to see how a play is put together.

There are people back here who think there's no value to that, you have to be fully invested in the action, *"You have to learn lessons the hard way."* **This other school of thought is to pull back the curtain, as you and Rich have done, and show how the play is constructed and that will help as well**.

Some of my clients call this "cheating."

There is that point of view; *"I don't want to know what's going to happen, because I can't learn from it if I do."* It seems like they're saying *"Aren't we cheating?"* It's like telling God to look the other way while you sneak around to get the candy.

But listen, the planet is in such a state as it is right now, on the verge of complete and utter destruction, I think it needs help and guidance and someone to think outside the box. **It cannot move into this next arena with billions of people who are going to be hungry with all the money in someone else's pockets. It will go through a huge turmoil until someone comes along and says "This is unsustainable."**

I try to avoid bringing up visions of a dystopian future as they call it; a world where everything seems to be going down the tubes. It's very popular in the culture right now, in the language of art and media, that the world is going to turn into some terrible place.

I'm just not of that ilk or frame of mind. **"Clap your hands if you think that happiness is the truth." I agree. I think the planet has a great opportunity to move forward with compassion for other human beings, and this is the fastest way to get people to be compassionate about others.**

That sums it up beautifully. Thank you.

"Thank you Scott!" That's what I hear them saying.

You are most welcome, and I thank you for your support and your guidance... Last thoughts?

Think about that formula that you saw on the chalkboard, how to ensure the crystal or diamond comes out of these elements in the right order. **This work has shown that it doesn't matter how much money you make; focus on creating the diamond and the good will come. Focus on your heart, focus on what's important, and you'll see that's where the gold is."**

…………..

I got a letter from a Minister in a large Church in the West regarding this information about Jesus, as I wanted to hear his opinion about it. I sent him a copy of the book and he wrote: "I like your history of Jesus in India that you put in this book. I had not read that before. It's a good transition into the material you present. The story I like best, that I would like to use in a Christmas Eve service as the meditation for the evening, is the reflection from "Mary the mother of Jesus" about what it was like in the manger with baby Jesus. That is very expressive and detailed and may be used in a traditional worship service I think."

It turns out this Minister has also had a between life hypnosis session. I applaud his openness with me, and I include this portion of his letter as well; he wrote about his own visit to the "Akashic" library during his life review:

"I know what you mean about the "library," having experienced that myself during an between life session. To me, it was like a vast library with millions of books going several stories high in a "Library of Congress" type building. When I chose a book on the third floor and opened it, I found myself standing within the scene it was about. It was sort of like a virtual reality experience. So perhaps these people are accessing that kind of "book" or "VR experience" in regard to Jesus from the "universal library." I had an interesting life review. I came reluctantly, with a sense of dread, to the life review chamber. This was after a lifetime (I saw where) I spent in Egypt as a construction supervisor on the pyramids in Giza. The 4 members of the divine council doing my life review dressed in carnival and medieval type outfits. One of them pretended to be a king, one a queen, one a knight, and one a court jester.

The message to me was "chill out," don't take all of this life on earth and evaluation of it so seriously. I thought that was a surprising but much needed message to me about the life review process. It reinforced the theme you often mention of how we are actors playing roles we choose to play and we should play them gusto and abandon. I got the feeling that such role play is also a large part of the afterlife. We learn and joke and have fun and delight in playing make believe, as we did when we were children, particularly in the afterlife.

Thanks for sending me the rough draft. I enjoyed reading it. I think you were wise to include the Jesus stuff as essentially part 3 of a long book where, as you mention, **if someone has stayed around long enough to read that far, they are less likely to be shocked or offended by the Jesus material you present**. Keep up the good work and stay in touch, my friend. Peace."

Well thanks Padre, I really appreciate it.

And finally… I got an email from a woman who appears in this book. She said that she was "doing her dishes" when out of the corner of her eye, "Jesus appeared" and gave her a message; "Tell Rich to go and see Jamie Butler when she's in Los Angeles. There's someone who wants to give him a message." I said to her "How do you know it was Jesus?" She said she didn't. It just *felt like* it was him.

I did not know Jamie Butler was going to be in LA, I've never met Jamie, but I thought it would be a great time to thank her for letting me use some of her work with Erik Medhus. Jamie is a medium from Atlanta, and tours the country doing events where people can ask direct questions to their loved ones no longer on the planet.[124]

During her event, she channels a number of different people, it depends who "wants to show up." On the evening I went, Erik Medhus showed up, (through Jamie) and saw me in the crowd. *"Richard! Love your sense of humor bro"* he said. Later, he sat (Jamie was sitting, but for all appearances, he was talking) with me for a few minutes. I recorded them with my cell phone.

Mind you; I'm not a person who has focused his research on Channelers. I've avoided the topic entirely, because they are contradictory by nature. (As I noted, I disagree with the concept that "time doesn't exist" outside

---

[124] As noted, earlier in this book, I spoke with a Channeler who claims to speak to Edgar Cayce. I know Jamie Butler's work as a medium, but in these evenings, she "channels" people no longer on the planet. I can't vouch for any of what is said, I can only compare it to what "these same people" have said to others. By comparing what they say to what they've reported said before, can offer a clearer picture to what's happening on the Flipside.

this realm, I argue that isn't what's in the reports. That time *does* exist, but relatively differently. Also that *the future is not set*, but there are *likely outcomes.* I won't belabor the point, but it's contrary to what most Channelers say.)

Me, Erik Medhus, Jamie Butler. Friday Aug 12th

Jamie/Erik sits down next to me. An embrace.

Me: Dude. How are you bro? I just want to thank you for your book "My life after Death." It's awesome and I recommend it to everyone.

Put it into a movie.

You gotta help me with that one.

Is this on? (into camera) Put my book into a movie and have this guy do it.

I'm a fan of you and your mom…

My mom is awesome.

I get an email from a woman, she says "Jesus just showed up in my kitchen to tell me to tell you to come down and see Jamie." That's why I'm here. So, like can you bring your pal in?

You mean you want me to dial Jesus?

If you want…

Maybe afterwards.

So dude, tell me, how can I help you? Is there something you need from me or some way that I can help you?

Dude, for me it's about my mom, totally about helping her get out what she wants to say, she's like this crazy inventor man. Popping with ideas; she's got movies, stories, she's ready to shake shit up about death.

It's great how she and you have figured how to talk in real time.

Do you think we could we get her into live streaming?

That would be great. People could ask you live questions.

That would be so cool to generate some funds, to support what she's doing. It would be cool to do like a live streaming event, to talk and everything.

And you could help her with that.

I'd stand next to her and be like "Bitch, you're on your own." (laughs, gestures to me) Dude, we're good together.

We are.

(Later, when time runs out on the session, Erik looks up, says *"Hey Rich, can you come back tomorrow?"*)

On a technical note, I recorded this conversation on my cellphone camera – a Samsung – but when I watched it, it was completely out of synch. I have the equipment to separate the sound from the picture, I have done so, but can't synch the words to the lips. It appears as if the sound was recorded at a different speed than the visual; I've never seen that happen before in a video. (Technically not possible as they both run at the same rate.) The battery was charged, the footage is all there, audio sounds slightly faster than my normal speaking voice.

After the session, as Jamie Butler was leaving, I mentioned to her that I found it fascinating when Jamie had done her "Erik and Jesus interview" (channelingerik.com) Jesus' physical presence overwhelmed her during the session. She couldn't breathe, tears came into her eyes – I noted that the same happened when he appeared to be speaking to my friend, medium Jennifer Shaffer; how she also lost her breath, cheeks turned red, tears came to her eyes. I came back the next day as per Erik's request.

CHANNELING GRACE/JESUS

A medium who lives in Atlanta, she has worked with Erik Medhus and a number of other people, Jamie tours the country speaking on behalf of the dead, so to speak.

After a few minutes, an English woman who lived in the 20th century named Grace "came forth." She speaks in a gentle manner, with an accent that is reminiscent of the actress Emma Thompson. She's gentle, yet precise, and later Jamie told me that she saw her as a young blonde woman from London in the previous century. After an introduction, Grace mentions "that there had been a request the previous evening for Jesus to come forth, and asked if the audience wouldn't mind him doing so." After they agree:

Grace: Thank you very much for joining us. May I say that his energy is in the room and he's very present for us, a lot of you already have a relationship with him. A lot of you understand that he is more than just a man, and **not just because there's a belief system designed around him or his actions, but because of the way that he viewed life, the way he viewed love and compassion on earth.**

He says "Hello to everyone." He's showing gratitude for being present. If you sense he's standing in front of me, you might feel his presence in front of you as when he addresses people, he goes directly to the source of communication … So Richard, do you have questions on the tip of your tongue? What were they?"

(I did not, as I had no idea he'd be making an entrance, so I just opened my mouth and spoke)

RichMartini: Is there anything he'd like to impart to us about his journey here? Or anyone in the room that might need his help or solace; if he could be so generous as to address their concerns, that would be fantastic.

He's saying "Thank you for giving him the time and the space to speak to all of you directly." Although I, Grace, have spoken to many entities, to be with one to translate for Jesus and other source entities, is always a joy and a challenge… What happens is, as Jesus says, that being in front of you in your presence, often the human body does not process such **a high vibration of energy, and sometimes people find themselves short of breath, teary eyed, feeling healed, expansive themselves...** and somewhat…" (Grace, aside) that's not an English word – we'll use the word *expansive* again then – "**full of unity… full of connectivity, where we are all one.**"

(Note: I realized later he was responding to the question I had the day before, about how he's able to change the frequency in a room.)

"A message that he would like to relay, first **Richard,** that **he did communicate to the woman for you to appear here. He feels that there's more of a story that *you* can tell, and not so much of the Catholic side of things for his story, but on the spiritual side of his journey.**"

Often," he says, "when one dedicates themselves into doing his life's work, in aligning themselves with who they are, **the masses will mistranslate** what has been happening and there are many situations where his presence in a certain situation has been mistranslated."

(Note: We've heard this point before, how his life's work has been mistranslated. Jamie has not read my book, nor was privy to any of the interviews in it, other than the one she participated in where Dr. Medhus asked the questions, and Jamie answered.)

"He's not asking for wrongs to be righted, he's asking that you yourselves, in this lifetime, as you're being taught and handed down stories from other people, from books, from other generations, from centuries ago -- that you not only hear the story in and of itself, but that you **hear where it is coming from; because the source (of the story) explains all."**

"If it's coming from a man, it will have a man's tone (pov), if it's coming from a woman, it will have the woman's tone. I myself..." he says, "want the tone of *all humanity*. I myself want to help all understand the value and importance of love. It is not about segregation in these days, but it is understanding that all people are human, that all people have emotions."

(Note: He's saying here "Consider the source." So if a man wrote a story that occurs in the Bible, or elsewhere, it will have a particular bent or filtered frame of reference, or if a woman tells the same story, it will have a different point of view, and to always consider the source of the story. In other words, the Bible isn't "the word of God" per se, but the word of people who were doing their best (or worst, depending) to put into words spiritual events.)

A lot of what **Jesus would talk about is based on love and acceptance**. He says "In these days... These specific days you stand and live in, are tearing apart; they're pulling apart at the seams. I wish for you," he says **"I wish for you to look at not what is being torn apart, but how it is mending."**

"When you look at people, (you can) start out (by) listening to their angry voices; they have their broken hearts, full of all emotions and maybe there are those you do not wish to engage with, (emotions) such as hatred and anger, rage. Know that what they are needing -- and **learn how to communicate (with them) in ways that are non-judgmental"** -- for this is what he is helping people with, in these days, these days that we live in now. "Meetings like this," he said, "are important. In halls, in homes, in churches, event spaces, that hold people who are seeking information, (the meetings) are so important. Find yourself in your community."

(Note: It's consistent with the report of considering God to be "unconditional love." The love that connects "everyone and all things." When someone is speaking with rage, anger or fear, to consider what they're saying or to reply in a non-judgmental fashion. Of course; easy to say, but hard to do.)

Grace: He would like to answer any questions people wish to direct towards him. I will assist with that.

Question: Today I came across two Mormons who asked about my faith; I grew up Catholic, thought it was a little strange that today they'd hand me their book. Just interesting how we're now having this conversation, a little synchronicity.

"Hello to you," he said "I love you. The synchronicity of today was to show you that it's time to find your faith again. **Though it does not need to be in any *religion*, it does not need to be in something that you *must* believe in, but to find your faith again.** He's hoping to help you with this, whether it includes him or not. ("Thank you.")

Question: When I close my eyes I see a cross and I see you on that cross. Is that you trying to communicate with me or something else?

He says "With all my heart; it is me communicating to you." He said "I would do that this way – I would do it with many of you. That you don't have the confidence to believe that you have a direct connection with me. **Though we do, we have a direct connection to all people, to all life on earth.**"

"The reason I bring to your mind a cross, is that **it causes such a deep emotional connection that you react to it in ways that words would not**. It is to remind you of the sacrifices that you are making and to align yourself to be more direct with where you want to go. That it does not (signify to) have to bear the cross of any sin or sorrow, that it could be aligned completely with joy." He said "Thank you, I love you."

Comment: I just have so much gratitude…

He said "Thank you. My heart goes to you."

Question: Any message for me?

He speaks about how we come to this earth and why. "**It is not just for yourself. You came to give of yourself to your family. And then extensively to your friends.** And your insight and compassion have healed wounds that no doctor could ever reach. His hope is that you'll find a life full of healing and compassion, because you do so easily with family and friends. He shows a deep compassion towards your ability to bring together people who would not necessarily come together."

(Note: This is consistent with the discussion of "choosing to come to earth" to help others through compassion or to be with friends and loved ones. That the very reason we're here on the planet may be to help others.)

Question: I'd like to ask him, what is the best way or method to shift our belief structure from fear and guilt into one of understanding and openness?

He said "Hello." He said "I love you." He's very open and grateful that you have brought this up. "Because this is not just an issue of today's times; this goes back centuries. **For so long the power has been in other people's hands to talk to the congregation and even the government - to talk to people, to keep them aligned with guilt and suffering so that the "uppers" as he put it, may find their way."**

In your society today, this is turning. You are now seeing, feeling, the *right* to be guilt free, to be connected to source, one on one. To be united, how one changes the belief system is also to look at why it was taught to you – **if you'd understand why it was spoken to you in place in the first place, then you can remove it from your head and remove it from your heart."**

"Understand that guilt - **that the direction to "keep you in line" was designed so that there was not a loss of control, by people who were above you. And if you knew there is a right and wrong on earth that then you'd walk a straighter line and give respect to those that had authority – but if you, my son, knew the truth, that there is no right and there is no wrong, the power that you possess would be more than what the authority had in you, and therefore there would be quite anarchy."**

(Note: Well there's the old Jesus we know and love. He's chastising those in power who've used language, religion to retain power, to keep the rich and elite in positions of power, and that by understanding the nature of reality, we don't have to allow anyone to "rule over us." But, as he notes, that might bring anarchy.)

"To know where the directions came from -- gives you the directions of how to remove it. Your belief system is very forgiving... it is very forgiving. If you can change it, it will do so for you. It will not anchor you back into old ways. One must look at their own light, one must look at their **own light** and then you will find the guidance." He said "I love you."

Question: "Do you have a personal message for me?"

"To the one who plays the swan, who pretends that in her space is all that she needs; to you I wish wings, I wish all the feathers in the world to build flight so that you may find your source in greatness through travel, through stories… But through your greatness, you will heal all the wounds that you've collected from your childhood. **All the things that you told yourself, will then come off you like old skin."** He said **"I gift you the snake. That you may renew yourself, and you may grow and you may travel fast and swift."**

Question; My heart is full of sorrow; can he help lift that sorrow for me?

He said "I love you. I will hold your sorrow." (Grace, aside:) This body is not going to let me get through this. "I will hold your sorrow, so that you will only carry less. Though I cannot take all of it from you, as it gives you lessons. **Understanding the darkness and the shadow, and the loss and the pretend separation, of being human, is understanding how infinite you truly are."**

"I do not wish to be the one to take it from you, but I will hold the sorrow as long as you wish, and above this I will bring back to you your love. Listen softly to your heart's ears, as that is where he speaks to you, and know that it is real. It is not a time of questioning, it is time of growing new relationship and path. **If one spends their entire days questioning, they're never going to experience it.** All my love to you."

Question: "Is my son going to be safe in his career and will you be with him?"

He said "My angel on earth, hello." He said "You yourself have suffered greatly before coming here. **I want you to understand that you have done great things for yourself by being here, knowing that you don't wish to stay human."** He says "Your son will navigate this human life with great strength, though he won't always have clarity but in that comes a lot of joy. He will find many things to do."

"Whether they are right or wrong in your eyes, he will do them and he will collect those experiences and he will be safe. **So the suffering and the worry that you have designed and created for yourself – you can go and find a good place in the earth to bury it - you no longer need it for him.** But for you, find ways that you love being human because remembering you're an angel is not going to help." He says "I love you."

(Note: "The suffering and worry that you have designed for yourself..." A pretty powerful indictment of all the people who design suffering for themselves.)

Question: "Could you help me understand what I can do to help my son who is autistic?"

He said "Hello." He says for others to listen to this, because it is not just a mother's love for a son, it's a love to help another. **"When they (a person with disability) are not having an equal experience of life that you are, when you can see someone struggling in ways, it cannot be compared to you and your experiences."** He says "I bring this to your attention, because I want you, every time you want to reach out to mend, to heal, to help, to cure; to step back and look at your hands." He said, "Notice that they're empty. They're empty for a reason; you are not to do the work for them."

"You are to be present with them, you are to encourage them to find their answers. Now if you're wondering how a mother to a young son is to give the power to a young child, what good would this do? **Autistic children come into this life, and they keep their light closely linked to the beyond; to *home*. They engage in this world as if they were on TV, but sitting in a room at home in heaven. They're not really on earth. So for them to act like you, or to have experiences like you, that is *not* what is needed.** That is *not* the level of success; the level of success is to be next to the person that holds the issue - the suffering, the disease, the mental imbalance, the need.

Advocate for them in the ways that they want, pay attention more to the child, to the person who needs, and not to what the doctors speak of. Though they are brilliant, though they are studied and very intelligent," he says, "what is most valuable is (to ask) **"What does the child need?"**

"This experience is all for great reasons. **It is not about suffering, and it is not to understand what loss is, it is to understand** *what light is,* **that is why this experience is in your life."** He says "Thank you. I love you."

Question about a personal message about her family and (loss of a child).

"Thank you for your and your family." He said "I love you." He said "Both of your children are great lights, are great beacons, but there is only one that is present with you (on earth). He says "This child needs your attention, needs to understand that you are still a family. For you to learn how to speak up in this life and make amends, and hold true to your promises and honor, though they may feel uncomfortable or disregarded. For you to take in stride and heal your family."

"Because **the amount of love that comes beyond us is unspeakable and that what you think cannot be healed, becomes healed and more than it was before.** There are no regrets for you; who you are is who you are. I look forward to the day when you love yourself so deeply, that your view, (with) your eyes, can distinguish who you are.

Question: Do you have any personal message for my family?

(Music coming in). Grace: *I'm trying to remain very plain, but I'm hearing the music (from outside) and when I see Jesus doing a wiggle, it's very hard to remain serious.* (laughter) **He's not the stick in the mud that a lot of ancient histories paint him to be.** He's very much like a – (to Jesus) well, why am I using words to describe you? You can describe you… - "You're granola people." (she looks down) *Is it because of the shoes?* I'm very loving. But don't mistake lust and intimate love with him, though it may feel like that on the inside, it's much more than that.

A message for your family? He says "Hello," says "I love your family. I love you more than ever that you've asked not on your behalf but on your family's behalf, because your family has a long line of stories. Struggle and success, we find that most families do, but with yours, there's an important reason why you incarnated together. I ask of you, that you keep everyone together, not distance-wise but emotionally. Do you have a question about the illness in your family?

Yes, my grandma's health.

He's showing me there are ways and medications to keep her sustained in the human body a long time, but it's not going to give her the longevity I think the family wants. So there's going to be a time, sooner than later, that you will be supporting her transition. He sees a lot of himself in you; ("thank you") he said you're quite creative, he looks forward to seeing what you're going to manifest in this life."

Comment: Jesus I noticed you said "I love you" to everyone but me… (Note, earlier he said to her "I give you my heart") and I just wanted to say that it upset me that you didn't say that to me, but I have to leave. (She gets and leaves).

Question: Is there a message I can give to my mom?

He says "Hello." (Pause, giggles) "The humor…" He said "I love *you twice as much*" (huge laugh). He says love is *unmeasurable*, so the joke and the joy of saying "twice as much" is the equivalent of saying "I love you singular" – but (said) to arouse the crowd… good thing he doesn't have a stick. (Grace, aside) You're here because we enjoy you. Continue, Jesus…

He has a message for your mother; *"The one he was teasing that he loves you twice as much."* He said "The message is that **"All the distance and all the loneliness that she has experienced inside of herself without sharing with others, was because that she has a connection to *home*, to (the) beyond, and she can feel, when she walks around in this life, it doesn't necessarily feel like hers."**

"He wants to remind her **"Find ways to love this life, find the snow, find the touch, find the travel, the joy of being human and allow this life to feed you in a way that she needs."** He wants to tell you again that he "Loves you four times as much and twice as much as the other woman."

(Grace, aside) *Can you imagine how wonderful it would be, Jesus, if your story was told in the words that you really have? You have such a clever sense of humor.* He says "Yes, those times of the bible were very different, these jokes weren't told then. Then there was a struggle that divided a nation, what it feels like to be in that time… - it really wasn't a time of joking, and he did his best to show love and compassion. **It just happens to be that *that* is the story that stuck. (It is) Not the life he had after, and not the life that he has now."**

Question: A personal message to my family about our future (with regard to life contracts)?

"There's going to be a lot of mystery, a lot of confusion and a lot of incomplete answers" he says. "Your purpose is to ask him (your father), how does he feel emotionally? You are the plug that turns this heart on and that is the most important role, and in doing so, you fulfill everything that you've come to this earth to do. Even above all (the) other contracts (that) you laid out."

He said, "**He wants to be clear that he's using the term "contracts" because it's a very common term that you've (all) created recently. It is simply the agreements that you've made in your own life; it doesn't have to sound so formal."**

Question: I have a hard time speaking up, do you have a message for me?

It's about commitment (to life). Once you have committed, you have put to rest any other option changing (the) commitment; **when change is what creates balance, alignment and joy.** So when you choose to commit, do so in a way where every day, you can look at a choice and allow you to grow in a way that supports you."

"This may require you to move, to invite family back in, or to invite family out. It may require you to grow, come closer to earth, or (be) higher than a sky scraper. **You came to this earth to experience love, not to experience hard work."**

"Though if you'd like to, you could create that for yourself. **You came to experience what it's like to feel separate, to find that you are not. And that is not "through me" or "only through me," it is through your *love of all*, of all that is.**

(Note: I really enjoyed this idea. You came here to experience separation, so you can see that it's false. You came here to experience love, not to just do hard work. And you won't find truth "only through me" – but through "opening your heart to everyone and all things." Loving all that is.)

Question: Any messages for me personally and how events affect my life adversely?

(Your question is about) "Control over yourself, but (you) cannot create change in someone else. **But through (experiencing) all situations, through all war, through all arguments, through all pain and suffering, you can change yourself.** You can show others what you would like to see in your space and in your home. **It is not going to be easy, but it is not meant for you to walk away from.** You know what needs to be done, and now it's finding the actions to follow through." (Grace, aside) *Do you understand what he's saying? Knowing the words, knowing what needs to be done?* ("I understand. Thank you.") He said "I love you."

I have a question. My grandmother passed away and I felt her, but my mother (is having a hard time).

"I love your grandmother." He says "Your grandmother is a wonderful light and she's already spoken to me about her daughter. (Your grandmother is) She is trying to seek closure, she wants to say a proper goodbye, she wants to close the relationship. She wants to show that there is a new one (that) is about to be created; but all your mother is sensing is fear. That is of her own doing, she is upset." He **says "It's not for me to interfere, but if you can explain to your mother to slow down, and start to say "Hello" and "I love you," and maybe this appearance of your grandmother, all the things she's trying to do will come through with clarity and not confusion.** It's simply about saying goodbye."

(Note: Pretty clear statement here: "It's not for me to interfere." Asking Jesus to step in and interfere is not his job or gig. He can't do that. He can help lighten the load, he can help show how to change your point of view, but he's not in charge of the outcome. As the Dalai Lama puts it "We can't control how others behave, but we can control how we react to them." A reframe of what his mission was, and continues to be.)

Question: "Do you have a message for me about my life?"

It is not asking you to change your position, but to stay true to who you are, and how much time you want to invest, and when to pull back. **He**

wants to be clear that this is not doing by something you've created or proven to you by words such as karma or any words of that nature.

Question: "I'm married with two boys; They're part of my soul family, want to know about our past lives."

He's smiling very big, he said "Hello and all my love to you and your family." He takes a lot of joy you can hear it in his voice - **when you talk about incarnations, the beauty of having soul families, and incarnation with other people time and time again, it allows you to have a level of comfort which goes beyond what you could create in human relationships**, this is the magic of finding your soul family on earth, and you will push your limits as both of your boys will push you."

"Both of them will seek your approval in their activities that you would never approve – do not give it to them. Do not give it to them. Let them know that here is where your opinion is, here is where you are their mother, you do not always need to be a friend. You also have four others in this life around you that in your soul family and the sense of healing," he says. **"(Over here) People know your soul, they don't just (only) know your name, they know your soul – there's a lot of peace in this realm as well."**

He nods his head and gives thanks to all that are here. He says **"This was a good surprise opportunity… and *very unplanned*.** All my love," he says. He says "Goodbye. I will see you on the flipside."

*   *   *   *

"See you on the Flipside." My sentiment exactly.

Where the gold is… (photo: NASA)

CHAPTER TWENTY-ONE: *The Martini Shot*

When I put this photo on our fridge after my friend Luana Anders crossed over, I said aloud "Well, that's the essence of our relationship." (Laughs, cookies and cappuccinos.) About a year later, while working on the Charles Grodin show on CNBC, Chuck had a medium connect to our mutual friend Luana during a live taping.

I called in from Santa Monica during the show, the medium accurately described her passing, where I was sitting, and said she was laughing about a "cocktail glass collection in your kitchen." (If I had a nickel for every Martini glass I own...) Then he said "She's telling me there's a photograph on your refrigerator she says "Is the essence of your relationship." Proof of Flipside communication comes in many forms.

"The Martini" is the last shot of the day on a movie set. They're about ready to finish, the crew begins to ask "Is this the Martini?" Imagine my chagrin when I directed my first feature film and answered "Yes, I'm the Martini. Who wants to know?" *But this is the last chapter. So let's call it The Martini.*

What does this all add up to? How can our knowledge about the Flipside help our lives? These words came to me in a dream recently: **"Respect the game."**

I was having a long involved dream, I'm not entirely sure what it was about. Earlier I had remembered what it was like to play Little League baseball, to put on a uniform, cleats, and take the mound. I pitched for a while, was really bad at it, until I altered my strike zone. I had been practicing throwing against the brick wall of our home, and had drawn a square on the wall and spent hours throwing at that square. I had a pretty good curve, and not a bad reverse curve.

But I rarely got strikes… until I moved the chalk that was the box. Then I started to get strikes in ball games. One metaphor here is "if you're throwing and not getting strikes, alter the chalk. Change the strike zone. Move it so when you are pitching – your idea, pitching your talent, or pitching your tent – you'll find your zone.

The last game I pitched, I was thrilled because I was actually getting the hang of it and pitching a great game. I had a no hit shut-out going into the ninth. I was thinking "Wow, I've gotten pretty good at this! I may actually BE a pitcher." Then Fred Waidner, a tall lanky kid with glasses, stepped to the plate and banged my best pitch out of the park. I can still see him rounding the bases of his walk-off homer. We lost 1 to nothing. It was the last game of the season, last game of my career. *"So that dream is dead."*

But it all came back to me in this dream. Sitting on a bench with the players, chewing gum, giving chatter. "Hey batter, no batter, swing!" Fingers hanging on the wire mesh of the fence, waiting for your turn at bat. Then I realized whomever I was talking to was trying to tell me something important.

"Respect the game."

What that meant to me; have respect for the journey, of what it means to be human. Of what it means to have life. The kinds of consequences involved, the amount of human endeavor involved.

I realized this voice was trying to remind me that when people come upon these reports – that we don't die, that there is an afterlife where we join our friends and plot our returns, that the Flipside is this pretty fantastic place we all return to – it can make this part of the journey, the one back here on earth - difficult for some.

Because they start to wonder *"If it's all worth it."* They start to wonder why they signed up to play the part in a game they're no longer enjoying. They're not that interested whether their teammate gets a hit, or gets hit, or when the ball is flying towards them whether they even want to lift up a glove and catch the damned ball. Little bit like Charlie Brown's baseball experience. *"Do I have to catch it if we're just going to lose?"*

Respect the game. We have rules to be sure on this playing field. We come here to learn and teach and share. We have uniforms to put on. Some of us get the brand new ones, some get the old ones. We all get a glove, and we have to learn how to use it. We have to learn how to catch a fly ball, learn how to get the ball out of the glove and throw it to a fellow player. We have to learn how to read how a batter leans, or swings, so we know where the ball might go before it leaves the bat.

We have to learn all the signs, we have to learn to respect the manager, perhaps not forever, not all of the managers, but while they're coaching the team, it's best we play along. Or play along so we can help our fellow teammates who are doing the same for us.

Respect the game. Doesn't mean you can't sit on the bench and say "Wait a minute. Why am I so worked up over beating this other team? This is only a game! I've got an amazing world in front of me, I don't have to wear this uniform, I can take it off and streak across the field naked if I want to. I can stand up in the infield and shout "It's all a game you nutballs!!! It's only a game and you're acting like it's the end of the world!!!"

Not that I would. I'm just saying.

But I have pointed out that by discussing these reports, it does feel a bit like I'm the guy running the lights in the ball park, running the organ and microphone – and suddenly I lean on the keyboard, blast everyone's eardrums and while turning up the lights to full *say "It's only a game people. That's all it is. Get over it."* Then I turn down the lights, go back to playing tunes, and get my Cracker Jack prize.

Respect the game because it's an important game. Every victory, every individual win means something to the overall universe. As one spirit guide put it *"Yes, the universe is a mechanism. But it's sentient."* If that's accurate, that means that every time I do something creative on the field, every time someone does something amazing on the field, the entire stadium learns it. Which if it doesn't make you respect the game, it should at the very least give us pause.

Recently I turned 60. As I said to one of my pals, "We're in the third act of this play now." Not everyone reaches this third act. Some of us leave the game early, get injured or hurt, or worse. But the rest of us are still on the bench, waiting for our turn in the outfield, waiting for our turn at the plate. But what's the third act in a play?

It's the act where everything comes together. It's the act where you realize all the loose ends and tie them all together. You can tie them together after you leave the theater ("Oh! That's how that all worked!") or you can tie them together in the theater and realize "Wow, wait a great story I've lived!" The third act should be the most fun act to watch… or live.

When I was in college I studied Beethoven's Ninth Symphony. As I listened to it over and over, I came upon the idea that Ludwig was summing up his own life in the three major acts of the symphony. There are four acts in his symphony, but the first three are instrumental.

The first act states the theme. Sometimes called an *"idee fixe;"* it's the theme of the symphony, the way we as children state the theme of our lives. As I've noted, I've asked many people when their "first conscious thought was of doing what they're doing now." And how one FBI agent said "I knew in preschool." I asked her why. She said "Because I kept extensive lists on everyone; what they wore, what they ate, what they did in their spare time."

I asked a banker what her first conscious memory was. It was playing the banker in board games like Monopoly. She had no desire to play the game, she just wanted to be keeper of the money. She said "I've led this boring life, unlike you in your film world." To which I replied, "But money is energy. You're helping people to organize their lives, organize their worlds, and in some cases helping them buy homes and build lives. The energy that you put into your work directly effects who people become."

So the first part of your symphony you state your theme. It may be athletic, it may be creative, whatever it is, it eventually informs the rest of your life. For me, I was assigned to be a hall monitor. I like the freedom of roaming hallways. I broke up fights, I asked people where they were going, and I issued passes. I didn't realize how similar that was to my life until I started directing films. The same gig. *"Can I see your pass please?"*

In the second part, Beethoven explores the various themes we get to in life. Becoming the person we want to be, elevating those themes into complex passages, the way we integrate who we want to be with our life's work. If you listen to that section, it's got the most complexity, but also the most yearning and effort. There are stops and starts, and notes left hanging.

Finally, the third act we synthesize who we are. It all comes together. The theme gets repeated by a variety of instruments and becomes the masterpiece that our life has been.

Ah, but there's a fourth act in Beethoven's Ninth, and it's Schiller's poem "Ode to Joy." It's where Beethoven combines the soaring words with the soaring music – as if he's stepped into the glory of heaven and is showing us all the various aspects of life. With a chorus of voices raised up, singing something that could only come from the deep regions of space, where Beethoven says he found inspiration.

"Joy, beautiful spark of divinity,
Daughter from Elysium,
We enter, drunk with fire,
Heavenly, thy sanctuary!
Your magics join again
What custom strictly divided;
All people become brothers,
Where your gentle wing abides."

As if Schiller was referring to our soul's entrance into the afterlife. It's a place where you can find a light filled with unconditional love, "divine joy," a sanctuary where everyone is equal, "all people become brothers" and where "angel's wings abide." I know I get chills every time I hear the "Ode to Joy" and now I finally understand why.

So what are we to make of this book filled with claims of speaking to the afterlife? Solving the mystery of Amelia Earhart? Or talking to a fellow known worldwide as Jesus? Have I lost my marbles?

I would suggest that indeed, I might have been looking for my marbles all along. I offer it as an *idee fixe*,[125] a theme so that others can explore, examine and go further. A jumping off place, an edge of a cliff overlooking a beautiful waterfall. A clarion call for others to find their inspiration in the Flipside, to take the time to examine these observations more closely, to find their own path to truth.

---

[125] Idée fixe, (French: "fixed idea") in music and literature, a recurring theme or character trait that serves as the structural foundation of a work. The term was later used in psychology to refer to an irrational obsession that so dominates an individual's thoughts as to determine his or her actions. (Britannica) I mean the former rather than the latter. Although the latter seems to apply to me!

So where's the "practical advice" that was promised in the title? I've taken too many pages to set this groundwork for the following "Afterlife Hacks." They're ideas meant as inspiration for those who want to explore these Flipside reports as a Rosetta Stone of what's really out there. An Akashic library if you will, of everything that's ever been learned on the planet.

HACKING THE AKASHIC LIBRARY WITHOUT A LIBRARY CARD

As noted, many between life sessions and a number of near death experiences include a visit to the "Library of souls." This is not a place per se, and it's definitely not a building floating in space – what the various reports tell us is that no one sees the same place. However, they all report the same essential facts about this location; a library. If we examine the word itself, library; "a place set apart to contain books, periodicals, and other material for reading, viewing, listening, study, or reference, as a room, set of rooms, or building where books may be read or borrowed." (Dictionary.com)

"A place set apart," check. "A place that contains books;" depends who is observing the place. "A place... for study, or reference..." that's accurate, as we've seen. What people observe in these libraries, is access to every lifetime they've ever had, as well as the lifetimes of others.

Imagine for a moment it's like the Library of Alexandria, which reportedly contained most of the books written. Burned in a political fire. Or the Medici library, which contained thousands of books purchased by Cosimo de Medici and translated into Italian. It was burned for political reasons. All of this knowledge apparently lost to humanity.

Except that it isn't. All of the people who wrote those books still exist. They may not be in their "full state" – since about a third of our energy isn't with us when we incarnate. They may have graduated up through the ranks to some other level. But if you have their name in your mind, their life story in your head, then those energetic elements (like a google search engine) are enough for you to be able to seek those individuals out.

I had a glimpse of how it works. One night, during a dream I found myself standing in front of an elderly sobbing woman. She was sad and looked lost. I asked "Can I help you?" She said "I can't find my husband?" She had that kind of inconsolable sadness about her where she wasn't really aware of me, but was just crying as if wandering in search of him.

I observed myself saying "Well show him to me." She looked at me, and then created an image in her mind of her husband. And I took that image, and processed it, opened my consciousness up to include the known universe – like opening ourselves up to an ocean of water, accessing all the droplets at the same moment – and found his energetic pattern. As if seeing him, like a dog sniffing a missing person's garment, or a detective poring over patterns, I instantly found this guy in his pod in the afterlife.

I say "pod" because that was the visual image. My search engine sought him out and found him in a pod in deep space. And I grabbed him – yanked him really, didn't ask him "Excuse me, your wife is looking for you" but literally pulled him out of his pod and returned to the woman, in a blink of an eye. Supersonic high speed beyond any possible version of speed. "You're looking for your husband... oh here he is." And I deposited him in front of her and went on my merry way.

Is that my occupation in the afterlife? I haven't a clue. Can anyone do it over there? I would imagine so, it seemed easy enough. Her energy was distraught so she couldn't "find him." Why her husband wasn't hanging around looking for her is beyond me – except perhaps she was so distraught after passing away, that she was just wandering around, and he couldn't reach out to her anyway.

But that's how it works. Searching the internet is akin to searching the Flipside.

It reminds me of the story in "It's a Wonderful Afterlife" where a woman rejoined her soul group that was in the midst of playing a game of "tag." Except she called it cosmic tag. The hypnotherapist asked "What's that?" She said "You can hide anywhere, be invisible doing so, and yet you have to find all five members of our soul group at the same time in order to win." Then she said "The twist is, they can hide in any realm, or any other universe."

How could you win at this game of tag? Well, as described, if you know the energetic pattern of your friend, loved one – like knowing the pattern of ones and zeroes that search engines look for – you'd be able to find them. Anywhere.

So the trick is to "find a piece of clothing" that was worn by the person you're looking for. That's pretty easy, because every time someone paints a painting, writes a song, sings a song, writes a book, some part of their energy goes into the action of creating that object. So if you can access that object – even in your mind's eye – whether it's a portrait of the person, or a portrait the person painted using words, music or some other means – you'll be able to track them down. And if you can't do it yourself, you can ask your guides to do so. Ask them if they can access this individual, and if they can't (they're very upfront over there, in my experience) ask them if they "know someone who can."

Everyone who has ever lived is back on the Flipside. We can access them as long as we know who to ask.

HACKING YOUR SOUL GROUP TO FIND YOUR SOUL MATE

You haven't found your soul mate in this lifetime? Not to worry. Your soul mate is having the same experience you're having, but somewhere else. "Why do I feel so alone?" Well, go back to your life planning session and you'll see why you insisted on not being together in this life.

You have found your soul mate but they left you. "Whaaat?" It happens. You meet someone you feel completely connected to, like you've known them forever, every beat of their heart is in synch with yours and… something happens. They died. They split. They go somewhere else. Or you freak out and run screaming into the night. Now what? Well, start with asking yourself "So why did I plan things this way? What can I learn from this? Or what was I thinking when I came up with this scenario? You don't have to like the scenario – you can hate the scenario. But you have to acknowledge that it's part of the scenario you designed.

When you get to the Flipside, by and large you're going to meet up with all those you've loved unconditionally and all those who love you unconditionally. It's not easy to say "be patient. Wait for the curtain." But sometimes that's the only thing that can be said. Be patient. *Wait for the curtain.*

The reports show that opening your heart up to whomever it is that you're supposed to reconnect with, is the correct path to take. If you can ask your guides about "where the heck your soul mate is hiding," they may tell you that you agreed to not connect in this lifetime because you wanted to learn from other relationships.

But if you'd like to get a direct answer to the question "Where is my soul mate hiding?" the fastest way to do that is with a hypnotherapist trained in the Michael Newton technique. One can be found at NewtonInstitute.com, they have a searchable database. Interview the therapist, see if they're compatible with what you're looking for.

I've seen a number of people who arrive at their soul group. It varies what the room or environment is, just as it varies on how many people are there to greet them. I've seen people literally "looking for their soul mate." Almost always, a figure appears that they can see the outline of, but not the face. The reason for that is obvious; if they recognized their soul mate standing in a room on the Flipside, how are they supposed to live the life they're supposed to live? Your soul mate may be standing right behind you as you read this sentence. The question is, are you open to finding them?

HACK THE FLIPSIDE TO FIGURE OUT WHY BAD THINGS HAPPEN

The topic of evil and sin comes up often. There was a clever scene in a play ("The Engine of our Ruin" by Jason Wells) where one character asks "If you could kill anyone in 1942, who would it be?" The main character (played by my pal Tim Ryan Meinelschmidt) says "Hitler."

The CIA station chief says "Ok. So Hitler's dead. His moderate generals sue for peace. The war ends and Germany retains all its territory and all its camps. Germany lost the war because Hitler was an idiot!" The point is, if you went back in time and killed Hitler in 1942, Germany might have remained some version of the Third Reich.

What we think is pure evil may serve some other purpose we can't fathom. I'm not arguing that there's no evil in the universe, but I am here to state that it just doesn't come up in the research. People are very attached to their "evil in the universe" beliefs, and I'm not here to change their minds. I'm just pointing out that it is a belief, as it doesn't show up in the reports. People who have NDEs or who have between life sessions tend to agree on that point: "there may be evil somewhere in the universe, but mostly what I've run into is unconditional love."

The first LBL session I filmed was a woman remembering her death in a gas chamber in Auschwitz. She described it in harrowing detail, but then between lives she asked her council and guardians "Why did I choose such a difficult life? I love everything and everyone I loved." Then she said "Oh. They're showing me through images that... as difficult as it might be to comprehend, in this lifetime it was harder to choose to play the role of a perpetrator than a victim. I see that every day in the camp was a heightened lesson in love, in courage, in compassion – From the perspective I'm viewing this, I'm glad I chose the side I was on." Hard to wrap our minds around, but worth examining.

If it's possible that bad things happen for a reason we might not be able to fathom, then it's about asking our guides to help us understand why something bad has happened. We have the answer to every question buried somewhere – either deep within us, or in the universe where our guides can give us some direction as to why something happened or didn't happen in our favor. The quickest way to understanding why, is to ask "Why?"

USE THE FLIPSIDE TO SCARE FRIENDS AND NEIGHBORS

Fears drives many people to ruin. (Also to success, but that's another issue.) Some fear "death" so much they sell their souls to purchase more stuff, more medicine, more toys to help them ignore death. But hang on a second – if death doesn't exist, per se – if we don't die, if our physical bodies are gone, but our spiritual selves live on – how can we take the knowledge of this to help us in our daily lives?

Think about it for a second. If you're going to live a thousand lifetimes, more or less, then how hard is it going to be to experience the end of this one? If you know for certain that there's not going to be an end, but a beginning and a journey back home, how much fear can you carry around on a daily basis?

So really, how much harm can one do to you? Yes, there's the element of pain, there's suffering, there's ill health – but these are for the most part relative issues. We normally don't stay ill for too long, either the illness takes our body or it doesn't. And when it doesn't we have a chance to come back and do more work here. But if it does, you're just going to get the chance to see it all from this other perspective. And once you're back home, you quickly get used to being there.

If you spent a good deal of time fearing death, what if you fully realized that it doesn't exist? If that's the case, how will that affect your decisions today? What are you going to be doing? Will that inspire you to enjoy every day of this lifetime as if it was a gift?

If you consider for a moment that when we return home we don't get a chance to experience nature, other than as a mental construct, it may give you more reason to spend time in nature. To go camping. To go and see the natural wonders you haven't seen but should see.

Imagine for a moment that earth is a tourist destination. You're here to have fun, you're here to go on an adventure, you're here to take advantage of the water, forests, greenery, trees. None of that exists per se back home – we see these things because we agree to the mental wavelength they're carried on – and we agree to participate in that wavelength – but there's nothing quite like rolling in the grass, climbing a tree, or breathing in fresh flowers. Is there?

If that's not something you've done in a while go and do it. I'll wait for you to return after you've done so. Smell the roses. Listen to the sound of the birds for a moment. This is a paradise that you've come to, and we forget that on a daily basis. If we didn't we'd get much more satisfaction out of being here, as well as understanding why it's important to keep it clean for our return. Who wants to come back to a dirty campground?

But use this knowledge to inform your voting, your decisions on a daily basis. Support those people who understand that the planet is a sacred place that we want to return to. Support those causes that take care of the Earth. Work to marginalize those individuals who don't see it that way, or who contribute to the earth's downfall.

Once we truly see that we choose to live here, we choose our lifetime, then we can see that the choice to come to the Earth is one that many people would like to participate in. Not just for the amazing adventures that occur here, but for other reasons.

As was repeated during one LBL session; "More life lessons can happen in one day of tragedy on earth than 500 years on some other boring planet. This is where the action is." If you think of it from that perspective, you can and will appreciate your journey here through fresh eyes.

Start to look around to see who your soul group might be. They're the people that you normally incarnate with – people whom you meet and feel as if "you've known them for your whole life and then some." Allow that to be your reality while you consider them for a moment – we all have people we feel like we've known forever from the moment we meet them. The truth is, it's very possible that we have known them for a lot longer than we imagine.

If you're having a rough go of it with an individual, step back and ask yourself "what lesson am I trying to learn by putting up with the angst from this individual? If it's possible that I've lived another lifetime with this person and suffered in the past, why would I agree to do it again?" the truth is you can always change the paradigm.

There's no hard fast rule that says "You must live out your lifetime as you've promised to do." On the contrary, if you learn a powerful lesson here, however you've learned that lesson, you don't need to learn it again.

If you're a soldier for example, and you see that you're going to likely die on the battlefield, as you have any other number of lifetimes (George Patton famously knew his previous lives as a soldier and wrote about them in his poem "Through a Glass Darkly.")

You can change that paradigm by resigning your commission, setting down your rifle and walking away from it. People change who they are all the time – and it may very well be that you've signed up to learn some lesson, and decide that you don't want to work on that energetic lesson any further. There's no one to tell you no, or "you can't" but yourself.

If you're feeling trapped in your life, in your situation, find a way to meditate, learn or understand why you've chosen this situation. Are you trying to assist or help someone else in their lifetime? Is there some reason that you've chosen a difficult life? What have you signed up to learn or teach? If you're feeling trapped in your body, meditate on it, ask your guides "So why did I choose me, then? What am I hear to learn as I am?"

The best way to understand the nature of fear is to examine it. It may require examining *many lifetimes*, it may require letting go of former fears. But the only way to conquer fear is to understand where it comes from.

USE THE FLIPSIDE TO COMPREHEND THE INCOMPREHENSIBLE

There are many among us who have a natural paranoia to whatever happens in the news. There's the feeling that "someone" has planned events to occur in a particular way, as if a "shadow government" may be behind what happens in our lifetime, or "people pulling the strings" that have the power over us. It may be as a result of "feeling that someone else is in control" when that "someone else" is our higher self!

When people feel "born to be" someone or something, like a politician, it may be that they're seeing what kind of life they had planned in advance. They make the appropriate steps to get to where they're supposed to be. That doesn't mean they can't change their mind, doesn't mean they will always fulfill what they set out to accomplish. But in general, they join the field because they feel like they were "born to do it."

Of course we are guided by, in some cases hampered by, who were are as humans. Greed, avarice, lust, gluttony, pride, jealousy, envy... remarkably fit any number of politicians throughout history. But that's what humans wrestle with on a daily basis. Can they overcome these constraints? Can they find a way to allow compassion, intelligence, humor to outweigh the unwanted characteristics? Certainly it makes for a better story to see the person who overcame their problems, then to watch a person wallow in them. But of course, that's how I like my stories to end.

People feel the need to run for office, feel the need to help or be needed – or to accumulate power and adulation, or love – not everyone has the same goals or desires when you take into account a sociological background, a genetic background and a spiritual background. For example, someone who is born into extreme poverty might spend their lifetime trying to break out of that box.

Someone born into a body that is imbued with beauty may use those genetics to change the paradigm – but it's equally possible that someone has signed up for a lifetime to learn about politics from a first-hand experience. So that they can teach or learn those particular lessons that are unique to politicians.

So the next time you vote, or find yourself involved in politics, try to eliminate the factors that come from a sociological or genetic background. Wipe that slate clean, to see who a politician truly is, or what motivates them. If they are people who care about other humans, who genuinely care about humanity, then I believe they deserve our support. But it also helps to understand that everyone signed up for a particular lifetime, to learn or teach lessons, and from that perspective it allows us not to be so caught up in the emotions of the outcome. "No matter what happens, we'll always be okay."

USE A FLIPSIDE HACK TO LORD YOUR MONEY OVER PALS

There's only one person to ask; that's you. Ask your higher self. "So am I supposed to be more successful? What's holding me back?" There are a number of ways to access that person; meditation, hypnosis, or a near death experience. Although I wouldn't recommend the latter.

Ask your guides or your soul group; "Is being wealthy going to help me on my path? What should I aim for?" Money is energy. It works like water, flows around the planet, moves from one place to the next. Some try to control that flow, but they eventually grow old, die, and then watch from the sidelines as others try to control that flow. Some are good at controlling the flow, at keeping more of it, and others aren't good at that at all. (*Ahem.*)

Let's pretend for a moment that someone has the notion of creating wealth or prosperity for other people. By creating an app, or building a site, or investing in other individuals. I would offer that by doing so, you'd be covering a number of bases in the life university. You've be affecting positive change in the life of others by helping them to help themselves.

In terms of depression or happiness, as cited, there's scientific evidence that shows that helping another person can alleviate symptoms of, or end depression. So that's one positive note. We may be able to create happiness and ease for other lives so that they don't have to spend all their time focusing on survival. We don't have to take a pill to do so – just the act of being selfless, or even the meditation on being selfless can have the same effect.[126]

A long way of saying "follow your bliss and you'll be happy whether you're rich or not." That saying has held up for eons and still applies. We live an era where people say "Money doesn't make you happy, but it makes life a lot easier." That's a bit like suiting up for a game, then going

---

[126] Studies at University of Wisconsin under Richard Davidson prove that "Tonglen" a form of Tibetan meditation where you pray and visualize the health of a loved one, actually changes the shape of the amygdala, reducing or curing depression.

on the field and saying "This game would be better if the bats were made of gold." It doesn't change the game. It makes the guy who values gold happy holding his gold bat, but it doesn't matter to the outcome of the game. Maybe more runs are scored. But the score of the game isn't the point. It's not who wins the game, it's who learns the most lessons, teaches the most skills, and honors their path and journey.

We've heard it a million times; do the thing that you love and riches will come to you. But *riches* aren't always measured in money; they're measured in love, in health, in compassion, in happiness. (And in my case *Richards*. How can I make myself rich when I already am him?) If your goal in life is "to be happy" then how hard can that be to achieve? If your goal is to "make others happy" it requires one step at a time. If your goal is to acquire a bunch of objects and have more objects than anyone else, then think about all the years you're going to have on the Flipside kicking yourself for wasting your time on the planet. *Don't worry. Be happy.*

USE A FLIPSIDE HACK TO CHOOSE A NEW LIFETIME

That's a trick question, isn't it? After all, these reports are not based on belief or philosophy. It's just what people consistently report from their journeys into the Flipside. If what people are saying is true; that we choose our lifetimes, then we've chosen to be who we are for a reason.

The question may be "How do I deal with the religion of my forefathers if I don't believe in it?" Or "Why did I choose such an uncomfortable journey?" I would offer that all religions have at their core the idea of liberating people to find ways to love each other unconditionally. If the religion of your forefathers allows you to do that – and almost all of them do – then allow that to be your guiding light. Remember that the words "Lord" and "God" and "Beloved" are interchangeable. Countless human societies have spoken about deities, avatars and holy people who have lived among them. As we've noted, these people appear to be composed of energy that is closer to source. They're closer to the energy that creates, supports and builds the universe – and when we're around them we sense that from them.

But when someone starts to tell you how to behave, how to dress, who to love, when to love – contrary to our experience on the Flipside which is all inclusive, and unconditional – then you should definitely let the person who's asking you to think or act contrary to your nature by telling them "sorry, no thanks." It's easy to so "no" if you add a "thanks" to it.

The idea that people are religious because some "higher power" is going to punish them, has been a motivating factor for centuries, millennia. What if there is no one who is going to punish you for your sins? What if the only punishment you might receive is having to relive all the pain and suffering you engender in others? Is that a motivating factor for living a good life?

How about the simple fact that the amygdala, the source of serotonin release in the brain, appears to react favorably to when people meditate on healing or helping others? Further that the action of helping others has the same effect on the brain? Literally loving your neighbor as yourself, or doing something that helps your neighbor, can alleviate symptoms of depression. That the fastest way to cure depression isn't in the form of a pill, it's in the form of helping your neighbor. If that's enough to motivate you to do good in the world, then it's pretty much what every religion teaches; kindness and compassion towards others.

IS HACKING THE AFTERLIFE GOING TO KILL MY KARMA?

I've grown up misusing the term karma like everyone else has. It doesn't mean "baggage" or "sins we committed in a previous lifetime." The universe isn't controlled by energy being willed to one place or another based on our human wants or needs. (Else everyone would win the lottery every day, wouldn't they?) We come here to be part of the ballgame, to learn from the day at the ballpark. We don't come here to manipulate it, or to make others not get what they want, but ensure we get what we want.

We aren't tied to karma like having some kind of third leg dragging around behind us. "Oh, I could be happy if I didn't have this bad karma following me around." Once we realize we choose our lives, we choose the kind of actions (karma means "action" in Sanskrit) we're going to examine during a particular lifetime. Like a painter browsing through colors. The painter looks at the canvas, says "It needs more red" and starts to apply it.

We can stand back and say "Hey! No! No more red, you're killing the rest of us with this red! We don't want any more red on the canvas!" But it's not our canvas to be part of. We have the free will to say "No thanks, I'm not participating in this lifetime with you. I totally get why you're doing it, what lessons you want to impart, teach or learn – but seriously. It's not for me. Have fun, I'll be in the stands watching."

The end of karma as we knew it. Not dictating who we are, who we were or who we're going to be. Sorry it that offends everyone, but it is what it is. The reports are consistent and replicable. If you want to understand why you've experienced "bad karma" in your lifetime, I sincerely recommend finding the right hypnotherapist who can take you to converse with your higher self to ask that question. I can't answer it. But you can.

Let's discuss artificial intelligence for a moment. There are scientists like Stephen Hawking who warn of artificial intelligence taking over machines and destroying humans. I can't imagine how that is a possibility – at least no one has explained it to me yet that makes sense. That somehow machines which are working so fast and have the ability to stop events from happening suddenly take it upon themselves to stop an event prematurely? I guess that's possible. But it has little or nothing to do with sentience.

If you call it artificial fear based mongering – perhaps that's more accurate. But a machine cannot be, will not, can never be sentient unless a person chooses to "inhabit" that machine as part of their own personal journey. And as we've heard life choices are not made in secret, nor are they made without the knowledge or advisement of our higher guides, or loved ones. So everyone would have to agree that living a life as a machine – that means coming into existence as a machine, and hanging around as long as there's an ability to do so – that's perhaps a possibility.

But why would anyone do it? Why would anyone choose that lifetime? As we learn in these reports, people choose lifetimes to help others. They don't do it to help only themselves. There are people who choose easy or simple lifetimes – almost "floater" lives – so they can be here, participate on some level, before going back home. Vacation lives.

But why choose Earth? There's a million vacation lives to choose from. Earth is a place of extremes, of lessons to be learned. Lives to be led and loved. I can imagine a scientist wondering how I can make the pronouncement there will never be artificial intelligence, in the sense that it's talked about – the sentience of machines or computers.

Because that's not how consciousness reportedly works. If we choose our lifetimes, then we'd have to choose to inhabit a robot for some compelling reason. Engrams are part of the brain's makeup.[127] And no number of engrams piled high constitutes sentience or consciousness.

There are many cases of people without higher brain functions who when they regain them report them.[128] There are many cases of people who remember lifetimes where they had no higher brain functions, but are able to describe accurate details about those lives. There are many cases of Alzheimer patients who spontaneously recover "their memory" prior to passing, but autopsies reveal their brains weren't capable of such memories. There are many cases of people with encephalitis, where their brain should not function, and yet does.

Compound that with the cases of people describing how consciousness works, and how these reports are consistent and replicable, then we have a clearer picture of how these events occur. By the way, if you're already this deep into the book and are asking whether or not the science exists that proves the afterlife exists, and the process of how souls come and go is knowable – then you really do have to send this book back to whomever gave it to you, or see if a refund is still available.

I'm writing this book for fellow travelers. *For people who've already come to the conclusion, as I have, that life continues on.* That life has been continuing on for a long time, and our awareness of the process is only now coming to light. That the idea that the brain is the source of all consciousness is not accurate in the least, and perhaps criminal in its insistence. After all, if people were aware of how consciousness really worked – if they were aware that someone might have chosen a lifetime where they would become a victim, and further they may have asked the perpetrator to participate in that life – then what does that do to the criminal justice system?

If people learn that they're conscious and aware of a vast amount of information, knowledge and history from the moment they arrive into the womb – and that information appears cloaked throughout their lives, what does that do to the educational system? If children are sentient, in some cases more aware than adults are – what does that do to parenting? As I'm

---

[127] en·gram (ĕn'grăm') n. A physical alteration thought to occur in living neural tissue in response to stimuli, posited as an explanation for memory. Also called neurogram. Dictionary.com

[128] See Mario Beauregard PhD's "Brain Wars" or Dr. Bruce Greyson's talk "Is Consciousness Produced by the Brain?" on YouTube.

fond of saying to my children *"Well, you picked me as your parent. What the hell did you do that for if you don't like what I'm telling you?"*

It doesn't win many arguments, I promise.

HOW CAN FLIPSIDE HACKS GET ME OUT OF GOING TO CHURCH?

As we've seen in this book, there is no one way to "experience the light." You don't have to have a religious experience, or go to church, or believe in any particular religion to access the Flipside.

Everything that you've ever believed is still intact. Nothing has changed by allowing your consciousness to open up to the possibility that there is more to our realm than meets the eye.

But allow this new information to temper your view of intolerance. Allow this new information to challenge those around you who define their dogma or their religious concepts as the only way to view reality. The only way to experience life in this realm. We know that's not the case. We know that they wish it was the case.

But that doesn't mean that someone who is a fervent believer in something that has no basis in fact is wrong. Consider for a moment that they signed up for a lifetime where this belief was everything to them. It was the essence of why they chose to be on the planet. By arguing with them about their choice to be on the planet or arguing with their beliefs of what they've chosen to do on the planet is to belittle who they are.

The best way to honor all religions is to allow everyone to get where they're going at their own pace. Doesn't mean you can't share what new information you might learn or experience from the Flipside. There's a long way to go before humanity might accept these reports to be accurate, that these reports from the Flipside might be correct.

Allow that to be the case for those who don't want to hear it, and for those who do want to hear it. The truth is there's a reason why you've been introduced to this information – the old or the new – and it's up to you to decipher what your role is and what to do with it. Is it to escape to a monastery in the mountains and spend the rest of your days meditating on the nature of reality? That's fine, there's nothing wrong in whatever choice you make. Is it to stop by a gun shop and pick up some ammo on your way to a shooting? I would hope that these reports wouldn't inspire anyone to do that. I would argue that if you can conceive of it, you can experience it – in your mind. There's no need to force others into your mindset, whatever it is.

Allow that all those things that have bugged you for so long, all those feelings of being oppressed, put upon, suffering – were all a choice you made when you decided to come here. All of it. If your suffering, or your feelings of suffering aren't moving you forward as an individual, then let them go. Or not. It's entirely up to you. If in doubt, ask your guides for help, ask Jesus for help, ask anyone that you know that was on the planet and is no longer here for help.

Just knowing that there's a deeper more profound reason for suffering, which may include your helping people out of their suffering, is a possibility. Don't blame religion. Don't blame humanity. Blame the powers that be that won't find this information useful to their power base.

HACKING THE FLIPSIDE TO SCARE SCIENTISTS

Many of these stories include someone declaring that "they slept on the idea" and woke up with the answer. A woman recently won a 400-million-dollar lottery after dreaming about what numbers to use. She woke up and wrote them down. What would have happened if she didn't write them down? What if she wrote them down wrong? Fact is, she didn't.

The same goes true for many scientists who talk about going to sleep thinking about a problem and waking up with the solution. Any rational person would argue that their subconscious came up with the answer. That could be true. But it's equally possible that while they were asleep, they consulted with their higher self, or asked questions of someone who knows the answers. By doing so, were able to clear the pathways to achieve the answer.

Dr. Anita Moorjani had a near death experience, and she claims that during the event, saw what the source of her cancer was. She was near death at the time of the event, but from the Flipside, she was able to diagnose the cause of her illness, and says that she "began to work on the cure" while she was in that in-between state. By the time she returned to consciousness, her illness had reversed itself and she eventually became healthy again.

No one is claiming that one should go out and create a "near death experience." However, the mechanism of having your consciousness review your health is something that everyone can do. It requires a bit of training in meditation, and the ability to concentrate and focus. But at some point, while meditating about the nature of existence, if you meditate about the nature of your illness you may come to the conclusion that it's part of the journey you chose to be on. At this point you need to ask – since I'm aware that I'm not going to die, that I can't die, then perhaps I can ask for help from my guides to learn how I can stay on the planet for this lifetime?

I'm not saying that guides will step forward and say "Oh, right, *sorry*, of course, *we forgot* that you were dying. *Here's the cure love*, now go on about your work…." The human body has frailties, has so many working parts, and certainly if those parts break down, if there's a certain number of toxic things in your environment that you may not be aware of – many factors come into play with regard to illness. There's the three factors that we deal with in health; genetic factors, what genes we're born with, the human body's foibles, and then the sociological factor – the environment we live in, whether toxic emotionally of physically. The history of medicine is dealing with just these two issues in pill form.

But if there may also be a spiritual element to an illness. If one looks at illness as one of three possible avenues – physical, sociological or spiritual – I think we'll be closer to the truth about the nature of our health. Certainly there can be a downside to choosing one modality over another – strictly focusing on sociological issues, or genetic causes may or may not alter a person's health. Or using pills to suppress the body's awareness. Why not ask the higher self, or higher sources to weigh in on a person's path to healing?

Now, because of *epigenetics* – the claim that genes retain a "soul memory" of past life traumas - we're about to have a new form of medicine prescribing pills to suppress our cell's "memories." Save your time. How about dealing directly with who we've actually been in previous lifetime and the traumas that are still with us? There is no pill to do that, but I can imagine one day people will try to market such a drug.

I think of understanding the spiritual reasons for our being on the planet as just another tool in a Doctor's bag. We have tools for physical ailments, we have medicine to correct physiological problems, we have the ability to take negative elements or toxins out of our environment and change our health – but we should not ignore the spiritual element involved.

Again; I am not a doctor. I'm not a philosopher. I'm a filmmaker who has been researching this topic for over a decade. Take my ideas with a bucket of salt – please! Consult with professionals, always. But be aware of the journey that you're on to best of your ability – and then when a professional makes a recommendation, you'll know in your heart whether it rings true or false to you. And always remember; I chose to be here, and I can consult with my spirit guides to understand that if I want to.

David Bennett notes in "Voyage of Purpose" that he had foreseen his cancer diagnosis 20 years before it occurred. When the new doctor came into the office – a doctor he'd never met, but whom he'd seen in his near death experience 20 years earlier – when that doctor said "I'm sorry but you only have so many months to live. Get your affairs in order" David was able to say "Actually, I know how this turns out. And I'm going to survive this."

To which the doctor said, rightfully so, based on his expertise; "You're in denial. I'm sorry but you are not going to survive this. You only have a few months to live." And David realized he wasn't going to get anywhere with this particular fellow.

Ultimately it was a combination of his own research into healing, along with traditional treatments (radiation, chemo, etc) that brought him around and healed him. His spine was fused at some point, and he survived the cancer, just as he'd foreseen that he would. But the doctor, with all his expertise, was inaccurate. I'm sure he'd been accurate in the past, and seen a number of cases like this – but because the doctor was unaware of the "spiritual element" that is part of all our journeys, as a scientist he just didn't know all the questions to ask.

That's all I'm saying about asking our higher selves for answers to scientific questions. They may not know the answer. They may say "I'm sorry, but that's not in my pay grade" or the "answer to that question is beyond my capacity to explain." It may even be that your higher self doesn't want you to see the answer to these questions because they'd (and you) would prefer to learn it on your own.

But I suspect they wouldn't have let you get this far in the book if that was the case. So for that reason alone, consider yourself lucky to be living at a time on the planet where it's okay to access people on the afterlife, and to ask them questions. They may not know the answer, they may be incorrect with the answer, but it's okay to ask them.

I've had spirit guides give me answers to questions based on their many lifetimes. As one guide said "I haven't lived all lifetimes. I've only lived the ones that I've lived, and the question you're asking me hasn't been part of those lifetimes. So there may be a person who can answer your question, I'm just not that person."

When someone passes away and reveals that they're still conscious, it doesn't mean they're suddenly omniscient. They may be able to access all of their lifetimes; they may be able to access all of the lifetimes of everyone in their soul group. But there are questions they cannot answer.

Sometimes when people are involved in this channeling exercise, they forget that. They ask a question to someone on the Flipside, and the person on the Flipside gives them an answer. But because we aren't there in person judging the answer – and by that I mean asking follow up questions – the answer may not apply.

As noted earlier, in Edgar Cayce's lifetime he answered a number of questions about health issues for many individuals. And for the most part, he was quite accurate about how to heal particular individuals. It's part of the data of his work. But on the other hand, when asked about predicting the future, instead of saying "I'm not really sure if I can predict the future, I'm just going to give you a likely scenario..." he answered questions in terms of what will or won't happen with the planet.

But we can't know those things because the future is not set. There are likely outcomes based on a variety of factors – like having your mother call you on your birthday, it's a likely event to happen, and you really notice it when she doesn't call on your birthday. But that doesn't mean for certain that she is going to call you, or that some other mitigating factor will change that outcome. We always have to allow for the possibility that things won't happen as predicted.

The same can be said for mediums. The ones who are the most honest about their abilities will explain that upfront. "I'm not really sure if this event will or will not occur, but this is what I'm seeing. I'm going to tell you these images, and if that makes sense to you, then it's possible that they will occur. However, it's entirely possible *someone changes their mind* and those events don't happen.

Again, if you dream up an app directly based on this information, don't forget to include me in the credits. My kids will thank you.

FLIPSIDE HACKING YOUR COLLEGE PROFESSOR

Key to remember, we are fully conscious prior to our lifetime (conscious of all or our previous lifetimes, that is) and when we're born, our bodies may not show that we're fully conscious, but we are.

When your child is old enough to speak, try this test. Ask them "Did mom and dad choose you or did you choose us?" If the child is not on the spot ("Dad, turn off the camera!") and is casually doing something else, you may be surprised by the answer. I made this same suggestion to a friend who is a fairly well known actor/writer. I said "so ask your 3-year-old the question." He did. His son nodded and said "Well I wasn't who I am now."

Then think about the history of raising children. For the past forty thousand years or so, many cultures have emphasized lessons by rote, lectures, pounding information into a child's mind. Some cultures seek out the reincarnated souls and drag them off to a monastery to "get back to school."

It's entirely possible that they chose this new life so they could have one "outside" the monastery. And when they get to a certain age, if they want to "go back to the monastery" or "into the church" or "onto the playing field" honor that choice as not just something that they've observed you as a parent doing, but possibly because they've done it before and chose a lifetime where they can do it again.

Then further, school curriculums need to be rethought. If a person wants to follow a path of mathematics and science, they may want to do so not because "that's where the money is" – but because "that's where the future is." The same goes for arts and music and every other endeavor a person might come to the planet to learn and observe. If they've been stifled, pent up, or discouraged from their path – then they're going to have a hard time with that.

And further, a parent needs to consider for a moment that the reason this child has chosen them is because they knew them from before. They may have been our parents in a previous lifetime, brothers, siblings, whatever. If you start to acknowledge that – you'll be closer to how the Hindus greet each other by putting their hands together and bowing, acknowledging the "eternal spirit" that is within the person they're meeting – not for the first time – but for the first time in this lifetime.

Perhaps it's time to consider talking about these topics in school. It's not sacrilegious or against anyone's religion to ask someone "So have you been on the planet before? If so, who were you?" Well, I can imagine some parents flipping out and marching down to the school, but teachers and students are clever enough to figure out a way to make these questions non-denominational.

I was lucky enough to get our daughter into one of the tony pre-schools here in Santa Monica. My wife and daughter had walked by the school and had a vision of seeing her in that school – painting something in the future. When she was old enough we applied.

A number of people said "You can't get in there. No one can get in there. Spielberg's kids went there. Ben Affleck's kid and Chris Martin's kids are in that school." We said "Yeah, we thought so too – except they had a vision of her going there." When the school called to tell us she hadn't gotten in, I was startled at first. "Really?" They said "Yes, sorry, perhaps next year."

We enrolled her in another school and she lasted about a month. She quit one day and said "This isn't the school I'm supposed to go to." Then a few days later we got a call from the head of the tony school and they said "I'm not sure how it happened, but a spot opened up for your daughter." She walked into her class about a month late.

Then some years later I was attending one of the classes that the head of the school organized. A renowned child psychologist, she was addressing the thoughts and issues parents were going through. And one of the parents said "My son claims he died in Africa. We've never been to Africa, but the other day we were watching a show on TV together and he said "I remember that place. I died there." She laughed nervously and said "What do I tell him?"

The renowned psychologist launched into the "kids say the darndest things" and talked about where dreams and imagination comes from. I raised my hand and said "well... actually, there is a growing field of evidence, about children's past lives."

The psychologist laughed out loud. "Oh c'mon, that's some screenplay or movie that you're working on."

Actually the body of evidence is much larger than it was when I made the comment in 2006.

Again, this isn't my belief, this isn't my philosophy, this isn't wishful thinking. This is my examining thousands of cases, filming 30 of my own, some of which you've heard about in this book. I don't really care if psychologists, psychiatrists, doctors, scientists, professors believe in what I'm saying or not. It's not about belief in the first place. It's putting the obvious on the table then allowing adults to have a conversation about it.

The data shows that we choose our lifetimes. That we choose our parents. That we've been here before, and will return again. The question I have for educators, professors and teachers – "Are you going to make the most of that time you have that returning soul in your classroom? Or are you going to shove them out the door with the same faulty data that you were taught in school?"

The history of our planet is based on two factors; genetics and sociology. That's what all science, medicine, law is based on – what your DNA does for your mind and health, or what sociological factors affect it. However, there's a third part of that model – it's "spirituality" for lack of a better term. It's the part of you that is not land based, but that is based in the spirit world. Is always in the spirit world, and has a hand in affecting your behavior here. So when dealing with issues of science, medicine, law, civics, society, politics, government; it behooves us to not ignore that fact.

USE A FLIPSIDE HACK TO GET OUT OF JAIL, FREE

People in prison for drug use? That's insane. Let them all out, give them therapy, let them understand why they've chosen this path.

Murderers, psychopaths, serial killers? Of course they need to be kept from harming other people, other individuals. But give them the opportunity to understand why these events happened, and how they could learn from their mistakes It won't happen again, or so that they can benefit someone else on the planet.

Since we don't die – then it goes without saying that no one should be put to death for any crime. *Put to use* instead of *put to death*, makes more sense doesn't it? Put to use helping others through their physical presence on the planet makes more sense than just creating a coffin shortage. I interviewed prisoners in Wallkill, NY prison when I was working on the Charles Grodin show.

One prisoner was working in an eyeglass factory and was extolling the virtue of the skills he'd learned. He said simply: "I'm going to be sitting next to you on the subway in a few years. Who do you want sitting next to you? A person who learned how to be a better criminal in prison? Or someone who learned the value of self-worth?"

Another prisoner was assigned to taking care of racehorses that had been "put out to pasture." The racehorses from Aqueduct and other race tracks find themselves being taken care of by prisoners in Wallkill. But the one man I interviewed said "In my entire life, I was never responsible for another human being. But I'm completely responsible for the life of this horse. I take care of him, I feed him, groom him, he is alive because I'm taking care of him. It's the first time I've learned how to take care of anyone else."

Rethink why a person should or shouldn't be in prison. It's not about breaking the law – because the law may refer to some arcane system based on the idea that humans are sheep like animals, a flock that must be tended, and the "bad ones" must be culled. There is no bad in this view of the Flipside, and the Flipside's view of us. There is only the learning of lessons about how we can or should relate to each other.

Prison should never be about revenge. The only way to examine *that* would be on a spiritual level – "Why did this event occur and is it possible that I had some prior involvement in it?" In terms of incarceration because someone is trapped in a cycle of criminal acts, perhaps based on the body they chose, or based on the sociological environment they chose – doesn't it behoove us to consider that in the equation when passing judgment?

Is putting someone in an isolate cell (or a violent prison environment) the best we can do as a civilization? Is there no logic to learning and teaching on another level? And once you're aware that there are mitigating factors involved in every crime, that must include a spiritual component – how can we pass judgment on people unless we ask them?

"Your Honor, we'd like the testimony to reflect that this criminal has done an extensive past life review and between life examination from a variety of sources. My client sees that he's been doing this for a few lifetimes now, and agrees that isolation would be of service to his figuring out why he continues to behave in such a fashion. But might I suggest that the court, sentence this individual to some years of taking care of animals who have been abandoned, left without care and are in danger of losing their lives. Instead of being put to death, he should be *put to use*."

Wouldn't that make a better contribution to society than staring at a wall, or being injected with drugs to give him a ticket to the Flipside? After all, the criminal isn't dying – as we've heard – they're just going home before the rest of us. Wouldn't it make more sense to give them an opportunity to commit acts of love and selflessness while they're still here so they can help mitigate the pain and suffering they've caused?

The justice system should be based on reality, not some archaic form of vengeance. If people act because of genes, because of sociological factors and spiritual ones – shouldn't all three be taken into consideration?

HOW FLIPSIDE HACKS HAVE ALTERED HISTORY

If no one dies, no one has ever died, then everyone who has ever existed still exists in one form or another. And I mean by that, many have elevated to a status that is not incarnating. Many do work that only discarnate beings can do.

So why do people get caught up in the mundane day to day fears and discriminations? Once we allow that everyone has chosen to be here – and chose to go through whatever their families, relatives, historical figures chose to experience, we can re-evaluate those ties that bind us.

Literally.

The idea is that we choose to be here, we've chosen to be with the people we're with. We tend to obscure this idea by focusing on what happened to people in the past, what others chose to experience in previous lifetimes.

Certainly it's worth noting that when someone starts to accumulate power, or wealth at the expense of others, then it's time to discuss with that person why they're doing such a thing.

It's important to have respect for everyone's path, for everyone's journey, because we can't be in their shoes. It's perfectly normal for them to identify with whatever group they feel the most connected to. The point is, that once we begin to examine how and why we're on the planet, we tend to see the usual stressful complaints as icing on the cake, or perhaps linseed oil on the stage that we might choose to avoid slipping on. Stepping over.

Consider for a moment, the historical events playing out in our country and around the globe as theatrical events. What is the premise behind the event, the way you'd examine the premise behind a play? Why are certain people involved, and what spiritual knowledge do they hope to gain from these events? If you take out the obvious issues or religion, gender, class, or any other sociological issue, and examine the events from a Flipside perspective – why did these events occur? How do these events, tragedies, victories, losses affect us in terms of our spiritual development? If "you can learn more in one day of tragedy on the earth, than 5000 years on some other boring planet where nothing happens" – how does that change our perspective on the "trauma" we hear every day in the media?

What if we could "see ourselves" in the roles other people play? Imagine ourselves as a person of color being stopped by a police car at night? Imagine ourselves a woman walking in a parking garage, and she hears footsteps behind her? Imagine ourselves as a child locked in a basement, frustrated from abuse? A family born without access to fresh water or food or medicine? Or a privileged golden-spooner who ignores everyone in eyesight for fear they want something from them? Or even the pet in our home – what does it feel like to be sitting on a rug waiting for someone to put some food in a bowl for you?

Just by shifting our consciousness into other individuals, and if not physically doing so (as they do in some esoteric Tibetan yoga practices) then just imagine it for a moment. Feel what *that feels like* to live in a city that has bombs exploding daily, drones chasing down friends or foes, or what it feels like to sit on a corner in the hot sun waiting for a quarter from an angry faced stranger? Or the angry gun owner, fed up with feeling isolated and ignored, loading his rifle to make someone else miserable? Or the person who looks up and sees the angry rifle bearer pointing a gun in their direction, knowing that they don't see you, they can't see you, because you're invisible to them.

We spend a lot of time on a daily basis judging others. From what people wear, to what they eat, to what they look like. And now imagine for a moment that you're living on some other planet, where everything is diametrically different – how people walk, talk, dress – and you come here to Earth for a moment and look around. What's wrong with this picture? Why are people walking around this planet in a constant state of anxiety and fear? (Except of course, for those who aren't.)

It's hard to have the perspective of someone no longer on the planet. They know what that feels like; their experience once they're off the planet is akin to being out of the theater, off stage, celebrating with your home team. Someone said to me the other day, "I wish my dad were here to see the Cubs winning baseball games." That's been a refrain for over a 100 years! What comedians are on the Flipside deciding who does or doesn't win the Pennant? *And do they really care?*

I said to my friend "Your dad is having wild adventures, flying around to different planets and universes; when he comes back to hear his son saying "Dad, the Cubs are winning!" He'd say "Oh, right. That's nice."" I'd argue his dad is more interested in seeing his estranged family members sitting at a ball game, having fun, enjoying life, then worrying about who is winning. Helpful to have perspective on how we might see our endless trials and tribulations over here, and how those on the Flipside might observe us from their perspective. *"Are you asking for help again!?"* I love how Jennifer Shaffer's guide said "She exasperates us, asking the same question if she can really hear us or not so many times. *And we don't get exasperated!*"

Who wants to go back in the theater and see how others are faring with the same props and costumes? You're done with that play, and no matter how many of your old friends might be calling you frantically from the stage, how many of us would really want to go back there and try to help them understand? "It's only a play. Enjoy it while you're on stage."

I come from Italian and Irish roots. Half and half. Irish pizza. I knew my Irish relatives, and I've known and spent time with many of my Italian ones. I've been to Ireland and experienced it on a cloudy day, when a shaft of sunlight emerged from the sky right down onto a deer who lifted its head and stared at me. Never seen anything so beautiful. The color of emerald – it's like everything sparkled at once in this bright green.

And I've walked the streets of ancient Rome at night, found myself standing under the giant pillars outside the Pantheon, hearing the ghosts of the ancient city call to each other using the voices of cats. I've strode the ancient roads of Pompeii, seen what the city used to look like in Herculaneum, and sat under the pine trees in the Alps having fresh polenta cooked over a wood fire outside in the Alpine air. I've been swallowed up by the Renaissance paintings in the Uffizi gallery in Florence, and slept on train benches from Venice to Naples.

But that was just in this lifetime.

After having four different past life regressions, I've seen lifetimes where I lived in India as a Brahmin priest in the region of Kerala, saw the face of my dear wife Miriam, spent time painting religious symbols on my face. Stood in a robe on the streets of Pompeii, a teacher of "logic and ethics" (as was Aristotle) married into a wealthy merchant family, who had me poisoned because I was too adoring of the ancient philosophy of the family's Nubian slaves.

Seeing myself as a failed sculptor in Greece, in the workshop of a great artist, overstaying my welcome and being banished from his employ for "borrowing" some of his tools to make sculptures of my own, living out my days crafting jewelry in Piraeus outside of Athens. Or my days as a young woman in Paris, who was raped by a wealthy patron, and sent to the convent to have my child, which I lost in miscarriage, but spent the rest of my days suffering under the boot of the nuns in the convent.

Or the Dominican friar who lived in Florence and spent his days painting – not famous, perhaps good enough to be remembered, but I had no access to his name, outside of imagining he might be one of the famous Dominicans who painted in Florence. I've visited with the callous member of a royal family in France, living near Calais, where he spent more time bedding women than he did learning culture, where he ignored his arranged marriage to an Italian countess, never bothering to learn to speak the language of our children – and dying at the sword of a rival who learned years after the incident, that the cad had dishonored his wife. As he lay dying I was thinking "But I didn't even like the woman he just killed me over. I just did it because I liked the game involved."

There are more, many more. My point in bringing them up is that they now no longer exist as "new information" to my brain when I was accessing them while under hypnosis. It's like I've opened up the gates of that garden, and can walk out there whenever I need to or want to. The value is that I can see incidents in my current life with a bit of humor, the downside is that I start to remember things that happened in a previous life as if they occurred in this life. I understand why it's important to filter all of that out – otherwise, we'd all spend hours in the game of "And where do I know you from again…?"

In this life when I run into someone familiar, I have to scan the decades of my life. From the film world? Literary world? Music world? College years? High school years? I was sitting at a tiny bar on the backside of the island of Corfu in Greece, when a young man sitting next to me asked my name. I told him. He said "Did you used to play football at St. Norbert's grade school?" I said that I did. He said "You hit me so hard in one game that I memorized your name."

I apologized and bought him a beer. Now just imagine if the filters were off – we'd be buying each other drinks until the cows came home.

What are the odds of me finding this fellow in this bar in Corfu? Perhaps we have more quantum entanglement in our lives than we thought we did. By that I mean the energy that goes into who we are, who we're going to be… is all part of a giant field, and we rotate around each other, and eventually find each other.

How can we use the knowledge that we've lived lifetimes as other people help inform the way we treat others today? If you consider that you were another gender in another life, or another race, or another color, or another income level – you can't help but start to consider that other people on the planet aren't any less than, or more than anyone else on the planet.

So our enemies, who view us as their enemies, become someone who "doesn't know us." If they did "know us" they would see that we don't hate them, in fact we believe in tolerance, in compassion, in understanding the roots of their rage. If the roots of their rage is based on intolerance, a lack of compassion, a lack of finances, a prejudice against religion or race or color… then who needs to do the rethinking about why we came to the planet?

Doesn't it make sense to consider the United Nations as an organization that allows people who are on the planet to find a way to live together We have a planet to come back to?

HACKING THE FLIPSIDE WITH JOE MEDIUM

Try not to connect with just any medium. Everyone is tuned differently. If you went into the stereo store (I'm dating myself here, I actually used to work in a stereo store, selling "hi-fi") and saw a hundred different receivers, you'd want the one that was suited most to you. Some unit that is just basic, no bells or whistles? Or some "unit" who walks and talks and thinks like you do – so when they give you their advice, you're more open to hearing it?

Every street corner where I live has a "psychic reading" sign in front of someone's house. Would you choose a dentist or doctor by driving by and seeing a neon sign out front? It may be someone that is delving into the most sacred part of your lifetime. Why not get a recommendation from someone you trust?

That's what I recommend. If you're going in for a past life regression or a between life session, I recommend speaking to the therapist, ask them about their history, how'd they come to this work? You'll hear from their replies if they're trying to sell you something, or if they're like you – on a spiritual path or journey. (I recommend the Newton Institute, they have a searchable database, and since I know how hard it is to get accredited, you have a good shot at getting someone well versed in both past life work and between life work, as that's required to become part of their organization.)

The same goes for mediums. You've seen the ones of television, but you haven't seen the outtakes. They film those shows so that you can't see what goes on behind the scenes. Not every medium is 100% correct – especially when it comes to predicting the future, because the future is not set. When a psychic tells you the future and doesn't say "this is what I'm getting, it may turn out this way, it may not" then they're not being accurate. Or as Jay Leno noted: why don't more psychics win the lottery?

That being said, you can find mediums, therapists and others trained in this work who do have an uncanny ability to speak to your spirit, or to speak to your guides. If you've lost someone, they're an excellent way of reminding you that your loved one isn't gone. But I would recommend not taking the time with the medium as a chance to "prove or disprove" something. After all, you sought them out – allow them to do what they do best.

If Uncle Pete does come through, ask Uncle Pete some questions. Don't let him off the hook. It's not enough for the medium to say "You have an uncle whose name begins with P." You reply, yes, that's Uncle Pete and while we have you in the room Pete, I want you to access your guide and tell us – why did you choose a lifetime where you borrowed all of my tools and never brought them back?"

There's no rules here on how to speak to the Flipside. None I'm aware of anyway. No reason for you not to talk to Uncle Pete the way you used to talk to him. It may startle the medium, but why not? They're used to being startled.

Some general thoughts on talking to the Flipside through a medium:

1. Mediums can access your loved ones. This is accurate and has been recorded since the dawn of time. The fact that people "don't believe in mediums" belays that data involved. It's not a matter of belief or disbelief. These folks are "hearing" "seeing" or "sensing" a message from your loved one. It may very well be that they are misreading, mishearing, not sensing the information accurately. That's possible in a game of telephone as well as in an actual conversation between someone not on the planet and someone who is.

2. People on the Flipside have a sense of humor. They may or may not be telling you things incorrectly on purpose. If you have a relative who used to pull your leg a lot, don't be surprised when what they tell the medium is absolutely false – but then turns out to be true later on. This is reported quite a few times – where the medium says something is accurate – the person hearing the information says "no, it's not" and then months or even years later, it turns out to be absolutely accurate.

3. Take it all with a grain of salt. The most important point is that your loved one still exists. Is still alive. Has not disappeared into nothingness. So start there. How cool is that? Then remember that you're getting the filter of your loved one – how they perceive reality, and remembering they're not suddenly omniscient – they

may want to play with you "Yes! The cubs will win the Series!" or they may not know the answer to your question but make one up because they're on the spot. After all – they've got people on this side of the fence shouting questions and they're doing their best to shout them back. Sometimes that can be boring so they'll just shout something to shut us up. "Yes I love you! Get on with it!"

4. As hard as it is, don't ask mediums to predict the future. Don't ask them to say what's going to happen. If they start to tell you "I see something in your future" stop them by saying "You see a likely event in my future, so please offer it in that fashion. You can't see the future because it's not set. You can see a possible future based on many events. So don't tell me it is the future when it isn't." That will usually stop a medium in their tracks.

5. That is, unless your relative or loved one is really trying to warn you about something in your future. If it's an event you've already planned, they're not going to warn you about it – because you *could warn yourself* if push came to shove. But if your higher self has been trying to communicate with you, and they've been trying to speak to you via dreams or other communications, and they say through the medium "They're trying to tell me something that's a warning to you, and you need to hear it." Take that with a grain of salt, but pay attention. If it rings true, it probably is.

6. A medium who talks about dark entities, or evil spirits isn't a medium. They're someone who may or may not sense things around them, and because they aren't familiar with these folks, they may categorize them in some 15th century nomenclature. Again, lots of salt here. No such thing as Satan, evil spirits, lost souls, entities etc. If they're talking about them, it's like having someone describe an elephant by the size of his trunk. They just don't have access to the whole picture to be able to give you advice. If someone insists that they've experienced evil spirits, entities, etc, good for them. It's just not in the data. It's entirely possible that these people have experienced something that was real for them, I'm just saying it's not useful or pragmatic to spend time dealing with things that are icing on the cake. Popcorn in the theater.

7. Never, ever allow someone to tell you who you should love or not love. The truth is that we are born from love, we all return to love,

there is no one in your path that you haven't asked to come there to teach or learn something from you. If you want to change that paradigm because it's not healthy for you – or turns negative – then send them waves of love and send them on their way. The love that you create doesn't end, and there's no right or wrong about who you fall in love with. There's sane love and insane love, but it's part of life to learn the difference.

8. The best use of a medium is in numbers. If you like one particular medium who tells you things about yourself that no one else has ever heard before, then ask them specific questions about your path and journey. Not about your love life, or where you're going to move, or the mundane things. Ask them to speak to your guardian, or higher guide. Ask for a name. Ask for some identifying feeling that can help assist you in the future. Ask them for guidance in your life to help you get to where you're supposed to be. And thank them profusely for coming through. Then do the same with two other mediums. If the same people keep appearing for you, if the same message keeps occurring for you, then it's likely that it's precisely what you're supposed to hear.

9. Remember that a medium is just acting like a receiver. There are vibrations in the universe, and for whatever reason they're tuned in such a way to receive them. Think of them as receivers, not as conductors. Meaning they aren't supposed to send out information into the universe for you – they're ability is to pick up on vibrations, thoughts and feelings that are meant for you. If you've lost a loved one recently, then absolutely, there's no quicker way to contact them, other than through your own thoughts, prayers and meditation.

10. Don't let a medium become your crutch. You signed up for this life, knowing that you weren't going to know what's going to happen, or why something happened in the past. That's part of the fun of it – reading a novel in real time without knowing how it's going to end. However, if you're someone who peeks at the ending because you can't stand suspense, fine – know what's going to happen to you in the future. But don't be surprised when it changes.

USE A FLIPSIDE HACK AS A YOUR FAVORITE DRUG

I had a conversation with a heart surgeon today who said he considers himself one of the few "holistic" heart surgeons he knows. We talked about all the modalities involved in the world of medicine – how we generally think of health in terms of two paradigms; genetic or sociological issues. Either nature or nurture. As I pointed out, there's another tool in the doctor's bag – and it's the spiritual aspects of a person's life.

If they've had a difficult previous lifetime that's influencing this lifetime, there are any number of illnesses, pains, unrecognizable illnesses that may be related to that previous lifetime. It doesn't mean that the spiritual aspect is more important than the other two – however, it's as equally important to examine. Especially if the doctor can't find any earthly reason for the person's illness.

I doubt many doctors are reading this book – or have gotten this far. But if they have, I refer them to Yale Psychiatrist Brian Weiss's book "Many Lives Many Masters" where he discovered he could cure or heal some patients while they were under hypnosis. I refer Michael Newton's first book "Journey of Souls" where he first understood how a previous lifetime might affect the health of this lifetime. I refer the reader to Psychiatrist Dr. Bruce Greyson's YouTube talk "Is Consciousness Produced by the Brain?" where he makes strong and effective arguments about how medicine hasn't begun to understand the brain, and how consciousness works.

The point is, there are many people who've had excellent advice from the Flipside about matters of health. As mentioned earlier, Edgar Cayce was famous for healing people with advice from the Flipside, but as noted in that chapter, that information isn't only accessible to people "channeling" Edgar Cayce – any one of us can work on asking and hearing answers from people who are no longer on the planet.

As noted previously, I met a "faith healer" from Iceland who was quite famous for "healing" or helping people just by touch and meditating on their health. I asked him how he became a healer, and he told me this incredible story about having a motorcycle accident, and how he had "prayed" for help from his relatives. He woke one day to find someone standing "in his room, operating on his leg." This fellow was etheric – but this fellow could see this man standing in his room, "His hands were inside my knee and repairing it."

He said that the operation was successful, however, it was "as if I had opened a door to the afterlife." Other people started showing up, and one day he awoke to find his bed hovering in mid-air. That was the last straw for his wife, and she left him.

He told me then he started having out of body experiences – he would feel himself floating around the bedroom, but at some point, these "light beings" would show up and take him somewhere. He would awake the next day not remembering where he had been.

So finally, he asked them to let him see what they were doing with him. He said he felt himself flying "a long distance" where they would go to a place to teach him healing exercises. I asked if he could describe them – after all, I was a tourist visiting his sister, an old friend of mine – and realized what a great opportunity it was to gain this knowledge without having to go through the experience myself.

Here's what he said. When a patient comes to him with a problem – like a sore back, he would picture the patient sitting in a chair in a room and then "call upon the white healing light of the universe" to come down and enter this fellow's back.

And he would see this bright light coming down from somewhere, and it would surround the patient, and he had learned how to "focus" the light to do the maximum work at healing.

I've encountered the reference "healing light of the universe" in a number of accounts. When speaking to a Tibetan monk about the meditation called "Tonglen" where a doctor would picture a patient sitting across from him, and then imagine the illness in the patient as a light or smoke. Then, during the meditation, he would "breathe in" the light or smoke from the patient, and as the illness would be drawn into the meditator, would "call upon the white healing light of the universe" to turn the illness into healthy energy, and then breathe that healed light or smoke back into the patient.

During a session where Scott De Tamble was talking to a woman about her healing abilities, she used the same words about describing "channeling the white healing light of the universe into her patients."

Finally, when I was in my first between life sessions, I found myself standing in a giant auditorium where my friend Luana was attending a class in healing energy. I consciously didn't have a clue where I was, or how I got there, but I started to answer the hypnotherapist Jimmy Quast's question; "Describe what happens here.'

And I said "this is a classroom where they teach students how to channel the white healing light of the universe so that a healer or shaman or doctor can use that energy to heal a patient." Now I had no clue as to what I was going to say, or why I was answering this question as if I did know the answer, but another unusual event happened as I said the sentence.

One of the students that I could see in my mind's eye sitting in the classroom turned around and glared at me. I realized that I was "speaking aloud" in that classroom and that I had interrupted the class. I could see the teacher with his arms folded, and I could see my friend Luana in the back row of the class, looking at me with hands upturned as if to say "What the hell are you doing here?"

It wasn't at all what I might have created if I was writing this scene. I froze, realizing I wasn't invisible, I was clearly visible, and I was interrupting a giant classroom by speaking aloud in front of all of them.

The student who had turned around and glared at me said "You don't have a clue as to what you're talking about." He said it with disdain, and I realized I hadn't been very polite about where I was, and what I was doing. I really didn't expect anyone to react to my presence standing in this large auditorium. I apologized, then said to the student "Yes, of course, you're correct, I'm describing this classroom too simplistically. The truth is that not everyone signs up to be healed, and not everyone signs up to cure their clients, especially if they need to understand or examine the energy of that illness. So while this classroom teaches these students how to help channel this energy, there's no guarantee that it will result in a healed patient."

The student nodded as if to say "Okay, that's better."

Then two years later, when I did another session with Scott De Tamble, he asked me where I wanted to go – and suddenly I was transported back to that classroom. It felt like perhaps 20 minutes had gone by. And Luana was introducing me to the teacher, and I apologized for interrupting his class. And at that point he asked "so what is it you want to know?"

My point isn't that I can answer these questions. It's to point out that anyone can answer these questions. They need to find a way to tune themselves into the right frequency to talk with their higher selves, or their guides, or they need to find someone who is tuned to that frequency. If it's a medium that can help with the transmission, it's important not to be caught up in the medium's own prejudices in this area – if you've got specific questions to ask your higher self, or your guides, skip the preliminaries, and ask.

USE FLIPSIDE HACKS TO FIGURE OUT WHICH BATHROOM TO USE

Our country is in the midst of a bathroom debate, which is hilarious if it wasn't Insane. I've traveled around the planet, and first Americans should appreciate they actually have a bathroom before they start telling who and who can't be in it. If you saw the toilets in Tibet, you'd be so happy to have a warm place to go, who was in there with you is the last thing on your mind.

That being said, there's a lot of young people who show up here with gender identity issues. Then there's others who realize they have gender identify issues later in life.

What's a gender identity issue of you choose your lifetime? *Good question.*

If you've already chosen your life, how confusing could that choice be? As we've heard often from people in these reports, people may show up here without a strong conviction of who they're going to be one way or another. Let's say that you've spent the past 5 lifetimes as a woman. And you show up here as a male to "check out what that would be like." But everything about your trip here reminds you of your lifetimes as a woman. And you can't help but want to return to that identity.

Or perhaps you've shown up here to teach others a lesson in identity – to help them realize that we are all equal between lives, and there's no reason we aren't equal in this life. So why not give them the hardest medicine they could take? They haven't a clue as to why someone might want to be a woman when born a man, or vice versa – and as long as the medical world completely ignores these reports, they'll never understand it.

There's a million reasons why someone might want to change their identity. I can think of a dozen arguments why someone might show up here and want to be someone else. Would a between life hypnotherapy session help them? It might. As we know, not everyone gets where they want to go. That person may be too young to have a session where they explain why they chose to be on the planet. And more often than not, the parents aren't going to be able to make that leap either.

So the answer is always love. How much do you love your child? Is it conditional love, meaning you only love your child if they behave exactly as you think they should? Well that's not unconditional love. Unconditional love is precisely what it reports itself to be – love without judgment or conditions.

Should you sit down with the child and ask them about their previous lifetimes? Why not? What possible harm could come from that question? If a child comes and says "I think I'm supposed to be a girl and not a boy" why not ask "Why do you think that? Were you a girl in a previous lifetime? Is this a choice you made before you chose to come here?"

But again, unconditional love is just what it is. Trying hard to not put any conditions on love whatsoever.

When a child comes and says they're "gay" or "straight" or "liberal" or "conservative" – that's great that they've lived on the planet long enough to be able to formulate the sentence. The idea is to love people as we love them between lives – without conditions.

So before you decide to "go under the knife" for gender reconstruction – which of course is anyone's right to do – seek out a professional hypnotherapist (I recommend the ones trained by the Newton Institute as they're trained to do this kind of work. They have a searchable database on their site, but like anything, get recommendations and speak to the therapist before you do a session.) The point is that the gender identity issue may relate to a previous lifetime experience. The reason a person feels "uncomfortable" may be because they've been a different gender for many lifetimes.

It's not going to change who you are if you decide to do this kind of between life exploration, but it will give you a second opinion – a logical easy step by step way to see what how this confusion came about. Something that you already planned? Something that you knew would be an issue? Or something that you're missing from a previous lifetime? Isn't it worth exploring that as well?

FLIPSIDE HACKS HELP FATHOM WHY YOU CHOSE YOUR PARENTS

If there's one factoid about what people say under deep hypnosis that bugs people; it's this one.

"Are you frickin' kidding me? Not in a million years! I would NOT choose those two people to ever be my parents. I did everything in my power to get away from them!"

I didn't say you had to like the idea. Just allow it to sink in.

If you chose your parents and they were horrible to you – think about that for a bit. If you've survived, and aren't reading this book from the Flipside, then chances are you survived them. Think about how many lessons you learned while trying to get away from them, trying to not be like them, or to somehow change the paradigm.

Then consider for a moment that they're just a couple of actors that you chose to play the parts of your nasty parents. Imagine yourself in the casting room going through the pairs that come through the door. "Oh, not you two – you're both too nice. Next!" Then finally your parents come in. And you say "Do you think you guys can play the roles of the nasty parents for me?"

We have free will. One of them may say "Yeah, I wasn't so sure about this, because you remember, I played your brother in the *Viking era*. That's when you wanted me to act like a crazy son of a bitch, and I gotta tell you. It wasn't fun." Then you remember – Oh right! You're Thor!!! Oh my god, you were fantastic. You were the best nasty brother I could have imagine. You've got to play this part, there's no one who's going to motivate me better!"

I made up that part about forgetting he played Thor. It's not something we'd forget. We generally remember everything about all of our lives – so when you run into the actor who played Thor you may get a visceral reaction to running into them again, in this life anyway. But the point is, *we ask them to play the role.*

They agree to play the role of the bad guy because we asked them to, because we begged them to, because we convinced them somehow that it would be cool to play that role. They may be such good actors that even you can't remember why you would have asked them to play such nasty characters! "What was I thinking? I totally forgot what a nasty *SOB* you are!"

But afterwards they come up to you and you embrace them. Because you know that you asked them to play the role. And you know that they did exactly what was asked of them, even though you had completely forgotten it back here – even though you spent a good deal of your life ranting and raving and going to therapy to complain about the role that they played.

Imagine if therapists could access this information.

Imagine if the psychiatrist said, instead of "so how does that make you feel?" asked "So why the hell did you ask them to play the role of your parents? Why the hell did you ask them to play the role of your parents if you didn't think you could handle it? If it's too much for you? What kind of an actor are you to ask them to put up with all the nonsense that they had to put up with so they could play the awful role of someone who hurt and maimed and tortured you in the ways that you perceived they did?"

Of course the person on the couch would say "But they did torture and maim and hurt me emotionally! Why would I ever ask them to do that?" To which the psychiatrist answers *"exactly!"*

The shrink says "So stop whining already. Stop complaining that your parents dealt you a bad hand, that the cause of your suffering is from somewhere else. That you're wounded, hurt, upset, traumatic because of something that happened to you – in the ballpark, in the war zone, in the bedroom, in the police station, in the church. None of it affects you negatively – it affects those who perpetrate negatively – they have to live with the energy of those actions. But none of it affects who you are – because you're someone who has live a thousand lives, who has walked the boards a thousand times in a thousand different roles. Sometimes you were the perpetrator, sometimes you were the victim. What have you learned from this journey? Why did you choose this journey?

Oh, sorry, time's up!

The psychiatrist lets you out into the street and invites in his next client.

It may be harsh to hear, and I have seen many people face these realities during these sessions – to fully understand that they are the architects of their lives, they are the ones who make the blueprint so they can learn from the mistakes, from the errors, from the drawing outside the line moments in their lifetimes. They do get to learn those lessons, because we always wind up back in the classroom.

We always wind up back with our loved ones in our soul group discussing what mistakes we made, what victories we had, and what people we saved.

So. You want to be someone regretting their lifetime during their life review? Or someone frolicking in the memory of it?

CAN I GET A HERNIA HACKING THE FLIPSIDE?

As I'm fond of saying, sometimes I feel like a guy in the theater standing at the back of the stage who turns on the lights and shouts "It's all a play! We're only in a play!" who then turns the lights back off.

It's not healthy to have the lights on all the time. Sometimes it's important to lean back in our chair, to be swept away by the drama, by the passion, by the dramatic choices those around us act out in front of us.

Sometimes we choose the life of monks. Which is a good thing. But you can't have everyone sitting around meditating about the nature of existence and not enjoying life, can you? I mean yes, some people are fulfilled doing that, and yes, many monks can teach people who are suffering in life how to live and not suffer. But we can't all be monks.

We can't all be chiefs either. Some of us relish playing the role of the rest of the tribe, of hunting and gathering and sharing and bringing back to the hearth while someone else puts on the headdress and plays the role of leader. It does seem these days that with the advent of social media, everyone longs for playing the role of chief, or knocking the chief down, or stomping on the chief's reputation. But that's a role as well.

When we examine what vanity really is; the idea that we need fame, fortune, good looks, lots of things to enjoy life – that's pretty ridiculous. If you're fortunate enough to live long enough to see how none of that matters, how the happiest people are not caught up in their possessions, how the laughter of a child, or a parent – or their tears – means more to us than any "achievement" placed in front of us, we get a perspective on what it means to be human.

I think it's important to think about these things, to observe the nature of reality from this new paradigm. After all, we have many places we could incarnate – according to these folks – so think about "Why did U choose this planet?" More importantly; "Why not enjoy it while we're here?"

Something I saw online today – Herbie Hancock, who was an old friend of my Luana Ander's (they were in the SGI division of Buddhism together) wrote about a time he played with Miles Davis and hit an off-key note. He said inside he felt terrible, *like he died* – until Miles took the mistake and somehow made it melodic. And it made him think of the old Buddhist saying "From poison comes medicine."

From poison comes medicine. To which I'd like to add "Turn your "clam" into an oyster. Turn your sand into a pearl."

A clam is a term musicians use for making a mistake while playing (I've had my share of clams, thank you very much.) But an oyster can only make a pearl when a piece of sand enters their world – and then they use *nacre* to coat the piece of sand and turn it into a pearl. They can't create the pearl without that annoying piece of sand entering their world.

Likewise, you can't make pearls if you don't have sand. You can't make beautiful things if you haven't had some grit in your life, some sand to push against. When you consider that you choose your life – it's up to you whether you're going to be a clam or an oyster (not literally, in these cases people claim we rarely if ever incarnate as animals. When I say "clam or oyster" it's your choice as to which metaphor applies.)

The sand that becomes your pearl is the obstacles, the stress, the lessons that you've agreed to learn or come in contact with your life. And you can either keep your seal shut your entire life, and tightly make sure that no sand comes in – or you can allow a little sand to enter your life and trust that you'll figure out how to make a beautiful pearl from it.

But allow for a moment that you chose this lifetime, you chose the people around you, and if you didn't choose the people around you, there's still time to find them. You don't have to have your head buried in a book to feel this to be the case, or sitting in a tent in South America under the influence of a drug, or even listening to me drone on about it on YouTube. You don't have to be aware of your previous lifetimes, your path and journey on the planet at all times; sometimes it's important to just float in the pool.

Or stop and smell some flowers. Or lie on your back in the grass and watch the clouds form. It's a pretty amazing place when you think about it – or allow it to invade your space. Hold someone's hand, give someone a hug. You'll get more energy from that single act than a thousand books on the topic.

HACK THE FLIPSIDE OR GET KICKED OFF THE PLANET

A note to scientists and religious folk; please get a refund. I'm not interested in debating the data with you. These reports come from over a decade of research; they're consistent and replicable. They're the kind of reports that drive materialist scientists or religious fundamentalists batty. It's the only thing I can get my atheist and fundamentalist friends to agree on; I must be batshit crazy. That's okay, we're on different paths.

But I believe we're at a point where we can ask people *over there* to help people *over here*. By asking people *over there*, we can get advice, help, science to help save us *over here*. There's no need to fear getting advice from "lower sources" as those sources aren't going to be giving out advice in this fashion. Because our guides wouldn't let them.

I've met people who've played guardians roles for the planet. One person under hypnosis remembered coming to Earth before it was fully formed, he was with a group of science souls, and they were discussing how the Earth would make a wonderful place for sentient beings.

I've met others who've had between life experiences where they see that their occupation over there is to travel to distant planets and seed them for future sentient beings to use. Seed them, meaning subtly making life form changes so that they will spontaneously turn into creatures' soul's they would like to inhabit.

I've interviewed people who claim they "normally incarnate on another planet" a planet in our Universe, outside our galaxy, where the life forms look more like the snapchat creature than humanoid. I was told by this person that on his home planet, they have much higher intelligence, but that he incarnated here to help earth with the "coming changes."

Michael Newton had had numerous people in his research with off world experience ("about ten percent") and Peter Smith, President of the Newton Institute told me the number has risen to about 30%. That's people who come in for an LBL therapy session and discover that they have "off world" experience – or they have incarnated on other planets.

Why has this number increased? It could be more souls want to come to Earth while it goes through a transition, perhaps people resonate with between life therapy. Perhaps the earth is going through some epic changes and they need to be here to help us get through them. I don't know why that number has increased. Perhaps it's because the veil is thinning.

I've also heard from people who saw or are able to see animals on the Flipside. Galen Stoller talks about it in "My Life After Life" and Erik Medhus gives a wonderful description of being in a sea of insects over there. Seeing or hearing them come out of existence over here, and into existence over there.

We've read about the person who claimed to be able to speak directly with the "soul" that was the Earth itself. This fellow spoke to someone or something that spoke of being an "oversoul" for the Earth. He remarked that all planets had the same form of oversouls, almost like a pool of water speaking on behalf of all the water molecules within it. What would happen if we started to see the earth as a closed system (which it is) where all the water, air, earth are things to be preserved, taken care of, tended to if not for your children, then for our own possible return?

Imagine for a moment that this is accurate. That the planet is sentient. Imagine further that there are beings out there in the universe who can help guide us here back on the planet, who want to help us back on the planet. That they see that we're causing distress or problems on the planet, and they're happy to help us fix or help heal the planet.

As mentioned, there have been failures on other planets, and I've interviewed one woman who remember living on a planet where the science "got out of hand" and ultimately destroyed their planet, and all the souls had to find somewhere else to incarnate.

So while there may be individual souls who are keeping an eye on our planet, or making sure that we aren't being slammed with asteroids – or perhaps in the case of the asteroid that supposedly killed off the dinosaurs, making sure that event would occur so that we could come into existence as human beings... I don't know. It may be that "higher souls" are capable of stopping cataclysmic events from happening to the earth. Perhaps we can ask for their assistance in guidance on how to keep fellow humans from creating cataclysmic events here.

What about the other creatures that inhabit the planet? Are animals sentient? Apparently so. Were the animals that were our ancestors sentient? Apparently so. So what event, or what change occurred on the planet so that we would decide "Okay, now is the time that we should start moving into the wombs of these humanoids and see if we can't make something of this place."

There are a handful of people who remember cavemen-like lifetimes. But none that I'm aware of who remember lifetimes as dinosaurs, lizards, etc. I mean they may exist; I just haven't run across any accounts like that.

I have run across one account, mentioned earlier where a hypnotherapist had a young lady come into the office and claim that her previous lifetime had been as a fox. That her parents had been fed up with hearing over and over how she "used to be a fox" and brought her to see this therapist so they could convince or demonstrate that wasn't the case. And this therapist told me that while under hypnosis this child gave pretty accurate descriptions of what her previous life was like – as a fox. The hills she lived in near an urban area, the brood that she created, the fences that caught her fur, the way she saw colors differently than she does as a human, everything from start to finish including fox pups.

So as an exercise this therapist asked her to regress to a previous lifetime, one that occurred prior to this fox life. And she remembered a different lifetime -- *as an Arctic Fox.*

I mention it to just say "You never know." It's easy to say "it's not possible." But it's more accurate to say "It's not something that's reported, in all the cases I've seen, one seemed to be a possible example of it." That's to say "Anything's possible; just not likely." Same goes for those claiming "What happens after we die." Ask to see some data. What are the others in this group saying? Are the experiences the same? It's not enough that someone "saw God" or "talked to Jesus" or "saw that nothing happened" on the Flipside. That experience was specifically designed for them alone. It's not the same thing that's going to happen to me or you.

Which brings us back to "how does these reports help the planet?"

First we have to acknowledge any of us *we like the planet*. That may sound silly, but we certainly don't treat it as a place we'd like to come back to. We ignore the poison that goes into the atmosphere, the toxins going into crops, or even the toxic way we pull oil out of the Earth. If as souls we view the Earth through the lens of thousands if not millions of years, why can't we do the same?

Easy to argue why we can't do the same. We can't all move back into tents and roam the planet like the indigenous people used to. (I know, I mentioned that lifetime as well. Yes, as a Lakota medicine man. And since having that memory, now whenever I hear their song, or see someone speaking Lakota, it's like a tuning fork goes off in my head.)

But we can ask indigenous people how to save our planet. We can start by looking at how they regarded nature – as if everything was imbued with the energy of the Great Spirit. Or as the indigenous Australians see it; when you're asleep reality happens, when you're awake it's "dream time." But if you can't find yourself seeing the planet as indigenous people do, then ask those who've gone before you.

Want to know how to create fresh water from salt water for pennies? Ask. See what your guides say. *If they can't answer, ask them if they know someone who can.*

Want to see how to find a way to holistically have renewable energy on the planet? How about finding a way to "unlock the cage" of animals who are being mistreated or used for experiments? Start with the animals who can communicate, and ask them. Then further, ask your guides how you can communicate with them. See what they have to say. If they can't answer, ask them if they know someone who can.

Want to know how to move energy through thought? In a number of sessions, I've heard people talking about their work on the Flipside as being someone who can "manipulate energy." I've visited classrooms in the afterlife where people are teaching how to do that. I've even seen formulas written on whiteboards on how to do that. If I was a physics professor, I might be able to understand what those symbols meant. But why not ask a physics professor to have a between life session? Direct him to a classroom. Ask him; "How does that work? Is there any way to find that same form of energy here on Earth?"

Want to know how to cure an illness? Find a way to help people access the "healing light of the universe"? How do we end pollution of our water systems? End climate change or stabilize it? How can we feed starving people holistically? How can we move income around so that more people have access to it? How can we use technology to better our existence on the planet? How can we offer a type of technology that would further benefit beings, as well as create work for them?

Ask. See what your guides say. If they can't answer these questions, then ask them if they know someone who can. Visit a classroom. Ask to speak to the teacher. Ask your questions. You'll be surprised by the answers.

You can always ask them the simple questions; "Where's my soul mate?" "How can I make more money to do the things I'm here to do?" "Why have bad things happened to me?" *"What are the lottery numbers?"* I suspect that even asking these questions you probably already know the answer – or why you haven't gotten the lottery numbers. But you can always ask. See what your guides say. If they can't answer the questions, then ask them if they know someone who can.

What are you waiting for? There's someone reading this sentence right now who will *say "that's a great idea!"* They will beat the tech giants to figuring out how to solve these problems, because they will begin to ask their guides the answer to these questions. They will be the people who create these apps, build these machines, or transfer that energy so that the earth is healed, so that mankind is helped.

You've gotten this far in the book. Maybe that's why.

Maybe it's you.

A sunset is nature's way of saying "It's a wrap."

EPILOGUE: The Final Frontier

BOOK QUOTES:

I asked Jennifer Shaffer if any of the people interviewed in the book might give a quote or "blurb" for the book cover. I wrote her (tongue firmly in cheek): "I assume no one spends time in the afterlife reading books, however, perhaps one of them might be able to give a quote I can put on the book?" She asked each person on my list for a reply:

Edgar Cayce

"Tell Richard that **his book has an appealing thunder** for controverting settings that are falsely depicted, for those that need (to hear) it. (Jennifer asks Cayce *"Need what?"*) The truth we need is, how we survive our bodies, (arrive) in the afterlife to different situations that make up (I think he means *comprise*) the past, present, and future outcomes of our spiritual existence. ("Controverting" may mean "contradicting misconceptions.")

Tell Rich not to fear the outcomes of what it is, that (the response to this book) **will have people questioning their own disbeliefs and belief paradigms**. And that we all have to, (and) at some point of our spiritual growth, need this "upheaval" to make a difference. **Rich, you are that translation of the ethers. For now; I'm "The Awakened Prophet."** (laughing.) (Note, Jennifer had a hard time with his syntax and I've done my best to unpack it. Edgar Cayce was known as "The Sleeping Prophet" so his comment "The Awakened Prophet" is pretty funny.)

Billy Meyer

(Billy is my life long pal who appeared to Jennifer when we were doing an interview live on German television moments after I'd learned he passed away.) Jennifer: He's smoking a cigarette. "Of course I am" he says. He's showing me your daughter by the way, Rich. *"Is it her birthday?"* (It is, in two weeks) He's showing me a depiction of.. not her birthday, or a previous birthday? *Your son?* (It was yesterday.) *What do you want to say to Rich?* He says "I want to tell Rich I'm watching over him. And I do care about what he publishes…" Jennifer asks *"Have you read it?"* "Yes, I was there when you wrote it – (and) many lifetimes before." *So Richard's written something like this before?* "(showing Jennifer) I'm seeing quills. "Absolutely... something they had to use a long time ago."

He says "He appreciates you talking to his family, last September. (That's accurate, I emailed his kids to let them know he came through to Jennifer). *He's showing me another female – is this the guy that...?* (I assume he's showing her a friend in high school who also dated another friend, Howard). *Why do I laugh with him so much?* "Because you get it," he says. He's hanging out with your other friend up there – Luana. Jennifer asks *"Luana's teaching you?"*

He says "He doesn't qualify for her classes, she's so much ahead of his spirit. He still likes being around here." He's super funny. He said "Rich did what I asked him to do. Yes, you checked up on his family and (that in turn) opened up a dialog between Bill and them."

Anything else Billy? He says "Tell him I finally have nothing to say. **And that Rich got it right this lifetime."** *Got it right?* "Right in terms of your soul purpose." He shows me a fence, like you were trapped (behind it) you lifted the fear factor and you're just going for it. He just high-fived you.

Tell me something else only Rich would know. "That you don't know when to stop. That it's working out better than anybody expected it to." He says tell him "I love you maaan;" like from that film; that's funny. He says "I hope to catch up soon after the reviews come in." He says "You did it Rich." He shows me an R with a circle, like the Radio Shack logo; like you're an antenna. He says "His heart is with you and **he thanks you and everything you're doing on both levels, with the spirit world as well**, and to not hold back... Ciao." (A phrase Billy used with me when saying goodbye.) He said "Good luck, but you don't need it."

Howard Schultz

Howard is a lifelong friend who grew up down the block from me. He came out to LA and became a successful TV writer/producer, creating successful shows "Extreme Makeover" and "Naked Dating." He offered to do a between life session with me, which I filmed and included in "Flipside" (but made him anonymous at the time.) We spoke often of doing a "spirit show" together, but it just never happened. We were talking about doing a show together the last time we spoke, but he passed away from a sudden heart attack a month later. Jennifer asked him for a quote:

Jennifer: Howard told me "**The beginning is near and the ending is nonexistent."** (I see this as Howard playing with "the end is near!" when it comes to talking about the Flipside.) It's something we all have to incorporate into the well of our being. Not to "look for the now," but to "live for the awakened shift." And not to use fear to have it... (Jennifer; "oh my gosh, he just showed me, a picture of a fear monger who's running for President") Not to use fear tactics within your soul's purpose to gratify who you are now.

He says "Tell Rich I support him in all his endeavors, even more so because I get where he's coming from. **Much luck to you... and you Jennifer... for making the unbelievable claim that *there is* even an afterlife.** (Jennifer laughs.) He's so funny; he showed me (a cover of) The National Enquirer; "The irony is that all the things we're afraid of are actually true in the afterlife."

Then he showed me the main characters from the movie "Men in Black." "Everything was true." "Truth" is written in big bold letters. **"Truth has now become a way of making fear and the lies are the fear's way of making truth nonexistent."** Then he showed me a wheel, he says "It's a never ending circle of stupidity in the population of the planet and the people in the afterlife are trying to make up for it." (Jennifer asks *"Of what you guys caused?"*) He says "No, of what's going on now; the past and the future, it's all one - in a nice bow that looks like it hurts. (She saw a picture of a Tiffany box with a bow that Howard pulled until the box bulged.)

He says "Tell Rich to keep listening, I'm there." *What else did you want to say?* He showed me Amelia Earhart and said "Tell Rich not to worry, everything will work out, ("I think he means financially") - spiritually he just showed me you were skyrocketing over him. Howard it was good to talk to you. He gave me that cute look of his. Gosh I love that... see you soon."

Prince

Since Prince and Robin Williams appear in the book, they're naturals to ask if they have a quote for the book. Jennifer sends me a file where she asks on her cellphone; *"Is there anything Prince can say about why people should or should not should read this book?"* "He says **"They should read it if they want to fly."** (Jennifer laughs "to the moon?") "then Robin Williams came in and said "That's mine!"

"Prince showed me the book opening up and then stars floating from the page, like it's magical." He says, "But it's history repeating itself." Jennifer: "He said put lyrics in the book from his song Purple Rain; it's the fourth section. (Jennifer: I hope I'm interpreting it right.) [129] He's showing me the magic of the purple rain going up instead of going down, with the sparkles that happen upon opening up **the book; it makes the reader open up.** They're calibrated, is what it feels like, into what you're reading. **"It's beautiful written music, Rich."**

He's also showing me an image of the Radio shack logo - that's so funny. He says "You're a transmitter of a spiritual language, hitting the masses in this dimension, which is hard to do unless you wear high heels like he did… which hurt his back. He's showing me it's ultimately what caused his death." Jennifer asks *"So you died from high heels?"* "Technically yes," he says. *"What would you have done differently?"* He said "I would not have used that piano (to jump from) … Ah, I see, it's a metaphor. He wanted more, so he jumped off of it; jumping off his favorite instrument, trying to reach the ethers. Jennifer asks: "So *you could have just done that by playing, no?* "Yes," he says, "he could have done that by playing."

He's showing your book at the piano. "Just do it" he says, laughing. *But what does Rich have to do with jumping off a piano?* He's says you're jumping off a different cliff, but he's showing me a trampoline (laughs) – that you'll be fine. Because you feel like you're jumping off a cliff with this endeavor. He said "Balls to the wall." He says "Tell Rich I can only have him hear me when he wants to listen." *"What does that mean?"* Oh, (that) you don't care to have things pushed on you. Jennifer asks *"Are you pushing him?"* "Kind of…" he says, "to the point where…" ah, I see, that's where the disbelief comes in.

He says he won't push you, he'll "Enchant your writings. Like on the piano, like a duo;" He showed me both of you guys side by side on the piano bench… (Note: Something I spent a lot of time doing with my mom who was a concert pianist who played duets.) **"Tell him that we're all doing this from all aspects."**

Oh… aw.. he just gave me a flower, I hope that was for me, I'm actually blushing… He gave me a daisy, not a rose. He said "The rose is saved for God." *What does that mean?* He says, **"God is all of us, in you and me.** The daisy is the enchantment of something. Something different in the

---

[129] Here's the fourth stanza: "You say you want a leader, but you can't seem to make up your mind. I think you better close it, and let me guide you to the purple rain." Song and lyrics copyright Prince Rogers Nelson. Purple Rain lyrics © Sony/ATV Music Publishing LLC, Universal Music Publishing Group

matrix." And then he showed me a beautiful array of flowers… wow. He said "Signed Prince." He made an x for a signature… "He'll know what that means," he said. (Like a sideways version of his signature of the "Artist known as Prince.") "See you soon."

Robin Williams

Jennifer: *I first want to say happy birthday to you, Robin* (It's his birthday as we write this.) *Do you have a quote for Richard's book, a direct message to your fans and friends?*

"I have only two words; "Love… Love." *Jennifer asks, "Love all?"* "No, love Love." He says **"That's the key ingredients for happiness; love the love. Find that. In everything that you are.** Whether you are in hell (metaphorically speaking) or in your prison cell, (physically speaking); find the truth. **Love is God's connectedness, love is God, it's every single one of us, even if we can't hear it. Love… Love. And then send it to everything.** *Oh my gosh, the sun just came through my window, my heart's pounding. I said is that it Robin*? He says "No; that's everything." Wow that makes me want to cry. Thank you.

He says "Tell Rich I'm here for him. He says tell him that I'll surprise him." *When?* He's going to visit this person, he's going to visit this person and then this person is going to come to you; that's *how* you'll know. He just winked. He says "Tell Rich it's exciting: the matrix, the connections, God…" -- it was so interesting when he said that -- and now he says "nanu nanu," and just did like a little thing on his head, over and out. **"Until now."** (A play on the parting line "Until then…") **"It's Over and yonder."**

(A pause) Robin showed me a record. "The record is your lifetimes. Playing over and over and then sometimes we scratch the record and then we have to get a new record." He's showing me how in this lifetime he scratched it and he left, and (then) you come back as like a CD or a Walkman. And then we end up all virtual. (Note: I think he means at the end of all of our lifetimes. Each lifetime is like a variation on a theme, like music on cylinder, on vinyl, on digital – variations on each them we choose as our lifetime, and eventually we become that recording in a virtual way.) The music keeps going, our souls keep going, that was such a great thing he just gave me – **we're all records, sometimes we scratch, sometimes we get broken, eventually we just live on to more**

instruments more human bodies, I love the way he shows me the Walkman, the cd player, then we go virtual... for millions of people.

"And you are that right now, Rich - you're now the virtual .. you're not the record player anymore, or the record, you're now in the virtual, you've made it, and you're sending it to everybody else. I commend your thoughts and love who you are and thank you and love to both of you." He showed me a pebble of some sort, he showed me a rock "You'll know what that means." Something with rocks. All right, bye. (I have a collection of rocks from around the world – world's cheapest souvenir, but reminds me instantly where I found it. I have one on my desk and my eye went straight for it.)

Amelia Earhart

She has the most beautiful eyes by the way. First thing she says **is "Don't find me." She says "it will disrupt everyone."** She says that her bones will be found or get shown soon. And that she's having fun with all the crazy people that want to find me, "I'm not worth that. They're spending too much on resources," *What about a tv show?* "That would be okay, I'll lead you; let them pay for it." *Oh I have the chills.*

She says that she wants you to lead (the search). You'll understand what not to look for. Not sure what she means by that. Oh, the plane. She's showing me the plane and one of the wings, like half the wing tip. She says something about it not being hers; something about 1948 (whatever that means to you, Rich.) *What else?* She says: "Tell him I love him." Oh, Luana came in by the way – both of you guys are conspiring something. They both just came in while I'm talking to Amelia.

Luana: they both love how you're channeling and actually thinking you're confirming what you already know. *What was that?* Luana just kicked you up to her class by the way. She wants you to ask for her tonight to ask what's going on; it's going to be another revelation before tomorrow's interview (on Coast to Coast AM radio). Um, aw... Ha, so Amelia just showed me her girlfriend and that you're correct. Whatever that means.

We are all part of this play, she just showed me how she did so much – **the last five years (of her life incarcerated in prison) she could live without** – she says. *But what about his book? Any quote?* **"Lift it to your soul. And see what your soul has to say. Hearing the words from the book; don't judge it, just listen to your spirit, it will guide you and tell**

you that the **"unthinkable" is real** -- and (she says) make sure that the unthinkable is in quotes; she's saying you're not thinking it – it's *unthinkable*. The things that you put in your head; it's the stuff you don't put in your head that's real.

She just gave you a kiss on the cheek and spun you around in the chair, She said "Bon Voyage… *to what?…* to the ethers." She says "I think we all have a lot in common. And we're lucky to have us in all dimensions, I am grateful." She says "**Be grateful for your breath**. It is coveted sometimes, (breathing) not the biblical sense of coveting of course. **Wanting breath is everything; it's your source, it's your power. Move and laugh, laughing's the best medicine don't waste time trying to dig up things**. Unless it's a TV show, she keeps saying; she's showing me September as well, not sure what that means. (Possible date of production of a documentary I'm helping about her). She says – "Au Revoir."

The Alpha and the Omega

I asked her; "see if Jesus has a quote for us…"

They're fighting for it, hold on, - oh, Mary Magdalene (is here), my heart always feels better when I feel her. She says "**Tell Rich he is not a saint….** Aw, that's so sweet, she says **that you're not a saint, but you're an etheric saint, and she showed me a statue in the ethers.** She showed me like a map of the US with lights, you know how like if you were pinning destinations everywhere, with all the destinations lit up? She says that you're doing that through your work. Then she showed me how **you reach all audiences in all the quantum fields** – she's showing me the dimension on top of our dimension and all the dimensions after that; so that's why you're an etheric saint… that's hilarious.

I'm being shown (Jesus) -- you know when I described him as he came to me with loafers and jeans and button downed shirt and his hair long, looks like a 1960's guy yet cleaned up? He has brown eyes, beautiful eyes, that's amazing, but they change.

First thing he says is "Tell Rich "**Thank you.**" *Why?* "**For allowing a different outcome in the way people can hear my story.**" He's showing me the Bible and showing me your work and how they stacked up against each other… that's so funny! Well, not funny.. but.. wow. He's showing me how my brain is like an antenna, *thank you,* and my heart as well…

"Tell Rich that his work is the truth. That people have become fearful and might say bad things (about it); it's one of many multidimensional truths that has to… heed the warning from *not* putting it out. That's where damnation happens - by not putting truth out there – it was taken out of context, (like) what was written in the Bible.

"You're a truth-gnostic." *What does that mean?* He's laughing. "Tell Rich that a truth-gnostic is someone who is unbiased and wants what others have to say, that resonates with his heart. You put it out there, even when you might not believe everything that you're listening to (or writing about).

Then he just showed me like lightning of some sort, like a lamp going out with a flash, just the frequencies bursting – what an amazing metaphor! He's showing how the frequencies (are affected), like your (way of putting things,) your language is making things crash, with people internally… You're breaking the old lamps so they can put a new bulb in, to bring forth the light, instead of (just) trying to dust off the old light. He says "Thank you for doing that."

"It is a challenge frequency that always hurts initially. Follow your spirit and only look back for the theater of history it plays in, or plays to. And know the audience members have to watch the play - the modern day version of it - enough times for them to have it sink in. Like (the Broadway play) *Alexander Hamilton* – using the different races that played the historic characters in Hamilton. People prep the stage for it to last.

He just showed me the Michelangelo painting where they're touching fingers in the Sistine chapel - where God imbues the human spirit with his touch – he says **"Everyone touches God and makes up (comprises) what God is."** He says "It's molecules of light in different shades, in different colors of light in different shapes and sizes. And some are big lights like you, so others can follow - not in a hierarchy way, but so they won't get lost on the path." He's showing me a dirt path. He says "Sometimes a dirt path is harder to stay on and being in a car is easier, but some people choose to keep walking up hill because they're told it's the only way."

(laughs) "You're giving them a hybrid choice - to question (reality) – nobody would have believed in the electric car (before it was made) – (Jennifer: He just showed me my electric car and said "but you already have one.") He says "I love you and everyone." He's showing me all the

U.S. presidents, and says "Everyone (of them) made a difference. In the quantum field of light and darkness, without one, you would not have had the other. So for you, for one, please do not judge." He showed me an image of Paul Revere. He says **"Do not judge the messenger and its contents to set you free; "free" meaning in your heart, where in the ethers is (always) "true."** We all are Shakespeare's love.

He shows me that we technically die and rise together. Whether in our hearts or in our spiritual uncertainty, or in our spiritual uncertainty or demise. We can rebuild. He says take my advice; Gandhi did it right. And we all have Gandhi inside our hearts. And he just showed me Robin Williams and said "Love the love. Within us all. And peace. And then peace has to follow."

"Thank you Rich. We are entertained by your thoughts." *Why was that shown to me? The Holy bible?* "It was a foundation." Now he showed me a lightbulb and breaking it with the frequencies, and showed me a new lightbulb and showed me your book, one of many books incorporated into – not "the new age" but "the new vulnerability." "Love the love. It's so simple yet dissected into a thousand different ways, thousand different shades of light that make up one… "Without darkness there is no light, and vice versa…. you get the drift."

He says **"Sing well. And listen more.** To your own advocacy. Of this multi-dimensional world." He's showing how you have to get along with all dimensions, not just this dimension, but you have to have the awareness that (reality) it is multidimensional. He shows me there is no stealing, everything is free. As long as your heart is (free) and you take action… "Like you, Rich. **More people will be changed by your words, than the ones who can't hear what you're saying**. That is their path. Maybe the next lifetime; but again, he shows me the contract between people that you have to have both; people who can hear and people who can't hear the difference, otherwise everyone would be following him or someone like him - like a saint. (Jennifer: hey, you're a saint in the ether, how's that make you feel?) I said I don't want them to leave but they'll be back. He just said **"Rich; you are an en-Richment."**

And finally, a quote from Luana Anders, which I heard in a dream six years after her passing: she said **"The hopes of a thousand generations are resting upon you."**

*   *   *   *   *

Reprinted from "Flipside: A Tourist's Guide on How to Navigate the Afterlife." What these reports show about the final frontier is consistent.

My grandparents (center) visiting the King of England 1933. I'm in their future.

1. *Souls don't die.*

We've been around for millennia; our souls continue on for millennia. In between lives we are fully conscious, with all of our memories intact. Yes, our bodies die, our loved ones depart from us in this life. But we reconnect with them in the Afterlife.

2. *After death we return to our soul group, where we recognize those we've been reincarnating with for eons.*

There's anywhere from 3-25 people in our individual group and we usually plan our next life with these same folks. We share laughs and memories of the life just lived and eventually plot with them our next adventure. We may even recognize them during this lifetime; usually identified with the thought "I felt like I always knew this person the moment I met them," or "I knew we would marry."

3. *In between lives, we all have a life planning session where we choose our next life; we are able to pick and choose what kind of life we want to lead for various reasons, as well as choose our parents.*

"Why would I choose those people who've made my life miserable?" is a familiar refrain. The answer is that you chose them so that you could be where you are today. Either far, far away from them - which is a gift in some cases, or their influence had directly put you in the place you're supposed to be on the planet. It puts a different spin on your parents' behavior when you consider you chose them because of it. As well as why your own children chose you.

4. *We each have our own "council of elders" who oversee our lifetimes, and engage with us in Socratic debate about how we did.*

Everyone has a council of elders, and everyone goes to see them at least twice; once upon our return so they can help assimilate all the lessons from that lifetime, and once again just before we take another trip into human form. They don't sit in judgment; rather they help you discern your path. Usually there are 6-12 people on any given council; it seems the younger souls have fewer.

5. *No humans are born without a soul, and we don't arrive at our chosen body until the fourth month (or sometimes later).*

Consciousness is something we've retained from our life between lives. Some kind of veil, or filter, prevents us from remembering those previous lives. However, through the process of deep hypnosis, we're able to bypass these filters and access these previous memories. The idea that we don't join the body until the fourth month would be controversial to advocates who believe life begins at conception. The human animal life may begin at conception, but the spiritual life does not.

6. *We don't normally reincarnate as other animals.*

Each species comes back with in its own pantheon; i.e. birds of a feather, fish in the sea, and animals on land can swap places with those in their group, but not within other groups. To the concept of being reborn in a "lower life form" as a result of negative karma - that's not what is reported. All life forms are sacred; there are no pejoratives when it comes to life. However, its reported you can access your animal friends at any time in the life between lives – they're an energy pattern as well, and can spend hours playing fetch once again. In all the cases I've examined, I've only known one where a person recalled in detail a previous life as an animal. I imagine it's possible, but statistically extremely rare.

7. *When we return to our home base, with our soul group, all actions and effects are left behind - we return to a pure state where we enjoy a world without pain, sin or suffering. There is no hell per se, nor a Satanic like region or persona.*

Those who've caused pain, sin or suffering, experience the pain they inflicted fully – as if they were the person being hurt during their life review. Afterwards they may choose (or it's decided for them) to be isolated from others in order to learn from their mistakes. There is no Satan or hell per se. Once you depart this plane, you no longer have access to the negativity here, or those who might perpetrate it. (For those Satanists out there, sorry, don't mean to offend.) According to the thousands who've journeyed into the afterlife, there's no evil waiting for us. But we may experience our own form of hell based on how we've treated other human beings.

8. *The process of reincarnation is planned by us, not subject to karma, past mistakes, or past injustices. People choose to be gay, choose to be crippled, or choose to be blissful depending on their spiritual depth.*

We don't travel up or down in any fashion, going from peasant to rich person, or unhappy soul to happy soul. Free will is the law of the Universe, and it's up to us who we want to return as, or even if we want to reincarnate. But inevitably, the pull of helping your loved ones and friends, brings us back time after time. Our life choices are up to us. That includes sexuality, physical type, body shape, etc. We may choose to struggle with these issues in order to progress spiritually, or to help those around us to progress. Those who live on the fringes of society are frequently older souls who chose to be there.

9. *Bad experiences, including suicide, murder, mayhem and other events are frequently worked out in advance, with the agreement of all souls involved.*

They claim there's no such thing as random violence. This may sound controversial, but according to the research, pretty universal. When examining a life between-life session, we get an opportunity to see those details, however heinous or upsetting, to be true.

10. *Our friends in our soul group frequently show up as pals in this life, relatives, brothers, sisters, loved ones or even as adversaries.*

In the "Gospel of Judas" (National Geographic 2006) Judas claims Jesus came to him and asked him to turn him over to the Romans. "If you truly love me, you'll do this for me." There are many reasons to be on the planet, we benefit from all our own experiences, but the main role might be one of assisting a loved one.

11. Our progression in the afterlife can be charted, in part, based on what color we see ourselves as - the earlier souls are closer to white, and through the spectrum, they wind up into the violet realm. But there is no hierarchy.

As therapist Jimmy Quast put it; "No one gets to hoard the jelly beans." The idea of someone being smarter, better, richer, happier, more famous, more revered, more anything is just not the case. You are the perfect self you're meant to be. All paths are sacred, and none is judged lesser than another. Just older.

12. We all have a spirit guide or "Guardian Angel," sometimes more than one.

Every one of us has a spirit guide who has agreed to watch over all of our incarnations. It gives new meaning to the sacrifice one does at the service of others - can you imagine becoming a mentor to a soul for all of their lifetimes? But the journey many of us are on is to eventually be a guardian angel (spirit guide) for another soul; no time like the present to start treating others like they might be a future candidate.

13. All of this movement and planning is based on energy.

Every thought, action, word or deed contains it, every emotion as well. Treat it with sacred intent, whether praying for deliverance, or to help another soul. If you think it, believe it, pray for it, sing it, act it or create it, you've put that personal energy out into the Universe. It can help, heal, or in negative cases, harm others.

14. There are other Universes and places we can reincarnate. Some religions have spoken of them, various planes in different dimensions Religion is a construct that mirrors the afterlife.

Earth is the best school, the best playground, the best place to advance our souls. *"You'll learn more in one day of tragedy on Earth, then perhaps 5,000 years on another, simpler planet,"* according to one interview. The argument has been raised, "There aren't enough souls to reincarnate. Where'd the new souls come from?" According to Newton's patients, there are other places to reincarnate and new souls are constantly coming into existence. When we graduate from our many lifetimes, the graduation ceremony includes being rewarded with (and offering to guide through many lifetimes) a new soul.

15. *Love and compassion turn out to be not just religious concepts, but words that explain how the Universe actually works; from energy transfer to why we choose a particular life.*

Love is the wheelwork of nature, and that attraction and energy is what keeps us going. Compassion is part of the fabric as it's included in many examples of what we give our loved ones by reincarnating by their side. The Golden Rule is actually golden for a reason, because it represents how the Universe works. Loving your neighbor as yourself, nature as yourself, your fellow beings on all levels as yourself, turns out to be not only a spiritual maxim, but a physical one as well.

16. *Religion is a man-made experience based on our god like nature.*

In light of these reports, world religions seem to be echoing the same thing; in the afterlife we have eternal qualities, and experience a heaven-like state of bliss. And while we're on Earth, we try to recreate or relive that experience. One could say we're "trying to get back to the Godhead," or "return to God." Religion expresses the inexpressible, examines the unexamined, and finds truth in the nature of all things. Science aspires to take the same journey, by making logical sense of what we are doing on the planet, how we got here, and where we are going. For those who believe that life ends in death, that's not what's reported. For those who think the stress of this lifetime is based on karma from a previous one; that too doesn't bear up under this form of scrutiny. Forgiveness, compassion and love for all people and things appears to be the universal law of the Universe.

17. *We have both an animal ego and a spiritual ego.*

According to these reports, we started incarnating on Earth millennia ago. Perhaps when humans became upright or adept; our spiritual energy melded with the human's, and thus began consciousness. Perhaps this event coincided with the formation of societies 60,000 years ago and is our "missing link."

Human life appears to be an agreement between the animal and spiritual ego. That fact helps to underline why people act a certain way, and could have a profound influence on the criminal justice system – if a person is struggling in this life with animalistic tendencies is there a way of examining a healing process that's not "Clockwork Orange[130]" but based

---

[130] The book by Anthony Burgess mocks criminal rehab in the future where prisoners are reprogrammed.

on helping souls discover their purpose? As mentioned, in Holland, they've already [131]begun to bring in psychics and past life regressionists to help cure career criminals.

18. *Curing and healing people is part of the work done by others in the Afterlife.*

People choose their lifetimes before coming here to continue their work in a particular field. Musicians may return to further their music knowledge, perhaps explaining child prodigies like Mozart and others. Doctors and Nurses are involved with healing energy transfer, and may have had many lifetimes where they continued their practice. Just the way Tibetan lamas might spend a lifetime studying esoteric practices, and then remember them in their ensuing lifetime, we can all tap into the knowledge of our previous lifetimes to help with our current one.

19. *There are no coincidences.*

What appears to be a matter of amazing coincidence, upon examination, turns out to be an incredible planned sequence, like a complex 3D chess or "Second Life" game being played on multiple planes where each move affects the other players. As a butterfly's wings in a rain forest may cause a hurricane in Asia, everything can be linked in cause and effect if one looks long and hard enough. By the way, is the reason you've picked up this book.

20. *You are doing pretty much what you set out to do.*

Time and again, people report the spiritual journey they're on was laid out in advance. This is annoying for anyone with a remote control - we all have the inclination to change the channel, to want to change our circumstance, get richer quicker - but the answer is: "You're doing fine, you're on the right path, relax." As hard as your path may seem, you're on it for a spiritual reason.

21. *These reports are the tip of the iceberg.*

For those who are interested in finding their soul's purpose – the reason they chose to be here on the planet – I can't think of a more effective way. Here's some collected insights from the therapists I interviewed:

---

[131] The Telegraph 22 Nov. 2010 "Dutch prisons use psychics to help prisoners contact the dead."

People come in because there may be a relative who recently died, or emotional trauma from losing a child. This work is not to supplant therapy they should receive from a licensed trained professional; it's intended to provide them with answers about their inner being. One of the things clients don't understand until they experience it is that there is a dual nature to all of us. We have our brain ego if you will, and we have a soul ego, and when they are combined it creates one personality and one lifetime.   Michael Newton

Someone can have a strong religious belief that doesn't include reincarnation, but when you take someone through one of these sessions, they have this mind boggling experience - it's a visceral experience on a soul and body level – they emerge knowing this to be true. It's far beyond a concept or belief. That's profound. One other common occurrence is a feeling of reconnecting to the whole. To know you and I are of the same essence makes it much more difficult for me to cause you harm, because it's harming me and the whole as well. That's a message for the entire planet; how we cause harm to others. It's more difficult to do knowing we are all the same. I'd love to see everyone have the opportunity to go through one of these sessions. It's wonderful that it's not a dogma, it's not a religion, but it's open to everyone.   Paul Aurand

I believe we are spiritual beings that live on this Earth. We're not Earthly beings who happen to be spiritual, but the other way around. So for me, this past life work, soulful work, is about that fact that at our core, we're this beautiful diamond and the mud that covers it are experiences in other lifetimes we 've encountered. And we create these negative beliefs we have about ourselves, whether it's shame or self-hatred or unworthiness, and sometimes we have to go all the way back to the beginning - our past lives - to wash away the mud We can uncover the beautiful diamond we are. Until you get to the source of it, you 're going to be in conflict with nature until you find the source of the diamond within you.   Debbie Haynie

Always wisdom is uppermost in mind. We choose to incarnate to harvest wisdom from the lifetime, to gain direct experience and knowledge so that we are improved as beings, so that we are expanded as beings, so that we have more wisdom, understanding and compassion.   Colleen Page-Joy

There's this very bright light everywhere I look; I'm part of it. He's showing me I'm part of a universal plan, I'm part of that light and it's everywhere, there's nowhere in the universe there isn't this light. He says "That's what you're working with, keep it as part of you and bring it back." We need to know there's nothing else but light and love. The work we're doing (as hypnotherapists) is about light, because it opens us up to understanding. We're on a mission to clarify and create more light and love and it's available to everyone; all we have to do is open ourselves to it. The light is clear and cleansing, loving and peaceful. Eventually when we become light all the other things go; sadness and such. It's very healing.   Morrin Bass

To date it's the single most important modality I can offer anyone. It gives them a sense of their immortality, of the importance of their life and journey, and it gives a sense of belonging to something greater than themselves. It's not a gifted psychic telling you who you are or what you've been, or going to a "Channeler" to tell you your past and background; it's experiential, the clients become their own channel. After every single client has an LBL, they aren't the same – some part of them has changed in a positive way and it's a resource that remains for them long after their Life between Lives journey is complete.   Chanda Nancy Berlatsky

I think traditional belief systems are breaking down all over the world; people are looking for something more, for a greater understanding of themselves, rather than being told by other people what to believe. If you can look at what you have within, that's got to be the real stuff because it's your own. If you can tap into that, have access to that, it's very empowering. The world is picking up pace and if we can have something that's centering, like an awakening and understanding of your immortal identity, that seems to be the most centering you could ever have. The more people discover the beautiful compassion and wisdom we hold within, that's got to be good for the planet.   Peter Smith

Me shading my eyes, mom Anthy, Italian grandmother Dionisia, Aunt Velia Martini, who the Italian Saint Padre Pio told "Your soul is pure; without blemish." She passed not long after this photo, all three are with my father now.

REFERENCES & LINKS

Scott De Tamble – LightBetweenLives.com
Peter Smith – NewtonInstitute.org
Mario Beauregard – DrMarioBeauregard.com
Gary Schwartz – DrGarySchwartz.com
Dr. Medhus – ChannelingErik.com
Jennifer Shaffer – JenniferShaffer.com
Division of Perceptual Studies – med.Virginia.edu
Carol Bowman – carolbowman.com
HackingTheAfterlife.com

RECOMMENDED READING

"Voyage of Purpose" by David Bennett. An amazing NDE from a science officer.

"Children's Past Lives" by Carol Bowman. Excellent case studies.

"Life Before Life" by Dr. Jim Tucker. Stories about Children's Past Lives from the Dept. of Perceptual Studies at UVA.

"Life After Life" by Dr. Raymond Moody. The book that inspired others to write.

"Life Before Life" by Helen Wambach PhD. Hard to find; her studies of subjects under hypnosis recalling past lives is the from the 1970's.

"Tibetan Book of the Dead," translated by Robert Thurman *"The Jewel Tree of Tibet,"* by Robert Thurman. *"Essential Tibetan Philosophy"* is equally terrific.

"Many Lives, Many Masters" by Brian Weiss. A Yale psychiatrist explores many cases of patients who spontaneously regressed during hypnotherapy.

My Son and the Afterlife: Conversations from the Other Side" by Dr. Elisa Medhus. Dramatic stories and interviews from the afterlife with her son Erik.

"After the Light: What I Discovered on the Other Side of Life That Can Change Your World." By Kimberly Clark Sharp. Her dramatic NDE.

"Journey of Souls" and *"Destiny of Souls"* by Michael Newton Based on over 7000 interviews with patients, he lays out a powerful case for his vision of the afterlife, and how to get there.

"Life Between Lives" and *"Memories of the Afterlife"* Edited by Michael Newton. A must read for all hypnotherapists.

"The Afterlife Experiments" and *"The G.O.D Experiments"* by Gary Schwartz with William Simon. The scientist explores scientific evidence of what ESP and psychic ability might be about.

"Brain Wars," by Mario Beauregard. Neuroscientist Beauregard proves there's not a single "God spot" and other case studies.

"The Near Death and Life of Jeremy Kagan" by Jeremy Kagan. The film director has a profound near death experience.

"The Soul of Wellness" by Dr. Rajiv Parti. Dr. Parti describes how his life changed dramatically after his NDE from "Hummer to hybrid."

"Proof of Heaven" by Dr. Eben Alexander. Dr. Alexander's fascinating NDE account which he has shared with many in the near death community.

"Journeys Out Of the Body" by Robert Monroe. Monroe is the Godfather of "astral projection" and has written many books on the subject.

"My Life After Life - A Posthumous Memoir" by Galen Stoller. Written by a young boy who passed away, edited by his father who is a renowned doctor.

"Afterlife of Billy Fingers" by Annie Kagan. Author's brother died and contacted her to prove that there's life after death.

"My Life After Death" by Erik Medhus. Fascinating look at the Flipside from a firsthand pov.

"Erasing Death: The Science That Is Rewriting the Boundaries Between Life and Death" by Dr. Sam Parnia. Parnia headed the research behind the "Aware Project;" medical case histories of NDEs.

"Beyond Physicalism: Toward Reconciliation of Science and Spirituality" by Edward F. Kelly, Rowman & Littlefield Publishers. A hefty look into the science of consciousness, a follow up to "Irreducible Mind."

ACKNOWLEDGMENTS - *A THOUSAND THANKS*

First and foremost Scott De Tamble. I bow to your skills as a therapist, a teacher and student, as well as your friendship. We've had many laughs during these sessions; nothing quite like hearing something profound and astounding, and being able to laugh about it. He's in Claremont, CA at LightBetweenLives.com. Michael Newton, thank you for your work and your research, and your kind words about the documentary.

This book was crowd funded! Thanks to everyone who donated to my GoFundMe page. Including: Pastor Rev. Jon Burnham, Shannon Walker, John Wylie, David Miller, Edmund Heron, John Melody, Chris Monaghan, Todd Bowden, Kari Krug, Basia Mosinski, Lyn (Tigg) Boyce, Maureen Johanson, Herbert Centeno, Lisa Yesse, Dave & Maryanne Patlak, Dani Dennington, Ian Bentley, Clara Ricker, Lucy Mattinen, Chris Rawls, Laurie Yehia, Billy Hunter, Tash Govender, Carin Levee, Rodney McCallum Jr, Sarah Jensen, Michael Flynn, Iris Libby, Linda Stone, Sally Stone, Sue Bodine, Michelle Rossi Eddins, Bill Vlasic, Sajjad Hussain, Cis Rundle! A thousand thank-yous!!!!

There are many crowds to thank: folks who wrote reviews on Amazon, who attended Flipside talks and passed the word along. Iands.org, Cheryl Birch. Thanks to George Noory, Coast to Coast radio show, "Flipside" went to #1 at Amazon after both shows. My appearance on his "Beyond Belief" was fun, now Gaiam TV is distributing the film "Flipside."

Thanks to Dr. Bruce Greyson, Mario Beauregard PhD, Gary Schwartz PhD, Bob & Nena Thurman, David & Cindy Griffith-Bennett, Prashant Solomon, Dr. Ken & Galen Stoller, Tim & Nancy Meinelschmidt, Chuck & Elissa Grodin, Bruce & Deb Haring, Abbie Adams Yaffe, Paul Tracey, Billy Meyer, Craig Ottinger, Howard Schultz, Minoo M, Edna Gundersen, P. R. Nelson, Bill Evashwick, John Rogers, Roger Jackson, Edward Oleschak, Sophie Bouris, Chuck Tebbetts, Angie C, Kevin Moore, Scherry & Jim Clarke, Mike Kramer, Duncan Clark, Doug Martin for his artwork and friendship. Dr. Habib Sadeghi; an early supporter. Pat & June Pothier, Shannon Johnson, Mary Grace, Erik & Dr. Elisa Medhus, mediums Pattie Canova, Jamie Butler and Kim Babcock. Medium Jennifer Shaffer, my new oldest best pal. Oh, and of course *Amelia, George, Fred* and *the Alpha and the Omega*, who makes everyone's path a little more interesting.

And to those of you who helped; *miei fratelli* Jeffry, Chas & Roberto and their families – my parents, Anthy and Charlie; thanks for all your support in this lifetime and others... And to my wife Sherry, Olivia and RJ – I love you. Thanks for choosing me.

This book is dedicated to **Ann Hayes Martini**, known to us as *Anthy* – (you can hear her play the piano at *AnthyMartini.com*) and to all our mothers, who may not be still on the planet but whom **are always with us.**

Thanks for always keeping an eye on me, mom.

Richard Martini is a journalist, author and award winning filmmaker. With a BA in Humanities from Boston University (Magna Cum Laude 1978), he was at USC Film School 78-80, returned for his Masters of Professional Writing 2008. He's written and/or directed eight theatrical films including "You Can't Hurry Love," "Limit Up," and "Cannes Man." Documentaries include "Journey Into Tibet with Robert Thurman," "Tibetan Refugee," and "Flipside: A Journey Into the Afterlife." He wrote for Variety, Premiere and Inc.com. His books "Flipside: A Tourist's Guide on How to Navigate the Afterlife" "It's a Wonderful Afterlife Volume 1 and 2" are available at all online or POD outlets.

His narration of his books is available at Audible.com. He has a number of book talks online at MartiniProds on YouTube. The documentary film "Flipside: A Journey Into the Afterlife" is available through Gaiam TV and Amazon. For further information, or to contact Richard, please visit RichMartini.com. He's married, has two children and lives in Santa Monica, California.

For further info: HackingTheAfterlife.com, RichMartini.com, FlipsideTheBook or FlipsideTheFilm.com.

Printed in Great Britain
by Amazon

27820607R00324